# MAX BRUCH
## His Life and Works

# MAX BRUCH

His Life and Works

by

## CHRISTOPHER FIFIELD

THE BOYDELL PRESS

© Christopher Fifield 2005
Typography © Victor Gollancz Ltd
(a division of the Orion Publishing Group) 1988

First published 1988
Victor Gollancz Ltd, London

New edition 2005
The Boydell Press, Woodbridge

ISBN 1 84383 136 8

The Boydell Press is an imprint of Boydell & Brewer Ltd
PO Box 9, Woodbridge, Suffolk IP12 3DF, UK
and of Boydell & Brewer Inc.
668 Mt Hope Avenue, Rochester, NY 14620, USA
website: www.boydellandbrewer.com

A CIP catalogue record for this book is available
from the British Library

Library of Congress Cataloging-in-Publication Data
Fifield, Christopher.
Max Bruch : his life and works / Christopher Fifield. – New ed.
p. cm.
Summary: "An updated reissue of this classic biography of Max Bruch, whose
violin concerto remains one of the most popular pieces in the repertoire" –
Provided by publisher.
Includes worklist (p. ), bibliographical references (p. ), and indexes.
ISBN 1-84383-136-8 (pbk. : alk. paper)
1. Bruch, Max, 1838–1920. 2. Composers – Germany – Biography. I. Title.
ML410.B87F53 2005
780'.92–dc22                                    2005008715

This publication is printed on acid-free paper

Printed in Great Britain by
Athenaeum Press Ltd, Gateshead, Tyne & Wear

*To Judy,*
*Dominic and Andrew*

# CONTENTS

# LIST OF ILLUSTRATIONS

*Title page* Silhouette of Max Bruch after a woodcut by Otto Wiedemann

*Following page 192*

## AUTHOR'S NOTE

All translations of letters and articles from the German are by the author unless otherwise acknowledged. Bruch's letters concerning his time in Liverpool, which were written in English, are quoted verbatim. His use of the English language has not been corrected.

C.F.

# PREFACE

WHEN MAKING PREPARATIONS for the first British performance of
Max Bruch's opera *Die Loreley*, which took place in February 1986, I
began by researching the composer's life. It was a matter of some
surprise to discover that in spite of the fact that Bruch's name is known
to virtually all lovers of music, no biography of the composer existed.
It was perhaps even more surprising to find that, apart from a
monograph by the eminent musicologist, Karl Gustav Fellerer,
published in Germany in 1970 as part of the History of Rhineland
Music, the situation in that country was no different.

Max Bruch is known principally as the composer of one work, the
Violin Concerto No. 1 in G minor Op. 26, a fact which caused the
composer much irritation during his own lifetime, not only because
he wrote nearly 100 other works, but also because of his naïvety at the
time it was published. He accepted a one-off payment for it, and lost
royalties that would have continued until 1990. Bruch was equally
well known during his lifetime as a composer of choral music. His
innovative choice of subject matter (in particular the sagas of ancient
Greece and northern Europe) aroused much interest throughout
Europe and America, generated a successful career as composer and
conductor on both continents and took the oratorio on a new course
away from the sacred works of Mendelssohn. What was true of the
violin concerto now became true of the oratorio; it was time for
change and Bruch provided it in both instances.

Bruch was a man of his period, but he was also a man who did not
change or adapt his ideas throughout his long life of 82 years. He lived
during the most turbulent times of his country and of Europe. He was
a boy during the revolution of 1848 and an old man at the end of the
First World War. He believed in Bismarck's political aim to unify
Germany which awoke an inherent nationalism during the 1860s and
1870s, but he was still clinging to these tenets 50 years later when other
political and social philosophies were in the ascendant.

His music suffered the same fate. He was a man who failed to adapt
to the startling changes which were taking place around him. He
stayed behind to defend the bastion of mid-nineteenth-century
Romanticism, and fly the flag of Mendelssohn and Schumann. He

thus became an increasingly isolated figure and an equally embittered one.

Max Bruch and his wife, Clara Tuczek, had four children. Margarethe was the eldest and only daughter. She became a writer and poet, who looked after her parents at their Berlin home until their deaths shortly after the First World War. She never married, and led a precarious existence as a writer during the stormy years in Germany that followed. She passionately believed in her father's music, and encouraged as many performances as she could to keep it before the public. Margarethe died in Berlin in 1963 at the age of eighty-one, impoverished and by then completely blind. The Bruchs' eldest son, Max Felix, was the only child to become a musician. He studied composition with his father at the Berlin Musikhochschule, but began his career as a clarinettist and a conductor of two amateur choral societies in Hamburg. Like so many sons of famous fathers, he suffered increasingly from living in his father's shadow, and soon abandoned all attempts at music as a profession. He eventually became the German representative for an international gramophone company and died in 1943.

Hans was the most gifted of the Bruch children, but his talents lay in painting. This he inherited from his father, who was faced, when only a child, with the choice between painting and music as a career. After an education at the hands of the best teachers at the Berlin School of Art, followed by an auspicious exhibition in the city, Hans was beginning to enjoy the success he deserved when he was struck down by blood poisoning caused by an insect sting. He was only 26 years old. The youngest son, Ewald, began his career in forestry, but the First World War intervened, and after active service he joined the police force and rose through the ranks. He retired through ill-health in 1943, and, after the conclusion of the war, set about gathering material for an archive of his father's effects. By his death in 1974 he had put together a considerable amount of manuscripts, letters and printed scores which he donated to the Institute of Musicology at the University of Cologne. Max Felix and Ewald were the only children to marry, but as neither had children themselves, the direct line from the composer ceased with their deaths.

My first thanks must go to Professor Klaus Wolfgang Niemöller for granting me unrestricted access to the Max Bruch Archive, which also generously supplied many photographs, and to Dr Manuel Gervinck and Frau Christiane Thiede for their considerable help. The Robert Schumann Institute in Düsseldorf was kind enough to grant me access to the letters from Bruch to Rudolf von Beckerath. I am grateful to Herr Matthias Schwarzer for helping me in Düsseldorf. I wish to thank Frau Ingrid Knierbein for providing me with copies of letters from Bruch to the Kölner Musikgesellschaft, and Dr Uwe Bauer for sending me material from Coblenz. Last but not least of my German sources is the Zanders Archive in Bergisch Gladbach. Early in life, Max Bruch befriended Maria Zanders and her husband Richard who, besides owning an extensive paper-works in the Bergisches Land to the north-east of Cologne, were lovers of music in general and of Bruch's music in particular.

Widowed at an early age, Maria Zanders together with her three children, Margaretha, Richard and Hans, devoted herself to philanthropic service to her workers. This included the founding of a choral society, the Cäcilienchor, which is still active today (though under another name). The Zanders family came to own a house atop a hill on the outskirts of Bergisch Gladbach. Bruch had often stayed at this house (known as the Igeler Hof) before they took it over, but now his visits were to become annual events. He wrote much of his music there and looked upon it as a sanctuary from the rigours of city life. Today the house is owned by Frau Renate Zanders, and I am exceedingly grateful to her, not only for the chance to see for myself why Bruch was so understandably obsessed by the beauty of the Igeler Hof and its surroundings, but for her permission to use the extensive family archive in gathering material for this book. The archive is run by the indefatigable Frau Hanna Rüstig, who has showered me with relevant letters and photographs. Without her considerable help, born of a passionate love for her work, this book would have been the poorer.

The Liverpool Public Library and the Royal Liverpool Philharmonic Society kindly granted me access to their records, and Mr John Hagan (of Rensburg & Co.) was good enough to undertake some research on my behalf relating to Bruch's Liverpool period. The music publishers, Richard Schauer, successors to Bruch's publisher Simrock, have helped me with information and in providing scores, and for this I wish to thank Mrs Irene Retford and Herr Wolfgang Peters. John Beckett has shared my interest in Bruch, and stimulated many conversations on the man and his music. Mrs Ursula Vaughan Williams has granted me permission to publish her late husband's few letters from the short period when he was a student in Bruch's composition class, and Mr Martin Berkofsky provided me with a substantial amount of material relevant to the curious history of Bruch's Concerto for Two Pianos. I extend my thanks to both, to my friends Jane Glover, Clive Brown and Geoffrey Chew for their help, and to Mrs Linda Watson, who has spent much time on my behalf at the Boston Public Library researching Bruch's visit to America in 1883.

I could not have written this book without the invaluable help of my mother, Mrs Ursula Fifield, who, together with our family friend, Mrs Vally Fischbach, has transcribed many hundreds of Bruch's letters into modern script before I could translate them. My thanks go to Dr Fred Wagner of the German Department at University College London who also helped in this regard.

My final thanks, no less sincere, go to Livia Gollancz for her patience and understanding, and to the British Academy, the Worshipful Company of Musicians and University College London for providing me with funds to research the book.

It is the occupational hazard of a biographer to encounter new material at a stage too late for inclusion in his completed work. Even as this book was despatched to the printer, several hundred letters to and from Bruch came to light in Germany. It is the author's intention to examine this collection and publish an article in an appropriate journal in due course.

C.F.

# ORIGINS

THE EARLIEST RECORDED ancestor of Max Bruch is Thomas Bruch. He was born a Catholic in Saarbrücken in 1560, converted to Protestantism (although his brother's descendants remained Catholic) and became a Provost, the first of several clerics in the family. Thomas Bruch's descendants included his son, Johann Adam Bruch (1635), Director of the Saarbrücken Hospital; grandson, Johann Balthasar Bruch (1624–84), barber and Court Surgeon in Zweibrücken, and great-grandson, Johann Paul Bruch (1668–1748), who, after studies in Basle, became a cleric, finally settling in Zweibrücken. His son, Johann Paul Bruch (1699–1755), was a doctor in Bergzabern, and the chemist, Ludwig Christian Bruch (1736), who settled in Pirmasens, was born of Johann's second marriage. The youngest of Ludwig's four sons was Christian Gottlieb Bruch (1771–1836), grandfather of the composer, and the most illustrious of his ancestors. He studied theology in Marburg and Jena, became Vicar in Bergzabern, military chaplain at the garrison in Breisach, and, in 1803, was called to Cologne as Superintendent and head of the Protestant community there. He was, by all accounts, ecumenical in his approach, and developed a bond of friendship with the head of the Catholic community, Canon Wallraf. He was summoned to an audience with Napoleon Bonaparte on 5 November 1811 during a visit by the Emperor to Cologne.

His eldest son was August Carl Friedrich Bruch (1799–1861), who, after his law studies, and several years in Berlin as a lawyer, became Vice-President of the Cologne police. His wife, née Wilhelmine Almenräder (1799–1867), was herself a singer and of a musical family. Her two brothers owned a music and instrument shop in Cologne, and, together with their father, they founded the Cologne Musical Society in 1812. The elder brother, Carl, was an eminent bassoonist and instrument builder. The Almenräder family came from the Bergisches Land, moving to Cologne in the second decade of the nineteenth century, at about the same time as the Bruch family. August Bruch and his wife Wilhelmine had two children, Max Christian Friedrich (1838–1920) and Mathilde (1841–1914), known as Till.

It has been erroneously recorded in such books as Kohut's *Berühmte jüdische Männer und Frauen*, Gunther's *Rassenkunde des deutschen Volkes*, and Zaleski's *Famous Musicians of a Wandering Race*, that Max Bruch was Jewish. This was refuted by the composer, by his daughter Margarethe and his youngest son Ewald, and by Professor Felix Bruch, a descendant of the composer's cousin.[1] During the Third Reich an attempt was again made to label Bruch a Jew, but in November 1933 this was corrected at the insistence of his family.[2] Bruch himself always considered that the composition of *Kol Nidrei* was the reason for the confusion.

# Chapter One

## CHILDHOOD AND YOUTH
### 1838–58

IN THE MIDDLE AGES there was a merchant named Richmodis, who lived in Cologne. During the plague, his wife succumbed and was taken from the house to be laid out in the undertaker's parlour to await burial. She had, however, not died, and recovered enough to make her way home. The housekeeper, aware of her presence at the front door, rushed into her master's study to tell him of his wife's recovery and that she was at the house. In total disbelief, Richmodis declared that he would only believe the news if his two horses left their stable at once, ascended the steps of the tower built on to his house, and looked out of the window at the top. Immediately a drumming of hooves was heard. To this day a tower has always stood at the same place, in Richmodisstrasse off the Neumarkt in Cologne, at the top of which are the modelled heads of two white horses. A house no longer stands on this spot, but it was here that, on Twelfth Night (6 January) 1838, Max Christian Friedrich Bruch was born, for at that time the Richmodishaus belonged to his family.[1] Max wrote the following description of his parents:[2]

> The eldest son of my grandfather (my father August) was a lawyer who studied in Marburg and Bonn, and then worked for a while in the Supreme Court in Berlin. Through a lack of good connections, he was diverted from his career, and later occupied the post of Police Chief in Cologne. He was an extremely loyal, keen, and conscientious official, willing (from an inborn benevolence) to mitigate the inevitable severity of police behaviour. He enjoyed the affection and trust of all sections of the community, and sometimes provided help for those in need. To his greatest misfortune, during the reactionary period of the 1850s, he once had to take over the censorship office. No one was more annoyed than he when the long proof sheets of the *Kölnische Zeitung* were handed over to him to seek out suspected sedition. The newspaper, which for a long time had at its head the excellent politician and poet Heinrich Kruse, often came into sharp conflict with the authorities during these last

years of the rule of Friedrich Wilhelm IV; it was therefore inevitable that occasionally the confiscation of an issue had to be enforced. Then the publisher, a genuine Kölner of the old school, would come running, wringing his hands and crying, 'Jesus, Maria, Joseph, dear Sir, this is too much, confiscated yet again, what are we going to do?'

. . . One day a small, nimble businessman appeared in my father's office with a tall boy, and said, 'Allow me, dear honoured Chief of Police, to introduce my son to you, he plays the cello very beautifully — a great talent — now he must go to Paris.' This boy was Jacques Offenbach, who later, through pleasant but at times less than beautiful operettas, achieved a special fame. As can be seen, it was a colourful mixture of people, who sometimes crowded into my father's small office to seek his sympathy and help.

In the same article Bruch described his mother:

. . . My mother was musical through and through, had a good soprano voice, and often sang as soloist during the 1820s at the Rhineland Music Festival. . . . To her great distress, however, she lost her voice early on, and devoted herself to giving singing lessons. For many years she worked in this way, and was much appreciated. For a long time she headed a private circle of music-lovers, who not only practised four-part choruses and folksongs, but also performed the great and beautiful ensembles and finales from *Don Giovanni*, *The Marriage of Figaro*, *Idomeneo*, *Cosi fan tutte*, *Fidelio*, *The Water Carrier* [Cherubini], *Joseph* [Mehul], *Euryanthe* etc. Among her effects I found piles of solo parts for these operas, all written very neatly and correctly in her hand for the purpose of these gatherings. This serious endeavour inspired musical friends and, in so doing, acquainted them with the greatest masterpieces of dramatic music, and earned her universal recognition.

Then follows a description of his sister:

My exceedingly musical sister, Mathilde, and I received our first piano lessons from our mother. As I had no other siblings, an especially profound bond developed between us. We studied everything together, music, languages etc., and there was nothing that, at that time or later, I did not confide in her. She had a naturally strong and penetrating mind, and the deepest sensitivity for the beauty of melody and the greatness in art; and she also possessed the ability to think sharply and logically in all artistic matters. She followed my artistic attainments throughout her life with the most faithful and penetrating understanding. In the years 1867–1870 she usually spent the summer with me in Sondershausen, where I was at that time Court Conductor, and where I was making progress through experience in the understanding of orchestral matters. In my charming country cottage, lying between meadows and woods, where I completed my First Violin Concerto, we spent many a happy day. Later we lived together for a few years in Berlin and Bonn. When, in 1878, I left my native Rhineland, unfortunately never to return for any length of time, she remained as a music teacher in Bonn, where she died in 1914. Men like Brahms (from whom she often sent me greetings in her letters), Philipp Spitta, Rudorff, Gernsheim and Sarasate valued her worth and respected her very much. As she later no longer wished to leave her homeland, and as I unfortunately had mostly to live in foreign parts, it proved impossible to live together during the second half of my life.

Between the ages of seven and ten, it appears that Bruch was developing his talents as a painter, so much so that his relatives described him as 'a second Raphael'. He idolized certain paintings, and copied them as material for practising his drawing technique. His enthusiasm was fired by works such as *The Landing of Ferdinand Cortez on the Coast of Mexico*, *The Ascension of Elijah*, *The Blessed Bonifacius Felling the Holy Oak of Hesse*, and others illustrating childrens' books, the Bible, and studies of world history. At the age of nine he wrote his first musical composition, a song for his mother's birthday, and from then on his first love became music, encouraged by his parents. He wrote many small works in a sudden burst of activity: motets, psalms, piano pieces, violin sonatas, a string quartet, and even orchestral works such as an overture to a projected opera *Jung frau von Orleans*. It was, however, at the age of eleven, in 1849, that work began in earnest on harnessing his talent and energy. Of the many works written during his childhood, very few have survived. When the widow of Max Bruch's eldest son died in 1968, the manuscript of one of these early works was found among her possessions. This was a Septet for Clarinet, Horn, Bassoon, two Violins, Cello and Double Bass dated 28 August 1849. The significance of this date is that it was the centenary of Goethe's birth, and it was therefore possibly written in homage to the great man. Bruch had a lifelong admiration for Goethe, and in his letters he invariably drew the attention of his friends and acquaintances to that date each year as a reminder of the respect all Germans owed to the poet. Though owing much to Beethoven and

Schubert, the Septet has the early hallmarks of Bruch's melodic writing, the freshness of his youth, and the charm of his Rhenish background. The scoring is remarkably assured, though he makes no distinction in the treatment of the three wind instruments, producing a horn part of some intricacy. In both the large-scale form and harmonic planning, the young Bruch was equally precocious.

He received his early training in the theory of music from his father's friend, Professor Heinrich Breidenstein, in Bonn. It was at this time that he first became acquainted with the Igeler Hof, a farm in Bergisch Gladbach near Cologne. Among his parents' friends was the lawyer Neissen, who lived in the house with his unmarried sister Thérèse. This farm (the name Igeler comes from Euler meaning an elder tree) was later bought by the Zanders family, owners of a large paper-making business, and throughout his life Bruch remained deeply involved with both the family and their idyllic home, perched high on a hillside among the woods and valleys of the Bergisches Land, where he journeyed whenever he could to write much of his music. In a letter to his mother, in the autumn of 1850, when he was twelve years old, he described how his father conversed with him in French on the journey back to Cologne from Bergisch Gladbach by the post-coach. His father also taught him English, his general education being provided privately at home by his parents and by visiting teachers from the Friedrich Wilhelm School in Cologne. As a result, Bruch did not matriculate officially from school, and this caused problems later when he tried to enrol at Bonn University in spite of the high standard of his work. Fortunately for him, the combination of a strong recommendation from the headmaster of the school, Dr Knebel, a glowing reference from the Cologne police, and the goodwill of the Rector of Bonn University, the Mozart biographer Otto Jahn, enabled him to do so at the age of twenty-one in 1859.

Meanwhile his musical education had progressed. In addition to working with Breidenstein, Bruch began studies with Ferdinand Hiller, who was to exercise a most significant and important influence upon him throughout his life, and to whom he frequently turned for advice. Hiller arrived in Cologne from Düsseldorf in 1850, and though he left for Paris shortly thereafter, he returned in 1852. Already, on 8 April 1850 he had noted in his diary a visit from 'Bruch and son', and his interest in the boy was immediate. He described perusing a piano sonata for four hands when on a visit to the Bruch household, where 'a string quartet written by the son for his mother's birthday was played', and on 30 November 1852 wrote of hearing a violin sonata and a string quintet performed at the house. It was largely through his recommendation that the 14-year-old boy was awarded the Mozart Foundation prize in 1852, to study composition with Hiller and piano with Carl Reinecke and Ferdinand Breunung for four years from 1853 to 1857. The Frankfurt-based Foundation asked Hiller to 'raise the Mozart-pupil to be an honest musician and composer', and awarded Max 400 florins a year for the four years. Max expressed his gratitude[3] in a letter to Hiller. He could 'no longer conceal the happiness of victory, and I know that I have you to thank for the largest part, because your excellent instruction on my early string quartet has brought me to my present situation . . . I shall do my utmost to justify the trust placed in me, and to work thoroughly under your guidance, as becomes a scholar of the Mozart Foundation.'

This was not the first time that the name of Mozart was associated with the young Bruch. In the *Rheinische Musik Zeitung*, a comparison was made between the 14-year-old boy, who had just had a symphony performed in public at a Musical Society concert, and both the young Mozart and Mendelssohn.[4] The same report described Max's family background, the encouragement of both parents, and the fruits of their efforts, with a description of the works the youth had written. He was 'a dear, sincere, merry, childish and ingenuous lad, who, though he lives for music, nonetheless shows talent and ability for other subjects', and it ended with the blessing, 'may he courageously set forth upon the journey ahead, serve his Art as a sublime and holy goddess, and find his goal in achieving the highest and best. This we wish him whole-heartedly, and with Heaven's blessing'.

From Hiller's diaries it is apparent that he thought highly of young Max, and lavished more attention on both his work, and his attitude to working, than on other pupils.

> 15 August 1853: Bruch came to me with an eight-part Mass and a Symphony. 8 September he brought them back improved.
>
> 20 October: After lunch M. Bruch came, parts of an Oratorio, long severe lecture on his way of reasoning.
>
> 3 December: Bruch came for the first of regular Saturday lessons, and I gave him a harmony and counterpoint exercise.
>
> 22 April 1854: After dinner Bruch [came], I took him through studies in musical analysis.

Most of Bruch's early unpublished works are mentioned in Hiller's diaries, as well as the first of his published material. His attempts at dramatic music (*Rinaldo, Jeri und Baetely, Die Gratulanten*), and an early trio, which received a performance at a Musical Society concert in

August 1855, also appear. The first mention of using texts such as *Die Loreley* and *Frithjof* appears in the diaries of 1855 and 1857, although these ideas were not to achieve fruition until 1863 and 1864 respectively, setting a pattern of long gestation periods for his compositions. In May 1856, Hiller wrote of a private performance of Bruch's setting of Goethe's Singspiel *Scherz, List und Rache (Joke, Cunning and Revenge)* at which Hiller played the piano accompaniment. On 28 February 1857 he was working on the orchestration of the work with his young pupil, whereupon it was officially designated Opus 1 (Hiller had earlier advised Bruch against allocating the number to a group of six songs). With Hiller's recommendation, and thanks to a subscription list circulated among Bruch's friends and the music lovers of Cologne, the one-act opera was printed by Senff in Leipzig in 1857.

Goethe's *Scherz, List und Rache* has been set to music by several composers over the years, starting with his contemporary, Philipp Christian Kayser (1786), Peter von Winter (1790), E. T. A. Hoffmann (1801–02), Peter Gast (1881) and Egon Wellesz (1925). Bruch collaborated with Ludwig Bischoff in abbreviating Goethe's text, and conceived the work as salon music with piano accompaniment, and in this form it was performed privately in various homes of the Bruch circle, among which was the Igeler Hof in Bergisch Gladbach, where he had completed the work in March 1856. Under Hiller's guidance he went on to orchestrate it, and it was successfully performed in the Stadttheater in Cologne on 14 January 1858. The orchestral version is lost, though there are a few indications in the piano score of instrumentation. The overture is written for four hands, and through its technical virtuosity, it gives an indication of both Hiller's and Bruch's pianistic abilities, though whether Max played the *secondo* part in the Overture and then went on to sing the Doctor in the performance, as reported in Hiller's diary of 4 May 1856, is unclear: 'Performance of Bruch's opera. I accompanied, Frau Mampe sang Scapine, Weber Scapin, Max the Doctor.'

Husband and wife, Scapin and Scapine (Tenor and Soprano) have been tricked out of their inheritance by the Doctor who tended their old nursemaid in her last days, and persuaded her to leave her savings of 100 florins to him. The couple are bent on revenge, and devise a plan to retrieve their money. Scapin, disguised as a beggar, enters the doctor's service as his assistant, and awaits his wife. She knocks at the door one day as the doctor is once again counting his money, and appeals to him for medical assistance. Scapin creates a diversion at this point, calling for help from another part of the house ('Hilfe, hilfe' to the notes F and B natural, which in German are F and H, the initials of Bruch's mentor Ferdinand Hiller) and the doctor rushes off to find the cause of the alarm. While he is away, Scapine throws away the medicine she has been given, and produces an empty packet labelled arsenic, which she leaves in view before feigning a serious worsening of her condition. The doctor returns with Scapin, in time to see Scapine 'die', and in a panic he promises Scapin 50 florins to dispose of her body. Scapin takes her to the cellar where he leaves her to effect their plan to obtain the remaining 50 florins. When alone, she cries out, and the doctor enters to discover her alive and well and threatening to reveal him as an attempted murderer unless he pays her 50 florins. This he is forced to do, and the lovers depart with their purpose achieved, whilst the doctor bemoans the loss of his hoard.

The work is written in one act (Goethe's original had four) consisting of three scenes, with sixteen musical numbers (arias and ensembles) interspersed with dialogue, and interludes to cover the scene changes. Bischoff described it as 'freshly grown in German earth' and full of 'melody, characterization, movement and life, and rich in truly musical comedy'.[5] He alerted not only the amateur music maker, but also the professional theatre to the work, which would enrich the repertoire of comic opera. He praised Bruch as the antidote to all that was happening in music at the time, namely the innovations of Wagner and the music of the future: 'At such a time as this, one must make doubly welcome a young artist, who does not look for overpowering material, but who is on the road of naturalness and simplicity. It is time to look back, and this cheerful kind of music paves the way to do just that.'

With his Opus 1, the years of study with Hiller came to an end, and young Max was sent on five years of travel to complete his musical education. In his recollections of this period he once again paid tribute to his mentor, grateful for having had the opportunity to sit at the feet of one who had been the close friend of Mendelssohn, who had studied with Hummel, met Beethoven in the last week of the great man's life, and had received Goethe's personal good wishes during a meeting in Vienna in 1827. 'Hiller directed my artistic development', Bruch wrote, 'with love and understanding, but like almost all my teachers, he expected too much of me, and later, by studying alone, I had to make up for this.'

# Chapter Two

## YEARS OF STUDY
### 1858–60

ON HILLER'S ADVICE, Max Bruch began his travels by going to Leipzig at the beginning of 1858, immediately after the first staging of *Scherz, List und Rache* in Cologne. With its famous Conservatoire, its Gewandhaus Orchestra, and its music publishers such as Senff, Kistner and Breitkopf & Härtel, Leipzig was a centre of considerable significance in the world of music at this time. His departure from Cologne had been marked by a farewell concert, given on 4 November 1857 in the Hotel Disch. The programme included several of his early works: a *Romanze* for Piano Solo, the *Capriccio* (Opus 2) for piano (four hands) played by Bruch and Hülle, the Piano Trio (Opus 5), two choral works, *Hosanna* and the Cantata for Soprano, Chorus and Orchestra *Die Birken und die Erlen* (Opus 8) performed with piano accompaniment on this occasion, two songs for tenor, a drinking song for baritone, the Doctor's aria from *Scherz, List und Rache*, and the finale from *Jeri und Baetely*. Max himself played Beethoven's Piano Sonata Opus 90 to complete the programme; and a report of the concert concluded: 'Under most circumstances it asks much to hold the attention throughout a whole evening of music by one and the same composer; that the involvement of the audience in no way flagged, but remained visibly active to the last sound, says much in the young composer's favour.'[1]

Although he was an able solo pianist and accompanist, Bruch was uncompromisingly harsh in his attitude towards the instrument. 'That unmelodious keyboard thing' and 'that dull rattle-trap' he wrote to Simrock in 1875 and 1883 respectively. He had a singular desire 'to set up a grand *auto da fé* of ten to twenty thousand pianos, so that this nineteenth-century epidemic, if not wiped out, might at least be reduced to manageable proportions.' His friend, Arthur Abell, recalled:

> I once asked [Max Bruch] why he, a pianist, had taken such an interest in the violin. He replied, 'because the violin can sing a melody better than the piano can, and melody is the soul of music'.

Others, besides myself, who had witnessed Bruch's virtuosity on the piano, wondered why he did not compose more for that instrument. . . . Bruch himself was still a magnificent pianist in spite of his age. He was then seventy-four, but he played that afternoon with a fire and *élan* that inspired Kreisler to give a reading of the Scottish Fantasy such as I have never heard since.[2]

With this negative attitude towards the piano, it is hardly surprising that his output for that instrument is small, although some unpublished early works featured the piano as a solo or chamber-music instrument. These works were, however, more an exercise in composition techniques than for publication. The first to appear in print was the *Capriccio* (Op. 2) for piano duet, written in 1858 and dedicated to the famous pianist Ignaz Moscheles. Max wrote to Hiller from Leipzig on 20 February 1858, soon after his arrival from Cologne, and among the many first impressions was this description of his meeting with Moscheles:

Among the artists the one who shows me the most goodwill is the worthy veteran Moscheles. He is always at home to artists on Sunday mornings (though it is no advice-giving session!). No less interesting than his playing, are his tales of former days, his diaries and family tree, so that every meeting with him is extraordinarily profitable and agreeable. I was often allowed to play my four-hand *Capriccio* in F sharp minor with him; this work appeared to have made such a good impression, that without my asking it of him, he promised to do all in his power to have it published. I learned from the manager of Kistner's that he did not leave it at that. I did not think it inappropriate to ask Herr Moscheles for permission to dedicate the work to him, and this I received in a most friendly manner.

Curiously Moscheles does not mention the *Capriccio* in his diary, though he did write that 'a young composer, Max Bruch, showed me a number of studies he has lately written. His Lieder are finely felt, and the two Cantatas, *Rinaldo* and *Jubilate*, are fresh and original compositions.' A feature of the *Capriccio* Op. 2 is its polyphonic structure. The three parts of the one movement consist of a fugato theme in the outer sections spanning a homophonous middle section in F sharp major. The use of fugato, and the organ-like treatment of the texture in the writing, particularly in the F sharp pedal-point leading to the climax of the work (bar 115 ff) reflect Bruch's current studies of the works of Bach, and the organ lessons he was taking. Yet his opinion of the great master was highly equivocal, if not extremely intolerant. 'I prefer a bar of Mozart to the whole of the *Well-Tempered Clavier*', he is known to have said, and his justification for turning to ancient Greece for the source of his oratorio texts was equally uncompromising: 'My annoyance with the Christian lamentation and poetic tears of Bach's cantatas, which I quickly saw through, with their narrow-minded and unpoetic sensitivity led me swiftly and of necessity to Greek poetry.' Yet such a sweeping condemnation did not prevent him from using such devices as imitation, *fugato* and polyphony in this early piano work and in his later compositions.

As a pupil of Hiller, the 20-year-old Bruch found himself thoroughly at home in Leipzig, where the influence of Mendelssohn and Schumann still dominated the musical life of the city. The Gewandhaus orchestra was under the direction of Julius Rietz at this time. He succeeded Mendelssohn both in Düsseldorf (1835) and Leipzig (1847) where he became conductor of the Opera and the Singakademie, a teacher of composition at the Conservatoire, and Director of the Gewandhaus concerts. The programmes were often devoted to the works of Beethoven, Schubert, Mendelssohn and Schumann, and performed to an exceedingly high standard. The enthusiastic Bruch described his feelings to Hiller: 'To hear masterpieces such as the great *Leonore* Overtures, or the C major Symphony of Schubert performed by this orchestra is truly a rare and real treat.'[3]

Young Bruch also met Ferdinand David, leader of the Gewandhaus orchestra, soloist in the first performance of Mendelssohn's violin concerto, and teacher of Joachim. The friendship led to David and his colleague, Friedrich Grützmacher, the principal cellist of the Gewandhaus orchestra, playing the first performance and receiving the dedication of Bruch's Piano Trio Op. 5. Both men, together with Röntgen and Unger, gave the first performance of his String Quartet Op. 9 in the Leipzig Gewandhaus on 10 February 1859. Bruch also met Moritz Hauptmann, another eminent musician living in Leipzig at the time. Hauptmann, a friend of Spohr and Mendelssohn, and teacher of David, Joachim, von Bülow, Sullivan and Cowen, was a celebrated theorist in his day, and a successor to Johann Sebastian Bach by holding the post of Cantor and Music Director of the Thomas School in Leipzig. All these men stood shoulder to shoulder opposed to the so-called 'New German Art' personified by Richard Wagner, and totally immersed in these conservative opinions and reactionary politics was the impressionable young Max Bruch.

Important as it was to make contact with the composers and conductors who were currently working in Leipzig, it was equally important for Bruch to establish a connection with a publisher for the many works that he had already written. Breitkopf & Härtel took him on and published Opp. 3–5, 7–15 and Op. 17 during the next five years. Some of these works had already been written while he was still in Cologne studying with Hiller, and he now succeeded in getting most of them performed, either in public or private, during his stay in Leipzig. The preference in the city at the time was for concerts of instrumental rather than vocal music, something that Bruch ruefully reported to Hiller, observing the similarity between this emphasis in Leipzig to that of the Rhineland, where vocal standards were less exalted.[4] He was particularly disappointed because he had two choral works ready for performance, the *Jubilate* and the Cantata *Die Birken und die Erlen* (*The Birches and the Alders*). The former had already been reviewed by Ludwig Bischoff in an article which praised Bruch to the heights, and must not only have put enormous pressure on the young man to live up to such praise, but also to have sown the seeds of disappointment which were, later in life, to produce such bitterness when his rising star had waned.[5] The article contained a long tirade against contemporary, so-called revolutionary composers, whose motives were strongly questioned and criticized, and whose followers were attacked for the necessity of having to place their 'dwarf-gods' on pedestals in order to both idolize them and give them superiority over others. Bischoff then described the virtues of a genius, all of which he saw in Bruch, who 'is a genuine musical being . . . for which he has to thank the Creator of all things, for it is a pure gift from God.'

The *Jubilate* Op. 3 is a short work for soprano solo, chorus and orchestra (double winds, two horns, two trumpets, timpani, and strings), and uses a German translation of a poem by Thomas Moore. The soprano soloist describes a walk in the country, and hears a choir singing a Vesper hymn far away beyond a river, woods, and meadows. This imagery is later used in exactly such a setting when Lenore first appears in the opening scene of Bruch's second opera *Die Loreley* (1863), though in this later work the distant chorus sings an *Ave Maria*. Bischoff described the *Jubilate* as 'a real little gem for choral societies', the orchestration as 'tender and beautiful', and concluded that 'the whole picture is one of Eichendorff romanticism'. The work was written in Cologne in 1856, and first performed (to piano accompaniment) on 1 May 1857 under Franz Weber, receiving a second performance (this time in its orchestral setting) the following year on 12 January 1858 under Hiller in the Cologne Gürzenich concert series. The ebb and flow of the dynamics in the text are well matched in the music, though the melodic architecture which Bruch later developed so strongly is lacking in this early work. The orchestration shows the composer's youth and inexperience, particularly in the string writing, where the violins (muted throughout) play continual arpeggios. In later works he might well have used a harp to achieve this effect. The predominance of the (unmuted) violas in the orchestral texture (a feature of later works) is already apparent, but the woodwind writing is chordal, and unimaginatively thickens the choral setting of the two words *Jubilate, Amen* throughout the work.

The other choral work in the group of compositions published by Breitkopf & Härtel during Bruch's stay in Leipzig during 1858 is *Die Birken und die Erlen* Op. 8, a setting of part of a poem called *Waldlieder* by Gustav Pfarrius, to whom the work is dedicated. It is written in six sections, the first and last of which feature a soprano soloist, the second and fourth a four-part male chorus, the third and fifth a two-part female chorus, the full chorus combining with the solo soprano in the last section. In its finale Bruch also introduces the hallmark of so much of his later work, the violin solo. The orchestration of the Cantata is that of the *Jubilate*, with an additional two horns. The male chorus is cast as the birch trees, the female as the alders, and the soprano soloist sings of walking early one morning and hearing the siren voices of the birches high upon the rocks, and the alders below at the stream's edge, all seeking to lure her. The calls of the thrush and the nightingale, and even the noise of the wind and a waterfall are stilled at the sound of the song of the trees.

The *Three Duets* Op. 4 (for soprano and alto with piano accompaniment) are one of five vocal works published by Breitkopf & Härtel at this time. The first song, 'Ihr lieben Lerchen, guten Tag' (You Lovely Larks, Good Day) — a poem by Count Schlippenbach — with alternating simple and compound duple rhythms, describes the feelings of the early-morning traveller in a sensitive, but not sentimental manner, according to Bischoff in his 1859 review in which he found this song 'the most successful of the group.' The second, 'Altdeutsches Winterlied' (Old German Winter Song), is 'of a quite contrasting character', whilst the mood of the third, 'Im Wald' (In the Wood) is 'at least original'. The *Seven Songs* Op. 6 (duets and trios for female voices) are prefaced as being suitable for 'the needs of senior schools for girls', and are dedicated to the Misses Schmitz who ran such an establishment in Cologne. These and the *Six Songs* Op. 7 (dedicated to his sister, Mathilde), are typical of his vocal output at this time, gentle and simple in style and relying much upon texts devoted to the praise of Nature or God, and written by Geibel, Lenau, Uhland, von Chamisso, Bone, von Fallersleben, and Silesius. *Hymnus* Op. 13 is a short piece for soprano or alto voice with piano accompaniment, using a poem by Auguste Kolter, to whom the work is dedicated. The outer sections of this prayer are accompanied by meandering first-inversion chords over a tonic C-major pedal, as if an organist were improvising. Only the contrasting middle section, a variation upon what has preceded it, has a pianistic accompaniment of gentle semi-quavers before the recapitulation returns its listener to the organ loft. The *Four Lieder* Op. 15 complete the vocal compositions published by Breitkopf & Härtel at this time, and are delicate settings of three poems by Bone and one by Emanuel Geibel, with whose poem *Loreley* Bruch was by now well and truly involved.

Of the various chamber works that Bruch wrote before the age of twenty, the Trio Op. 5 in C minor, for piano, violin and cello is the first of significance. The three through-composed movements are unified harmonically and thematically, but were received with circumspection by the audience at the performance on 4 November 1858 at the Hotel Disch:

> The soirée began with a Trio for piano, violin, and cello which appealed more to us in its earlier form, than in its present one, where the somewhat long Adagio forms the first movement, and is joined to a really fine Scherzo and a fiery Finale. The impression of the first movement, which otherwise has truly beautiful moments, is obviously spoilt, for the audience did not really know what to make of it; an initial movement in such a slow tempo and such dimensions was somewhat unexpected as the first, and therefore, main movement of a trio. We cannot approve of this form, and sincerely hope that the talented composer will not be inclined to an interest in searching for new forms.

The three movements are unified through many harmonic links and thematic references. The first movement (Andante molto cantabile) in C minor flows into the second (Allegro assai); this produces an immediate modulating introduction at the beginning of the movement, which flows into the main key of G major. In turn the third movement (Presto) is reached without a break through a short modulation from G major to C minor. The thematic linking of the movements occurs through the repetition of the augmented first subject in the middle section of the Finale. The main theme appears in its original form, in the tempo of the first movement (Andante), before the work finishes in a final *prestissimo*, the tension being well maintained from beginning to end by an ever-increasing tempo indication. Whereas the first two movements are clearly defined in form (the first ABA¹B¹, the second ABA) the third has a free Rondo form (ABACBBA). This middle section of the Rondo (here called C) is the climax of the work, recalling not only the main motif of the Trio, but other elements from the work. Bruch is unusually bold in his harmonic creativity, concealing at times to the last moment the direction of his keys, as in the last movement where the second subject only establishes its E flat character seven bars after its introduction. Similarly the second subject of the first movement is revealed to be in A flat major only by an excursion through its supertonic of B flat minor. His use of the enharmonic change and the upwards–resolving passing note is striking, with the resolution of a dissonance to a consonance frequently delayed over several other interposed and connected dissonances, producing an increase in harmonic tension. Brahms had written the first version of his Piano Trio Op. 8 in 1854, and the similarities of Bruch's treatment of the three instruments (using both extremes of each instrument's *tessitura* and the texture of the chordal piano writing to achieve a near-orchestral sound), together with rhythmic complexities of two against three, and harmonic twists and turns, are striking.

The entry in Cobbett's *Cyclopedic Survey of Chamber Music* (1929) for Bruch's two String Quartets Op. 9 and Op. 10 is as follows:

His published chamber works are one and all distinguished by beauty of tone and musical architecture. They are naturally modelled on classical lines, and are not especially prominent among the mass of similar productions. The first quartet begins with an introduction, *andante*, tinged with pathos, followed by a powerful and energetic Allegro ma non troppo, the best points of which are the delicate transitions and a beautiful cantabile theme. The richly melodious Adagio is a sort of song without words, relieved by a quicker interlude. The rhythmical Scherzo is sufficiently described by its superscription, *allegro molto energico*; but there is grace in the melodious middle section. The last movement, in the major, is a really jolly Rondo, in which the chief melody resembles a tarantella, the second has a rocking movement, and the third is lyrical in character. The second quartet is a more effective work. If the first movement, Allegro maestoso, has touches of Mendelssohn, it atones by its almost orchestral breadth and vigour. The slow movement opens simply like a song, but is treated with a wealth of elaboration, particularly in the repeated portion, while a fine contrast is provided by the middle section, with its important entry and its broad melodic design. The third, scherzo-like movement, *vivace ma non troppo*, has a fascinating rhythm; it has two trios, one smooth and flowing, the other again remarkable for its rhythm;

here the influence of Schubert was probably at work. The movement, which is in E, ends with a coda in G sharp minor. The lively finale is distinguished by its elaborate figure work and incisive rhythm.

Bruch wrote his last works for solo piano during this period of study and travel. They are the *Fantasia* for two pianos Op. 11, and two solo piano works, *Six Pieces* Op. 12, and *Two Pieces* Op. 14. During the year 1859 Bruch was enrolled as a student at Bonn University, where he was often to be found hard at work practising the organ, 'two hours a day from the beginning of May to the middle of August on the little University organ'. This naturally drew him once again to the works of Bach, in spite of his distaste for the Cantatas and the *Well-Tempered Clavier*. 'There was a five-part fugue of Bach that I loved so much, that I could not leave the organ bench each night throughout the whole term without playing it.' During the winter of 1859–60 he paid several visits to the Curtius-Matthes family in Duisburg, where he played Bach's works for two and three pianos with the family. The *Fantasia* for two pianos, dedicated to Frau Matthes, is the result of his hours in the organ loft during those summer months. The work is in three parts, and opens with a powerful and richly dramatic D minor section, interrupted by rushing triplet passages recalling the famous D minor Toccata and Fugue of Bach. The movement continues with these alternating chordal and flowing figurations until, by a Neopolitan sixth, the relative major key of B flat is reached and a slow, lyrical movement with a syncopated main theme begins. A short reference to the powerful chords of the first movement bridges the second and third movements. This last section is an energetic fugue, cleverly constructed to fit against the recurring triplets of the first movement. After developing fragments of the fugue, the pianos combine to full effect with Bruch the organist pulling out all the stops, and in headlong flight rush through a five-bar coda with a final statement of the fugue's subject.

The *Six Pieces*, dedicated to Bruch's cousin, Bertha Krupp, are short and disarmingly simple works in Schumann's style. Only No. 3 (Impromptu) and No. 5 (Waltz) have titles, and apart from No. 1, all are very short in length. The *Two Pieces* have titles, namely Romanze and Phantasiestück. The former is simple and lyrical, the latter, the most effective of all Bruch's piano works, virtuosic and exciting. His discomfort with the piano as a means of his musical expression is apparent in all these works, limited as they are by their lack of harmonic exploration and by their stylistic eclecticism, so often recalling Beethoven, Schubert, Mendelssohn and Schumann. Nevertheless melody is their strength, lyricism their beauty, the orchestra or the organ their inspiration.

Upon his return from Leipzig in 1859, the 21-year-old Bruch decided on a short break from further studies of music, opted instead for Philosophy, Art and Architecture, and succeeded against the odds in getting himself registered as a student at Bonn University. What stood in his way was his private home-based education, with no evidence of matriculation from a school, though the private tuition he did receive from outside the home was from teachers at the Friedrich Wilhelm Gymnasium. The acting Director of this School (Professor Hoss, successor to the late Dr Knebel) was one of those who provided Max with a reference for the University. Another came from the police, no doubt through August Bruch, the composer's father. This attested to his moral and political virtue, and assured the University authorities that the would-be student had never indulged in illegal activities. It was stipulated that Max could seek higher education only within his chosen profession as musician, and was specifically prohibited from employment in State or Church service at any later stage in his life. This appears to be a hangover from the nervousness of the immediate post-1848 revolutionary period a decade earlier. The final signatory to his enrolment documents was the Rector of the University, the Professor of Archaeology and Classical Philology, Otto Jahn, whose famous biography of Mozart had been completed just four years earlier.

On 28 June 1859 Max Bruch was enrolled as a student of Philosophy, and took lodgings at 408 Cölnstrasse, the home of an obstetrician, Dr Schilde. It would appear, however, that in spite of all the trouble it took to get himself enrolled as a student, he did not stay long at the University, for by the winter of 1859 his name no longer appeared in the University Register, and his file was closed on 6 December 1859. A lasting memory were the lectures of Anton Springer on the history of Art in the Rhineland. The lectures were so interesting, and the lecturer so riveting that Max often could not tear himself away from the 'blazing eyes' in order to take notes on a speech which poured out 'like a mountain stream'. He kept his exercise book containing the notes he did manage to take, recalling conducted visits to Cologne with fellow students to visit Romanesque churches and crypts under the supervision of the enthusiastic Springer. His passionate interest in literature and poetry was awakened during the few months in Bonn, fuelling his own creative ideas as he worked on the two significant compositions gestating at this time, *Die Loreley* and *Frithjof*.

The years 1860–62 were the last that Bruch was ever to spend living in his native city, Cologne. As this became increasingly apparent to him over the years, his bitterness and resentment grew against the city that would not give him the permanent post he sought, and which consequently prevented him from living in his beloved Rhineland. In 1861 Max's father died, and it appeared that the young man would have to take on the financial burden of his mother and sister. Fortunately for the family their distant relative, the Essen industrialist Alfred Krupp, gave them the support they needed, and enabled Max to resume his travels to such cities as Berlin, Dresden, Leipzig, Vienna and Munich, to broaden his education, develop his contacts, and to compose.

# Chapter Three

## MANNHEIM
### 1861–63

---

IT WAS HIS aunt's sister who married Alfred Krupp, and the result was a welcome injection of finance into the ailing Bruch household. It was now possible for him to resume his travels, and, encouraged by his mother, he set off for Berlin. Recently widowed, she began a correspondence with her son which became a mixture of maternal advice on methods of washing nightshirts and keeping his feet warm in winter, encouragement to pursue potentially useful contacts (especially if they would help in overcoming the difficulties he was having in getting Geibel's permission to set the poet's own *Die Loreley*), and warnings against money-grasping landladies and their untrustworthy servants. She urged him to pay his rent monthly as well as the bills for hiring a piano, and the costs of breakfasts and other daily meals taken at his lodgings, but bills from the shoemaker and the tailor should be paid on the spot. She even reproached herself for ever having considered his chosen profession unwise, for her past short-sightedness and impatience at his choice, and whilst recognizing that her own life had never been easy with its toil and worries, she acknowledged that the sacrifice had been, and would continue to be worthwhile. Her letters are full of the anxieties of a mother hen. They are preoccupied with his clothes ('bring home the seven shirts with the cuffs when you come') and his health ('a few times daily you must drink some really good Bordeaux with a little bread, for this strengthens the body; but it must be a good wine, no matter if it is expensive'). Her own health was already failing (she died in 1867) and she now wore blue tinted spectacles in an effort to stave off encroaching blindness. Amid the domestic guidance in her letters, however, there were telling comments on the decisions he was faced with at this time, and no shortage of her own opinions on what he should do.

No letters from Bruch to his mother have survived from the early 1860s, but he did write on two occasions to Hiller from Berlin in December 1861 giving an account of his travels. His early symphony (unpublished and since lost) had been finished during his journey to

Leipzig via Essen and Paderborn that autumn. He arrived in Leipzig on 18 November 1861 where he met once again with Reinecke and David. They organized an orchestral rehearsal of the work which went well, and a performance two months later in January was proposed. Bruch was already now enjoying the luxury of full orchestral run-throughs of his works, something he put more and more value on in the coming years, even to the extent of having his choral works played and sung so that he could then correct and reshape before submitting the work for publication. David had also played Bruch's String Quartet Op. 10, and was impressed enough by it to promise a performance during the coming winter season. Bruch renewed his acquaintance with Moscheles ('we spent pleasant hours playing Mozart's Sonata for two pianos'). On 24 November he left Leipzig for Berlin where he spent a month living at Zimmerstrasse 38. The social and musical life became more hectic ('concerts in abundance, with free tickets flowing from every source to those thirsty for them') and he was granted a rehearsal pass for the Opera. He played his symphony to Wilhelm Taubert described in Grove (1899) as being 'one of those sound and cultivated artists who contribute so much to the solid musical reputation of Germany' though 'a want of strength and spirit, with all his real musicianlike qualities, his refined taste and immense industry, has prevented Taubert from writing anything that will be remembered.' Taubert (not surprisingly perhaps) did not convince Max with his comments on the work whereas Reinecke gave him practical suggestions and tips on orchestration ('I had much work to do on the woodwind writing in particular. I have virtually rewritten the first movement').

As well as attending concerts at the Court, he heard the cathedral choir ('quite excellent'), and went to a soirée at which Joachim's Violin Concerto was played by Ferdinand Laub. He attended three such soirées at von Bülow's house, and ruefully commented to Hiller: 'A piano stood on the right and on the left, because one instrument could not possibly withstand the orchestral treatment it got for a whole evening. He played very well, but it's a bit much to expect one to listen to piano playing for 2½ hours!'[1] This same letter was largely devoted to recommending to Hiller a man from Paderborn who wished, at the age of twenty-nine, to change profession from lawyer to musician. Bruch took a great deal of trouble to write at length on the abilities of the gifted amateur (a Herr Turnau), and showed much consideration at a time when he himself needed all the help he could get in furthering his own career. In spite of all his effort, it does not appear that Herr Turnau was successful in his attempt to be enrolled at the Conservatoire in Cologne, although Hiller auditioned him at Bruch's request.

He heard Haydn's *Creation* given by the Singakademie ('which, according to a local malicious gossip, consists of the old virgins of Berlin breathing their last'). He saw the final performance, at the Opera, given by Leopoldine Herrenburg-Tuczek on 6 December as Susanna in *The Marriage of Figaro*, at which the king himself threw her a laurel wreath, and sent her a miniature laurel-tree in silver, bearing 65 leaves on which were inscribed the roles she had sung during her career. Little did the 23-year-old Max realize that he was watching the aunt of his future wife Clara Tuczek, but that marriage lay twenty years ahead. As Frau Herrenburg-Tuczek's star waned, so another rose — that of Adelina Patti, at whose début he was also fortunate to be present at this time. 'The voice is sharp, however, and the technique not yet complete, so the brightness of this star is not undimmed.' On New Year's Day 1862 he saw *Don Giovanni*, the following Monday *Figaro* once again, followed by *Lohengrin*, though in his letter of 3 January he called Wagner's opera 'Mein lieber Schwan' rather than use its proper title. The letters of 13 December and 21 December 1861 asked Hiller for comments on the as yet uncompleted score of *Die Loreley*. He entrusted it to his former teacher, saying that his sister Mathilde would collect it, when Hiller had read it through, and return it to her brother. 'I cannot be without it in Munich.' The year 1862 was to be a watershed in his career — it saw the completion of his next work, the opera *Die Loreley* Op. 16.

When Emanuel Geibel asked Mendelssohn, after a performance in the autumn of 1845 of *A Midsummer Night's Dream*, why he was not writing an opera, the composer replied, 'Give me a good text and I'll start writing one at four o'clock tomorrow morning.' Whether this motivated Geibel's version of *Die Loreley* is unclear, but the poet certainly set to work at once, using as his source Clemens Brentano's 1802 novel *Godwi* in which the poem appears. Mendelssohn's relationship with the opera house was not a happy one, in spite of a long and close friendship with one of the foremost actors, directors and theatre administrators of the time, Eduard Devrient (who also wrote the libretto, rejected by Mendelssohn but accepted by Marschner in 1833, for the opera *Hans Heiling*).

It was his dissatisfaction with the texts offered him that drove Mendelssohn into an increasingly negative frame of mind on the subject of opera and virtually condemned every project before it stood a chance of success. His association with Geibel over the text for *Die Loreley* was no different, although what eventually put paid to any further discussion or correspondence on the subject was the composer's death in November 1847. During the years 1845–47 Geibel sent Mendelssohn many draft revisions of the work, and went through moods of elation and frustration at the composer's comments in their frequent correspondence. It becomes apparent from these letters that things were not going well, and that, given half a chance, Mendelssohn would rather have nothing more to do with the idea. He was particularly dissatisfied with the first act of Geibel's draft which he received in January 1846. That year he was also distracted from the project by conducting the Aachen Music Festival in the early summer and the first performance of *Elijah* in Birmingham on 16 August.

The correspondence between the two men was resumed in September 1846, when, along with a receipt for 20 louis-d'or (100 gold thalers) on account of his future participation in the opera, Geibel sent the amended draft of the work to the composer. Again it was the first act that troubled Mendelssohn, 'indeed the opening itself appears to me neither interesting nor necessary', so he proposed starting on the composition of his 'favourite bits from the second or third acts'. The rest of 1846 was taken up with revisions of *Elijah*, but an interesting letter written by Mendelssohn to Jenny Lind (the 'Swedish Nightingale') on 31 October is full of enthusiasm at the idea of writing an opera for her: 'If I do not write a good opera now, and for you, then it will never happen.' Whether he saw her as the first Loreley, or whether he was already considering an alternative suggestion from the English impresario, Benjamin Lumley, for an opera on Shakespeare's *The Tempest* is unclear. Certainly the possibility of the latter project coming to fruition appeared in the newspapers, and created a strain in the relationship between Geibel and Mendelssohn. Lumley had, however, been premature in telling the press, and the beleaguered composer, now sick of the whole business, physically very tired and with his spirits at an extremely low ebb, was forced to smooth Geibel's ruffled feathers. By the middle of February 1847 Mendelssohn had the draft returned to him amended yet again. His reaction was described by Devrient.[2] The composer, 'with a very resigned expression brought me the poem of *Loreley* which he had received from Geibel shortly before. "There it is," he said. "Look at it and do not call me obstinate or whimsical if I tell you I cannot compose it as it is." . . . Felix became really ill-tempered over his constant bad luck with opera.'

In desperation, and with another journey to England imminent, Mendelssohn suggested the services of an unnamed third party to save the situation and get the results he wanted (perhaps it was Devrient). Geibel rejected any suggestion of bringing in someone else, and proceeded to make further alterations to try and satisfy his collaborator. Tragedy was now to take control of events, for Mendelssohn's sister Fanny died in May 1847, and the shock weakened her brother's already deteriorating condition, plunging him into even greater depths of black moods. Even so he made another attempt in June to obtain an agreement on the problematic first act. Geibel sent yet another draft, Mendelssohn replying in August that he wanted a meeting to discuss his latest ideas; but nothing appears to have come of this either. The last letter, written 22 October 1847, is from Mendelssohn's wife, Cécile. She pleaded her husband's serious illness but hoped that he would be well enough to meet with Geibel at the end of November upon his return from a concert engagement in Vienna. That meeting never took place, for the composer died on 3 November, and with him the idea for an operatic setting of Geibel's text. He left just three fragments which he had set, perhaps the 'favourite bits' with which he assured the exasperated librettist that he would make a start. They were an *Ave Maria* for female chorus, a drinking song for the vintners, and the Finale to the first act with its chorus of Rhine Spirits. These fragments were performed a year after the composer's death by his successor at the Leipzig Gewandhaus, Julius Rietz.

For the next thirteen years Geibel did nothing with *Die Loreley* other than to reject requests from many composers (among them Marschner) for its use as an opera libretto. Then in the autumn of 1860 he had the text published, and one of its early purchasers (who read it eagerly 'like a wild animal devouring its prey') was Max Bruch. Naïvely he seems to have ignored the copyright clearly printed in the book forbidding any setting of the work, and went ahead with his composition in an 'ecstasy of inspiration'. He went for the heart of the material by setting the chorus of Rhine Spirits, which was dramatically the most effective part of the work (an element for the most part sadly lacking elsewhere in Geibel's text) and which no doubt featured in Mendelssohn's 'favourite bits' for the same reason. On 8 December 1860 Bruch belatedly asked permission to set the work which he had already begun. Geibel replied on 11 December:

Your lines of the 8th of the month place me — I must sincerely confess — in a difficult predicament. For although I wish to thank you for the friendly interest you show in my poem, I must nevertheless regretfully inform you that, on the grounds of my relationship with the Mendelssohn family and on other grounds which I shall not go into now, it is not possible to agree to any proposal concerning your composition of *Die Loreley*. By publishing my poem I no longer gave any thought to a musical setting of the work, on the contrary I felt myself rid of such a necessity, and at last concluded my hard work of many years in a literary manner. If I add that I rejected a request from Marschner years ago to set the work to music . . . and others were all refused the text, you will see that under the circumstances I am in no position to give you a favourable reply; without in any way doing you any unkindness nor underestimating your talent, it is a misfortune that I sincerely regret. How could I possibly think that, in spite of the clearly expressed safeguard of my copyright, a musician would undertake such a task without first obtaining my permission? Once again regretting I am unable to send you more comforting news, I remain in highest esteem, your servant Geibel.

Max was devastated when he received Geibel's letter, and it was cold comfort to read of the rejections sent by the poet to thirteen other composers. His determination grew to try to change Geibel's mind, for although he was unaware of the difficulties and misgivings his eminent predecessor had experienced, he concluded that what had been good enough for Mendelssohn was good enough for him. 'As I placed all my hopes on this opera, I did not wish to leave any possibility untried in getting Geibel's agreement.' Hearing that the Mendelssohn family might have rights in the text after all, he wrote at once to the late composer's brother Paul asking if he would intervene on his behalf and persuade Geibel to change his mind. He received a 'scornful' reply, short and to the point; Paul Mendelssohn was 'not in a position to change the reply sent by Herr Geibel to Herr Bruch'. With no literary contacts to intercede for him, the New Year of 1861 began very inauspiciously for Max.

On 14 January 1861 he wrote from Cologne to his friend, Rudolf von Beckerath, for help, reporting that he had 'composed Geibel's *Loreley* (complete, including the first act Finale, to the hair-tearing fury of the Mendelssohn fanatics)', but had come up against the poet's refusal of permission to use his text. 'Much has been written hither and thither; through Moscheles and Härtel I turned to the Mendelssohn family to put in a word for me. . . . What is to be done? I must do all I can to get *Loreley* heard, even if it means doing it unstaged. This opera, conceived in the heat of an extraordinary inspiration, is unquestionably the best thing I have produced till now.' It appears that Hiller, to whom he naturally also turned for help at this time, suggested that Bruch should try for a concert performance of extracts from the work in the hope of favourable reviews, news of which would spread until it finally reached the intransigent poet. Bruch agreed that this would be his best hope, if only because he believed that 'good operatic music, even if stripped of all scenic elements, can and must work musically on its own merits'. He then proposed the idea that Beckerath, through his connection with the Choral Society in Crefeld, might be able to organize such a performance. By 19 January Bruch was writing once again to Beckerath, grateful this time that such a performance would indeed take place in the spring, but also cannily suggesting that a 'private performance' take place at an even earlier date to heighten public interest. He himself would sing Reinald 'and, where necessary, Hubert', perhaps Beckerath himself 'with Herr Seyffart' would sing Otto, and he took the liberty of suggesting his sister Mathilde as Lenore. 'She knows my intentions as no other . . . the voice is not big enough to sing significant roles on stage, but for a room it would suffice completely.' With two voices on each chorus part, the private sing-through of the first act took place in Crefeld at the beginning of February 1861.

No further significance can be attached to these Crefeld events, other than their benefit to Bruch in his refining of the orchestration of the work. For the rest of the year little happened to encourage him, but events took a new turn in January 1862. After returning to Berlin and Leipzig he received an invitation to Munich from Count Ludwig von Stainlein, not only for a social visit to this keen amateur musician, but for a first meeting with Emanuel Geibel. Bruch was firmly instructed by Stainlein to select 'only the simplest and the most intelligible parts of the opera' to play to Geibel who was 'not very musical and imagined a plain and simple folksong-like setting of his poem'. So Max chose a little song, 'Wir grüssen dich fein', as a sample of his craft.[3] Bruch took up the story in a letter to Rudolf von Beckerath: 'Since 24 February I have been in this noisy, happy, colourful capital city of Vienna. The main outcome of my journeying is that I have come to an arrangement with Geibel and made a friend of him. *Die Loreley* is free! Geibel told me directly: "Your obstinacy overcame my own; if you had not come to me with the finished work, even though I had already forbidden any such setting, I would never have given you my permission."'[4]

He had received the permission verbally on 25 January, and was to receive it in writing on 1 May 1862. Geibel encouraged Max to believe that Munich would give the first performance in the autumn of 1862, but the North German poet was no welcome figure in the Bavarian capital, and the work found no champion in Franz Lachner, the Court Conductor, former close friend of Schubert and now the dominating figure in the musical life of the city (Grove calls him the 'Hiller of the south'). In the autumn of 1862 Max went to Mannheim, where he met Lachner's brother Vincenz, and the result was far more successful. As Court Conductor in Mannheim it was through his instigation that the opera was accepted for performance and the première planned for 14

June 1863. Lachner's influence on Bruch at this time and in the immediate future was as considerable as Hiller's had been earlier in his career, for he was a highly experienced opera conductor, and taught Max not only the technique of conducting, but also showed him the pitfalls of over-orchestrating his works and how to keep the textures thinner and more transparent. This becomes apparent in *Die Loreley*, with its skilful woodwind writing.

Matters could not have been helped by his mother's gloomy letters, sent throughout the period of doubt over the future of the opera: 'I am anxious to hear from you and know if you can bear your ill-fortune calmly, for recently I do not believe this to be so. Misfortune rarely comes once only, as can be seen in your case.' 'The cough which I have now laboured under for four weeks will not go away, in spite of the medicines, powders, and tea that the doctor gives me to take . . . I will gladly bear all these little troubles if only we could all sit together and listen to your news.' When the matter of *Loreley* was resolved, however, she became more constructive in her concern towards the successful outcome of its staging:

I pray the good Lord will send us a blessed result! How I implore this of Him daily and hourly. I cannot conceal from you how your happy confidence delights me on the one hand, and worries me on the other. Forgive me, dear Max, if, after so many dashed hopes, I do not speak of more positive and shining expectations. These past nights I have spent less time sleeping than worrying about *Loreley*, and the more I think about how dear the music has become to me, the more I think how dear it must become to other people. Let that not be a false conclusion! What a shame they postponed the performances of your opera until after Whitsun. The people like to treat themselves to something special on such public holidays, and many would have undertaken the trip there to hear it, when later they will not have half the time to do so. I am glad you speak so well of Michaeli [who sang Lenore], for on her rests so much importance in the success of the opera. Schlösser [who sang Otto] will leave much to be desired . . . I am concerned that the Loreley rock cannot be brought nearer the front so that her voice is not lost in the effective ending.

The opera was well received at its first performance on Sunday 14 June 1863, and was given three further performances that season. At that on 4 July several eminent musicians attended, among them Clara Schumann, Anton Rubinstein, Ignaz Lachner, Hermann Levi, Friedrich Gernsheim, Johann Kalliwoda and Joseph Raff. Geibel attended none of them, expressing a preconceived opinion that 'the folk-song way of writing which the text presupposes, is hardly the way of the modern musician to write.' The opera appeared twice in each of the next two seasons at Mannheim, and was also staged in Hamburg, Leipzig, Cologne, Mainz, Weimar and Coburg. Abroad it was staged in Rotterdam and Prague before it disappeared from the repertoire for just over twenty years.

The opera is set in the heart of the wine-producing Rhineland. Ever since a chance meeting in the hills above their respective homes, the Count Otto has been pursuing a passionate obsession with the peasant girl, Lenore. As his steward, Leupold, reminds him, it is now the eve of his wedding to Bertha, Countess of Stahleck, the bride whom society has selected for him. Otto, however, is determined on another meeting with Lenore, to whom he has neither revealed his true identity nor the truth of his impending marriage for fear of losing her love. Whilst far away in the valley below a choir sings the Ave Maria, Lenore arrives for her meeting with her lover. The encounter ends with Otto's impulsive departure, tormented by the guilt of deceiving this innocent village girl, and she, bewildered at his manner, is left alone to pray for him and their love. The scene then changes to the river bank where the peasants are assembling a shipment of their finest produce for the wedding feast. Lenore's father, Hubert the ferryman, supervises the operation but is unable to account for his daughter's strange and solitary behaviour. When she arrives the village girls select her in a folk ritual as the maid to present the ritual goblet of wine to the bridal pair, Otto and Bertha. At that moment the wedding procession passes by the assembled villagers on its way to Otto's castle. Recognizing her lover, Lenore confronts Otto, but he denies all knowledge of her and orders the procession to continue. Lenore falls in a faint, whilst the ballad singer Reinald, hired for the nuptial feast, observes these events with interest and senses the unease and ill-feeling of the people.

In Act II Lenore arrives at the river, shocked by the nightmare of her predicament, and calls upon Evil to avenge her. She summons the Rhine Spirits and enters into a pact with them in which she sells her soul and the ability to love for a sensual beauty that will ensnare a man and drive him to his death.

Act III begins with the wedding feast at which Reinald sings his ballad, heavy with innuendo and the cause of much displeasure to the increasingly nervous Otto. The Count calls for the bridal cup and is confronted by Lenore, who now has everyone present enchanted by her appearance. Through her sensuous singing she brings the deranged Otto to a pitch of madness in which he challenges all assembled for her hand. As a fight begins, Bertha's uncle appears — he is the Archbishop of Mainz, the symbol of supreme spiritual and temporal power. He condemns Lenore as a witch and convenes an ecclesiastical court to try her, despite Otto's continued irrational championing of her. As the trial is about to begin, Bertha mourns her lost husband and love, and contemplates suicide. Her ally, Reinald, fails in his attempt to get her to leave by revealing that Otto has come to attend Lenore's trial. This now begins, and Lenore makes no defence, and indeed it is her openness and resignation together with her newly acquired power over men which touches everyone, including her judge the Archbishop, and she is acquitted. The Archbishop tries to call Otto to his senses and restore him to Bertha, who now also pleads with her husband in an attempt to win him back. She is cursed by Otto and thrown to the ground, whereupon the Archbishop turns his wrath on him with sentence of excommunication and proscription.

The final act begins with the peasants celebrating the grape harvest, but Hubert has lost all his sense of fun since the tragedy which has exiled his daughter from the community, and he laments his lost optimism and leaves to join Bertha's funeral procession. She has died of a broken heart, and even Otto feels such a sense of shame at his treatment of her that he arrives to pay his last respects from a distance, though nothing can drive from his mind the vision of Lenore. He resolves to find her, and to win her once and for all. Lenore is awaiting him, and the fulfilment of their tragedy. His attempts to recapture their former happiness bring her to the brink of forgiveness, but she cannot escape the destiny she has chosen for herself, nor can he avoid the fate she has selected for him. The Rhine Spirits claim him as he flings himself into the river, and Lenore on her rock becomes irrevocably wedded to the spirit of the Rhine.

The opera is through composed with arias and ensembles linked by recitatives. These latter, unaided by Geibel's poor dramatic sense, are unhappily also Bruch's weakness. They possess rare moments of adventurous chromaticism, and have somewhat inconsequential, meandering melodic lines which do little to propel the action forward. The strength of the vocal writing lies in the choruses, richly textured, often beautiful in melody, and owing much to composers such as Bach, Beethoven, Weber and Spohr. The short second act is highly derivative of the Wolf's Glen scene from Weber's *Der Freischütz* or Faust and Mephistofeles' scene with Sycorax in Spohr's *Faust*. Already Bruch was showing a preference in writing for male chorus, of which there are several in this opera. All the characters have arias ranging from Hubert and Reinald with their strophic folksongs to Otto's dramatic *Heldentenor* aria in the last act. This role, like that of Lenore, is particularly demanding. Lenore, in spite of her more lyrical moments (such as the opening *Ave Maria* and the Song of the Loreley) comes into her own in the second act with the Rhine Spirits: accompanied by a full chorus, and with dark, dramatic chords and rushing string passages from the orchestra, the soprano is tested to her vocal limits. The role of Bertha, with her beautiful Cavatina in Act III recalling Mozart's aria for Pamina in *Die Zauberflöte*, 'Ach, ich fühl's', is contrastingly lyrical. This aria (No. 16), 'Komm', o Tod', was used by Bruch in his earlier opera *Scherz, List und Rache*, though in this original form it was a duet for Scapine and Scapin (No. 14), 'Nacht o holde, halbes Leben'. In spite of the exceptionally fine aria Bertha is given, the character is dramatically too pallid to sustain interest and it is Lenore who dominates the opera.

At the beginning of 1862, whilst in Munich, Bruch wrote a *Canzonetta* for orchestra which is a preliminary sketch for the Prelude to *Die Loreley*. The main theme of the opera's overture is also the kernel of this short orchestral work, and makes three appearances during its course, initially by the first horn and twice by the full orchestra. A short coda incorporates the opening four bars of the second subject before concluding with the beginning of the main theme, which is once again entrusted to the principal horn.[5]

*Die Loreley* is scored for double winds, four horns, two trumpets, three trombones, timpani and strings, with an offstage organ used in the ecclesiastical scenes. Apart from a few cymbal strokes in the Rhine Spirits' scene of the second act, no further use is made of percussion in the orchestra. The instrumental writing owes much to the young Wagner. It is typical of the press at this time to use Bruch as a means with which to whip the New German Art of Wagner, and the reviews for this work were no exception. Bischoff (in the *Niederrheinische Musikzeitung*) once again placed it in the line of Mozart, Beethoven, Weber and Marschner, contrasting it with the 'anti-musical system of Richard Wagner'. 'There are,' he wrote, 'no shrill dissonances, no torture of the ears, no ugliness on the ears or nerves of the listener.' There were also no motivic references 'which trumpet "I am the King", "I am the good person", "I am the evil one", no eccentric couplings of heterogeneous instruments such as piccolo with timpani and similar trivial hocuspocus. In a word: the law of beauty is never broken. Let this beautiful and pure German work make its own way forward! Our great theatres will not regret taking on this patriotic work of art.'

After attending the performance on 4 July 1863, Clara Schumann reported to Hiller:

As you can imagine, the opera by Brughk (!) interested me very much; there are lovely moments in it; throughout the work the orchestra and chorus are so masterfully handled, I can scarcely believe it is by such a young composer. Its length is considerable, and if I may say so openly, I miss a creative power in the music. Throughout I felt I was more interested in the lyricism than being musically particularly affected. I will certainly not miss the chance of hearing it again, for now I can only speak of my first impression, and please do not believe I would let this stand as my verdict. I will gladly retract if proved wrong. The text, by the way, is dreadful. The characters Bertha and Reinhold are downright disturbing; however I found certain moments of *Die Loreley* wonderful.

Half a dozen theatres in Germany, besides Prague and Rotterdam, took Bischoff's advice, after which the opera disappeared from the repertoire to be replaced by the more progressive works of others. In 1887 Max Stägemann staged the work in Leipzig in a refashioned version, in which scenes and even whole acts were transposed with the composer's blessing. This was no doubt an attempt to improve upon the weaknesses of Geibel's pallid drama rather than Bruch's music. The theatre in Leipzig was at a low ebb at the time, and Stägemann needed a work to boost its fortunes. Musically well prepared under the leadership of the young Kapellmeister Gustav Mahler, the performances were justly praised, though none thought the work had been improved by the reorganization of the plot. In this form it was performed in Leipzig, Breslau, Cassel and Cologne.

Nearly thirty years later the work found an unlikely champion in Hans Pfitzner. Appointed Music Director to the Opera House in Strasburg in 1916, he immediately put Bruch's opera into the repertoire. He had been devoted to *Die Loreley* since childhood, ever since he discovered the vocal score at home. He entered into correspondence with Bruch, by now an old man of seventy-eight and living in retirement in Berlin. Bruch had no love for Pfitzner's music, which he held in contempt along with that of Reger and Richard Strauss, but immediately warmed to the idea of a revival of the work and developed a cordial relationship with the younger man. He agreed completely with Pfitzner that the first version of the opera must be used, revealing that after initially agreeing to Stägemann's reworking of the drama, in 1887, he subsequently regretted doing so and never again wished the second version to be performed.

After the première in Strasburg on 26 March 1916 the work received five further performances, whereupon it once again vanished into obscurity, though not before Pfitzner had somewhat rashly written that 'any theatre which from now on does not take up *Die Loreley* sins not only against the composer but above all against Art'. When Bruch received this report he rather sardonically wrote in the margin, 'they will all be sinners, for until now all is still and silent.' Nevertheless it did the old man much good during the dreadful suffering of the years of the First World War to witness Pfitzner's enthusiasm for staging the work: 'Your actions in this matter are psychologically remarkable for me, uplifting to see in these times what one man can achieve through an honest, pure will, unbowing to consequences and with an indestructible idealism in spite of so many difficulties. My only fear is that indifferent or partisan conductors, completely unmusical, asinine producers and theatre managements would ruin it; for Hans Pfitzner is a rare bird in this gloomy company.' Some extracts were broadcast by Pfitzner from Munich during 1938 (the centenary of the composer's birth) and in 1984 the work was staged by the joint theatres of Oberhausen and Remscheid. The British première was given by University College Opera, London, at the Bloomsbury Theatre in February 1986, using the original version and conducted by the present author.

# Chapter Four

---

ιττεmpt at opera had received mixed fortunes,
)se just one more (in 1870) before abandoning the
form for ever. He enjoyed the generally favourable reception of *Die Loreley* in the various German cities which took it up; in fact he became somewhat bored by its success. 'Yesterday *Lorelips* was played for the sixth time in Cologne,' he wrote to Beckerath in September 1864, 'am heartily thankful I did not have to be there. Next in Aachen; from the tenth performance on I get 5 per cent of the gross takings. I'll be a rich chap; advise me whether I should buy Government Stock or Railway Shares.'

While the fifteen published compositions preceding *Die Loreley* consist of piano solos and duets, a trio, two string quartets, and various vocal and short choral works, the group of compositions which separate the opera from his next significant work is exclusively vocal. In writing them, Bruch attained that facility for vocal composition (using either solo or choral forces) with which his fame and fortune were to spread over the next twenty years, not only throughout Germany but also to England and America. It was at this period that his love for folksong manifested itself in the *Twelve Scottish Folksongs*.[1] His source was the collection entitled *The Scots Musical Museum* (Edinburgh 1787–1803) compiled by James Johnson. Much of the taking down of the airs was done by Robert Burns, whose involvement in the compilation of the six volumes, each containing 100 airs, became so close that he was its virtual unpaid editor. It was George Thomson, Secretary to the Board of Trustees for the Encouragement of Arts and Manufactures in Scotland, who contacted Beethoven in 1803 with a commission to set Scottish folksongs, and it was Bruch's new mentor, Vincenz Lachner, who now directed and encouraged the young man to set twelve of the original melodies to his own accompaniment. In December 1875 he was to write to his publisher, Simrock: 'The influence of folksong upon my melody is unmistakable – happily so!!' In November 1884 he wrote again to Simrock:

I am pleased that others are now taking the same path that I took twenty years ago with the publication of my *Scottish Folksongs*. As a rule a good folk tune is more valuable than 200 created works of art. I would never have come to anything in this world, if I had not, since my twenty-fourth year, studied the folk music of all nations with seriousness, perseverance, and unending interest. There is nothing to compare with the feeling, power, originality and beauty of the folksong. . . . This is the route one should now take — here is the salvation of our unmelodic times — all is ruined, only true Melody survives all the changes and behaviour of these times! The least creative recognize that they are groping in the dark, and do not see this eternally bubbling source, 'like the thirsty in the desert'.

In contrast to the English revival of the folksong which was to occur around the turn of the century, Bruch belonged to those musicians of the nineteenth century who made use of the folksong, rather than respect its autonomy. It was a means to an end and its use exonerated the motives of its arranger; it was there as a servant to be reworked into the musical identity of its master, and was used as a purifying sword against the heresy of the modern movement, a bastion of the conservatives on the attack. At the beginning of 1863, although preoccupied with the forthcoming première of *Die Loreley*, Bruch was overjoyed to receive a collection of folksongs for perusal from the poet Paul Heyse whom he met and befriended in Carlsruhe. 'I look upon this collection as a holy relic,' he wrote as he began his studies of them, and 'this treasure chest of folksongs' gave him the 'liveliest stimulation. You could truthfully not have done me a greater service.' He was, however, careful to make the distinction between the working of a folksong into a composition and a straightforward arrangement. Citing Brahms as an example, he observed to Fritz Simrock in May 1897:

What you say about the free use of folksong and folk poetry is quite true. In such cases neither the poet nor the musician really needs to reveal his sources, because through the medium of his spirit something different and new has been recreated from the often modest original material. With the Hungarian Dances, however, the case is different for, as far as I know, Brahms has only arranged them without somehow changing the musical substance or adding anything of his own. I remember quite clearly that in 1865 I was with Brahms in a restaurant in Vienna, and heard the first G minor 2/4 dance played by a Hungarian band exactly as Brahms later published it. And without a doubt that's how it is with the other dances — we are talking unmistakably about arrangements.

Of the six hundred folksongs in the Johnson collection, Bruch selected just twelve for voice and piano accompaniment. Among them were two of which he was to make fuller use in the *Scottish Fantasy* sixteen years later, 'Auld Rob Morris' and 'Scots wha hae'. This latter is the only song which specifies the type of voice intended to sing it, namely a tenor. Bruch's accompaniments vary from the straightforward chordal quality of 'Marion' and 'Auld Rob Morris' with the frequent use of the harmonic suspension for sacred rather than secular effect, to the suggestive portrayal of folk instruments such as the harp in 'Scots wha hae' and 'Highland Laddie'. His selection from the volumes favours those with unusual rhythmic patterns and eccentric phrase lengths, and whilst in 'The Wedding Day' voice and piano chase one another in a canon, in 'Mary's Dream' and 'O saw ye my father?' they meander and interweave in arabesque. Throughout his life he was often to refer to these songs and the significance they held for him, but never more passionately than in a letter to Beckerath at the time of their publication:

As a little keepsake I am sending you an example I have just received of my Scottish [folksongs]. If you sing and play these melodies through . . . you once again experience the holy respect for the power, simplicity, and beauty of the genuine folksong. Don't you agree? A melody like, for example, 'The Beds of Sweet Roses' literally strikes dead hundreds of modern melodies, stone dead I say. Where do we all stand? I consider I have revealed my musical Credo quite clearly and loudly through the publication of these wonderful, unknown melodies.[2]

Bruch's association with Paul Heyse and Emanuel Geibel also led to publication of the *Ten Lieder* Op. 17, five Spanish, two Italian and three German poems by Hermann Lingg. Heyse and Geibel were responsible for the translations into German of the Spanish and Italian songs. Hermann Deiters described the songs in the November 1864 issue of the *Allgemeine Musikalische Zeitung* as being 'drunk with a mixture of southern heat and the warm intimacy of the German soul'. He went on to praise the composer's ability to produce a good and singable melody, his care in declamation and modulation, and the way he 'frequently makes known his understanding and interpretation in a few fine strokes', recognizing in the songs 'a highly gifted musician of taste and culture', though adding that he was as yet immature and young enough not to have tasted life to its 'depth of suffering'. Once again Bruch was being overpraised, overrated and openly used as a weapon in the war against the progressive factions of mid-nineteenth-century musical life.

The ten songs were followed by four more, this time for baritone (dedicated to the singer, Julius Stockhausen) with piano accompaniment. They appeared as Op. 18 and consist of settings of two poems by Geibel (the first of which, 'Volker's Nachtgesang' becomes very Schubertian in Bruch's hands), and two by Heyse. The latter's contribution is once again a translation of a Spanish folksong, but this time coupled with a troubadour's song from Provence. These four songs are suddenly far more self-assured; the piano writing is more interesting, the songs more declamatory, the result more satisfying. They show a new maturity in Bruch's facility to blend voice with accompaniment, something which had largely eluded him hitherto.

The direction Max was taking at this time was towards a work which had preoccupied him for several years, *Frithjof* Op. 23. After the settings of solo songs and piano Opp. 17 and 18, came four choral works. The first are the four male voice choruses with orchestral accompaniment Op. 19 composed for the Concordia male voice choir in Aachen. The first, (*Römischer Triumphgesang* — the text once again by Lingg), is scored for full orchestra and chorus, whereas the remaining three appeared as Op. 19 Book II and are accompanied only by two horns, two trumpets, three trombones and timpani. The last of the three draws once again on Scotland for inspiration, being a setting of the folksong 'Scotland's Tears — a Song of Mourning after the Battle of Culloden in 1746'. The two works Opp. 20 and 21 appear to have been two parts of an unfinished trilogy based on the Christmas story and are respectively *Die Flucht der heiligen Familie* (The Flight of the Holy Family) and *Gesang der heiligen drei Könige* (The Song of the Three Wise Men) again for chorus and orchestra. The manuscript of the former is dated 19 July 1863 and dedicated to the Choral Society in Crefeld, the director of which was Leonhard Wolff, uncle of Max's friend, Rudolf von Beckerath. It was to this organization, to Wolff and to Beckerath that Bruch had been so grateful for the opportunity to run through Act I of *Die Loreley* earlier in the same year. Bruch himself conducted the first performance of *Die Flucht der heiligen Familie* there in December 1863 as part of a concert which also included his own *Die Birken und die Erlen*, Mendelssohn's overture *The Fair Melusine* and arias from Spohr's *Faust*.

The Cantata is a tenderly romantic setting of a poem by Eichendorff, and tells of the flight of the Holy Family into Egypt. As they traverse the meadows and groves, the wings of angels create a gentle breeze for them, flickering fireflies light their way by night, and all Nature feels blessed by their passing. The reviewer in the *Niederrheinische Musikzeitung* was moved to write that 'a tender breeze of poetic feeling runs through the entire work. The overall effect, which the choir produced on the audience, is above all proof of the truth and purity of expression with which this composer has rendered his feelings. This choir, particularly the ladies' chorus, ranks with the best in the Rhine Province, and that is both for the choir and for the conductor no mean praise. Performed with vigour and accuracy the Bruch works (under the composer's direction) created a charming impression.' Vincenz Lachner performed the work in Mannheim in February 1864, and Max reported to Hiller: 'Lachner is continually friendly and well-meaning. This week he is performing my *Flucht*. I have considered it my duty, out of gratitude, to dedicate the opera [*Die Loreley*] to him — without his beneficial interest in me, I would hardly have got as far here as I have.'

The *Gesang der heiligen drei Könige* (to a text by Schenkendorff) was written in January 1863, but, to generate an income during the hard times of the First World War, he revised and orchestrated the work in February 1915, five years before his death. He then inscribed the manuscript to his daughter Margarethe, adding 'to the preservation of better times'. It is written for a trio of male soloists, a tenor and two basses representing the three kings. It was highly thought of by Brahms, who urged Joachim to 'look at this beautiful piece of music!'[3] According to a letter from Bruch to Beckerath, Joachim took Brahms' advice, but found the work 'quite horrible'.[4] The letter went on: 'This strange mystical work is way above the horizon for the critics, but at the same time it is quite unsuitable for the concert hall. It pleased neither the public nor the King; as a result an audience with the King came to nothing.' The work was dedicated to Johann Naret-Koning, leader of the orchestra (Konzertmeister) in Mannheim, with whom Bruch became a close friend. It was Koning who introduced him to a detailed study of the works of Brahms at this time, as well as setting him on the path of composing for the violin, which led to the First Violin Concerto four years later. In a letter to Rudolf von Beckerath he wrote:

Recently we have had much enjoyment here in studying the latest works of BRAHMS. We (I mean Koning and I) have got to know one after the other the excellent *Variations on a Theme of Schumann*, the *Variations on a Theme of Handel*, the Sextet, the two Serenades, and the two Piano Quartets. As the opportunity for you will be more or less lacking in hearing these thoughtful, beautifully crafted and

masterly constructed works in their original version, try at least to
get to know them in their four-hands [piano] version. You will
derive much pleasure from them.[5]

The *Five Songs* for mixed *a cappella* chorus Op. 22 were once again
based on folksongs (Geibel, Rist, Lingg, an Irish song by Thomas
Moore, and one from Herder's *Stimmen der Völker*).

The first performance of *Frithjof* Op. 23 took place in Aachen on 20
November 1864 with Bruch conducting the Concordia male voice
chorus, soloists and orchestra. By the time it was published the
following year, Bruch had been working on the cantata for some eight
years. The epic poem, based on a thirteenth-century Icelandic saga,
was the work of the Swedish poet Esaias Tegner, and appeared in
1820. The basis of the German translation was by Gottlieb Mohnike,
although Bruch himself adapted it freely for the six scenes he extracted
for his work from the 24 in Tegner's original.

King Helge keeps his beautiful sister Ingeborg in Baldur's Temple
and Grove, safe from strangers' eyes. She and Frithjof are in love and
want to marry, but Helge is incensed because the lovers have
desecrated the holy Grove by their secret meetings at night. Frithjof is
banished by the King and told not to return until he can bring with
him the tribute withheld by the rebellious Jarl Anganthyr.
    Meanwhile Helge has mocked old King Ring, another of Inge-
borg's suitors. Offended at his treatment, Ring has waged war on
Helge and defeated him in battle. Helge flees, destroying Frithjof's
home and court in a spiteful rage. He then buys his peace by promising
Ingeborg to Ring. Tearing Frithjof's bracelet from his sister, Helge
dedicates it to the god Baldur, and then sends the maiden, now
resigned to being sacrificed for her brother, in a festive procession to
the old King.
    The heroic Frithjof, having fulfilled the task set him by Helge,
returns with his brave companions on their ship *Ellida* to find his home
razed to the ground and his bride sold. In a fury he storms the Temple
and kills Helge. The Temple goes up in flames and Frithjof is
condemned for this blasphemy by both priests and people. He is
sentenced to exile, and, taking his faithful companions, embarks for
southern climes.
    The protagonists of the saga are limited to two soloists in Bruch's
setting, Frithjof (baritone) and Ingeborg (soprano). As in a Greek
drama, the chorus relates the tale as events occur. The orchestral
introduction portrays Frithjof's sea journey home and his landing,

whereupon he gives thanks for overcoming the elements that, in response to the prayers of his enemy Helge, have tried to wreck his ship. His recitative leads into a lyrical aria interspersed with the chorus praising their ship *Ellida* for bringing them safely ashore to their native land. After an introductory processional march, the second scene begins with the chorus describing how pale Ingeborg appears as she is led unwillingly to the old King Ring. She sings of her suffering at the events which have torn her from her beloved Frithjof, and the chorus join with her in a plea for justice from the Almighty. In the turbulent scene which follows, the chorus take the part of the priests watching with horror as the vengeful Frithjof burns down the Temple around them, triumphant that he has slain Helge for the wrong done to Ingeborg and himself. The chorus divides into Frithjof's followers urging on the elements to help in the destruction of the Temple, and the Priests and the People bemoaning its fate, urging the upwards drifting smoke to tell the Gods in Valhalla of all that is happening below. The fourth scene begins with a quartet of choral soloists describing how the wind and the sea are now favourable for Frithjof's departure into exile, and the warrior once again bids farewell to his homeland in a poignant aria. Ingeborg's Lament follows, an aria often extracted for separate concert performance in later years and the precursor of Penelope's aria in the oratorio *Odysseus*. The work ends with Frithjof and his sailors at sea bound for unknown lands far from their own.

Bruch's mother pleaded with him not to turn down the opportunity to conduct *Frithjof* in Aachen the following year, something about which he had obviously not yet made up his mind. He was at this time still studying musicianship, conducting and orchestration with Lachner in Mannheim, and had not yet been responsible for conducting an important première of one of his compositions:

> We [his sister Mathilde and his mother] are both of the opinion that this work in particular, which is straightforward and splendid, with no changes in *tempi*, will offer no problems at all in its direction; we are absolutely convinced that with it you will make the best, most rewarding beginning as a conductor. You know how much I value the virtue of modesty, and how much I want it to be an integral part of your inner being. But this refusal seems to me to be weakness. You must make a start once and for all, and this is such a wonderful chance to do so. Here [Cologne] it is assumed you will conduct your work in Aachen — please, please take this step forward. You have nothing to lose.[6]

He yielded to his family's persuasive pleas, and four days before the première wrote to Laura von Beckerath, wife of Rudolf, 'Yesterday I heard *Frithjof* for the first time sung by the chorus. I was very pleased, mainly because everything sounded exactly as I had thought it would, and thought it should.' On the same day he wrote to Clara Schumann, 'May I permit myself a great favour from you? I am so grateful to you for your delightful interest in *Frithjof*, that I wish only to send the work into the world in your name. If you will permit me to dedicate *Frithjof* to you, you would make me very happy and indebted to you forever.' The permission was received and the work duly appeared dedicated to the famous widow. It was once again reviewed by Ludwig Bischoff.[7] He had translated Tegner's text in 1850, and this was certainly used by Bruch as a source, particularly during the period of study with Hiller in the second half of that decade. In the year before the first performance of *Tristan* he was able to write that 'the greatest law of music, Melody, has not been broken. It sounds almost laughable that [these days] we have to assert that Melody must be a basic ingredient in music, as if it no longer goes without saying.' Four months later Bischoff reviewed the performance, once again conducted by the composer, which took place in the Redoutensaal in Vienna before an audience of 2,000 people.

Its success can be measured by the deafening applause after each scene, and the recall of the composer by the public three times at the end, and further by the verdict and good wishes of the orchestra during the rehearsals, confirmed to me by verbal reports from eyewitnesses and by the famous soloist [Frau Dustmann who sang Ingeborg in the performance]. *Die Presse* reported 'the public took to the piece so well that Herr Bruch can be proud of his success'. *Die Neue Freie Presse* said 'the performing forces co-operated sincerely in helping Herr Bruch to a successful début in Vienna'. The *Recensionen*, while admittedly ignoring the exceptional applause, reported nevertheless 'that the work can rejoice in honourable recognition'. . . . We also in no way acknowledge Max Bruch to be at this stage a complete master, but we place great hopes on his future.[8]

With *Frithjof*, Bruch's reputation suddenly grew. At the age of twenty-six he had acquired an extraordinary power and facility in the manipulation of large vocal masses; his choral writing was now the work of a completely accomplished musician, solid and earnest as well as spontaneous, tuneful and effective. With it he reached to the heart of amateur music-making current in Germany by writing for chorus, and by the appeal of his choice of subject-matter, namely a saga of love, vengeance, heroic deeds and pride of country.

With this success behind him, and with his most recent works receiving performances, Max began considering the opportunities of taking up a post wherever one might fall vacant. This aspect of his career was to preoccupy him for the rest of his life, the restlessness of the composer/conductor forever travelling, forever worried about money, forever weighing up the advantages and disadvantages of either being a freelance artist or having a permanent position. In the period leading to his first successful application he was to suffer several disappointments, among them Mainz, Elberfeld and Aachen. 'I like this gentleman [Bruch] very much,' wrote the publisher Franz Schott to Ferdinand Hiller, 'and I also do not doubt that, as well as having a serious exterior, he is very sociable. My colleagues, however, have a different opinion on this, and as I cannot convince them to the contrary, it would please me if you would have the goodness to describe the situation to Herr Bruch at an appropriate moment. The people in Mainz expect a lot, they want a gifted conductor and an amiable person in one man. The successor must therefore be perfect, so that interest in the Society will grow once again.'9

Shortly before this Max had written to Beckerath, 'I have thought seriously about Mainz, and informed myself about the place and the post; however so much was unfavourable and forbidding, and Lachner and others who know Mainz and the people there well advised me so strongly against it that I did not apply. For the present I do not need to be worried or act impetuously on material grounds by going for every possible appointment.' In the same letter he reported that he only had to give a few lessons in order to make ends meet, due to the current success of his compositions and the favourable prospects of further performances. Towards the end of 1864 he considered the Music Director's post to the Choral Society known as the Elberfeld Liedertafel, but a letter to Clara Schumann revealed troubles with the committee.10 He was neither the first nor the last musician to encounter and be defeated by problems with committees, indeed they were to plague him throughout his life everywhere he went. Once again he withdrew his application.

Aachen was a different matter. He had recently enjoyed the triumph of *Frithjof*, and had successfully worked with the Concordia chorus and orchestra. The vacancy was caused by the departure of Franz Wüllner for Munich as Hofkapellmeister, and the appointment attracted 42 applications. The selection committee decided to ask Franz Lachner in Munich and Julius Rietz in Dresden to choose one of the eight shortlisted candidates, among whom was Bruch. He immediately set about canvassing support, writing to Clara Schumann, Rudolf von Beckerath, Ludwig Bischoff, and even Lachner himself. A lesson he appears to have learnt from the affair is that contacts made should be contacts maintained, for although he had met Rietz in Leipzig some six years earlier, Max did not keep in touch and feared that Rietz was not fully apprised of the musical progress and success he had since enjoyed. 'At that time,' he wrote to Clara Schumann, 'I was quite an immature child of Art seeking his way through the mist. In the six years since, I have honestly taken the trouble to make profounder judgements, achieve greater clarity in our Art, and hope through my latest successes to have proved that between then and now there is an appreciable difference — that I have now laid a firm foundation, on which I can build and for which I can strive without qualms.' He asked her to write to Rietz on his behalf, and then added:

> You know what superb forces there are here; excellent orchestra, a large lively chorus, that is why Aachen is a Music Festival city — all this is very attractive and explains the dreadful rush of applications. Naturally I cannot have much actual experience in conducting, though I have conducted often, and Kapellmeister Lachner in Mannheim gave me some tips. *Frithjof* went well enough under my direction, as anyone will tell you; so I can hope in the not too distant future to get the necessary experience, for in the end conducting is not witchcraft.[11]

To Beckerath he confided, 'I am assured that I am preferred by the city. Of the ten votes of the Music Committee I am sure of six or seven, and that ratio can be improved if Lachner and especially Rietz do not ruin everything.' Later, he revealed that Frau Schumann had responded to his request for help, and had written on his behalf to Lachner and Rietz.[12] 'May my warm intercession,' she wrote, 'about which you need have no doubts, lead to a favourable outcome.' Her optimism was, however, misplaced. The post went to Ferdinand Breunung, and Max suffered yet another disappointment at the hands of the factions and cabals of musical life in the Rhineland. At this stage in his life he was able to recover from such setbacks relatively quickly and with sufficient optimism to forge ahead with his career. Later this proved more difficult for him to do, for his feelings bruised more easily and he became less thick-skinned.

In March 1865 he wrote an extremely long letter to Beckerath from Breslau reflecting on the events of the past winter, the change in his opinion of *Die Loreley* and the prospects for his immediate future:

Best of all is that *Frithjof* was really and truly a mighty striking success in Leipzig. The best proof lies in the fact that the Gewandhaus repeated the work, owing to its brilliant performance in a Pauliner Concert, and in spite of poorer soloists, it was as decided and as brilliant a triumph. How happy I am about it! Orchestra, public, singers, and all the Leipzig critics, with the exception of that desiccated schoolmaster Bagge, were quite united in warm recognition, David and Reinecke at their head. One day I will tell you the details of these wonderful weeks in Leipzig. . . . Instead of Paris I must now go to Vienna; on the 25 March I conduct *Frithjof* there, and have planned in the meantime to leave Vienna at the beginning of April, travel through southern Germany to Paris, stay there for six weeks, and at any rate be in Cologne in time for the Music Festival. . . . In Vienna I should still see the beginning of the Italian season, which usually has good singers; in Paris I should get the best impression of the Opéra comique and the Théâtre lyrique, at which the French excel. . . .

If *Frithjof* proves a success in Vienna, which I do not doubt it will, I will have achieved more in a very short time than I could ever have dreamed at the beginning of the winter. Already in the first few weeks of my travels, in Hamburg and Hanover, the thought always nagged me that in the end Aachen was not the right place for me. Everything was progressing so unexpectedly and brilliantly, that the news of my fiasco, which I could scarcely have borne in December, I took at the beginning of February with great calmness and *aequo animo*. . . .

A propitious Destiny always brings some good with it! . . . I have completely given up Mannheim; first it was unbearable and downright destructive for my spirit, second I could not bring myself to go back to the same people. . . . What is going to happen later on I do not know . . . Who knows the future?

*Die Lorelips* should be on in Hamburg some time now for the eleventh time. It is coming back in September in Leipzig. If I could, at the stroke of a pen, rid the world of *Die Loreley*, I would do it without a thought, that is my true and sincere opinion. You cannot believe the pain it gives me to have to answer for, and to be interested in, a work that lies so far behind me. What I merely sensed in *Die Loreley*, I expressed clearly in *Frithjof*. Now I understand all the internal and external ingredients of Art better than at that time. . . . Would you believe that already two years ago, a few months before the première in Mannheim, I had the idea to withdraw the opera because it dissatisfied me? It was not possible; it was a rash idea. Koning talked me out of it, the sets were nearly finished. . . .

Dearest Beckerath, you must allow me these outpourings for there is no one else to whom I can or would want to express them. [13]

In the same letter he mentioned meeting Joseph Joachim for the first time. 'In Hanover I got really close to Joachim and have learnt to respect this great and simple man.' The two men began a professional and private association at this time which was to continue until the great violinist's death over 40 years later. It was not always an easy friendship, particularly during the period when Joachim was divorcing his wife Amalie, and sides were inevitably taken. Through Joachim (as well as through Clara Schumann) Bruch came to know Brahms on a personal level, and he was able to centre his own artistic circle on the town to which he now moved, having at last secured an appointment. This was Coblenz, where he lived from 1865–1867. He had travelled far and wide throughout his own land since 1857 when he set off for Leipzig. He had met or befriended all the important musicians with whose musical ideas he was in sympathy (including Berlioz and Rossini during this most recent trip to Paris) and he had formulated his musical philosophy by developing and maturing his own personal style of composition. He had concluded that the consummate musician was the composer/conductor (the 'rostrum virtuoso' was not for him) and at last he could put his ideas into practice by being in control of the musical activities and facilities available to him. Coblenz was a beginning.

# Chapter Five

## COBLENZ
### 1865–67

IN THE SUMMER of 1864 Max Bruch left Mannheim and in August, during a visit to his friends Laura and Rudolf von Beckerath in Crefeld, he wrote to Hiller asking once again for a reference for another vacant post. Ferdinand Hiller seems to have been the centre of the musical universe to whom all in the conservative anti-New German Music camp turned. In Cologne he sat, spider-like at the centre of his web, weaving and spinning the futures of his pupils and protégés, foiling plots, creating intrigues, and promoting or even destroying careers. After the failures of Mainz, Elberfeld and Aachen (and it is worth noting that Hiller did not respond to Wüllner's request for suggestions regarding his successor in Aachen by putting Bruch's name forward) Max turned his attention to Coblenz, a town at the confluence of the rivers Rhine and Mosel. Queen Augusta of Prussia, who had a castle there, was actively interested in music and encouraged an enterprising musical life in the city. After visiting Coblenz, he wrote to Hiller of his intention to apply for the post:

> These past few days I have been in Coblenz, to get myself informed about the place and the post. All in all, the results of my enquiries were pleasing; the committee members were friendly to me, appeared to be half-expecting my application, and to wish for my selection — so I have decided after all to apply in writing within the next few days. The Queen, who takes a lively interest in the musical life of the city, let the committee know, when she was here at the beginning of August, that they should not hurry over making a decision, and that they were welcome to her advice before coming to a definite conclusion. They would probably have done that anyway, without the royal suggestion, as any committee in that position knows that sooner or later an urgent need arises which depends on the support of its master. So I write to ask you something which I am sure is necessary, and which I beg you not to refuse, to write a friendly word on my behalf if you are requested to do so.[1]

Though he had decided to proceed with his application, Max reflected yet again on the alternative of remaining freelance, and proposed to 'try my luck in Paris or Vienna', no doubt dreading the prospect of yet another rejection and the ensuing disappointment. 'I must however concede,' he went on, 'that the thought of continuing this random existence becomes increasingly unbearable. As I am not a good enough pianist to earn my living at playing, I should not depend upon being able to earn enough at giving lessons. When I was in Paris I thought it possible to write a great operatic success there. But those were plans for the future and, now I am back, I think each man must have a specific occupation when he gets to a certain age. In any case I can learn in Coblenz. I can ascertain if I have a talent in leading, I have the opportunity to become known to the Queen, and the prospect, if I do my job tolerably well, of better posts than now.' This time Hiller was pleased to recommend Max, who, as one of 49 applicants, was offered the post on 2 September 1865 and accepted it, starting immediately.

His official title was director of the Royal Institute for Music and of the Coblenz Subscription Concerts. The orchestra consisted of 60–70 musicians of whom half a dozen were amateurs, and a chorus of 150 amateurs. The Director was obliged to give ten concerts between October and March each year, and to train a women's chorus for six hours each week. This chorus was regarded as a source both of potential solo and chorus material. Bruch's salary was fixed at 367 thalers and 15 silver groschen, with opportunities for private teaching. Max decided to train the chorus from the piano, and, as a result Richard Kugler, hitherto the choir's repetiteur, was made redundant. The choir, which met each Friday evening for two hours, was very evenly proportioned at 38 sopranos, 30 altos, 27 tenors and 29 basses.

One of the first invitations to appear as soloist in a concert was sent to and accepted by Hiller, who played his own Piano Concerto in F sharp minor in November 1865 under Max's direction in one of the first concerts of the season, and returned the compliment by putting on *Frithjof* in Cologne on 16 January 1866. Queen Augusta received Hiller favourably, presented him with a golden snuff-box and invited him to play at the castle. The concerto he played was dedicated to another pianist invited by Bruch to appear in Coblenz, Wilhelmine Clauss-Szarvady, whose playing of Chopin he greatly admired. Clara Schumann also accepted an invitation to perform, and their friendship broadened by making music together. Max reported to Hiller that he had to sort out 'a hundred stupidities in the way of making music here' in his initial period in the post, though in taking on the role of a new broom, he had 'not lost sight of his goal'.[2]

The orchestral fare for his first season consisted of works by Beethoven, Mozart, Mendelssohn, Gade, Schumann and Schubert. In the same season the choir performed works by Handel, Mendelssohn, Schumann, Hiller, Cherubini, Mozart, Brahms and Bruch himself. The two years in Coblenz were spent mainly in practical music making, and as a result his output of new compositions diminished in quantity if not in quality. Three works were completed during this period, the first two of which were choral. The year 1866 saw the short and decisive Austro-Prussian War with Bismarck's crushing and humiliating defeat of the Hapsburg Emperor Franz Josef's forces at Königgrätz on 3 July, and it is no small wonder that the patriotic fervour aroused by events during that year should have inspired *Schön Ellen* Op. 24 and *Salamis* Op. 25.

The Ballad of *Schön Ellen* is once again the work of Emanuel Geibel, but was based on recent historical fact. The story is set in the Indian Mutiny of 1857–58 and describes the Siege of Lucknow. The rebellion was largely due to a decline in discipline among native troops, together with discontent and suspicion over British measures affecting native customs, caste and religion. The accumulated grievances were sparked off by the issue of cartridges to the Sepoy soldiers, the tops of which had to be bitten off before use. Rumour had it that the cartridge tops were smeared with the fats of animals sacred to the Hindus or untouchable to the Moslems. The Sepoys (soldiers of the East India Company) rose up and, having taken Delhi, set siege to the city of Lucknow, trapping an English garrison of over 1,700 men, women and children in the fort for two months under the command of General Havelock. On the day Lucknow was relieved by the Highland Regiment under Sir Colin Campbell, Havelock died of sickness and exhaustion.

Geibel's version of events centres on Fair Ellen who, when the garrison is in the direst straits, claims to hear the distant drums of the advancing relief column of the Campbells. In spite of her reassuring words, no one else can hear what she hears or believe in her vision, and it is only at her third outburst that she is seen to have spoken the truth. Both Geibel's text and Bruch's music have a full palette of emotions ranging from despair and hope to fear and elation, and much is made of the Scottish folksong, 'The Campbells Are Coming'. The work, like *Frithjof*, is set for baritone and soprano soloists with chorus and orchestra, and ends with a glorious transformation of the dominating folksong from the familiar 6/8 rhythm to an augmented 3/4 setting for chorus, soloists, and full orchestra (with obligatory 'Scottish' harp) to bring the work to its grand apotheosis and triumphant conclusion.

The Ballad received its first performance in Coblenz on 22 February 1867. Both Hermann Levi and Clara Schumann had kind words to say about the work. Levi wrote to Max from Carlsruhe to say that '*Schön Ellen* pleased me very much. The sound of the Ballad is well-caught and maintained, the musical form (your understanding of the relationship between chorus and soloists) correct throughout. I cannot conceive how it could have been bettered. Regarding the instrumentation, one cannot fault you, for it is all masterly.'[3] Clara Schumann reported her pleasure at hearing the work to Brahms in a letter from Coblenz: 'Today Bruch, who thanks you for your greetings, played me several new works and pleased me very much with some of them. I especially liked a Ballad for soprano, baritone and chorus called *Schön Ellen*.'[4]

Hard on the heels of *Schön Ellen* came *Salamis*, subtitled 'A War Song of the Greeks', and in its powerful setting for a quartet of male soloists, male voice chorus and full orchestra it uses a poem by Hermann Lingg. Very much in the mould of *Frithjof* and looking ahead to *Odysseus*, the work depicts Greek soldiers sailing home in triumph after a victory over the Persian king, Xerxes. With these choral works Bruch mastered the marriage of music with text; his word painting and sensitivity to descriptive moods are supported by the consummation of his expansive melodic writing and developed powers of orchestration.

The time had now arrived to explore another musical form, the concerto. A letter Max wrote to Hiller in November 1865, soon after he had begun his duties in Coblenz, ends 'as soon as you can show me a bearable text, over which I can get excited, I will compose another opera, but not before. My Violin Concerto is progressing slowly — I do not feel sure of my feet on this terrain. Do you not think that it is in fact very audacious to write a Violin Concerto?' Clara Schumann's letter to Brahms describing her pleasure at hearing *Schön Ellen* also referred to the nascent Violin Concerto and to *Salamis*. '[I liked much] in his Violin Concerto. It appears to me that in these current works he has made significant progress. I was also very interested in a victory chorus about the Battle of Salamis.'

The genesis of the work by which Max Bruch is known to all lovers of music spans the period just prior to and just after the two years in Coblenz. He later wrote to Fritz Simrock in response to a request for an opinion of a certain composer, and suggested the man should try his hand at writing a concerto for the violin. 'It is a damned difficult thing to do; between 1864 and 1868 I rewrote my concerto at least half a dozen times, and conferred with *x* violinists before it took the final form in which it is universally famous and played everywhere.'[5] Johann Naret-Koning, Konzertmeister in Mannheim, was one of the first of the violinists to encourage and advise Bruch on matters concerning the composition of the concerto, but it was not long before he turned to Joseph Joachim, whose role in the creation of the work, with that of Ferdinand David, was to be of paramount importance.

Bruch began work on the concerto in the summer of 1864. At the beginning of 1866 he completed the first draft, and on 24 April it was performed from the manuscript in Coblenz with Otto von Königslöw as soloist. Dissatisfied with what he had produced, Bruch sent the manuscript to Joachim during the summer of 1866 for his comments. On 9 July Joachim wrote pleading for more time, for 'in addition to political excitement [it was barely a week after Königgratz] I have household cares. In September I expect to be in Hanover again, though how it will go with the concerts only the gods, Bismarck and Napoleon know.' Because the Hanoverian King George had allied himself with Austria against Prussia, he was dethroned by the victorious Bismarck, and without a Court Joachim suddenly found himself no longer Director of the Royal Concerts but once again a private citizen. It was August before he wrote a long and detailed reply to Bruch:[6]

At last I am sending back your concerto. I wish that instead of writing I could come myself, not because I am a lazy correspondent, but because I really believe that a few hours together would settle all doubtful points regarding the violin part. As a whole the piece is very violinistic and as such, I believe it will make a splendid effect. Well, it will no doubt be best if I answer your questions in the order you put them:

I too would prefer the tutti on page 20 to be considerably longer. Coming after the broad pedal point, it is to be expected, and fortunately there is plenty of material. The pregnant phrase:

Ex. 1

and the broad second theme will help to give you the proper suggestion. On page 25 I have written a cadenza in pencil; this can (like all subsequent notes from my hand) quickly be erased, and awaits your judgement. Should not the last B flat of the first violin on page 29 be carried over into the Andante? Undoubtedly! In that event, the second violin would, of course, have to be changed accordingly in the first bar. On page 38 it seems to me also that there is a bar missing, yet each attempt on my part to supply it proved inadequate.

Ex. 2

This is after all only a prolonged *ritardando* and therefore pleases me best. I shall especially enjoy hearing the Andante, that I can say most sincerely.

In the last movement I heartily agree with L[evi] concerning page 61. As the part from the second principal theme to the violin passage now stands, the flow of the movement which precedes the energetic impetus, seems to me too greatly retarded. The cut which you yourself suggested perhaps helps best here; only then the cheerful bit is lost (which, by the way, is very violinistic and effective):

Ex. 3

Too broad a melodic treatment of this part would, moreover, be detrimental in the beautiful middle movement in C minor which follows. By way of suggestion I have written an alternative on a bit of paper, but of course it is only intended to give a general idea of what I mean and is not to be taken literally. It is thrown off too hastily for that! For the first three bars on page 69, however (and to speak plainly), I should prefer something better. Is this not a rather superficial filler? Also the somewhat parallel case on page 101 does not satisfy me yet either, and I hope that you will not disagree with

me on this point. The passage work, on the other hand, I find very
delightful and have taken the liberty of making only a slight
alteration here and there for the sake of fingering and bowing. I
have changed the end of the solo, because the rapid scale which runs
over into the tutti might be considered a bit reminiscent of the
Mendelssohn concerto. Do you think me too outspoken? Also an
occasional passage:

Ex. 4

etc. etc. reminds one of the above mentioned piece, and I have made
partial suggestions for alterations, for as it is, the player is
stimulated to uneasiness rather than sprightliness. I have also risked
re-writing the beginning of the final passage. Moreover from this:

Ex. 5

something very violinistic might be worked out, and I have not the
least fear that a beautiful and effective ending will suggest itself to
you.

Finish it very quickly and then allow me, if you do not find my
request too forward, to write out a solo part so that I may learn the
concerto before we meet, which I hope will be soon. As to your
'doubts', I am happy to say, in conclusion, that I find the title
Concerto fully justified; for the name 'Fantasy' the last two
movements are actually too completely and symmetrically developed; the different parts are brought together in a beautiful
relationship, and yet there is sufficient contrast, which is the main
point. Spohr, moreover, calls his Gesangszene a 'Concerto'.

And now I beg you once more, do not be angry with me because
the manuscript has been in my hands for so long, and that perhaps I
make myself tedious with these copious comments. I shall be very

glad to hear from you again soon. If concerts were to be considered
in Hanover this winter, I should ask you for one of your new
works, which interest me greatly. But as a private citizen I cannot
do this. As from yesterday I am no longer Royal Concert-Director
in Hanover (according to notification from the Chamber of
Deputies), but I shall always remain that which no one can take
from me.

In an interview with Arthur Abell, for an American journal in July
1911, Bruch sanctioned publication of the letter from Joachim.[7] Abell
prefaced it with an excuse for not including the music examples given
by Joachim: 'I am quoting the letter in full, but I am not giving the
illustrations which Joachim wrote out, because Bruch did not adopt
any of them.' This is clearly untrue from Bruch's reply to Joachim.[8]
As Bruch himself suppressed publication of this letter in 1912, it
explains Abell's unwittingly inaccurate statement of the year before:

I am indebted to you for your detailed letter about the concerto;
nothing makes me happier or more comforted than the certainty
that you are prepared, after carefully and sincerely looking through
it, to take an interest in it. I have now renewed work on it with fresh
enthusiasm, and have gratefully used your good suggestions. I have
taken the liberty, at your request, to send to you alone a new solo
part. I have put in all the tutti where appropriate, so that although
you provisionally have neither a full score nor a piano reduction,
you can follow the thread of the whole work. Allow me briefly to
give you the changes:

  1) In the first movement I thought the octave passages

Ex. 6

somewhat rigid; I have provisionally put in a few sextuplet figures
at this point, which link the melody, but four more bars in D minor
are probably very difficult. If you think I have bowdlerized the
passage, it can be easily restored to what it was.

2) The conclusion in D minor

Ex. 7

appeared somewhat dry to me, the more so since the tempo is obviously slower than I had thought when I wrote it down; I mean the three bars I inserted instead

Ex. 8

are decidedly better.

3) The repeated passage immediately following

Ex. 9

I have placed entirely in the orchestra. It must appear strong and meaningful, and already at the play-through here did not sound as I wanted. I also now believe that the solo violin enters much more beautifully and effectively with the second subject. Do you not agree?

4) When it continues after the *cantilena* in B flat major, the rhythm

Ex. 10

which previously was only in the solo violin, must of necessity be brought out more — exactly at this point. I allow the beginning of this motif to appear in the four horns, answering the solo violin thus

Ex. 11

5) The figurations in the solo violin leading to the tutti, are to be found in the part exactly as your instructions.

6) The *tutti* has become longer. I have taken your advice by working the motif into the basses.

Ex. 12

I deliberately did not want to abandon the main key for too long, it must be well established here.

7) Your alterations to the last cadenza are written as if from my soul.

8) The first violins must remain on B flat in the first bar at the beginning of the Adagio. It is changed.

9) The *rit.* bar is a strange thing. To make two bars out of it, I believe one is too aware of the intention. Perhaps it suffices to stroke out the '*poco*' and to allow the *rit.* to begin somewhat sooner (on the last quaver of the previous bar), thus

Ex. 13

10) I also think that the present (first ending) is the best. One must hear it. By way of experiment and according to your thoughts, I have written the last two chords *pizzicato*.

11) I also think that the cut

Ex. 14

is not to be avoided. At first I wrote your alteration into the score; I found it excellent and was pleased that the motif

Ex. 15

had been preserved in this way. When, however, I played the whole of the first part in context, I had the irrefutable feeling of protracted length exactly at this point, and I had to concede Levi's indicated cut. I really believe that by going to B flat major and then later returning to D, the movement falters significantly. It is also perhaps better not to touch B flat major at all here, as the tutti which begins soon after modulates to B flat immediately. So the modulation in the first part of the Finale takes shape quite simply, and the feeling of the main key will at no time substantially irritate.

12) I was hesitant whether I should keep the figure

Ex. 16

However as it is violinistic, and as you believe that anyway the charm will work well here as a necessary contrast, I have provisionally left it so, and have gratefully used your changes at the end of the section.

13) I have changed the next eight bars of the next tutti, so that now the solo

Ex. 17

enters on the 6/4 chord and C minor now appears for the first time as the tonic at the beginning of the melody.

Ex. 18 [*sic!*]

I really believe it is significantly better.

14) At the repeat of the main movement in the solo violin, I have made an important change. This appeared to me to be the place to

do something with the main theme. I am curious to hear how this place pleases you.

15) I think it is very good if the second subject only appears once in G major, and is then taken up and developed by the solo violin in the eighth bar. From here, it seems to me, everything should rush on to the end without stopping. If you play the piece through in sequence, you will certainly have the same feeling.

16) I have yet to work on the whole ending; I have no talent in contriving beautiful new figurations. I will write an ending — in the end it will come.

I would place invaluable worth on the chance to speak with you about the final details . . .

In 1912 the proofs for a book of letters to and from Joachim were prepared by Johannes Joachim (son of the late violinist) with Andreas Moser and sent to Bruch for approval, including the foregoing reply. Bruch replied to the editors expressly forbidding publication of this particular letter:[9]

1) Regarding my *Violin Concerto No. 1* in G minor Op. 26, I only value the publication of that letter from Joachim in Harzburg in August 1866 which violinists of all Schools and all countries will find the most important and the most interesting; and this letter will indeed appear with the other letters from Joachim to me.

2) I did not know that such a detailed reply from me to the Harzburg letter existed, and knowing it now gives me no pleasure; for in this reply I appear dreadfully dependent (not to say schoolboy-like) on Joachim. To be sure the discussion is only of details, often trifles, for the essentials, the thought content and the form remain unchanged. But the reading public would not have this impression, and would judge wrongly my whole relationship with Joachim (which later became quite different). The public would virtually believe when it read all this that Joachim composed this concerto, and not I. The truth is that I gratefully used some of his suggestions, not others.

3) I am surprised that Herr Moser picked this particular letter from the masses of others. I never authorized Herr Moser to publish it, I decidedly refuse my authorization now, and ask for the letter not to be printed.

Obviously still highly concerned at the knowledge that the letter was at large, he wrote again to Johannes Joachim:[10]

Everyone would say upon reading the letter: 'Ah this work took a lot of trouble and difficulty in its completion. M.B. never in fact knew what he wanted, now one can see how little initiative and self-dependence the man had, he probably never did anything alone throughout his entire life' (whereas exactly the opposite is true!). This version would become universal, and would be hawked about with leering satisfaction to hurt me . . . I have always considered it fully satisfactory, that regarding the first Concerto, Joachim's beautiful, interesting and useful letter of August 1866 would be published; what I used from it, anyone wishing to take up the matter can see easily and clearly enough by comparing this letter with the printed work.

Following the correspondence during the summer of 1866, between Joachim and Bruch, the composer travelled to Hanover to confer with the violinist. During his stay, and after numerous rehearsals with piano, the two men received the permission of Hans von Bronsart, Intendant of the Royal Orchestra, to play the work in a private performance at the Royal Theatre, with the Court Orchestra conducted by the composer and with Joachim as soloist. Even at this late stage Bruch was writing to Levi:

My violin concerto was with Joachim long throughout the summer; now David has it, and he is talking of another basic revision of the solo part. The gods alone know what will come out of all this in the end. I shall soon be getting bored with the whole thing; I no longer thank Koning for setting me to work on something to which I was not equal. I will treat David's criticisms with great care. Genuine David-type violin passages would fit damned badly into the concerto.

Difficult and impatient though Bruch was in seeking advice from his professional colleagues, Levi nevertheless persisted in offering it, though his manner hardly helped. 'Was I not right,' he wrote, 'in my prophecy about the violin concerto? I consider the concerto form to be the hardest, and gave you timely warning. But why throw the baby out with the bath water? I have the greatest trust in David's practical suggestions, wait until he writes to you!'

In January 1867 Max replied to Levi, grateful for more ideas he had received from the conductor concerning the Finale of the concerto:

. . . at that place (in the Finale) I feel you have hit the nail on the head, as a result I have done a lot to the movement in the interest of shaping the form, and really believe it would satisfy you more now. Joachim and Frau Schumann are quite pleased with it, I am less so, for I still have the distinct feeling that I am standing on very insecure ground.[11]

At this point, however, Levi began to stir up Bruch's insecurities to a point of no return, and the temperature of their friendship dropped dramatically. This can be seen in a letter from Bruch later that year. The source of their estrangement lay in Levi's letters, such as this one:

Write still more violin concertos or sonatas; one cannot have enough of working at one's own weaknesses . . . what you lack is apparent in all those places in your vocal works where the musical invention could not emerge from the text, in all preludes, post-ludes, interludes, in short in all the inessentials. It is a big step from a beautiful imagination to a beautiful work of art. What the master does is to rein in the imagination and exclude it from the work of art. Do not regret having written the Violin Concerto; its failures should not override your beliefs, nor place you on strange territory contrary to your 'nature'; cultivate the earth and it will bear you and us lovely fruit. What you learn with a string quartet, will benefit each vocal work. What was hardest for you in working on the Violin Concerto, what caused most trouble in achieving it, the invention or the form? Certainly the latter.[12]

Bruch chose to ignore the criticism and responded:

'I have at last edited the Violin Concerto with Joachim; he takes a lively interest in it, has accepted the dedication and will play it soon in Vienna, then in other cities. The printed score will appear in January. That is good, is it not? Cranz has paid me 250 thalers for it.'[13] He continued to ignore the criticism, dwelling only on how well matters concerning the progress of the Violin Concerto were developing, and how much improved his instrumental composition had become through writing it:

You will know that Joachim played my Violin Concerto on 5 January in Bremen, on 11 January in Hanover and on 13 February in Aachen, with, as he writes, much resounding success. He wants to play it more often. It appears (with the printed full score) in two weeks' time with Joachim's markings. I spent eight days in

Hanover in October, and completed the definitive version with Joachim.[14]

> *En attendant* I have been free enough to write a Symphony. The Concerto gave me the courage to write instrumental music, although you once believed it was lacking. All developments which are not in the Concerto, nor need to be there, you will find in the Symphony. The Concerto is beginning a fabulous career. Joachim has played it in Bremen, Aachen, Hanover and Brussels, plays it next in Copenhagen and at the Cologne Music Festival at Whitsun, which pleases me enormously. Auer is doing it on the 17th in Hamburg (Philharmonic Concert), Straus in May in London (Philharmonic Society), David (!) in Leipzig (at the beginning of next season), Léonhard and Vieuxtemps have ordered it — in short it advances brilliantly.[15]

This exchange produced a strain in their friendship and a lessening of trust by Bruch towards the conductor which now became irreversible. Levi placed Brahms on a pedestal and was forever quoting him as an example from whom other composers should take their lead, an attitude which did little to satisfy Bruch's ego or appeal to his fast developing vanity. 'Try to forget that Mendelssohn and Schumann ever lived, tie yourself directly to Bach and Beethoven,' Levi advised, adding not only an exhortation to use Brahms as a model, but repeating a criticism made before that Bruch's instrumental music was influenced too much by his own vocal music. Bruch's reply was unequivocal:

> It is not easy for me to find the right answer to your admonition. No artist should find reproofs from competent friends unwelcome, but in this case I have the distinct feeling that you no longer understand me. In the final analysis that is not surprising, for the whole world knows the extent to which you are a fanatic for Brahms' music; but now we have completely gone our separate ways and it is not possible for you to do me justice. You say I cannot write any beautiful music without the support of words. I find this viewpoint very strange, especially when considering the Violin Concerto, particularly the Adagio.
>
> You appear to believe that I have a low opinion of hard work. I must say first of all that I started work on the Violin Concerto in the summer of 1864, and only now, after truly a lot of hard, patient, loving, often interrupted then resumed hard work is it published. I wrote three or four developments for the Finale, cut them, could

never do enough until it was as I wanted to have it, but now it is good, and exactly as it should be. And because it is good violinists play it everywhere with the greatest pleasure, and because it is good the people love it everywhere; they do not stare at it from a cold distance like they do with some of the works of your idol! They feel a heartfelt happiness towards it, I should think that is worth something. Short and sweet (I will be cheeky). *Sit ut est, aut non sit.* Not another note![16]

By April 1868 Ferdinand David, in his own words, had the concerto 'well in his fingers' in spite of his 'ninety-eight years' (he was in fact fifty-eight years old) and was a great admirer of the work. Bruch described David's playing of the work, at a Leipzig Gewandhaus concert in the autumn of 1868, to Abell during their encounter in 1911:

Dr Bruch still has a very vivid recollection of the event, and he tells me that the venerable violinist played the novelty with great enthusiasm, but scratchily, and technically very badly. He was already in his dotage and his fingers were old and stiff, and he was no longer equal to the technical demands of the Finale. However his enthusiasm for the Concerto was infectious, and soon every violin player in Leipzig was hard at work on the novelty.[17]

David also publicized the work during a trip to London in the summer of 1868: 'The night before I left London, only a week ago, Sullivan accompanied me in it. The listeners, among whom were Mr Manns, Mr Grove and the Secretary of Sydenham Palace [*sic*] were delighted with it.'[18]

The advice he received leading to the decision he subsequently took to sell the Concerto outright to Cranz for 250 thalers was the source of much regret and bitterness throughout his life. In 1874 he wrote to Simrock that Cranz had sold the work to Durand in Paris 'and I have got nothing out of it'. When he retired from his final post in Berlin in 1911 he decided to sell the original manuscript to raise some capital. Interest in purchasing it came from the violinist Ysaÿe and also from a group in America anxious to donate it to the National Library in Washington. Neither venture came to anything and the manuscript remained with the composer. In April 1920, six months before his death, he allowed the American Sutro sisters to take the manuscript back with them to the United States where they were to sell it and send the money back to Bruch, by now in dire straits through the combined exigencies of old age, inflation, and the aftermath of the First World War. Bruch's youngest son Ewald wrote an account of the incident in 1970:

I was rather sceptical about the matter, but my father reassured me: 'My boy, soon I shall be free of all worries when the first dollars arrive.' The unsuspecting man just smiled. My father sustained this good faith until his death in October 1920. He had neither received the promised dollars, nor had he seen the score of his G minor concerto again.

In December 1920 my brother, sister and I received the ostensible proceeds from the score: we were paid out in worthless German paper money. Where from, we could not find out — some bank somewhere paid us the worthless money. For years experts tried to find out the whereabouts of the score in America, but in vain. The Sutro sisters abruptly rejected every request for information, and hindered any enquiries. About twelve years ago I received the address, through friends, of a German-American music publisher, who apparently knew the current owner of the manuscript. He replied politely that a short while before it had been sold through him, and the present owner had sworn him to silence regarding his possession of the score. The Sutro sisters are no longer alive. They took the secret of this outrageous deception, the victim of which was my poor father, with them to the grave. That is the fate of the score of the G minor Violin Concerto by Max Bruch.

A happier end to the story lies in the present known whereabouts of the score. The Sutro sisters had indeed kept the manuscript for nearly 30 years, and had not fulfilled their promise to Bruch. In 1949 they sold it to the New York dealer Walter Schatzki, who was acting on behalf of Mary Flagler Cary. She then placed it in her considerable collection of rare books and manuscripts. Upon her death in 1967, the Mary Flagler Cary Music Collection was donated by its Trustees to the Pierpont Morgan Library in New York, where it has been since 1968, ironically at the time Ewald Bruch must have been preparing his piece for publication.

The Concerto was naturally significant in ensuring the fame and reputation of its composer, even if there was no comparable financial remuneration. The trouble began for Bruch when it put all his other music in its shadow, and in time he became seriously concerned and genuinely upset by the unbalanced adulation the work was receiving. It was the direct successor to the Mendelssohn concerto of twenty years earlier (time perhaps indeed for a new addition to the repertoire) and remained so until Brahms threw his hat into the ring with his own Violin Concerto ten years later. By then even Bruch's considerable reputation as a composer of choral works was being threatened by the success of the Concerto. What also irritated him in later years was the reluctance by violinists themselves to play his increasing number of compositions for that instrument. In a letter to Fritz Simrock he wrote:

> Nothing compares to the laziness, stupidity and dullness of many German violinists. Every fortnight another one comes to me wanting to play the first Concerto; I have now become rude, and have told them: 'I cannot listen to this Concerto any more — did I perhaps write just this one? Go away and once and for all play the other Concertos, which are just as good, if not better.'[19]

He expressed the same sentiments to his pupil, Leo Schrattenholz, about another violinist wishing to audition for him. Bruch would do so 'on condition that he does not play my world-renowned Concerto in G minor, because I cannot hear it any more.'[20] Italian violinists lay in wait for him in Naples where he went in 1903: 'On the corner of the Via Toledo they stand there, ready to break out with my first Violin Concerto as soon as I allow myself to be seen. (They can all go to the Devil! As if I had not written other equally good concertos!)'[21]

Against the critics, however, he was the mother hen protecting her brood. Hanslick had written ill of the work, and Bruch responded in a letter to Simrock, ' . . . when, in *Anno Domini* 1884, he writes about my first Violin Concerto, a work which for the past eighteen years has been the common property of all the violinists in the world and survives criticism, [and says] the following unspeakable stupidity: "we cannot warm to the spiritless cleverness of the Bruch Violin Concerto", he can go drown himself! "The Finale of the first Concerto has no temperament" — now that really is the end!'[22] In his next letter he was still smarting from the insult, but this time curtly dismissed Hanslick's opinion as 'barbaric nonsense'.[23]

Bruch's music speaks for itself in terms of its lyricism, harmonic language and rhythmic motifs, and these elements hold no surprises. What is novel is his concept of the first movement as a Vorspiel (Prelude) to the slow movement, the use of sonata form for all three movements, and the Hungarian flavour of the last movement owing much, no doubt, to Joachim's influence. Joachim had written his own 'Hungarian' Concerto Op. 11 in 1854, and ten years after Bruch's Concerto the violinist exercised a similar influence on Brahms in the composition of his Violin Concerto. The juxtaposition of the openings of the last movements of the concertos by Bruch and Brahms makes an interesting comparison:

Ex. 19

The essence of Bruch's musical language, the beauty of melody, lies in the inspired opening of the slow movement. It caught the imagination and attention of its listeners then, and has done so ever since.[24] The following review appeared in the Bremen newspaper (*Weser Zeitung*) after the first performance of the final and definitive version on 7 January 1868 in Bremen, with Reinthaler conducting and Joachim as soloist:

> . . . with Bruch there is no fear that he is lost in the chaos of the formless music of the future, but uses his own form in which the composer moves with moderate assurance and, by an abundance of harmonic and melodic beauty, never loses the thread to his audience. The two main movements, the Adagio and the energetically clever Finale-Allegro are excellently contrasted; the former will, on its own merit, pioneer a way through Music.

It is worth quoting Tovey at this point, not only for the pleasure of reading his masterly style, but also for his astute and accurate assessment of Max Bruch:

> When Max Bruch died at the age of eighty-three [*sic*], the news came to many as a surprise that he had lived so long. . . . It is really easy for Bruch to write beautifully, it is in fact instinctive for him. . . . Further, it is impossible to find in Max Bruch any lapses from the standard of beauty which he thus instinctively sets himself. . . . Max Bruch's First Violin Concerto thoroughly deserves the great success it has always had. Nobody who can appreciate it will believe for a moment that its composer has written nothing else worthy of the like success.[25]

*Chapter Six*

## SONDERSHAUSEN
## 1867–70

BY THE TIME of the first performance of the definitive version of the first Violin Concerto in Bremen (7 January 1868) Max Bruch was no longer living or working in Coblenz. On the first page of the elusive manuscript of the Concerto the dedication reads 'Joseph Joachim in Verehrung zugeeignet'. The word 'Verehrung' (respect) is crossed through and 'Freundschaft' (friendship) substituted by Joachim, according to a note by Bruch in the top right hand corner. Then follows the work's title and the genesis of the various versions:

> Komponiert 1866 in Koblenz, umgearbeitet 1867. I Auff[ührung] (in der alten Form) Febr. 1867 in Koblenz. Beendigt Herbst (im October) 1867 (in Sondershausen). Von Joachim auf dem Nied-errh.[einischen] Musikfest in Köln gespielt (Mai 1868).

At the end of the manuscript Bruch wrote: 'Sondershausen 22 Oct. 1867 M.B.'

April 1867 was a bad month for Max. On the 6th his mother died, and in spite of hurrying from Coblenz to Cologne, he was too late to be with her at the end. On the 26th of the same month he conducted a performance of *Frithjof* in Hamburg (in the second half of the concert he included Schumann's Fourth Symphony, 'a special favourite of mine'). It was in Hamburg that he entertained hopes of being appointed as successor to the singer/conductor, Julius Stockhausen. In spite of a recommendation from the departing incumbent of the post, it was not offered to Bruch.

The possibility of leaving Coblenz for Sondershausen first appeared in a letter Bruch wrote to Hermann Levi primarily to obtain the orchestral parts for Beethoven's Emperor Concerto, to be played in Coblenz on 21 December by Clara Schumann.[1] He also wrote of Brahms, 'What is he doing, and where is he hiding?', and praised such works as the 'excellent waltzes' (for which Bruch was making 'loud propaganda' both in Coblenz and Cologne), the G minor Piano Quartet and one of the Serenades for orchestra. 'When you write to

Brahms, greet him heartily from me, my sister, and from other Cologne friends, and urge him to write a great, splendid Symphony, which will directly strike the hearts of the people, and shake and jolt the philistines so that they will not know what hit them!' Brahms did just that, although not for another ten years when the First Symphony appeared. The letter then turned to the subject of Sondershausen:

> I would like to ask your advice. I have received an offer of the post of First Court Conductor in Sondershausen.[2] Provisional salary, the Court Chamberlain writes, of 800 th[alers], three months' probation, the appointment to be taken up from 1 January 1867 according to their wish. Naturally I cannot leave here this winter. After Easter matters could be re-arranged, although I am contractually bound here until September 1867. I have written to Sondershausen to this effect; should they be in a position to wait (Marpurg [who currently held the post] leaves on 1 January), I must consider the question seriously. For the present I do not feel any special enthusiasm to bury myself in Sondershausen. It is a backwater, a very small backwater, very out of the way, does not even have a railway station; it takes seven hours by post-coach and train to reach Leipzig. Artistic activity is very modest. On the other hand, a good orchestra as I hear, only little to do. Here at most only average potential at my disposal, but the greatest cities in the Province are near, and I always have agreeable artistic projects. If I were to decide to go over to the Theatre completely, then I would definitely have to take Sondershausen as a stepping-stone, and do everything to ensure my priorities there. Frau Schumann, to whom I wrote on the subject, is decidedly against it and paints a picture in shocking colours of the trivialities of a little court. However when she says 'better to eke out a living in a big city than to be on a bed of roses in a small one', I can only go along with that to a certain point. The worst and most worrying of all is giving lessons: if that is the only way for me to keep body and soul together in a big city, I would rather never live in one, no matter what the long-term effect might be perhaps. Conducting gives me so much pleasure, and is becoming so easy, that from now on I would not like to be without a permanent post. Without one it would be difficult to acquire orchestral knowledge and a facility in the artistic requirements of orchestral methods. By that, however, I do not mean to say that I have a liking for Sondershausen. Meanwhile I must await more details. It would, however, be very valuable for me to know your opinion.

It is worth noting an interesting comment made at the end of this letter about Hiller, to whom Max's attitude was already changing. The pupil was no longer willing to sit quiescent at the feet of the master.

On Tuesday Hiller performed his *Saul*. How much my standpoint on Hiller's music has changed in the course of time was made very clear to me. In '58 I enthused unquestioningly for *Saul*, with all the feelings of a pupil, now (apart from a few places), the whole thing left me unspeakably cold. Rudorff and Gernsheim do not feel differently, and the worst of it is that so much could be better, if only he had taken it more seriously.

Levi replied to Bruch[3] with his usual mixture of sound advice and schoolmasterly reproach:

I know very little about the situation in Sondershausen, I remember only that Marpurg did not speak very enthusiastically about his post there. Little goes on in winter. On summer afternoons there are open-air concerts, during which the royal family and the inhabitants of Sondershausen and its surroundings attend by wandering about.
   Marpurg's predecessor was a 'futurist', and Marpurg himself must also be a member of this extreme party; the Liszt symphonic poems are always in the repertoire. I do not know any more. But the little I do, does not appear tempting to me. You can easily establish if it is true. A great advantage is that there is little to do in winter, and you could go on holiday for months; but that does not wash away the odium of the 'Garden Concerts'. The remoteness of the place is also to be considered. In short — *caveant consules*. I do not quite understand your sentence: 'If I were to decide to go over to the Theatre completely, then I would definitely have to take Sondershausen as a stepping stone.' Believe me, there is no connection between concerts and the Theatre, and if you conduct symphonies for ten years, in the eleventh in the Theatre you have to start again from ABC.

On 27 May 1801 Count Günther Friedrich Carl I von Schwarzburg-Sondershausen founded the Harmoniekorps for his own ceremonial use. This was a wind band comprising pairs of clarinets, oboes, bassoons, horns and trumpets, a trombone and a bass horn (a variant of the serpent, later displaced by the bass tuba). A flute was also added. The reputation of the wind band grew with the appointment as its

Director of the famous virtuoso clarinettist, Johann Hermstedt, for whom Spohr wrote his clarinet concerto in E minor Op. 26. In 1815 Spohr extended his admiration to the full band by writing his *Notturno* for them. With the establishment of an Opera in Sondershausen in 1815, the band was extended to orchestral proportions by the addition of a full string complement.

It was quite out of the question for Bruch to give such short notice to Coblenz (it would have been less than a month) and take up the post at Sondershausen, and so further discussion on the subject was stopped. Three months later, in March 1867, the post was offered to him once again, and this time he accepted. This period was a busy and eventful one for him. On 22 February he conducted three scenes from *Frithjof*, the Adagio from the Violin Concerto, and *Schön Ellen* together with choruses from Schubert's *Lazarus* in Coblenz, on 2 March he was in Bremen conducting the *Römischer Triumphgesang* and *Salamis*, followed by *Schön Ellen* three days later. In the middle of March he was in Mannheim and Heidelberg conducting *Frithjof*, in April he was in Paris, in June in Zürich with *Frithjof*, and on 24 October he conducted *Schön Ellen* in Düsseldorf.

Judging by the mood of a letter to Laura von Beckerath, he was ready for a change: 'I got back yesterday evening, and sang this song to Coblenz: "Weh, sitz ich in dem Kerker noch? Verfluchtes dumpfes Mauseloch!" [Alas am I still in this prison? This confounded stifling mousehole!] The daily routine makes me slink back to my room with a bored face, and again I have to learn how to bear it.'[4]

Two months later he wrote to her again, but this time in quite a different mood:

I present myself to you as Court Conductor at Sondershausen! Respect! . . . I did not want to stay in Coblenz, the Committee in Hamburg did not want me . . . so I took Sondershausen. Excellent orchestra, a lot of winter holiday (so that I can go to Paris, Berlin and Crefeld), a salary of 1000 thalers, lovely surroundings, only for one year, ample library, very friendly obliging people, a lot of time to work — they are the many advantages, but it is only a transitory post once again.[5]

A letter to Clara Schumann provided an explanation of his reasons for accepting the position when it was offered to him a second time. While acknowledging her point of view favouring a career based in a larger centre rather than a smaller one, Max nevertheless pointed out that he should seize the chance of benefiting from the association with a good orchestra like the one in Sondershausen. 'I have made the choice of a career as a Kapellmeister, and I will pursue it thoroughly. He who does not know an orchestra inside out will one day find it difficult to use his facility for his higher goals. There may be exceptions, but I have no right to include myself among them."[6]

He then went on to describe how history had repeated itself when (as in Aachen) the committee in Hamburg, though not the public, had rejected his application for the post of Music Director. He could no longer remain in Coblenz:

> I had battled long enough with bad amateurs and wretched musicians, and had learned long ago what a budding conductor had to learn. So I journeyed to Sondershausen . . . on 6 June I arrived and conducted my first rehearsal within a few days. Every Sunday between Whitsun and the end of September I have Symphony Concerts to conduct, some in the Court, some in the Theatre. I am free from the end of September until Christmas, and can travel as much as I want. The Theatre operates from 1 January until 31 March — April and May are quite free, and even during the Theatre period I can get away easily, substitutes are provided. I have a fixed salary of 1000 thalers, enjoy the invaluable title of 'Hofkapellmeister', have a lot of time in which to work, can be away often as you see. I conduct an excellent orchestra, am with them almost daily, perform all the good music which exists, am quite independent in the selection of programmes, and, in all that I undertake, I am certain of the complete agreement of our musically inclined Princess.

After describing the period of three months between the two offers made to him, during which time a pianist called Blassmann had filled the post to everyone's dissatisfaction, Bruch related how Princess Elisabeth of Schwarzburg-Sondershausen had written to him 'a second time (in March of this year) and offered me the position with a guarantee of quite unusual advantages and amenities'.

So on 23 May 1867 he wrote to the committee of the Music Institute in Coblenz, informing them of his resignation. He asked to be released forthwith ('as it is urgently required that I start in my new post in June'), and pointed out that little is demanded of him in Coblenz during the summer months. The committee waived the contractual three months' notice, and released him forthwith.

With the death of his mother and his departure from Coblenz occurring more or less simultaneously, his sister Mathilde decided to go to live in Sondershausen with her brother, and take on the role of housekeeper as well as helping him with artistic matters. The period of three years he spent at the Court was a particularly fruitful one, with the creation of his first published Symphony, and thereafter a return to the composition of works for chorus and orchestra. The three earlier symphonies he wrote as part of his studies with Hiller and dating from the years 1852, 1853 and 1861 are lost.

Before producing the Symphony, Bruch wrote a scene for baritone, women's chorus and orchestra entitled *Frithjof auf seines Vaters Grabhügel* Op. 27 (Frithjof on the mound of his father's grave). This was a postscript to his Cantata Op. 23 and is best described as a Concert Scene in which Frithjof seeks forgiveness by invoking the spirit of his father. In answer to his call the spirits of the air order Frithjof to rebuild the Temple of Baldur, after which he will receive celestial pardon in expiation of his sins.

Like the first Violin Concerto, the first Symphony Op. 28 in E flat was begun during Bruch's time in Coblenz and completed in Sondershausen. Once again Hermann Levi had been the catalyst, spurring the composer to write a Symphony to broaden his experience away from the choral medium to that of the instrumental. The work is in four movements, the first is in sonata form, the second a scherzo and the third (marked *Quasi Fantasia*) leads directly into the boisterous Finale (*allegro guerriero*). The tempo indication of the last movement is a reminder not only of the *Twelve Scottish Folksongs* written not long before, but also of the last movement of Mendelssohn's Scottish Symphony which carried the same marking. Bruch was to use it yet again in the final movement of the *Scottish Fantasy*, twelve years later. Scotland was a country close to his musical heart.

The first movement of Bruch's Symphony No. 1 begins with a slow lyrical introduction over an E flat tonic pedal, and with its gradual build-up of sustained chords (the organ once again) looks back to Schumann's Rhenish symphony or forward to a symphony by Bruckner. Devices such as harmonic suspensions, *tremolando*, *arpeggiato* accompaniments and the doubling of melody by horns and woodwinds (or horns and strings), are by now becoming a recognizable characteristic of Bruch's creative vocabulary. What Bruch, with Levi's strong encouragement, sought to achieve was a satisfactory thematic development in his instrumental works, and by closely adhering to the principles of sonata form (exposition, development and recapitulation) he achieved his goal with this movement alone.

The second movement makes no apology for recalling Mendelssohn's scherzo from the *Midsummer Night's Dream*. The movement is in three parts, the first and third dominated by a perpetual staccato string motive, the second by an expansive melody given in octaves (as in Spohr's Third Symphony) initially by the strings against the continual quaver accompaniment of the winds and horns, and then with roles reversed with the melody taken up by the winds and horns accompanied by the strings.

The short slow Fantasia in the tonic minor key of E flat begins with a sombre, thickly scored passage for strings and winds leading to solos for cello, oboe, viola and clarinet before the violas quote a melody from the first movement. After a densely scored climax for the full orchestra, the solo instruments heard earlier (with horn and bassoon now included) calm matters down to a quiet timpani roll on the dominant to link this movement to the Finale.

Like the first movement, the last contains two contrasting themes both worked in detail in the development section, and both returning exchanged with one another in the recapitulation. Spohr is once again recalled in the character of the strong rhythmic emphasis of the theme, whilst the influence of Schubert and Mendelssohn lies in the perpetual triplet accompaniment of the strings. Bruch's originality is not absent, however, as at (rehearsal letter) D where a marvellously syncopated variation of the accompaniment occurs between the second violins, violas and cellos whilst horn and clarinet intone the second theme.

Ex. 20

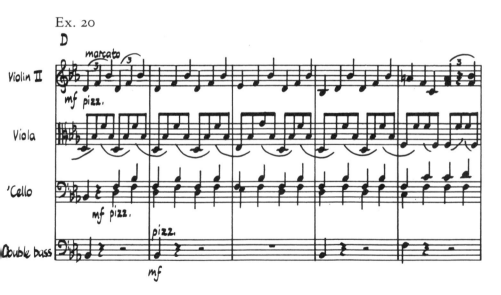

The work is scored for conventional symphony orchestra, with particular emphasis on the writing for horns (fast becoming a favourite melodic instrument), woodwinds and strings. The trumpets, trombones and timpani are less adventurously used, appearing mainly at climaxes. Kretschmar referred to the Symphony as 'one of the best known symphonies of the period'.[7] The first performance took place under Bruch's baton on 26 July 1868, in Sondershausen, using manuscript score and parts. Bruch dedicated it 'in friendship' to Brahms:

> At the same time as you receive these lines, honoured friend, the score of my Symphony will have reached you. I have taken the liberty of dedicating it to you before asking you beforehand, and hope that you will not accept it less amicably as a result. Inasmuch as I decorate my work with your name, dear Brahms, I wish you to know how highly I regard your gifts and your achievements — how much I receive pleasure and take delight, as an equally striving Artist, in your truly significant and steadily increasing productive powers.
>
> I am especially moved to say this to you at this time; your powerful *Requiem* lies before me, excellent through and through, greatly conceived, deeply felt, and it brings me an artistic joy which I have not known in a long time. What should I, what can I say about it? I can only shake your hand in spirit, and express my thanks once again for such a work, for such a valuable work of art.
>
> It would be understandable and forgivable if you, who for years have pursued your own way so energetically, were to have little interest in the labours of your artistic colleagues. It pleases me the more that you so clearly proved just the opposite to me in Cologne at Whitsun; your lively interest, your sincere, warmly expressed pleasure in my Symphony gave me an especial happiness and already then it awakened in me the wish [to dedicate it to you]. And so I ask you once again, dear Brahms, to accept the dedication of the Symphony as it is meant. . . .[8]

On Christmas Day 1868, Brahms replied from Vienna to Bruch, who was now back in Sondershausen:

> It can hardly have been your intention, dear Bruch, to surprise me on Christmas Eve. I went indoors . . . and found your letter which was the loveliest festive present, one pronounced in great seriousness, and I think and feel nothing but the most vivid joy and heartfelt feelings of thanks. I must, however, await the music (because of the holiday), but in the meantime memory and fantasy help me by playing, the best it can, trumpets and drums in E flat and certain appropriate melodies.

After the Vienna performance on 20 February 1870 Brahms wrote again:

In spite of my shyness of paper I cannot prevent myself thanking you in a few words for the Symphony which we heard here yesterday. . . . [It] went really quite exceptionally well throughout. All the movements were applauded unopposed. The Scherzo in particular received a quite unusual applause, which not only the piece but also the splendidly stirring performance earned. . . . Has a four-hand version [for piano] still not appeared? I see with much joy (and some envy) how busy and hardworking you are. I have seen all your new works . . .

When Bruch replied he not only thanked Brahms for the report of the Vienna performance, but also made an observation about piano versions of works not originally conceived for that instrument. His point of view is not unnaturally somewhat coloured by his instinctive dislike of the piano. 'The Symphony sounds pitiful in this form; I hate nothing more than piano versions, and yet one must overcome it and send them out into the world.'⁹

A long letter to Hiller provided an interesting insight into Bruch's work at Sondershausen, and further confirmation of the high regard he had for Brahms and his *Requiem*.

On 31 March our 'Opera Season' ended. It sounds first rate — it was not first rate at all! Average soloists, miserable chorus, but in contrast there was our good orchestra. I conducted eighteen operatic performances and fifteen different operas, and believe I have learned a good deal from doing so. And that is the most important point for me. I may now say that there is no area in the art of conducting with which I am unfamiliar.

. . . from Leipzig I travelled direct to Bremen where many of Brahms' friends had gathered to hear the Good Friday performance of his *Deutsches Requiem*. Frau Schumann, Joachim and his wife . . . were there among others. The work is very greatly conceived and deeply felt. It makes a meaningful impression not only on artists, but also on the people. It appears that Brahms has achieved something here which had failed him hitherto. Nevertheless I believe that one will feel more respect and awe for this work of his, rather than love. I am frank enough to say that a powerful ravishing melody is preferable to the most beautiful imitations and contrapuntal tight-rope walk. There is now a Philistine Party in Germany which places work above all else, and gives at best a disdainful shrug of its shoulders to every fresh, impartial, uneducated expression of Life in Art. As far as I am concerned — I can truly be in love with Walpurgisnacht [Mendelssohn], ensembles from *Figaro*, or bits of [*William*] *Tell*, but not with pieces by Brahms, as much as I raise my hat to his brilliant talent. You will feel the same, as others also do. However I am pleased that, after so much bad luck, Brahms has a success for once. I am convinced this success will be the same elsewhere as in Bremen.[10]

In spite of his letter to Levi of 6 December 1866 in which he criticized Hiller's oratorio *Saul* and questioned the change in his own relationship to his former teacher, a letter to Hiller in May 1869 desperately sought the reassurance of his mentor that the pupil had not fallen from favour. Hiller had neither reacted to, nor expressed an opinion of the performance Bruch gave in Cologne of the Symphony on 16 February of that year (in the same concert Hiller conducted Brahms' *Requiem* and Handel's *Jephtha*). Max was unsettled by this and sought to know the reason. Hiller was also rumoured to be leaving Cologne (he did not in fact do so, but retired in 1884, one year before his death), and it is not inconceivable that Max would wish his own name to be firmly in Hiller's mind in case advice regarding a successor might be sought by the city authorities. It should never be forgotten that Bruch always wanted to be in charge of the musical life in Cologne. As the years passed during which he was rejected time and again, he had to contend with seeing others in that coveted post, and this naturally gave rise to feelings of bitterness and frustration at his native city. 'If you do really leave Cologne,' he wrote to Hiller, 'I must then seek to introduce myself there without you. That will be difficult.' He then cautiously raised the matter of Hiller's opinion of his Symphony, though this trepidation soon gave way to candour and frankness:

I performed my Symphony in February in Cologne. You were kind enough to be with us that evening. We spoke about much, only you said nothing at all about the Symphony. I must therefore assume that it totally displeased you. If that was so, then between our current musical thinking and feelings a gulf has now obviously occurred, which appears to be difficult to bridge. Do not, for God's sake, think that I wish to be only praised. I know full well the value of open discussion between artists. I do not delude myself that the Symphony is perfect — one could take another point of view of the dramatic development in the Finale — but I also do not believe that it deserves to be silently ignored. Many of my artistic colleagues (including Joachim, Brahms, David, Dietrich, Reinecke, to say nothing of my close friends) acknowledge in this Symphony substantial progress since all my early works, in particular the aspect of thematic material and the use of polyphonic elements. I know full well, as I have said, that some things in the Symphony give full scope for discussion — it would have been so interesting after the performance to have heard the opinion of such an honoured and important master as you — the opportunity offered itself, for we sat next to one another and were often engaged in conversation — but you said nothing, and so I can only take it that you had so much in your heart against the Symphony, you did not wish to distress me by saying so. Later however, you said: 'You are too spoilt for me' — a remark I have already heard expressed before. If you should understand by that 'spoilt by the Press', then you are mistaken. It is impossible to call someone 'spoilt' who, within a week, receives bad reviews from Breslau, Leipzig, Vienna, Cologne etc., and is attacked in the city of his birth by a wretched ignoramus in a particularly awful way, without raising a finger for himself. If you mean the success that *Frithjof*, [*Schön*] *Ellen*, the Violin Concerto etc. have had with the public, then I must say that this pleases me but in no way has it, nor could it dazzle me. Do you believe that artists spoil me when conductors perform my works, and violinists play my Concerto everywhere? Thank God, I am not yet used to the most talented and best artists taking the sincerest and friendliest interest in my works. That is my good fortune!

All this taken together gives me pain. I had the definite impression that you had formed the view that my career had been unjustly favoured by luck until now — as if you wanted to attribute the main role in this to luck. It is true that without luck one makes no progress, but in Art, he who from within and without wants to get on, must take honest trouble, be constantly putting finishing touches and improving, and always be eager to recognize the truth and do the right ting. And if he wanted to object to this constant toil, then this so-called 'luck' would come to an end.

I hate airing my views verbally; and as I could not bring myself to talk to you about superficial, trivial matters so long as this insecurity between us remained, I decided to write quite frankly to you upon my return. Honoured Kapellmeister, consider this pronouncement merely as the reproduction of my earlier mood. I had to say something to you about it, however, to explain my absence. Perhaps, if he has erred, you will forgive a young artist, whose soul lies in his works — I wish for nothing more.[11]

At the end of the year Max sent Hiller some new works for perusal and comment, and in his accompanying letter it appears that peace had been restored, fears and agitations dispelled, and misunderstandings forgotten and forgiven. One cannot, however, fail to sense Bruch wanting to have the last word in declaring a grudging truce. The whole episode is typical of Bruch's sensitivity and overreaction to criticism, which in later years bordered on paranoia. 'I may truly assume,' he wrote, 'that today you no longer stand by the hard and extreme remarks with which you replied to my (as you yourself said) "friendly" questions of the New Year, and on this assumption I look forward from my heart to be able to shake you by the hand with former sentiments of gratitude and devotion. I am after all not as bad as you described me at the time. I have never been. I had much to tell you today, but far be it from me to return to matters of the past.'[12]

The period to 1870 in Bruch's life is, by comparison with the years after that date, relatively poorly documented in the known archives and collections. The explanation for the disparity of the quantity of documentation lies almost exclusively in the extant collection of the letters he wrote to his publisher, Fritz Simrock, between May 1870 and November 1904 (though by that time Fritz had died and had been succeeded by his nephew Hans). These letters, covering a period of 34 years, give an insight into Max Bruch the composer and the man, though the emphasis is decidedly on the former. Details of his private and domestic life are relatively hard to come by, but occasionally a glimpse is to be had. Reference has already been made to the letters he wrote to his friends Laura and Rudolf von Beckerath in Crefeld. This correspondence took place between 1861 and 1877, when Max severed the friendship because he felt that the Beckeraths were attending Brahms' concerts in preference to his own. It appears that he did not keep any letters from Beckerath though he may well have destroyed them in a fit of pique. There are hardly any letters from Simrock, but those that do exist are included among the seventeen volumes Bruch put together containing letters and programmes sent to him by colleagues and personal friends covering the period 1866–1891.

He certainly planned memoirs in his last years, and began dictating his reminiscences to his daughter Margarethe near the end of his life. They do not however constitute very much in terms of the number of years they cover; they are neither detailed, nor is any reference made to the emotional side of his life. His father is barely mentioned anywhere, not even at his death in 1861, and although more is to be read about his mother, it is hardly in proportion to the important influence she had in the years to her death in 1867. His sister Mathilde appears to have stepped at once into her late mother's shoes. She became both housekeeper and adviser in her brother's artistic affairs, and it appears she had a role to play in the first serious romantic involvement in Max's life, which occurred in 1868 when he was thirty years old.

There are just two references to Emma Landau in letters from Bruch to Beckerath, and both refer to the breaking off of an engagement. The first was written in Brussels:

These few short words follow yesterday's sad telegram from me. I still cannot write much. Tilly [Mathilde] has received more detailed news this morning, and is authorized to inform you if you wish. If you telegraph her early on Saturday, she can come in the afternoon. She will long to do so, particularly to be with you at this time. Briefly, for today, the following: What the mother wanted, the daughter did not. It was too late. Emma had long ago come to a decision. As she did not hear from me for so long, she suppressed her liking for me with the utmost energy, and she succeeded in doing this surprisingly well, so well that hardly a trace of her inner feelings were to be noticed. Can I complain? May I complain? No! A loving girl demands feelings, and may demand exclusive feelings from her beloved. Love knows nothing else, tolerates no other feeling, nor understands other feelings which seek to stand in its way or put it aside. The mother understood me fully, she spoke to me with such gentleness and goodness! The daughter did not understand me, and could not understand me (because she loved me deeply and seriously) — who could blame her?

At the time, in the New Year of '67, I said A and then very soon had to say B. At the time I had it all in hand. Therefore I am greatly to blame — only the certain knowledge that Emma has never understood my sister, helps me over it somewhat. I also consider it possible and probable that she can still be happy after her feelings for me have been pulled up by the roots. She is twenty years old, lives in the big wide world, and is successful; she will yet be happy. She is no longer unhappy, but the fact that she was so, for a time, through my fault, is a horrible thought. If possible after all this, like the mother, do not think worse of me. I have written to Tilly what you wrote. Your words comforted me somewhat, and lifted me up again. I was a mad fool to think that Emma would still take me back. Suppose, after my long explanation, she had accepted my offer of marriage; could that have been a happy marriage? After all that had happened; hardly! There is still much to say, but I shall stop. I must work and write music to lift myself out of all my sorrows. . . . I had never thought to go through hours like those of yesterday. But such experiences also have their good side, inasmuch as they widen the horizon of sincerity and truth. Little by little one gets used to seeing everything in shocking clarity, but in fact this selfsame clarity cannot be shocking to the man seeking absolute truth.[13]

One can only surmise who Emma Landau was, where she lived and how they came to meet. From this last letter it would appear that she lived in Coblenz, for that is where Max was in the New Year of 1867, and his move to Sondershausen would explain their separation at the time. Another clue to where she lived might lie in a letter to his publisher, Fritz Simrock, in which Bruch asked 'for a piano score of [my] new (Second) Symphony to be sent to Frau Jetty Landau in Coblenz (a cousin of Joachim).'[14] By January 1869 he had emerged from the gloom of two months earlier, and his perspective of Emma Landau had been changed. 'After all the worries and confusion of the past months,' he wrote, 'a friendly bright star now shines; the solicitous hand of my good, understanding and noble-thinking Princess smooths the way to the most Beautiful. I believe my friends can wish me luck at this turning point. If I were engaged, or had been tied down, then it all could not have happened. Be assured, dear friend, that I feel myself once again wholly as an artist and to have found happiness once again, which is surely the greatest thing. It is good that the matter with E.L. came to an end, anything else would have been bad. Invisible forces drive and impel determinable Man without his knowledge. But from now on, no one and nothing shall so easily cloud my view of my objective.'[15]

His intentions may have been to put Emma from his mind, but two years later (towards the end of August 1871) his determination not to see her again weakened. In two letters to Laura von Beckerath, he reported two frustrated attempts to be alone with Emma if only to talk matters through.

He was holidaying at Bad Godesberg at the time, and the first meeting was on the platform of the railway station in the company of her uncle, Heinrich Landau. The result was an arrangement to meet again in Bonn the next day, but poor Max was once again denied the opportunity to be alone with her; this time it was her mother who came between the lovers (Max was not to have much luck with potential mothers-in-law). Emma was whisked off to Brussels by her mother, while Max resumed his moping. In June 1872 the boot was on the other foot, and Max was having to fend off the advances of another lady (known only as Franziska), and during the course of the narrative to Laura von Beckerath (by now probably used to her role in his life as an agony aunt), he declared himself to be 'still battered and bruised by the recent Landau business'. After this, Emma vanished into history.

The period in Sondershausen was proving fruitful both in the continuing experience on the rostrum and in the number of compositions Bruch was to produce in his three years there. His time at the Court began with the First Symphony, and ended with the Second (if the Violin Concerto is to be credited to Coblenz), but in between came works entirely for solo voice or chorus. Yet no matter how conducive the environment was to composing, it was with another place back in his beloved Rhineland that Bruch now began an association in earnest which was to last the rest of his life. The Igeler Hof in Bergisch Gladbach was from now on to be forever associated with Max Bruch. Many of his compositions were the fruits of visits to this house high on the hills overlooking the Bergisches Land. It lay in complete isolation and utter tranquillity, the silence disturbed only by the sounds no sensitive artist finds disturbing, those of Nature.

## Chapter Seven

## BERGISCH GLADBACH:
## IGELER HOF

---

IN AN ARTICLE written in 1960, celebrating 75 years since the founding of the Cäcilienchor in 1885, Edwin Redslob described the countryside surrounding Bergisch Gladbach as 'a picturesque, beautiful region, from which the streams of the Bergisches Land flow down to the valley of the Rhine; undulating hills with bright green meadows in broad valleys, mysterious, shadowy beech woods and mixed woodland which ascend leisurely to a height at which old settlements lie.'

There were several strands drawing Max Bruch to the house called the Igeler Hof, which stands among the hills of the Bergisches Land. His mother, Wilhelmine Almenräder, was both singing teacher and friend to Katherina Theresia Neissen, and the Igeler Hof was in the possession of the Brussels-based Neissen family until 1888. Katherina died in 1859, and for the next ten years Max rarely visited the house, Frau Neissen's death having affected him deeply (it gave rise to the *Messensätze* Op. 35 dedicated to her memory). In his old age he wrote in some notes he made about Katherina for his projected memoirs: 'Thérèse's life lived in a spirit of sacrifice for her brother August. Thérèse good, understanding, a music enthusiast. To me she was Earthmother, friend. The years 1850–1859: a beautiful, too beautiful adolescence; [I was] also spoilt too much.'

In 1888 the house was bought by the Zanders family, in whose possession it remains today. The heavily wooded countryside is a natural resource for paper manufacture, and at the beginning of the nineteenth century there were several mills in the area. One of these (Schnabelsmühle) was owned by Johann Wilhelm Adolf Zanders until his untimely death in 1831 at the age of thirty-five. His widow, Julie, promptly let the mill and moved to Bonn with her son Karl Wilhelm Richard (born just four years earlier in 1826). When he was eight years old Richard suddenly began to lose his sight, and, during the time before he became totally blind, his mother called in highly eminent teachers to provide the child with the all-round education which normally lasted until the beginning of University studies. Ten years

later, at the age of eighteen, he underwent an operation which
restored his sight, but it remained very weak and left him seriously
disabled throughout his life. Though blind, he had nevertheless
managed to study. A friend taught him Greek by tracing the
characters of the Greek alphabet on to the palm of his hand. Even
when his sight returned to him, he had to forego any further studies
which involved reading, or any ideas of a career in the clergy or
music, both of which had seriously interested him. In 1856 he met
Maria Johanny, and after a short engagement they were married on
17 June 1857, whereupon Richard took over the management of the
family paper business.

Maria Johanny was born on 9 March 1839 to the cloth manufacturer Julius Johanny and his wife Charlotte (née Walter), in the small
town of Hückeswagen on the river Wupper (coincidentally the home
of Bruch's cousins). She was brought up in a highly cultured
environment of music, painting and literature, before leaving home
for Düsseldorf to complete her education. There she stayed with the
Mangold family during her school years, and further enriched her
musical background in the company of this family of music-lovers
(Charlotte Walter had also received her initial musical education at
their hands). In 1856 Maria returned home, where she met and
married Richard Zanders the following year. Their first few years
together were troubled by the problems of Richard's eyesight and
the worries of rebuilding the family business, but they also brought
the joy of four children — Margaretha, Richard jun., Hans and
Marie.

Happiness for the Zanders family was short-lived, for tragedy
struck two dreadful blows with the death from diphtheria of the
youngest child Marie in 1868, followed by Richard's own death from
consumption in 1870 at the age of forty-four. After just thirteen years
of marriage, and at the age of thirty-one, Maria was alone, caring for
her three surviving children and running the paper business. After a
period of mourning, she vigorously renewed her interest in music and
art. She travelled to Cologne to take singing lessons and to Düsseldorf
for instruction in painting. She took her daughter Margaretha to Italy
to discover the treasures of Florence and Rome. Meanwhile the
business had expanded with the purchase of two more mills (Gohrs-
mühle and Dombach) to become a thriving enterprise. It was now that
the young widow began to devote herself to the interests of her factory
workers, both on and off the shop floor. Dining facilities were created,
a cookery school for the female workers was built, the factories were
landscaped with rest areas, and gardens and fruit trees were established. Her philanthropy eventually embraced her love of music, for

she began to teach singing and rudimentary theory to those female
workers who showed an interest.

From her initial three pupils (Adelheid, Margarethe and Elise)
grew the beginnings of a female chorus, which gave its first public
performance in the autumn of 1885 with the angels' trio from
Mendelssohn's *Elijah*, 'Lift thine eyes to the mountains'. Of the
twenty ladies who sang that night on 25 September 1885, Adelheid
was described as the 'pillar of the sopranos', with Gertrud Kierspel
holding the same responsibility in the alto section. By merging her
ladies' chorus with an established male chorus in Bergisch Gladbach,
called the Liederkranz, Maria Zanders (now called 'Mother' by her
devoted workers) created the Cäcilienchor. At first the two groups
would rehearse separately for a sing-through of the work being
studied, only combining when each had been thoroughly prepared
by its own conductor (Jacob Breuer directed the male chorus). The
success of this enterprise led to a concert at the end of 1886 conducted
by Breuer, with Maria Zanders discreetly hidden on stage behind a
potted plant and helping her ladies through the hardest parts of the
music. The choir then began performing the established repertoire of
Palestrina, Bach, Handel, Schumann and Mendelssohn, as well as
those works of contemporary composers such as Bruch and Brahms.
In 1889 a professional musician from nearby Cologne, Arnold
Kroegel, was selected by Maria Zanders as the choir's conductor,
and with this appointment the standard of performance by the
Cäcilienchor was enhanced, creating for itself the high reputation
which it has maintained ever since. In 1966 the choir was re-named
the Chorgemeinschaft Bergisch Gladbach, and in 1985 it celebrated
its centenary with a performance of Max Bruch's *Das Lied von der
Glocke*.

The energetic and determined Maria Zanders espoused another
cause during her life, namely the rebuilding and restoration of the
thirteenth-century Cistercian cathedral in the small town of Altenberg. Towards the end of the nineteenth century the Altenberger
Dom had deteriorated to a mere shell of a building, lacking its
original Gothic roof, windows, ridge turrets, its organ and its bells.
Relentlessly Frau Zanders pursued and hounded bureaucrats in Berlin and elsewhere in her efforts to obtain funds to restore the
cathedral to its former glory. In 1894 she formed a committee
chaired by her son Hans to co-ordinate all the means at her disposal
to achieve her goal. By 1904 she had succeeded and the festival
celebrating the completion of the project began on 13 June. Maria
Zanders was by now exhausted and suffering the effects of diabetes,
together with periodic bouts of depression. Too weak and ill to

attend the festivities celebrating the fruits of her own tireless labours, she could only listen to descriptions of the new façade, the new west window, roof turrets, choir stalls and the three new bells, all of which were installed as a result of her efforts. Six months later, on 6 December 1904, she died in the certain knowledge that she would rejoin her beloved husband Richard.

Shortly before his death in 1920, Max Bruch wrote a short article entitled 'In the Bergisches Land' as part of his projected memoirs.[1] His life at this time was full of sadness and misery. By now all those closest to him had died: his wife, his eldest son Hans, his sister Mathilde, Richard and Maria Zanders and all their four children. Yet in spite of his dreadful loneliness and bitter despair, he was able to look back on his days in the Bergisches Land, and to assess the influence of Maria Zanders, the house on the hill called the Igeler Hof and its surrounding countryside, on his life and work. His feelings were born of a deep sense of gratitude and a sincere love.

If you climb up from Gladbach through beautiful beech trees along tranquil woodland paths, you will see above you between the walnut, the lime and the ash trees, meadows, fields and orchards surrounding a modest old country house, the Igeler Hof. If you look from here to the west, the view opens out on to the flat plains of the Lower Rhine, with the majestic towers of Cologne Cathedral upon the horizon. To the east, however, from the wooded heights you are greeted with the sight of little white churches and chapels, and the turreted Palatinate hunting lodge at Bensberg. Beautiful woodland paths lead down to the Igel Mill and the charming, peaceful valley of the Herrenstrund. In my youth the Igeler Hof was owned by an artistic, German family resident in Brussels; in particular the sister of the owners (a former singing pupil of my mother) took the warmest interest in my artistic development and called herself my 'maternal girlfriend' [this was Katherina Neissen]. Under her faithful care I was allowed as a boy and a youth to live, to think and to work for weeks or months on end in the lovely house between the walnut trees. It was a refuge for quiet spiritual work, which one could not imagine as more beautiful, and from this it is understandable that I have loved the Igeler Hof above all else for the whole of my life. One by one the former owners passed on; I was robbed of my maternal friend through her death in 1859, and for years the Igeler Hof stood lonely and deserted. Quite unexpectedly, however, I experienced one day the dawning of a new life for the house, and in a manner of speaking I too received the same new life. The eldest son of my Gladbach friends, Richard Zanders jun., a

richly talented, aspiring young man, and his first-rate young wife
[Anna] (the worthy daughter of the great inventor Werner von
Siemens, a man of whom Germany will always be proud) acquired
the Igeler Hof and restored it to its former beauty. Very often I
stayed, reflected and worked with them up on the green hill as a
grateful guest, and whereas I enjoyed the true friendship of the older
generation of the Zanders family down below in the valley, I was
now also able to enjoy the younger one up on the hill. Both Man
and Nature worked together to create in me a great and deep
dependence upon my homeland, and I would have considered
myself fortunate if my life could have been played out in this place
which is so dear to me. But that was not to be — I had to go off into
the world, 'to see the play of Life enacted in its wildly exciting
streets' — and so I could only now and then succumb to the magic
of my former homeland. But wherever I was, I never lost the
homesickness for beautiful Gladbach and the Igeler Hof, both
places of my happy youth. From however afar, I always went back
as long as my health permitted, and always with those feelings of
inner happiness.

Bruch fled to the Igeler Hof to escape the chores of his daily duties or
the wrangles with officialdom in Sondershausen during his last two
years in the post (1869–70), and in Bergisch Gladbach he found the
peace and solitude necessary for composing. His friendship with
Maria Zanders, after her husband's death in 1870, blossomed into a
twinning of souls and a relationship of spiritual depth which inspired
the composer for 30 years. It has a similarity to the friendship between
Johannes Brahms and Clara Schumann. Although Frau Schumann
was fourteen years older than Brahms, and Maria Zanders was a year
younger than Bruch, there is a common element in the platonic, deep
relationship which both couples enjoyed without any intrusion from
others in their lives, in Bruch's case even his own wife. Indeed when
Clara Tuczek married Max, she was warmly befriended by Maria.
The composer understood and encouraged Maria's philanthropic
activities, particularly when they touched upon music and painting.
She in turn loved his music, took care of him when he was in material
difficulty, and sustained his creative impulses by providing him with
an environment conducive to bringing them to fruition. In his letters
he addresses her as 'Mama' or 'Die grosse Vergolderin' (the great
gilder or painter in gold). Often they referred to one another by using
two names from Nordic sagas; she was 'Bele' and he was 'Thorsten'.
'With her intuitive, almost Greek sense of what is beautiful,' he wrote,
'she perceived through listening to and studying the deepest, truly

musical works of art, the beauty of melody, the nobility and strength of architectural structure, the symmetry of formal construction, the purity of composition, and the exquisite filigree work in elaborate thematic development.'

The importance of the value he placed upon his visits there was fully appreciated by Frau Zanders, who told Max's sister Mathilde:

Today it is decided that Max will remain here over Christmas and the New Year — it is so cold, and it would be so bleak for him in Berlin. Here he is in the best mood for working, he has as much solitude as he wishes, and is as happy as a sandboy. . . . You know Max in his working and creative moods, so you are clearly able to imagine how he lives like a hermit down in the library. Most evenings we are downstairs together reading, making music or chatting . . . otherwise it is a matter of complete seclusion for him. I am happy to be able to provide this solitude for my dear friend.[2]

Her death on 6 December 1904 shattered him and he wrote to her son Hans two weeks later:

I am an old tree and do not know if I will ever recover from this blow to my innermost core — nor whether or how I shall live on without her heartfelt interest, her moving and sincere friendship, and her understanding. I read, but I do not know what, I work but I cannot concentrate my thoughts, I look around me and I see everywhere nothing but a vast wasteland. Everything in this world goes on in its accustomed way; it is only one person that the world has lost — but what a person!

In the summer of 1889 when the Igeler Hof had just been acquired by Richard Zanders jun. and his wife Anna, Bruch compiled a list of works he had written, revised or worked on during visits to the house during the years when it was owned by the Neissen family. He also listed the occasions when he worked on his compositions down in the valley during visits to Maria Zanders. Entitled 'Igel memories' it is dedicated to Anna Zanders, who, after the deaths of Maria and all her children, took over the management of the Cäcilienchor.

1850 (Summer) My first visit to the Igel (12 years old).
1851 Lieder etc. composed
1852 Quintet for Piano and strings, Lieder etc.
1853 Various works, e.g. Lieder and piano pieces.
1854 *Rinaldo*, cantata by Goethe.

1855 Various works, e.g. Ingeborg's Lament from Tegner's *Frithjof Saga* (first version, later revised). A Piano Trio.

1856 Overture, March and Entr'acte to Schiller's *Maid of Orleans* (performed in the City Theatre, Cologne in the New Year 1857).

1857 *Mondbeglänzte Zaubernacht* [Moonlit Night of Magic] by Tieck, for soprano, chorus and orchestra (composed partly at the Igel). Scenes from the *Frithjof Saga* (first version, used later for the work published as Op. 23).

1858 Worked on the *Frithjof* scenes among others. String Quartet in C minor, later revised and published as Op. 9.

1859 (Easter) *Hymne* by Auguste Kolter for voice and piano (published as Op. 13).

1859 6 July. Death of Thérèse Neissen. During the next ten years no further work at the Igel.

1869 From 15 April to 8 May at the Igel. Composed: *Normannenzug* by Scheffel (Op. 32), Lieder for baritone (Op. 33), *Die Flucht nach Aegypten* (poem by Reinick for soprano, women's chorus and orchestra) and *Morgenstunde* by Lingg for the same forces. Both works published as Op. 31. *Waldpsalm* by Scheffel (later part of the collection of choral songs published as Op. 38).

1871 In November down at the old house [the Zanders Mill known as the Schnabelsmühle, which was demolished to make way in 1873–74 for the Villa Zanders] all the main scenes from *Odysseus* Op. 41; the scene 'Odysseus in the Underworld' written up at the Igel.

1875 From mid-August to mid-October worked on the secular oratorio *Arminius* up at the Igel (published 1877).

1877 *Das Lied von der Glocke* [The Song of the Bell] down in the new house [the Villa Zanders], written for the most part (in July), much of it conceived up at the Igel.

1880 (Second half of July) stayed two weeks in the Igeler Hof, wrote Scherzo of the Third Symphony, and *Kol Nidrei*.

1888 (July) Worked on the score of *Das Feuerkreuz*.

Several of the early works on this list have since vanished. Later works which are known to have been composed or worked on in Bergisch Gladbach include the *Serenade* for violin and orchestra Op. 75, the piano score of the *Canzone* for cello and orchestra Op. 55, the *Adagio on Celtic Themes* for cello and orchestra Op. 56, and possibly the simplified version he wrote for piano duet of six Hungarian Dances by Brahms. Many autograph scores were presented to Maria Zanders or to her family after her death, as a token of Bruch's gratitude. These, with photographs and many letters to and from the composer, now form part of the Zanders family archive housed in the Villa Zanders in the centre of the town of Bergisch Gladbach.

It would appear that in the period between the death of Thérèse Neissen in 1859 and 1888, the year in which the Zanders family bought the Igeler Hof, Bruch would visit Bergisch Gladbach and spend the nights at the Villa Zanders in the town, and work during the day up at the Igeler Hof (still occupied by Thérèse Neissen's brother). This is evident from the letters he wrote from the Hof to Maria when she was away from Bergisch Gladbach for the summer. In spite of her absence, she would nevertheless put her own house and servants at his disposal. When she was at home, she would sometimes send a servant up to the Igeler Hof with a lunch-tray of soup and bread for the hard-working composer, and when she was away he would write asking for permission to have his laundry washed down at the Villa. When Herr Neissen was also absent, leaving him quite alone, Max would ask Maria for 'a piece of meat and a few potatoes' each evening, and then spend the few hours before retiring 'by reading in the corner room'. Such was his love for the Bergisches Land that in August 1875, Bruch came close to buying a rectory in the village of Sand, not far from Bergisch Gladbach. He had been introduced to the rector, Pastor Fussbahn, who thought that the rectory would become disused and put up for sale, but the plan came to nothing. Had he bought a property there, the Igeler Hof might not have played such a significant role in his creative output.

Max Bruch stayed at the Igeler Hof for the last time in the summer of 1909. Old age and illness prevented him from returning throughout the last eleven years of his life, although it was often in his mind to do so. He corresponded regularly from Berlin with Maria's son Hans and his wife Olga, and to them and indeed to all the younger generation of the Zanders family he was known as Uncle Max. In 1914 he wrote, 'I would be the happiest man, if once again in my life I could see the beloved Igeler Hof — but I do not know if it will come to pass.'

To celebrate his eightieth birthday, in 1918, he was granted honorary citizenship of Bergisch Gladbach in recognition of his musical association with the town, and in 1935 a memorial to him was erected there. On Whit Monday (9 June) 1919 he wrote one of his last letters to Olga Zanders. It can be regarded as his Testament, not only to the Igeler Hof but also to his life:

How beautiful it must be now in the valley and up on the hill in

Gladbach. How often, in past happier years, I experienced those early summer days, and how unhappy I sometimes feel now that Fate has unrelentingly robbed me of what was loveliest and dearest to me. But things cannot be otherwise. Above the gates of old age the sad word 'Resignation' is written. When one such as I has to forgo so much, one gradually becomes a virtuoso in the art of resignation. I do not have to tell you that I think of you and your troubles with my former lively interest during these terrible, abnormal times, for Destiny has laid much upon you. Is it not as if a quite exceptionally heavy Fate has befallen three generations of the Zanders family in Gladbach through the same great ill-fortune, ever since [the death of] J. W. Zanders? Time and again the men heading the increasingly important family business were taken prematurely in the fullness of their work and achievement during the best years of their lives, and they left behind them young widows on whom the work and responsibility now fell. That is how it was first in 1831 when the husband of Frau Julie Zanders (the grandmother whom I still knew between 1862 and 1868) suddenly died. At that time she was only 32 or 33 years old, but she leased the factory out and moved to Bonn with the children. In 1870, immediately after the Battle of Gravelotte during the French War, your mother-in- law, my unforgettable friend Maria, met with the same fate. Her husband died of consumption and at 31 years of age she was a widow, and the same lot fell to you when our beloved and brilliant Hans was torn from you quite unexpectedly during those most difficult times of 1915. A man whose apparent vigorous nature appeared guaranteed to grant him a long life. Sometimes it is really as if Fate has made up its mind to plague certain families (particularly the best ones) especially grievously. The matter will become ever harder, for the future looks very dark in reality. The Social Democrats have ruined Germany politically, militarily, economically, commercially and financially for future decades — perhaps for ever! The workers are completely mad; the proletariat throughout the whole world is preparing a struggle everywhere for the annihilation of ownership, intellect, education and the employer, and we are propelling ourselves evermore towards chaos. . . . I only see *la bête humaine* all around me in its ugliest, basest form; who will undertake to reason with these narrow-minded, fanatical, brutal minds, and who will restore us to normal perceptions?

It is now already ten years since I had the pleasure of staying in your house. It was the summer of 1909; at the time I still had hopes of returning each summer, and it was a fond thought for me to have the lovely Hilla [daughter Hildegard, born in 1897 to Hans and Olga Zanders and god-daughter to Max Bruch] around me at the Igeler Hof, for you know how much I always loved the child. But nothing came of it all, for since 1910 I have become a slave to the infirmities of my old age, and could no longer go to those places so dear to me: Gladbach, Lehrbach and the Igeler Hof — and for the past five years no longer to beloved Oberhof in Thuringia. I am a man who throughout his life could not be without hills, trees and mountain air, who always loved most to be with Nature and amidst Nature. All this I must now renounce, and continue a miserable existence in this cursed Brandenburg desert [Berlin]. Only do not ask me how! I would give everything if once again in my life I could see Gladbach. How deeply my homeland is buried in my heart, my song of the homeland ['Nirgend ist's lieblicher ja, als in der Heimath' — the final chorus from *Odysseus*] is proof to you of that. It came from my heart and has made its way into many hearts, not only in Germany but in all the countries where *Odysseus* resounds.

# Chapter Eight

## SONDERSHAUSEN: THE COMPOSITIONS
### 1867–70

WITHIN SIX MONTHS of the successful première of Bruch's First Symphony, in July 1868, further performances were either planned or given in the cities of Leipzig, Bremen, Oldenburg, Dresden, Vienna, Mannheim, Carlsruhe, Lübeck and Hamburg. This success encouraged him to begin another, which he completed towards the end of his stay in Sondershausen during 1870. In the two years between the two symphonies Bruch reverted to the composition of choral works, although some of these had been started during the years prior to his appointment to the Court in Sondershausen. These works are *Rorate coeli* for chorus and orchestra (begun in Mannheim in 1863), *Die Priesterin der Isis in Rom* for alto solo and orchestra, *Die Flucht nach Aegypten* and *Morgenstunde* for soprano solo, women's chorus and orchestra, *Normannenzug* for solo baritone, men's chorus (unison throughout) and orchestra, *Four Lieder* for baritone with piano accompaniment, *Römische Leichenfeier* for chorus and orchestra (also begun in the years 1863/1864 during his stay in Mannheim), and the *Messensätze* for chorus and orchestra (the Kyrie dates from his university days in Bonn during 1859, the Sanctus from the period spent in Cologne the following year).

The first work in this group, *Rorate coeli* Op. 29, is a translation from the original Latin into German by Karl Simrock (uncle of the publisher, Fritz Simrock), of the Introit to the Mass sung on the fourth Sunday in Advent. The work is dedicated to his friend, Rudolf von Beckerath, and was first performed on 22 February 1869 under Bruch's direction in Crefeld. The First Symphony was also played in this concert. *Rorate coeli* is written as a single movement, beginning in C minor and ending in C major, with excursions to related keys in between. The movement can be divided into two contrasting sections, the second beginning at the point where there is both a key change from tonic minor to major, and a time signature change from four to six crotchets in a bar. The choral writing throughout is alternately chorale-like homophony and contrapuntal polyphony, which Bruch by now had completely mastered. The orchestral texture is excessively thickened by the busy string writing (Schumann's same weakness had obviously exerted its influence on Bruch in this regard) and the work would perhaps have benefited from an orchestral interlude here and there. In a letter which largely concerns the Vienna performance of Bruch's First Symphony, Brahms questioned Bruch about *Rorate coeli*.[1] Brahms' own setting of the Introit appeared in 1879 as the second of Two Motets Op. 74, and was probably written between 1860 and 1865. 'I have seen much of your new things,' wrote Brahms. 'Do you know the old, beautiful melody to Rorate coeli? I have by chance set an older German translation (which I prefer) in the form of a Motet and Variations.'

The next group of works features a solo singer, and the first is a short dramatic concert Cantata entitled *Die Priesterin der Isis in Rom* (The Priestess of Isis in Rome) Op. 30 using a text by Hermann Lingg. The work is dedicated to Amalie Joachim, wife of the violinist, who was herself a highly successful professional concert singer. The Cantata is a short through-composed work consisting of *arioso* interspersed with recitative and, like its immediate predecessor, it has no orchestral interludes. The theme of the poem is a familiar one to Bruch, homesickness for one's country: in this piece the enslaved Egyptian Priestess prays for her return to the banks of the Nile. In 1870 Hanslick reviewed the work, acknowledged its 'dubious success', but compared it unfavourably with its predecessor, *Schön Ellen*, as being 'without effect', and having only 'average freshness and originality'. 'Only through force,' the critic went on, 'does this long poem with its historical-philosophical reflections lend itself to music. What Bruch gives his Egyptian priestess to sing also sounds forced and prosaic.'

The Egyptian theme is continued in the next work of the group, another concert Cantata, to a text by Robert Reinick, *Die Flucht nach Aegypten* Op. 31 No. 1. It is in three sections, richly melodic and using three contrasting instrumental groupings: strings; one each of flute, oboe and clarinet; three horns. The first section (*andante tranquillo* in E flat) interweaves solo voice with chorus, the second (in the mediant minor key of G) is for the soloist alone, and the third section is a repeat of the first. The poem entreats Nature and the birds and beasts of the field to greet and guard Mother and Child on their flight.

Nature is once again the theme of *Morgenstunde* Op. 31 No. 2 but this time using a poem in five verses by Hermann Lingg. 'A work of flowering melody and truly lyrical magic', is how Rudolf von Beckerath described this piece.[2] Dawn is evocatively portrayed at the start of the work by sustained pedal notes over which the homophonous ladies' chorus introduces the soloist's description of the waking blackbird, nightingale and lark. As day breaks, soloist and chorus join forces accompanied by the full orchestral texture. Both works are dedicated to Bruch's sister, Mathilde.

Josef Viktor von Scheffel's text from his *Ekkehard*, which Bruch uses for *Normannenzug* Op. 32, also has as its theme a longing for homeland, though this time the subject is once again Nordic (as in *Frithjof*). Solo baritone with unison tenor and bass chorus tell of the dying Nordic race yearning for far-off Iceland, the 'ice-cold rock in the sea', where they seek a last refuge for themselves and the worship of their gods. The chorus plays a very secondary role in this work, either repeating what the baritone solo has just sung or doubling his melodic line. The accompanying figuration in the strings is, on the one hand, either a continuous *tremolando* of repeated quavers or, on the other hand, arpeggios in triplets or syncopated double-stopped chords, all of which results in a leaden, thickened texture. Kretschmar described the work as 'one of several off-shoots which came out of *Frithjof*', and 'as one of the most successful, simply and powerfully drafted and developed'.

Von Scheffel was also the author of *Frau Aventiure* and *Der Trompeter von Säckingen* from which Bruch took four poems to set for baritone with piano accompaniment as the *Four Lieder* Op. 33. The year 1190 is the period for the first song ('Biterolf encamped before Akkon') with the familiar theme of men far away from home pining for their loved ones. The subject of the second and fourth songs ('An old German harvest dance', and 'May night') is the countryside and Nature, whilst the third ('I think of you, Margaretha') is a love poem.

The last of the group of concert Cantatas written at this time is *Römische Leichenfeier* (Roman Funeral Rites) Op. 34. Although this Cantata does not apear on Bruch's 1889 list of compositions associated with the Igeler Hof in Bergisch Gladbach, a letter to Maria Zanders written from the house mentioned it as 'an old work' (he began composing it two years earlier in Mannheim) which he had now 'kneaded together and changed significantly'.[3] A printed score owned by the BBC in London has the following lines written on the title page in Bruch's handwriting:

Componirt April 1869, Igel. Erschienen [appeared] Winter 69–70

*Römische Leichenfeier* is dedicated to Bruch's friend and future collaborator, the Bach scholar Dr Philipp Spitta, who was a teacher at a senior school in Sondershausen at the time. In 1874 he moved to Berlin, where he founded a new research department in musicology, and earned Bruch's respect by giving the first performance of his next work, the *Messensätze*. 'It is very surprising,' he wrote to Brahms, 'and pleasant that, in spite of his continual serious preoccupation with the distant past, he still has the freshest sensitivity for the works of the present day.'[4] With his Kyrie, Sanctus and Agnus Dei, or *Messensätze* (movements from the Mass) Op. 35, Bruch broke free of the secular Concert Cantatas, with their unvaried subject matter and consequent similarity, and put together three movements of the Mass for double chorus, two soprano soloists and orchestra (with organ *ad libitum*). He dedicated it to Princess Elisabeth von Schwarzburg-Sondershausen. Later, on 29 March 1881, Max was to write from Liverpool to his friend Emil Kamphausen (a manufacturer by profession, a leading member of the Choral Society in Barmen and no mean amateur musician, who also handled Max's financial affairs, particularly during his period abroad in England): 'My movements from the Mass (which in fact are a kind of Missa Brevis in concert form) may well belong to the best I have yet produced in my life.'

Bruch had reason to be grateful to Dr Spitta, who conducted the first performance of the work on 9 May 1880, eleven years after its completion. The concert took place at the Hochschule für Musik in Berlin. By this time Bruch had no hesitation in being critical of his old friend Joachim, who, together with his fellow Hochschule Director, Hermann Kretschmar, had been less than enthusiastic about performing the work. 'The ever-procrastinating, petty-prejudiced Joachim would never have decided to do it,' wrote Bruch in the ill-tempered style that was to become all too familiar in later years. In another letter to Emil Kamphausen[5] written before the Barmen performance of the work later that year, Bruch gave a highly detailed history of the chronology of the three movements. The Kyrie was written in response to the death of Thérèse Neissen, sister and housekeeper to the owners of the Igeler Hof. 'My grief was deep and unremitting, and to the memory of this dearly loved woman, I wrote the Kyrie in Bonn in the summer semester of 1859.' Bruch obviously had second thoughts overnight, for the next day he wrote a long correction to his letter and recalled in greater detail.

The truth is that thoughts of a Mass for double chorus and organ often preoccupied me in my boyhood during the fifties. I still remember clearly today that, whilst on visits to the Mores' in the Palatinate in 1853 and 1855, I worked on a Gloria for double chorus in C major and 3/2; also a Benedictus in D flat major, 3/8 Andante, but which has now completely slipped my memory. The Kyrie in A minor, which now features as the opening of Op. 35, was not a piece on its own, it was also no beginning of anything, but took the form more of a sequel to a work begun long before and often interrupted. I know I definitely wrote my Kyrie before 1859. Now listen further: one of the main purposes of my stay in Bonn in the summer semester of 1859 was to play the organ often. I practised on the University organ two hours a day from the beginning of May until the middle of August, and went so far as to conquer the hardest of Bach's works. . . . It appears now that I was inspired by Bach, and that I worked further on, and indeed completed the double chorus Mass in 1860 — probably in the summer of 1860, I do not know any longer. What I do know quite definitely is, that in the autumn of 1860 I gave the manuscript of a completely finished Mass for double chorus, strings and organ to Leibl, the Cathedral organist in Cologne, and asked him to perform it. The frail old man fed me a friendly story, and the Mass was never performed. I do not know what happened to the manuscript. The whole thing was forgotten after my father's death in 1861. Our house was given up. Mathilde moved to Brüderstrasse, my mother went for a time to friends in Duisburg, and I set off in October 1861 on a year-long journey to Leipzig, Berlin, Munich, Vienna etc. with money from Krupp. The manuscript is either with Mr J. Bel in Cologne (at that time treasurer to the Cathedral choir), or (which I do not believe) it was given back to me, in which case it must be lying in a trunk with innumerable other old manuscripts, which Mathilde is looking after. I see the broad format of the manuscript before me now. Your questions have revived definite memories in me that, before this Missa Brevis, a complete Mass by me existed, and that these three movements [Op. 35] are nothing more than a proposed critical reworking of that earlier composition.

Bruch's motives for writing the Sanctus appear to have been inspired by a desire to improve on his teacher Hiller's own Mass of 1859–60. Max thought it a poor work, and he set about writing his own 'real Sanctus, which would be worthy of being sung by the Cologne Cathedral choir and truly elevate the soul. . . . The idea of the Divinity lived in me then as now,' he continued to Spitta, 'and it found here a natural outlet for expression. Every serious artist will permit himself at least once in his lifetime, to express the best and deepest feelings of his innermost soul through the medium of his Art, by combining noble representation with ancient established text.'

The depth of his religious sentiment is to be found in the sensitive writing for chorus, the richness of the orchestration and expressiveness of the melodic writing. In this work Bruch speaks as a Romantic in the spirit, language and musical structure of the pre-Classical. Like his contemporary, Josef Rheinberger, he looked for a marriage of the two styles by using his own idiomatic harmonic and contrapuntal language, and although deeply motivated by the religious nature of his subject matter, it is a work destined for the concert hall, not the church. Tovey's article on the Violin Concerto mentions few of the many works by the composer, but one is the *Messensätze*. Curiously it is erroneously described as Bruch's 'last choral work' by the celebrated musical analyst. 'I have not the slightest doubt,' he wrote, 'that a revival of Bruch's *Odysseus* (which the writer regards as his most successful work), and perhaps still more of his last choral work, a Kyrie and Sanctus, which I heard in Berlin in 1907, would make a fresh and stirring impression on any audience that will listen naïvely to beautiful music for music's sake.'[6]

Philipp Spitta was himself just thirty years old when he conducted the first performance of the work in 1870. He also wrote an extensive analysis of the work for the *Musikalisches Wochenblatt* that year. Though lacking Tovey's dry humour, he was to become as eminent an analyst in Germany as Tovey became in Britain. Spitta regarded the *Messensätze* as the best of Bruch's vocal works which were currently appearing (the Concert Cantatas Opp. 29–32 and Op. 34), and praised him for setting selected parts of the Mass, rather than following dogmatic, traditional precedent in composing the complete text. Bruch's religion is best described as militant Protestantism, which was true to his ancestry. There is no Credo in the *Messensätze* because, as he wrote to von Beckerath,[7] 'I can only compose what I feel deeply, but the Credo of the Mass is not my Credo.' Although Bruch himself described this work as 'a Missa Brevis in concert form', and was emphatic to von Beckerath in the same letter that the movements 'are expressly and exclusively meant for the concert hall, not for the church', a performance in a church setting with that unique acoustic could only enhance its impact upon the listener. Spitta was himself moved to describe the magical effect of the two soprano solo lines soaring above the double chorus in the beautiful Sanctus as having 'something of that mood in it which surrounds one in the high walls of a Cathedral building, when soft full sunlight breaks through a stained glass window.'

The year 1870 was a watershed in Bruch's life for several reasons. He no longer depended on his former teacher, Hiller, of whose compositions he was beginning to be highly critical. His own self-assurance was developing, and he was more confident in both composing and conducting. His musical creed was firmly established, although he saw himself as far more progressive a composer than did his critics (who rightly attributed this role to Wagner, Liszt and their adherents). Not only were his musical ideas fully formed at this time.

His political philosophy was now firmly conservative, staunchly patriotic and loyally dedicated to those who were to unify Germany after the Franco-Prussian War of 1870. Bismarck was rapidly becoming a hero.

Max Bruch's music was now reaching a far wider audience thanks to his new association with the publisher, Fritz Simrock. The publishing firm had contracted Bruch during 1869, and for 21 years held exclusive rights on his compositions. The agreement after 1890 was changed, the exclusivity being confined to works written for the violin (although Simrock did in fact take other pieces). Simrock's publishing house was firmly in the conservative camp (Brahms was another famous client) and this isolated Bruch even further from the opposing New German Art of Wagner and Liszt. In the continuing controversy, his combative senses became honed against his critics, his reactions became more aggressive in defence of his corner, and he made few friends.

After the success of the First Symphony, Bruch began his Second in F minor Op. 36, completing it in the summer of 1870. Bruch then wrote to Simrock:

> The last (fifth) rehearsal of the Symphony took place last Saturday in the presence of our admirable Princess Elisabeth and a few local artistic friends. The orchestra played so exquisitely, nothing was left to ask of them regarding expression, fire and the finer nuances; if we only had a stronger body of strings, the overall sound would also be completely perfect.[8]

After its dedicatee, Joseph Joachim, had undertaken the bowing of the string parts, the first performance took place three months later on 4 September 1870, and it was well received. A further performance on 24 November that year, when Bruch conducted it in Leipzig at the Gewandhaus at Carl Reinecke's invitation, was not so successful. Bruch blamed the failure of the work here on the Leipzig public, whom he considered had reacted badly to the absence of a Scherzo in this three-movement work. 'A Scherzo,' he wrote to Hermann Levi, 'does not fit into the construction of this symphony; so there is none, to the great annoyance of the Leipzig public, who always want to dance on a freshly dug grave.'[9] Bruch may well have highlighted one of the work's shortcomings in his explanation, for earlier he appears to have intended some revisions to the work such as inserting a 'shorter, friendlier movement' between the first and third movements. These intentions also included cuts in the Finale, but he considered the first two movements to be completely satisfactory.[10]

The use of sonata form in all three movements creates a structural monotony to the work's detriment. Kretschmar considered it to have a programmatic content, which was so concealed that it defied understanding. Bruch indignantly denied this to Philipp Spitta: 'I can swear this time that extra-musical concepts were far from my thoughts. I have only perceived and written music, and there is nothing else in it other than the unceasing weighing and balancing of passions.'[11] The most successful movement is undoubtedly the beautiful lyrical Adagio, Bruch's predilection for the alto *tessitura* manifested in solos for clarinet, horn, viola and the upper register of the cello. Neither the opening movement with its dark and sombre mood, nor the last in the tonic major key, which emerges without a break from the slow movement, had yet broken the rhythmic and thematic moulds of both Mendelssohn and Schumann. Although it was Brahms whose own First Symphony was labelled Beethoven's tenth (because of the main theme of its Finale), it is worth examining the last movement of Bruch's Second Symphony, at letter A, and noting the same similarity.

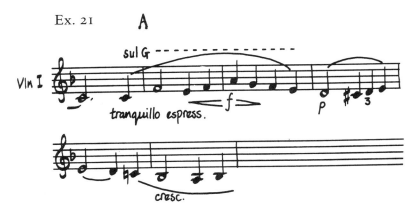

Ex. 21

Wagner's *Kaisermarsch* was written as a direct consequence of the Prussian victory in the war with France in 1870, and was his tribute to Wilhelm I, Kaiser of the newly unified Germany. Bruch's response was to set a poem by Emanuel Geibel for chorus and orchestra. The work is full of patriotic fervour and phrases such as 'Deutschland, Deutschland, die schön geschmückte Braut' (Germany, Germany, the beautifully adorned bride). It apostrophizes Germany as a sleeping bride being awakened by the drums of war and, to the joy of thousands of patriotic hearts, being led to fulfilment by the Kaiser — 'Nun führst du sie heim, mein Kaiser' (Now you lead her home, my Emperor). It was published as *Das Lied vom deutschen Kaiser* Op. 37. Although he was caught up in the jingoism of the time, Bruch felt restrained enough to write to Simrock, tempering his approach to this hymn to the Fatherland. 'I did not wish to associate myself with the swarm of busy musicians who wanted immediately to release their miserable occasional songs and one-day wonders into the world; I wanted to wait until the end of the war, and then put something more ordered together, which would be worth singing at the victory celebration, and would retain the ideal expression of its patriotism for a long time thereafter.'[12]

The *Five Lieder* Op. 38 for unaccompanied mixed chorus have texts from familiar sources (Scheffel, Scottish folksong, Lingg and Geibel) for the first four ('Waldpsalm', 'Der Wald von Traquair', 'Tannhäuser' and 'Rheinsage'), and Schiller for the fifth ('Feierliches Tafellied'). The great German poet was currently much on Bruch's mind; the influence of Beethoven's Ninth Symphony (using Schiller's 'Ode to Joy') on the shape of the main theme in the last movement of Bruch's Second Symphony may seem far-fetched, but the next work he produced (*Dithyrambe*) used a text by Schiller, and he was to continue setting the famous poet's work in such future compositions as Op. 45 (*Das Lied von der Glocke*), Op. 80 (*Szene der Marfa*) and Op. 87 (*Die Macht des Gesangs*).

In October 1873 he was able to rehearse the *Five Lieder* with the Elberfeld Chorus. The lessons he learned from rehearsal and performance prior to publication were stressed once again: 'I now have a secure knowledge of the final sound and the problems of the individual songs, and I see anew how important it is to hear everything first.' When, shortly thereafter, he performed them with the chorus in Barmen, he seriously considered orchestrating them; for instance, setting No. 1 ('Waldpsalm') for strings and four horns, and the Scottish folksong ('Der Wald von Traquair') for strings alone, but he eventually changed his mind and they were published as unaccompanied choruses. In a letter to Simrock, he said, 'like all true folk melodies, it is best left in four-parts.'[13] He added the interesting information that 'Boïeldieu, as is generally known, used this same melody (but not in its entirety) in *La Dame blanche*.' Bruch had already set Lingg's 'Tannhäuser' as one of his *Ten Lieder* for solo voice Op. 17, and its appearance among the Op. 38 collection is no more than a rescoring from piano and solo voice to four part unaccompanied chorus.

The original intention for *Dithyrambe* Op. 39 for tenor solo, six-part chorus and orchestra (dedicated to the Barmen Chorus) was to link it into a cycle incorporating some of the *Five Lieder*, but Bruch eventually settled for a separate publication of the Schiller ballad. A dithyramb is an ancient Greek hymn in honour of Bacchus, and an account by Kretschmar described the work as 'a characteristic and beautiful setting, beginning tempestuously and brightly, but ending calmly and clearly, thereby contrasting the agitated stress of [poetic] inspiration with the contented peace of Heaven.'[14] A substantial orchestral introduction establishes the contrasting moods which are later to be found in the text, the initial section consisting of a hectic motif passed among the upper strings against an equally restless accompaniment in the lower. The tenor soloist (the poet), envious of the life led by the Immortals, sings to Bacchus, Amor, Phoebe and the other gods, begging to be permitted to drink from the fount of eternal youth, to live far from the shadow of the river Styx, which haunts earthbound humans, and to repose forever in the sunlight of Olympus. The entry of the heavenly chorus is, according to Kretschmar, 'the most beautiful part of the work.' The moment when the choir disappears 'in the softest *pianissimo*, as if behind a veil of cloud' is also written with striking effect. Kretschmar ended his assessment of the work with the sardonic observation that, 'for performance a solo tenor is required for whom the top [of the voice] is easy', though he concluded regretfully that 'this valuable work has not found its place in the concert hall.'[15]

By the middle of 1870 Bruch was beginning to feel restless in his Court post at Sondershausen. He never changed his regard for the Princess or her family, but he became as impatient with Court officialdom as he was to become with committees running musical organizations with which he came into contact. In the year leading up to his departure from the Thuringian town, he wrote twenty letters, covering a variety of subjects, to the von Beckeraths in Crefeld, and they provide a fascinating insight into the man and his character.

A singer by the name of Anna Strauss (with whom he worked in Leipzig and Crefeld during February 1869 — 'the little one is musical through and through') would appear to have passed briefly into his love life, though the relationship ended unhappily for Max when she became engaged to another man. An understandably biased view of the lady was given in a letter to Laura von Beckerath.[16] It also contains the first mention of Shakespeare's *The Winter's Tale* as the source of the libretto for his next opera:

I have been here about a week, that means I sleep, breakfast and eat (evenings at 7 o'clock) with the Zanders; I am staying with Richard alone at the moment, as Maria and the children are in Leutesdorf with her parents. Each day I go up [to the Igeler Hof] about 9 and come back to Gladbach about 6 or 6.30. In this way I get something done; I hope to be able to show you good results soon. Did you know I was in Leipzig and Berlin for ten days? The pressure to come finally to definite, dramatic decisions was suddenly so strong in me, after I had somewhat recovered from the Strauss matter, that at the beginning of April, instead of travelling to Paris, I went to Leipzig where I found both advice and help. You and Rudolf should know that I have definitely decided on Shakespeare's *The Winter's Tale*. . . .

I thank you, if belatedly, dear Laura, for your news about Anna Strauss. In order not to attract public attention to her, I visited her in Cologne on Good Friday, when she sang in Rudorff's concert. She was in the company of a woman. Have you not discovered who the favoured one is? Probably some stupid little Swiss from a hidden corner of the Zürich or Aargau Cantons — perhaps an early engagement, which now at all costs must be obtained honourably. Frau Moschelas, with whom she stayed for a week, could not discover anything about her closer friendships; what is certain is that she has many pressures to bear, the father is common and not a generous chap. She evidently longs for her 25th year, in order to marry the man of her dreams, but until then she can only hope to have acquired him. To rid myself of the thought of this one girl has been particularly difficult, because I believed with an almost fatalistic certainty that we were meant for one another. So much seemed to have come happily together; in the highest of matters it appeared that our souls met so exactly, and this magic of pure womanhood, this grace, this girlishness, all part of such an outstanding talent! It was bad enough that I felt all this so deeply, and was careless enough to nurture such feelings, but it was only natural. As long as she publicly favoured me in Leipzig so that everyone noticed (and for the week I was there she wanted me around her almost constantly) it was all right for me to deceive myself. As if I were a young artist made of wood or stone! As if it were possible to set exactly the limits and to maintain them all the time; all this kindness, this affection means nothing to a man, only to an artist! But in reality this girl does not appear to know what huge powers she possesses. That is the nature of her magic. But precisely because of this, she is not destined for a great artistic career. Too much ambition is not good, but too little is even worse. Will you let me know in the next few days what you have discovered about her? Although I must observe the development of this lovely person from afar, I would nevertheless like to know as many details as possible.

Poor Max did not have long to wait for 'further details', for two months later he wrote that '*Die Signale* carries the official engagement of A.S. with Musikdirektor Walter in Basel. Have you read the announcement? She seems to have handled her father. Other people than I (who anyway may not talk with them openly) consider this engagement is madness. She must know it.'[17] Bruised but unbowed, Max picked up the bits of his life and stuck them back together again very quickly. 'My productive powers have not suffered; on the contrary they are bubbling away quite happily and will not stop . . . I think I shall achieve much this year. I see more great projects before me, and have been encumbered with no more than a few sad memories — that does not matter much.' His suffering was, as on the occasion with Emmy Landau, short and sweet while it lasted. He was aware of the romantic image he wanted to project to the world at large, and a successful relationship or even marriage with either girl would not have been part of it.

One of the circumstances he took into consideration before making a decision to leave the security of a fixed post in Sondershausen, was the success he was having with the publication and distribution of his music. 'Next week,' he wrote, '[Op. 35 and Op. 31] are going for printing in Leipzig. In July other miscellaneous things will follow, and in August I hope to be about 700 or 800 thalers richer — you see the Jew in me is powerfully aroused!'[17] The variety of publishing houses with which he was concurrently dealing in 1869 is remarkable. 'Cranz was here from Bremen at the same time as Reinecke,' he wrote on 6 August 1869. 'He is printing the *Lieder* [Op. 33]. Breitkopf & Härtel are printing the *Messensätze*; Kistner Op. 31 (the women's choruses); *Normannenzug* Op. 32 Härtel again; the *Römische Leichenfeier* probably Herr Sander.' This last assumption was correct, for Sander did publish Op. 34 under the auspices of his firm F. E. C. Leuckart, but it was with Simrock that Bruch finally threw in his lot for many years to come.

It was to take him a little while to find a librettist for his projected opera on *The Winter's Tale*. In August 1869, he rejected the work of a certain Dr Klengel from Leipzig, just as he had done with the Viennese Mosenthal in 1866, whose suggestion of an opera on the subject of Prince Magnus of Sweden had not been to his satisfaction.[18] He finally decided in favour of Emil Hopffer, 'a very talented young writer' whom he met in Berlin, and 'who has been involved with stage matters for years, and combines the most important theoretical insights with great practical skill.'[19]

He had much to say about Berlioz at this time. He described a performance he conducted of *Harold in Italy*, 'which gave us (Spitta and me) much lasting thought. His Symphony *Romeo and Juliet* is monstrous in its form, crosses all boundaries, but has charming beauty in its details.'[20] In January 1870[21] he answered von Beckerath's request for a recommendation of a Berlioz overture:

> As for Berlioz, I advise the overture to *King Lear*. *Waverley* is not suitable anywhere as a first introduction to Berlioz. . . . The overture *Carnaval Romain* is a happy well-known piece, which you could perhaps perform sometime. The *Lear* overture has something magnificent and striking about it, and is, like almost all Berlioz's orchestral works, filled with the spirit of its literary source; some unfortunately appear powerful and mammoth-like; on the other hand there are too many disagreeable details to call them important works of art. You cannot do without a good principal oboe in this overture, for there is a beautiful and important solo in the Andante introduction. As far as I remember, there is no cor anglais in the *Lear* overture.

Another letter contained an observation on Wagner, whose opera, *Die Meistersinger*, Bruch had heard at its first performance: 'I experienced the whole scandal,' he wrote. His assessment of Wagner was to the point, if somewhat patronizing: 'A brilliant man, who strives with great energy and exceptional talent for undoubtedly the wrong goals.'[22]

In spite of writing a work such as *Das Lied vom deutschen Kaiser* in celebration of the German victory in the Franco-Prussian War, he revealed a considered sensitivity to the futility and senselessness of war as a means to an end:

> What a war! What a time! We think we are dreaming when we look about us in Germany; how by a miracle, we are united! Only a step further, and the unification of the States of our glorious country, so unhappy for centuries, will be complete — more integrated and more beautiful than any German dared hope to experience. But regrettably: 'all the great documents of Mankind are written in blood', and this wonderful document, at whose head will be written in letters of gold that from now on Germany is a great nation, will only come about after rivers have flowed with blood. It always feels strange to me, when I think back to my boyhood, how war in our highly civilized century was considered quite unthinkable; this was the generally held and often stated belief of the peace-loving citizen. Then came that little blood-letting in 1848 and 1849 with its evidence that the race of guns and cannons had not yet died out. Certainly if one looks at the undeniably considerable progress in many areas (e.g. legislation or moral concepts), one asks how it is

possible for men today to suffer the unspeakable barbarism of war. If this question were put to the world at large, it would remain as unanswered as a thousand others. So let us bear the calamity, and hope that palpable and splendid results will grow forth.[23]

Bruch's letters during these two years of 1869–70 often mentioned the progress of his next opera, *Hermione* Op. 40. Considering his dubious success in the field of opera, he was extraordinarily optimistic and self-confident both about its assured success and also his own abilities. In view of what was going on around him in the world of opera at that time, the kindest that can be said of his attitude is that he suffered delusions of grandeur. 'The main thing is that this winter the opera will be begun,' he wrote in the excitement of having just contracted his librettist Hopffer. 'Once it is completed, I hope to bring a new one out every year; this would most satisfy my ambition.'[24] The following year, when he was halfway through the work, he expressed his belief that 'when I have established *Hermione* on the opera stage, which I wish and hope for with all the power of my soul (much depends upon it), I shall no longer fight shy of the Theatre. The German Theatre still has a future, and I am one of those who have work to do for it, and who will develop a new honour for the newborn Nation in this domain.'[25]

There is more than a hint in this same letter that all had not been going well for Bruch in Sondershausen. His success with so many music publishers culminating in his contract with Simrock, the flow of works emanating from his pen, and the good prospects ahead all encouraged him to make the decision to resign from the position he held at the Court, and to concentrate solely on composition. 'What wretchedness I experienced in resigning my post,' he wrote. 'The position was untenable in spite of its favourable conditions for me; certain sycophants harassed me incessantly, and eventually won. But I remain on very friendly terms with both the Court and the orchestra.'

An interesting exchange of correspondence now took place between Bruch and Brahms. It had come to Brahms' attention that Bruch had resigned his post in Sondershausen, and, although Brahms knew that he himself was being seriously considered as Herbeck's successor as Director of the Concerts given by the Gesellschaft der Musikfreunde in Vienna, he considered applying for the vacant post in Sondershausen instead. He wrote to Bruch, asking for more details:

A few words in haste with the request for a swift reply, as short or as suitably detailed as you wish. I hear, or I have read that you have given up your post and that you now wish to live in Berlin. It goes without saying that I want a post (i.e. a job). Would you write me a few clear, unhindered words on the subject, among other things, whether there is a chorus in Sondershausen, about the countryside, the state of relations with the royalty, holiday leave, duties, salary — whatever occurs to you. You can believe that I am not especially keen on Sondershausen; it is under no circumstances a place in which to remain, and my age reminds me of that. Between ourselves, I can tell you that I am being thought of for Herbeck's post. That job has so many serious considerations, I wish the people there would spare themselves the official invitation, and spare me the pondering.[26]

Bruch replied immediately:

Right at the start I must tell you that in my opinion you could only consider the post if you are accorded the same amount of freedom that I have had. . . . You could endure it here in the summer, with good orchestral music, attractive countryside surroundings, and continual, heartening conversation with Spitta; on the other hand, in winter the place is really monotonous and oppressive. . . . The Court orchestra is very good — one of the finest orchestras in Germany. It is superbly disciplined, the members are co-operative and enthusiastic. It is possible without any great trouble to bring off the most difficult works because of the splendid ensemble playing of this orchestra. There is no place in Germany where, in the course of a concert season, one could play so many orchestral novelties as here. The Ninth Symphony, the Schumann works (why can I not yet do the Brahms Symphonies?!) go very well. Thuringia is a real 'musician's state', there is no large orchestra anywhere, nor a Prussian or Saxon Music Corps without players from this district in it. Here there are quite inconspicuous, modest musicians who play several instruments very respectably, have a very capable knowledge of counterpoint, play Bach Toccatas on the organ without difficulty, and nevertheless live here quite peacefully, without wishing to try and become famous elsewhere. You can get more details of these circumstances from Spitta, who has made a thorough study of Thuringia in connection with his Bach studies. Dealings with the orchestra are easy and enjoyable. I am on the best terms with the people, and will remain in friendliest contact after my departure. Princess Elisabeth (daughter of the sovereign) is a simple, kind, splendid lady and a great friend to Music. I have nothing but the best to thank her for during the past three years; I will never forget that of her. She has no actual aesthetic education, but her noble nature itself decisively crushes everything in Art which is bad and impure, and she has the strongest and deepest feeling for that which is excellent. She has founded a small choral society, which also sometimes takes part in the Court concerts. The Princess sometimes sings the soprano solos herself, with her small, but melodious voice. . . . Strange how you, with all your freedom, long for my captivity, whilst I, in my captivity, long for all your freedom!

To conclude, may I make a suggestion and make you a friendly and sincere request, dear friend: visit us sometime this summer! Spitta and I would be exceedingly happy to see you here; we would do everything in our power to make your stay pleasant. In the event that you want to rehearse the orchestra, I would be delighted to place it at your disposal; this summer I am able to do so. You should hear your Serenades [Opp. 11 and 16], and perhaps you would play your Piano Concerto [No. 1 Op. 15] in a rehearsal. It would also be wonderful if you would decide to rehearse your Symphonic Movements [these were the sketches for his First Symphony] with us first. Joachim could come over from Berlin perhaps. There would be no lack of lovely evenings in my charmingly laid-out cottage garden, with good friends, cold drinks, and good conversation.[27]

It does not appear that Brahms gave the matter any further thought, for soon afterwards he accepted the proffered post in Vienna, where he remained until 1874.

By the beginning of October 1870 Bruch had come to terms with his decision to leave Sondershausen. In spite of an instinctive preference for material and financial security, he was now leaving for Berlin, and a new phase of his life was about to begin. 'A strange meeting of different circumstances,' he wrote, 'appears to say that the old times are at an end, and that one should neither waver nor take rash decisions, but create new and finer ones through one's own powers. . . . I am leaving Sondershausen after I have learnt there what I could use for my purposes.'

## Chapter Nine

## FREELANCE COMPOSER: BERLIN
### 1870–73

THE YEAR 1870 was important for Max Bruch, not only because he now chose to become an independent freelance musician, but also because it saw the preparation and publication in the *Musikalisches Wochenblatt* of a biography of his life to that date by his friend Rudolf von Beckerath. In helping the author put the article together, Bruch had the opportunity to sit back and reflect on his thirty-two years, summarize his musical successes and failures, consider the decisions he had taken in the shaping of his career, and assess with hindsight the value of the influences which had worked upon him throughout the development of his life as a composer.

He considered himself to be half-way through his life (on this point he was wrong by eighteen years) and saw this project not only as taking stock of his career, but also as valuable publicity for the promotion of his music. His notes for von Beckerath are comprehensive:[1]

1838   Born in Cologne 6 January (Died: With God's will, before He thinks of removing my creative powers!!)

1852   Scholar of the Frankfurt Mozart Foundation

53–57  Hiller designated by Mozart Foundation Committee as teacher

57–58  Winter stay in Leipzig

58–61  Apart from small journeys, mostly in Cologne (unfortunately!)

61–62  After my father's death, a long journey through Germany (with Krupp's money, which in my opinion should in no circumstances be mentioned; if need be, a suggestion of generous support etc. I believe Krupp or v.d. Leyen should not be named now; in years ahead perhaps). (1861/2) Visited Leipzig, Berlin, Vienna, Munich.

62–64  Mannheim. First performance of *Loreley* (June 1863). From there it found its way to several German stages, among others Cologne, Hamburg, Leipzig, Prague, Weimar,

Gotha can be named. The larger Court Theatres held back. *Loreley* could not maintain its place in the repertoire of these named theatres (except Mannheim, which I think stages it now and again). My reasons, but maybe you know others: 1. Although the libretto contains text worthy of Geibel, and some really effective theatrical scenes (and it also has the advantage of engaging nationalistic tendencies) all this is not enough to compensate for the lack of a good dramatic framework. As a theatrical work, *Loreley* stands on weak ground. 2. As far as the music is concerned, I stand by much of what I wrote (between ourselves); but it was impossible for me, at twenty-two . . . to have mastered theatrical and orchestral technique sufficiently to achieve exactly what I perceived. Now things are quite different . . .

62–64 Living in Mannheim. Theatre and orchestral studies. Theatre at the time had an excellent repertoire. Vincenz Lachner can be named.

64–65 Journey through Germany, and visit to Paris . . . November 1864 first performance of *Frithjof* in Aachen. Conducted *Frithjof* on this trip in Leipzig (Gewandhaus) and Vienna. Great success. Since then this work has been performed everywhere, also in America. In 1865 I met Rossini, Berlioz, Szarvady in Paris . . . Will you say that Rossini took an active, kind and warm interest in the then new *Frithjof* scenes? That is piquant! Think about it, O biographer!

65–67 Music Director in Coblenz (composed *Schön Ellen* and the Violin Concerto there among other things).

67–70 Court conductor in Sondershausen. Here you must say a word about the excellent orchestra and artistically sensitive or sympathetic Court. Perhaps mention works such as the First Symphony Op. 28, *Rorate coeli* and other smaller choral works, the Second Symphony (new) in F minor. You could briefly mention that I have recently resigned the Sondershausen post, without giving further details.

Bruch, having described this potted history as the 'outward appearance of his life to date', then proceeded to give the 'important innermost' detailed notes, which were strictly for Beckerath's eyes only.

After I, like all German musicians, had long written anything and everything possible, and had searched (like a mule in the mist) for my path, I finally asked myself (after *Loreley* in 1862) where in fact lies the ever-flowing beauty of a work which is called classical? Were the great masters of the past men or gods? If the former, then on what basic principles did they proceed, and how did they make use of their talent? How did they begin to uplift and make thousands happy, and why can we of today not do so? What is Truth? What is Beauty? Are we of today always to be content with the products of a few specially selected performers, or of a few cliques? I had thought to recognize that true melody is what is lacking in modern music (perhaps the influence of that modish instrument, the piano), and now I do not hesitate to study genuine melody at its source: since 1862 I have exclusively preoccupied myself with folksong (Munich and Mannheim). I seriously studied hundreds of songs from all nations in the search for characteristic expression, periodic arrangements, rhythmic construction, etc. Today I still believe that the melodic beauty of genuine folksong is only rarely achieved in creative works of art. But everyone today should at least refresh themselves at this source. . . . The works 1862–67 show signs of this study.

Bruch reminded Beckerath that the *Twelve Scottish Folksongs* in particular were the fruits of his labours with folksong, and if he was to be credited with a strong sense of melodic line, it was entirely attributable to this influence. He next turned to Bach and the organ studies he undertook, the results of which were to be found in his works *Rorate coeli* and the Cantata *Gesang der heiligen drei Könige*. He wrote that 'this strange, mystical work, like *Rorate*, was written in homage to the memory of a late and, to me, highly valued lady in Cologne. For long she had drawn me (perhaps more than was necessary yet nevertheless harmlessly) into her mystical, poetic, Catholic point of view; but as everything about her was alive, and her life was in keeping with her belief, so I developed the highest regard for her and took her death most painfully. Although a Protestant, I never lost the ability to sympathize with the purely poetic content of the Catholic myth.'

The *Messensätze*, he reminded Beckerath, was the product of 'the troubled winter of 1868–69', by which he meant his unhappy affair with Emmy Landau. In writing the work, which itself consisted of sections written at different periods of his life to date (and one of those was the the sad times following Thérèse Neissen's death), he purged himself of his troubles and saw ahead of him 'the possibility of further happy creative achievement. All the little things which followed during that wonderful spring of 1869 (at the Igel): *Normannenzug*, *Flucht*, *Morgenstunde*, *Leichenfeier*, the *Lieder*, are nothing more than a sigh of relief in the splendour of spring after an all too unhappy winter.' The Second Symphony also stemmed from that period even though it was completed much later.

The next day Bruch wrote a long postscript. He considered that during 1866–67, with *Frithjof* and *Schön Ellen* behind him, he had nothing of significance to say in that style of work. This troubled him, until he realized that it was his concentration on melody without the infusion of polyphony that was the root of the problem. He had, it is true to say, written polyphonically in some works (such as the two string quartets and the piano pieces), but it was not until the First Symphony of 1868 that both elements were integrated to his satisfaction, and that he felt that the emphasis was now properly balanced.

He went on to complain that Hiller's influence had seriously restrained him for some time, and until he began his journeying throughout Germany, he considered his compositions to be stylistically too much in his master's mould. In a letter written the previous month (14 September 1870) one of his other former teachers, this time Breidenstein, had also come in for criticism by Bruch, who was now becoming quite adept at biting the hand that had once fed him.

> . . . please leave out the name of that old ass from Bonn, Breidenstein, who unfortunately gave me some harmony lessons in 1849. That was one of the numerous sad mistakes (made with good intentions but by amateurs) that took place during my education. My first lessons were entrusted to a man who throughout the Rhineland had the reputation of an ignoramus, finally made a fool of himself as a practical musician during the 1845 Beethoven Festival in Bonn, and was on bad terms with virtually every good musician in the district.

Turning on his teachers, accusing them of dangerously and irresponsibly impeding his progress by expecting too much of him too soon, Bruch regretted the early death of Mendelssohn ('he died too soon for me'), making the assumption that he would have been a pupil of the great composer. Other regrets included staying too long in Cologne and in Mannheim ('two whole years there was unnecessary. What was to be learned there could have been achieved in one'), the failure to win a competitive post in Aachen, Rotterdam or Elberfeld, and the time spent in Coblenz ('hated from the start'). 'A beginner's post,' he called it now, 'a wretched orchestra, average chorus, amateurish arrogance, impossible to do anything well there.' In spite of these harsh criticisms, he urged Beckerath not to print them, 'the time is not yet come to speak openly of them', but rather emphasize the Court and 'our most gracious Queen' (Augusta of Prussia), pointing out that it was through Bruch that such artists as Clara Schumann and Wilhelmine Szarvady appeared in Coblenz. 'You could also lie by saying,' he concluded, 'that the beautiful countryside and the beautiful city on the Rhine and Mosel (to quote Baedeker) had an auspicious influence on my work; everyone would be happy to think that the walls and cannons of Ehrenbreitstein had inspired me to write *Schön Ellen*. Unfortunately this was not the case.'

The tact and unselfishness so lamentably lacking in Bruch's personality was abundant in Beckerath's, and the period spent in Coblenz was summarized in the article in a totally inoffensive manner. 'Whether the rural character of the area surrounding Coblenz, with its majestic ruins of the fortress Ehrenbreitstein and the experience of the war in 1866 fed the composer's fantasy or influenced the works of this period, is not to be conjectured by us; but it is surely more than a coincidence that during the Coblenz period of 1866 *Schön Ellen* and *Salamis* first saw the light of day.'

Sondershausen at least escaped any savagery by Bruch, who credited it with 'helping him enormously' and giving him a secure knowledge of the orchestra. Bruch had a few afterthoughts, and asked for greater credit to be given to Princess Elisabeth von Schwarzburg-Sondershausen for her understanding and sympathetic attitude to music and musicians.[2] He showed little concern for the absence of any mention of Ludwig Bischoff. It was Bischoff who had promoted Bruch so vigorously in the press during his early years, but who was now regarded by Bruch as a tool of 'Hiller's propaganda', and who had brought little credit upon himself by opposing the 'modernists' Schumann and Brahms. Bruch now considered that mentioning Bischoff could do him more harm than good, and although he half-heartedly suggested that Beckerath might wish to name him 'in passing at the appropriate place', his name is nowhere to be found in the article. He also asked for emphasis on the immediate international success of the Violin Concerto ('for a change some works achieve a quick success'), and a detailed description of the two String Quartets. 'I heard them both recently after a gap of ten years. The invention in the second did not appear bad to me, the form is right, but it is very impracticable, difficult, and has too much double-stopping throughout.' Finally he assessed the importance of his piano music:

My piano music is stupid and insignificant. For ten years I have not written a note for the piano. I have no interest in the instrument, so I cannot produce anything for it. My domain appears to be the orchestra and large choral works. I believe this is where I stand absolutely contrary to Schumann. With him and his followers everything stems from the piano, which was also true of his contemporaries Chopin and Hiller, who also started from the piano. Now I can no longer think for the piano. I also maintain that it would be foolish and absurd to use it as a substitute for the orchestra, which would then lose its true character, and in any case the piano in no way has the charm nor the unlimited expressiveness of the orchestra. Naturally I have the greatest respect for the beautiful piano pieces of others, for example Brahms.

Before Beckerath went into print, Bruch sent a final request. 'It is unnecessary to tell you once again most sincerely to be careful; the world should not know the innermost motives. On the other hand one should not have the feeling that I have influenced the article directly. Make me a little bad from time to time, so that the public is not suspicious!' Quite what Beckerath made of this editorial interference is impossible to judge, as no letters from him to Bruch remain. The article is surprisingly fair and dispassionate, considering all the pressures Bruch was exerting in his self-promoting approach to the project. When the first of the three instalments appeared in November 1870, Bruch declared himself to be well satisfied with the author for his 'objective biography'.

We also have an opinion of Bruch at this time from Ernst Rudorff, a friend and colleague. Rudorff was based in Berlin at the Hochschule für Musik, though at this period he was going through a difficult time with that institution, and was looking for possible alternatives elsewhere. When he heard that Bruch had resigned his post at Sondershausen, he decided to apply. Hiller recommended both Rudorff and Breunung (currently in the post at Aachen which Bruch had earnestly contested and coveted), and Rudorff wrote to Hiller gratefully acknowledging his support. As it happened, neither Rudorff nor Breunung subsequently went to Sondershausen. The master of ceremonies' office in the Court sought advice from Carl Reinecke in Leipzig, and he recommended a gifted pupil of Ignaz Moscheles, 22-year-old Max Erdmannsdörfer, who was appointed to the post on 15 February 1871. During the course of Rudorff's letter, he described the legacy of damage left by Bruch at Sondershausen. Rudorff was justifiably irritated by the tarnished image any composer now had to contend with in applying for the post, thanks to Bruch. 'I can scarcely believe,' he complained, 'that Breunung wants to give up his post in Aachen for Sondershausen, especially as conditions there are no longer what they were in Bruch's time. Between ourselves, Bruch behaved so unbelievably arrogantly whilst there, that his successor will on no account be accorded the freedom that Bruch himself enjoyed. My own personal connection to Bruch is already known, but what also harms me in Sondershausen is the fact that I am a composer, and I hear it is feared that I only wish to use it to my own ends.'[3]

Rudolf von Beckerath's article for the *Musikalisches Wochenblatt* ended with an assessment of Bruch's operatic output, and after dealing with *Scherz, List und Rache* and *Die Loreley*, entreated the reader to await the next work in that genre (*Hermione*) with 'the greatest expectation'. Unfortunately Bruch did not live up to such an expectation. Once again he had encumbered himself with a weak libretto, (taken from Shakespeare's *Winter's Tale*) which was best left alone in its original form as a play because the librettist was simply not equal to the task. Bruch must, however, take his share of the blame for not recognizing Hopffer's poor attempt at setting the work, for he described himself as 'completely happy' when he received the completed libretto.[4]

Bruch set to work at the end of June, and a month later he was able to inform Beckerath that it 'fills my thoughts so much that I neither can nor wish to stop. About half the opera is already completed, and most of that is already orchestrated.'[5] After a trip to Amsterdam at the end of April 1871 (where he conducted *Frithjof* and his First Symphony), he returned to Sondershausen at the beginning of June to rehearse the entire opera with the orchestra. He was fortunate in being granted permission by the Court to try out his new works, and to use the facilities even though he was no longer employed there. He completed the work by the summer of 1871, and it was printed immediately. Although he had hoped to have the first staging of *Hermione* in Leipzig, it was eventually given in Berlin (in spite of strong misgivings on the composer's part), on 21 March 1872. Performances followed at Bremen in April, Cologne on 12 December 1872 and Dresden on 24 January 1873. Rehearsals for the Berlin première were fraught with troubles, and did nothing for Bruch's opinion of Berlin as a place for a musician to live. He told Simrock: 'All those tales of Berlin asses like Taubert, Eichberg, Hopffer [his current librettist], Hülsen, Gumprecht, Lienau, etc, have produced such an aversion to the aforementioned city, that I want to return there in the autumn only as late as I possibly can.'[6]

He considered a negative critical reaction to the new opera as a foregone conclusion if it were to appear in Berlin for the first time, rather than at Leipzig or Dresden. It is not surprising that he was soon thinking of leaving the city or even of going abroad. 'It does one good to meet such cordiality and interest abroad, while at home one is treated by the press either as a schoolboy, or as a scoundrel . . . I have always found all my works to be well known in Holland, but none in Berlin.'

Like *Die Loreley* before it, *Hermione* is an opera in four acts, its 22 numbers consisting of arias, duets, trios, quartets and larger ensembles in the Finales, all linked by recitatives. Comparing the opera to Shakespeare's play, it is clear that the omission of certain characters was bound to weaken the dramatic impact of the work. Paulina became Irene in the opera, and being widowed in the transition, the character of her husband Antigonus was omitted. An immediate result was the unfortunate loss of that memorable stage direction of the Bard, 'exit, pursued by a bear'. Quite why Bruch decided to avoid casting a bear in his opera (thus robbing himself of a box office winner) is hard to imagine. If it was a matter of expense, the alternative upon which he decided must have set the theatre budget back a pretty penny. In a short dream pantomime, and according to the opera's stage directions, the back wall of Hermione's cell opens up to reveal the scenario of a raging storm at sea. As a boat containing Hermione's baby Perdita is about to go under the waves, mermaids appear to rescue the infant, and she is safely placed at the base of a rainbow on the nearby shore, where she is found and raised by Tityrus (the unnamed shepherd of the play). The cell wall then closes once again, and Hermione awakes in the joyful knowledge that her baby is safe. None of the original rustics from the play is found in the opera, so Bruch could not exploit the dramatic contrast between tragedy and comedy in this problematic work. With no Autolycus, Mopsa, Dorcas and Clown there was no opportunity to set some of the original songs from the play, nor were there any set dances in the Spring Feast. From his comments about the 'miserable Ballet' in the Bremen performances (April 1872), it is to be assumed that they danced to the pastoral chorus in the Finale of the third act.

Hopffer's libretto (with its use of rhyming couplets in a lamentable attempt at translating Shakespeare) more or less follows the play. The first act of the opera (prefaced by an orchestral introduction) combines the play's first two acts. Leontes' jealousy is given full reign in its build-up to an extended aria. Polyxenes (King of Bohemia) is warned by Camillo (Leontes' aide) that Leontes suspects his regal friend of adultery with Hermione, so Polyxenes hastily flees to Bohemia taking Camillo with him. The act ends with Leontes' accusations of infidelity directed publicly at Hermione, who is led off to prison.

After Hermione's opening aria in Act II, Irene (her confidante) tells her mistress that the newborn baby (Perdita) has been entrusted to a servant to be taken far from Leontes' wrath. Left alone, Hermione dreams of the baby's adventures at sea, though in the play it was Antigonus who had a dream in which Hermione appeared, naming the baby Perdita and warning him of his own impending death. Hermione wakes up, now able to bear with fortitude the burden of her imminent public trial. As in the play, Leontes rejects the verdict of the Delphic Oracle exonerating Hermione, but when the news of the death of his son Mamillius is brought to him, he repents and begs forgiveness from his wife. Hermione faints upon hearing news of the death of her son, and is led away. Irene now effects her plan to make Leontes suffer for his false accusations against his faithful wife. She pretends Hermione has died, and now Leontes has nothing to look forward to but his own death.

In the play Time is personified and introduces the fourth act by moving the action forward by sixteen years, but no such help is afforded the opera's audience. An orchestral entr'acte sets the pastoral scene of Act III of the opera and introduces first Perdita (now a teenager), then her lover Florizel (son of Polyxenes) and finally Tityrus (the shepherd who found the abandoned baby Perdita). King Polyxenes and Camillo (both disguised) join in the Maytime festivities until the king's wrath is aroused by his son's betrothal to Perdita, a humble shepherdess. Camillo then advises the young couple to flee to the court of Leontes and seek his help. The wheel has come full circle.

All is resolved in Act IV when Polyxenes, in pursuit of his son Florizel, arrives at Leontes' court and identifies Perdita as the daughter of the now repentant monarch. Irene duly leads the assembled company to view a lifelike statue of Hermione, which indeed it is. To the accompaniment of the harp (used in *Die Loreley* in the last act for similar dramatic effect), Hermione steps down from her pedestal to be reunited with her husband.

There are strong similarities in Bruch's dramatic and musical setting of the chorus in both *Die Loreley* and *Hermione*. There is much good choral writing in both operas, where it is used in similarly dramatic situations. The public trials of both wronged women (Lenore and Hermione) involve choruses of priests and populace, and the peasants' paeans of praise to Nature in the first and fourth acts of *Die Loreley* and the third act of *Hermione* are treated similarly in both operas.

After the Dresden performance in January 1873 the *Allgemeine Zeitung* reported that 'as in Berlin, it had no sweeping success. Even if the music is noble, clever and careful here and there, a monotony and lack of an actual dramatic life is too noticeable. The brilliant instrumentation forces interest in the singing roles completely into the background, a defect from which *Die Loreley* also suffers.'

The conductor Julius Rietz also had misgivings during the preparations for the same Dresden performances. The cast were apparently dissatisfied with the music and their roles, and it was feared that the lack of form in the music would produce an ineffective result. A year later, however, Rietz wrote again (when Dresden were restaging the work on 15 January 1873) and praised Bruch's music, much to the composer's satisfaction. It is nevertheless undeniable that the harmonic interest of the work is rarely heightened by any novel ideas on the part of its composer. Risks are never taken and the result is a mixture of missed opportunity and harmonic dullness, with Bruch's usual emphasis on melody. It is evident that in the seven years between *Die Loreley* and *Hermione*, he had learned little about the operate *genre*. He was never again to be tempted back into the theatre as a composer of opera. Still, he showed himself capable of preserving a sense of humour even in the troubled days leading to the first performance: 'I have nothing at all against an Italian translation,' he wrote to Simrock. 'As far as I am concerned it can be translated into Chaldean.'[7] 'When is the *Hermione pot-pourri* for two piccolos and double bass appearing?' he asked in December 1871.

Years later in his projected memoirs, Bruch, while acknowledging Hopffer's poor libretto, wrote of the opera:

> Best overall was the melodic third act (the charming love scene between Perdita and Florizel), the other acts were dominated too much by the declamatory element. The material did not impress me on the whole, and besides I had already (before the completion of this opera) been totally spellbound by Homeric poetry. I now lived only for the *Odyssey*, the *Winter's Tale* and the whole concept of opera had become indifferent to me, and once again (and for many years to come) I turned with all my powers to big choral works.

Bruch had settled in Berlin at No. 52 Königin Augusta Strasse during the period of the composition and staging rehearsals of his opera. Though surrounded by a stimulating circle of artistic friends and acquaintances, he longed for the rural solitude of the Rhineland. It appeared that wherever he was, the grass on the other side was always greener. If he was in a city, it was the countryside he missed, and if he was amidst Nature, he wanted only to immerse himself in the hustle and bustle of a great city and its artistic traffic. His publisher, Simrock, lived in Berlin, and Bruch was often in his company together with Joachim and sometimes Brahms. Bruch's opinion of Brahms the man was rapidly differing from his view of him as a composer. Indeed it is apparent that they both had difficult temperaments. Bruch described to von Beckerath a dinner at Simrock's to which Brahms was also invited. 'Unfortunately,' Bruch wrote, 'the personality of Brahms impressed us this time as being far more conceited than before; I can absolutely no longer reconcile this cynical, mocking personality with the spirit that conceived the *Requiem*.'[8] He envied von Beckerath's move from Crefeld to the more rural Rüdesheim on the Rhine: 'you can thank your Creator that you are spared the society monkeys and all the glittering servitude of a large city'. In June, after visits to Amsterdam and Cologne, he holidayed in the Bergisches Land, and from there he wrote that he would find it 'difficult to endure the daily life of Berlin once again.' In November, with his sister Mathilde's health in a poor state, he considered the possibility of leaving Berlin: 'would that the winter months had wings. . . . It is wonderful here. The lovely Bergisches Land is displaying itself just once more in its full magic, before the much-too-long winter sets in. . . . I am scared of all the Berlin tittle-tattle, all those semi-friends and the social tomfoolery.'[9] For the present, however, he was to remain in Berlin, and endure the real or imagined problems he believed existed there.

His current project was the first of his secular oratorios, *Odysseus* Op. 41 for mixed chorus, soli and orchestra, in collaboration with the poet Wilhelm Paul Graff. He conceived the idea in September 1871, began work on it immediately with his customary great enthusiasm, and finished it at the end of November 1872. On 6 May 1872 a performance of six finished scenes took place in Bremen under Carl Reinthaler. The first performance of the completed work was given in Barmen (Wuppertal) on 8 February 1873 under Bruch's direction. Amalie Joachim (for whom the part of Penelope was written) and Julius Stockhausen were scheduled to appear as soloists, but both were forced to cancel late in the day. The work, which was dedicated to the Choral Society in Bremen, did as much for Bruch's reputation as a composer as he had previously experienced with the first Violin Concerto. It was immediately taken up by many choral societies, particularly in the Rhineland, and was a catalyst in furthering his music abroad, especially in Holland, England and America. The première was not only a significant occasion for Bruch personally, but it also represented a change in the position of the oratorio in the literature of music.

The oratorio, from the beginning of the seventeenth century to Mendelssohn, had been concerned exclusively with religious subject matter, and indeed oratorio can be defined as an extended setting of a religious text in an unstaged dramatic form. Though not requiring a scenic setting with costumes and action, Handel's oratorios were conceived in dramatic terms, and performed unstaged in theatres. In the mid-nineteenth century the oratorio was affected by the musical and political world around it. Liszt attempted a transfer of dramatic elements of the 'Music of the Future' from his symphonic poems into his two oratorios (*The Legend of St Elizabeth* 1865 and *Christus* 1873), and Schumann began the move to the secular oratorio with *Das Paradies und die Peri* (1843) and the uncompleted *Scenes from Goethe's Faust* (1844–1853).

The mood of unified Germany that followed the Franco-Prussian War was understandably euphoric. Wagner had celebrated with his *Kaisermarsch*, Brahms with his *Triumphlied* Op. 55 tauntingly (described by Wagner as 'Brahms running around wearing his Handel's Hallelujah wig'), and Bruch's contribution was *Das Lied vom deutschen Kaiser*. The war reparations from the French created an economic boom. Nationalistic fervour was at its height, and wealth, leisure and optimism created an atmosphere which encouraged social contact, for example in the increasing number of choral societies. It was also a period, in German literature, of the historical novel and historical retrospection (Felix Dahn and Georg Ebers). Bruch's choral ballads and cantatas, such as *Salamis*, *Normannenzug*, *Römische Leichenfeier*, *Frithjof* and *Schön Ellen*, had already fired his imagination with the secular and heroic past, and it was only a matter of time before his attention turned to ancient Greece as a source.

On 22 January 1873 Bruch wrote to Hermann Deiters on the subject of his choice of material and his view of the oratorio since Mendelssohn. 'Biblical subject matter,' he wrote, 'was and is far from my mind; the old masters have achieved so much in this field, that we are only able to attain such success and originality through the use of other material. It is no coincidence that all oratorios since Mendelssohn have failed.'

In September 1871 Max wrote, from the Beckeraths' new home in Rüdesheim to his sister Mathilde in Berlin, that he had hit upon 'incomparable material' for a 'concert work.' 'Do not be shocked,' he continued, 'if I tell you that it is the Odyssey!' It was as if 'scales fell from my eyes' when he read the Homeric poem, and he seized upon it as the antidote to the 'Christian lamentation and the poetic tears of Bach's cantatas' which he hated. He then outlined a preliminary plan of the work:

Part I
1. Overture (Greek, blue!)
2. Odysseus on Calypso's island
3. Odysseus in the Underworld
4. Odysseus with the Sirens
5. Storm at sea

Part II
6. Odysseus with the Phaeacians
   *a.* Nausicaa
   *b.* the feast
   *c.* departure on journey home
7. Penelope
8. Final scene. Reunion. Revenge. Large resounding final chorus, glorification of marital love and fidelity, and of the homeland.[10]

In November and December 1871 he was in Bergisch Gladbach, and from there he wrote to Till in highly enthusiastic terms of his progress with the composition. 'I have forgotten that since last Thursday I have been thinking quite exclusively of the Odyssey, and I sit here up to my ears in the music. It is an indescribable wonder! The final chorus . . . has such a melody, and is a large and quite simple ensemble movement to the words, 'There is nowhere lovelier than the homeland', which will give people joy for a long time to come . . . I sit here at work in the stillness of winter . . . The Odyssey truly pleases me no end, and I believe one can see that it is all born of my spirit.'[11]

Bruch's *Odysseus* is subtitled 'Scenes from the Odyssey', and although his selection was ostensibly random, it was nevertheless made with great care and deliberation. He never wished to transfer the detailed dramatic effects of the operatic stage to the concert hall, but rather to rely on the fantasy and imagination of his audience. In spite of these intentions, there is a similarity between some of the choral music in *Odysseus* and the second act of his opera *Die Loreley*: the Rhine Spirits and the Spirits of the Underworld are kinsmen. More in keeping with his wish to fire the imagination of his audience are the rushing waves of semiquaver arpeggios and scales in the strings, which depict the maritime scenario of the Phaeacian sailors transporting Odysseus back to Ithaca. To sustain this desire not to become too operatic, he had to make the startling omission of Penelope's suitors as characters in the work. By excluding them, he could omit both their Bacchanale and their murder by Odysseus, although these events are referred to by the chorus. The result is an enhancement of the role of the chorus in the oratorio, both as participants in the drama (during the course of the work, they are cast as the companions of Odysseus, the spirits of Hades, Phaeacians, Sirens, maidens of Nausicaa, Oceanides and the people of Ithaca) and as narrators in the original manner of the Chorus in a Greek drama.

In choosing his scenes carefully, he avoided the danger of the work becoming too dramatic. In a letter to Deiters he explained that he had chosen 'the scenes deliberately following a law of contrasts, and the order of the scenes was considered mainly from a musical viewpoint. I then made an exact lay-out for each individual scene . . . and presented the detailed plan to my friend Graff with the question whether, within the limitations drawn by me and by the musical considerations, he could and would, with poetic licence, present me with a poem. He agreed, and gave me one which in all aspects has turned out very well.'[12]

The orchestral introduction is drawn from the work's final scene in which Odysseus is reunited with his wife Queen Penelope. In the first scene Odysseus is found on Calypso's island. A chorus of nymphs sing of the delights of the place, and of the beauty of their sister, the golden-haired Calypso. But Odysseus can sing only of his longing to return to his home on Ithaca and to his wife. The gods, moved by his song, take pity upon him. Hermes appears and enables Odysseus to escape, on a raft, from the lure of Calypso's enchantment. In the second scene Odysseus and his companions have descended into Hades. As his men sing of their horror and fear, and as the Spirits of the Dead lament their fate in the Underworld, the blind sage Tiresias and the ghost of Anticleia (Odysseus' mother) urge him to flee with his companions, and continue his journey homewards. In the third scene Circe sends a wind which carries the ship of Odysseus and his companions close to the island of the Sirens. By filling his men's ears with wax, and having himself bound securely to the mast, they escape the intoxicating seductiveness of the song of the Sirens, whose island is strewn with the bleached bones of previous voyagers who succumbed. Part I concludes with Odysseus sailing alone on the raft on which he escaped from Calypso's island. Soon he is caught in a mighty storm stirred up by Poseidon, god of the sea. Just as he believes himself lost, the sea goddess Leucothea intervenes to protect him. He is swept into the raging waters and thrown up on the island of the Phaeacians, where he drags himself beyond the reach of the waves and falls into an exhausted slumber.

Part II opens in Ithaca, where Queen Penelope mourns the loss of her son Telemachus, who has set off in search of his father. She beseeches the gods to lead home her wandering husband Odysseus, should he still be alive. In the following scene Odysseus is found emerging from his sleep on the island of the Phaeacians. The tempest has subsided, and in the bright sunlight he wakes to the dancing and singing of Nausicaa, daughter of the Phaeacian king Alcinoüs, and her handmaidens. Odysseus is overwhelmed by her beauty and grace, and greets her as both queen and goddess, whereupon she invites him to her father's court. In the name of Zeus he is welcomed at the court of the king. A great banquet is held in his honour. When he reveals his identity, and tells his hosts of the sufferings he has endured during his prolonged wanderings at the mercy of the angry gods, they take pity upon him and provide him with a ship to take him home. Back in Ithaca, Penelope sings as she unravels at night the garment she weaves by day. In this way she has been able to remain faithful to the absent Odysseus, for she has promised the suitors who surround her that on the day she finishes weaving the garment, she will accept one of them as husband. This scene is followed by Odysseus' arrival on Ithaca. The Phaeacian sailors carry him tenderly to land as he sleeps, after which they depart silently. When he wakes up, he does not recognize his whereabouts, fearing he has once again been led astray by the fickle gods. But Athene appears to assure him that he is at last at home, in his own kingdom of Ithaca, and that she will protect him. She tells him of the suitors who desecrate his palace and molest his faithful wife, Penelope, and he swears murderous vengeance. The scene in which he carries out his threat, using the great bow which only he can string, is omitted by Bruch, and the work ends with a scene of universal rejoicing in Ithaca, incorporating a tender duet between husband and wife, the music for which has first appeared in the orchestral introduction to the oratorio.

The original plan of the work was slightly modified in its final form. The orchestral introduction lost both its subtitle and its numerical designation, but the rest of Part I remained in its original form. Part II was more extensively reshaped by starting with the change of scene back to Ithaca and the mourning Penelope. In his final version she has two scenes which come before and after those with Nausikaa and the encounter with the Phaeacians. All the scenes are self-contained, with the implication of dramatic continuity only evident in scenes six and seven (when Nausicaa leads Odysseus to the court of the Phaeacians), and in the last three scenes of the work (nine, ten and the choral finale) when Odysseus has returned to Ithaca.

The ingredients of conventional oratorio are to be found in *Odysseus*, though the formal boundaries between recitative and aria or *arioso* are blurred to give the work more flow. What little recitative there is lends to the work a dullness and stagnation of the drama, largely through the unimaginative chordal accompaniment. Recitative is interestingly used at times by the chorus, for whom Bruch writes in three distinctive styles. The first is recitative with the chorus singing in unison or octaves in a rhythm determined by the text. The second is the chorale style of block homophonic chords, and the third is contrapuntal polyphony using *fugato* and imitative counterpoint, the choice of style being determined by the dramatic situation of the moment. There are only two solo scenes in the whole work, and both are for Penelope. *Arioso* sections for the remaining soloists (Odysseus being naturally prominent among them) are found in all the other scenes interspersed among choruses and recitatives.

*Odysseus* abounds in melody, which by now is to be expected of anything from the composer's pen. The work's strength lies in melodic power either when it surges up to the surface from the orchestral accompaniment, or when it lies in the mournful simplicity of Penelope's music. The *Helden* or heroic bass-baritone role of Odysseus, indicates the calibre of Julius Stockhausen's voice (who was in Bruch's mind when he wrote the work) and also that of George Henschel who often sang it in the years to come. It is a highly demanding and taxing role, and requires a voice with the qualities of a Wotan; and indeed there are moments in the work, such as Odysseus' fury at the news that Penelope is being molested by her suitors, when Wotan can be heard in equally black mood berating Brünnhilde for trying to protect Siegmund from his appointed death in *Die Walküre*.

The interval of the third is a unifying feature of the work. First it plays a prominent part (from the very first three notes of the work) in the melodic or motivic structure of each scene. Second, the intervallic third is used frequently by Bruch in its harmonic relationship between tonic and mediant keys, the mediant (third note) of the tonic key becoming the tonic of the mediant. Without modulation, Bruch continually slips into and out of the two unrelated keys. Finally it is the only ingredient in the chord of the diminished seventh (which is a construction of four superimposed minor thirds), the chord which Bruch uses continually for dramatic effect throughout the work.

Bruch's friend Anton Krause (music director in Barmen from 1859 to 1894) prepared the chorus for the first performance in Barmen on 8 February 1873, in which Josef Bletzacher replaced Julius Stockhausen, and Adele Graf stood in for Amalie Joachim. They acquitted themselves well in spite of stepping in at the last moment, and the concert (sold out to an audience of 1,250 people) became a significant day in the history of the oratorio. The Bible (both Old and New Testaments) was, for the present, displaced by myths, legends and world history as a source of text. Bruch felt so strongly about the association between the Bible in literature and oratorio in music, that he subtitled *Odysseus* with the phrase 'Scenes from the Odyssey' rather than describing it as an oratorio.

The popularity of *Odysseus* was instant, but lasted only until about the beginning of the First World War, in spite of predictions of everlasting success by the reviewer in the *Allgemeine Musikalische Zeitung*, Hermann Deiters. The reviewer in the *Barmer Zeitung*

(Barmen's local newspaper) wrote of the 'resounding success' the work had achieved at its first performance, and of the 'electrifying effect it had on its large audience, who responded with lively applause that increased with the passing of each number.' A chorus and an *arioso* for Odysseus were repeated on demand. The ladies of the chorus publicly presented their conductor/composer with a bouquet at the conclusion of the performance, whereupon the full chorus crowned him with the tribute of a victorious laurel wreath. A large contingent of musicians (including Hiller) came from all over Germany, but particularly from the Rhineland. The rift between Hiller and Bruch grew wider when no review appeared in the *Kölner Zeitung* after the performance. Bruch strongly suspected his former teacher of having a hand in the affair, attributing the omission to jealousy of Bruch's success. Of the Rhineland towns which performed the work, Cologne was the last to stage it, on 27 January 1874. 'I have now had enough of the old dog,' he had written to Simrock about Hiller a month earlier.[13] Simrock nevertheless urged Bruch to accept Hiller's invitation to conduct the work himself, even if Hiller was making life as difficult as possible (there were problems with Bruch's fee, Cologne's choice of soloists, and the preparation of the chorus).

Bruch heeded Simrock's advice, swallowed his pride, and conducted the performance. As it happened the concert went well: 'Cologne is transformed. *Odysseus* made an enormous and lasting impression. Orchestra and chorus were very good,' he wrote to Simrock.[14] It also received a good review, and for once Cologne was back in favour with the sensitive composer. Apart from the Rhineland, *Odysseus* received performances in every city throughout Germany and began to be heard in other European countries (Holland, Belgium and Switzerland). It brought Bruch the Gold Medal for the Arts and Sciences from the Grand Duke of Mecklenburg after its performance in Schwerin. An accolade he valued highly was accorded him by Brahms, who chose to perform *Odysseus* in his farewell concert with the Gesellschaft der Musikfreunde in Vienna on 18 April 1875. Bruch was less happy that Brahms could not perform the complete work owing to restraints on the concert's length. He pleaded for Part I to be given complete, and that Part II should at least include the 'Phaeacian Banquet' and the Final Chorus. He was very unhappy at the idea of excising Penelope from the performance (a problem of finance) and urged Brahms not to do so, but he sanctioned Nausicaa's omission, again with reluctance. He looked forward to being present in Vienna: 'Of course I am very keen to come; to see you and Vienna again (I have not been there since 1865), and to hear *Odysseus* performed by your brilliant chorus will give me exceptional pleasure.'[15] Like so many events in his life, this one also turned sour. Henschel (who took the title role in this performance) informed him from Vienna, in March 1875, that the role of Penelope was indeed to be cut, and as Bruch had received no word from Brahms or the Committee on the subject, nor even an official invitation to attend the concert, he decided to stay away.

Bruch listed the 42 performances of *Odysseus* which had either taken place since the Bremen première of the incomplete work, or were projected ahead to the end of 1875.[16] Among those countries listed were America (New York 25 January 1874) and England (a projected performance in Manchester for March 1875). Sir Julius Benedict (on a visit from Liverpool) met Bruch in Cologne, and confirmed that a performance of *Odysseus* would be given in the Merseyside city in March 1875 under Benedict's own direction. This was the beginning of an association with Liverpool which was to culminate in Bruch's move there in 1880 as Benedict's successor.

When *Odysseus* was first published, it appeared with translations into French and English. Mrs Natalia Macfarren (wife of the eminent composer and musicologist, George Macfarren, and a singer herself) was responsible for the English translation. Bruch expressed his complete satisfaction with her work, and she maintained her association with him by translating some later choral works. Though his name was already known in England through his Violin Concerto, his fame was to spread with his choral compositions. The proliferation of choral societies throughout the land, and the existence of a translation in the vocal scores of his works, both contributed to the dissemination of his music in England and America. J. A. Fuller-Maitland[17] was full of praise for *Odysseus*:

> The work . . . is that by which Bruch's name is, perhaps, best known all the world over. Again he reached his highest point in setting . . . a story that appealed strongly to his imagination. A close study of this masterpiece of Bruch's genius will shed some light on his failure as an operatic composer. . . . On its production in Bremen [*sic*] in 1873 this beautiful work was received with much enthusiasm, for it is of a kind that makes its effect immediately. . . . The success achieved by it wherever it has been given has been very remarkable.

## Chapter Ten

### FREELANCE COMPOSER: BONN
1873–78

IN 1873 THE failure in Berlin of his opera *Hermione* still rankled with Bruch, so he decided to leave the 'north-east centre of all hatred, envy and meanness . . . Brahms is better off there: he has a strong following. In several other places in Germany, as well as in Switzerland and England, I am in the same situation, but not in Berlin . . . for the Wagnerians hate me and only Brahms exists for the classic high society.'

The success of *Odysseus* in Barmen in February 1873 ensured further performances throughout Germany in the following months and years. Bruch was often asked to conduct it by various choral societies, and it was the combination of this busy conducting career together with his increasing unhappiness in Berlin that led him to move with his sister to his beloved Rhineland. The ten years 1873–83 were the least productive in terms of the number of compositions completed and published. They were however highly active years, filled with conducting engagements, travel, permanent posts, and a change in his domestic situation through his marriage.

Before he met the woman who was to become his wife, he had one further love affair which ended unhappily. The girl that the 35-year-old Max Bruch now fell in love with and proposed to, was 19-year-old Amalie Heydweiller. Between the end of October 1873 and the end of January 1875, the saga unfolds in letters written in moods ranging from elation to deep depression. There is no doubt that Bruch's lack of creative output in this period is directly attributable to the uncertainties resulting from the on–off engagement between the two lovers.

The first mention of 'Lally' Heydweiller (though initially without naming her) occurred in a letter Bruch wrote to Simrock in October 1873. 'For a short while,' he wrote, 'I have been secretly engaged to a very charming 19-year-old girl from one of the first families of the Rhineland. . . . We are as one, and do not want to let one another go — however the family has put up some resistance; above all her mother (her father is dead) is demanding proof of a secure income (not necessarily a post, as my name suffices), something which, as a mother, she can and must expect.'[1]

Max was convinced that Lally's mother was only interested in marrying her off to anyone from the Rhineland who was rich ('einen rheinischen Geldsack'), although von Beckerath tried to assure him that this was not true. Matters were obviously serious enough for the two lovers to have to communicate secretly with one another ('behind her mother's back'), but Lally, the inexperienced *ingénue*, was firmly resolved to marry him. Max in turn was naturally flattered by this romantic response, and enjoyed himself regardless of the consequences. 'The dear girl is true and constant,' he observed, 'and does not think of leaving me, in spite of all the sermons; she loves me with a passionate warmth, which makes me very happy, for how could I, in my somewhat complicated situation, expect to find this supreme human happiness again!'

Max then put forward a proposal to Simrock, which, if accepted, would help solve his pecuniary problems. If all that Frau Heydweiller wished to see was a guarantee of a secure annual income, would Simrock not grant him a retainer for the next five years, payable in half-yearly instalments? Unfortunately for Max, the idea was rejected, in spite of a guarantee of exclusive rights being given to the publisher by the composer. It is not known what Simrock's reasons were for refusing the proposition, though it should have been obvious to Bruch that, in spite of the success of *Odysseus*, their commercial relationship had begun very shakily with the indifferent success of the Second Symphony and the failure of *Hermione*. If the money spinner, the first Violin Concerto, had been part of the Simrock catalogue, no doubt his response might have been more favourable. In spite of the fact that Bruch was currently working on a second violin concerto (which ultimately became the single-movement *Romanze*), Bruch expressed 'little inclination towards instrumental music. All my projects, small or large, will favour vocal music. I no longer think of opera.' Having tried to tempt Simrock with his current musical ideas (he also revealed plans to set the *Iliad* after the success of *Odysseus*), Bruch turned to other potential sources of work to supplement his income. The towns of Barmen, Elberfeld, Crefeld, Düsseldorf and München Gladbach were planning to unite in an annual Music Festival each spring in Düsseldorf, and, according to Bruch, he was considered the obvious candidate for the Music Director (at 500 thalers per year). At the end of his letter, Max's attempt at secrecy gave way: 'Shall I tell you now, little Simrock, who the girl is? Amalie (called Lally) Heydweiller from Crefeld. Mayor Bredt in Barmen is her uncle, her mother was born von der Leyen . . . she [Lally] is beautiful and simple, and loving. Have you now recovered from your astonishment? Odysseus the "Impervious" is in love, engaged, and loved — if our Berlin friends only knew!!'

Max wrote to Simrock again, having received a negative response from the publisher.[2] His first letter had not specified a particular sum for a retainer, but now he wrote, 'I had not thought of much, 600–700 thalers, the other 700–800 I would have guaranteed myself in other ways, producing a secure income of 1,500 thalers. With a 500 thaler allowance from her mother, we could live quite nicely in Bonn, for we are both happy if we only have one another.' But from then on it became increasingly clear that hopes of marriage were doomed. Max half-heartedly applied for posts in Detmold and in Rotterdam ('I hate this post before I have it, and even before I know if I shall have it'). He wanted to stay in the Rhineland, 'in a place where my works will grow daily more popular, and where I live so easily.'

It now transpired that Lally Heydweiller was heiress to considerable wealth, and it seems probable that Max was regarded by her relations not only as an impecunious artist but also as a fortune hunter. Her father had died in October 1872, and various relatives now began to advise the widow Heydweiller on financial matters. Lally would come of age in two years' time, on 16 October 1875, and (together with her four siblings) stood to inherit not only the 80–100,000 thalers from her father, but also (upon the death of her mother) nearly a quarter of a million from her maternal grandfather who had died in the spring of 1873. Knowing her mother's demand that he obtain a permanent post somewhere, Max showed a rather unhealthy interest in discovering from Simrock (evidently also a legal expert) whether Lally would be able to claim the inheritance from her father under 'the French law which prevails here' when she came of age. His letter to von Beckerath, reporting Simrock's rejection of his proposal, also included an estimate of his income for the following year, 1874. It is of interest to note that of the 4,000 thalers he anticipated in fees, 600 would result from the Violin Concerto. Even his friends now joined Lally in urging him to take a post: 'Now philistine friends like Emil Kamphausen, and the girl herself come and make my heart heavy with their cries of "a post! a post!" The girl is a pure child; she knows nothing of anything.'

His aversion to the trappings of a position were aired more strongly in a letter to von Beckerath, which he wrote whilst staying in Elberfeld:[3]

I see here once again the meaning of a post: Hell on Earth. This unspeakable tittle-tattle, this wickedness, this insulting of one another, this interfering in local stupidities, this dreadful incompetence . . . this lamentable provincial behaviour with its stupid envy of Barmen (and there the opposite towards Elberfeld), this eternal carping at anything done by the Music Director of the place — all this I reject . . . I really can no longer live like all these people, who have no ability for achievement, yet run around in circles with a God-given right as the local Conductor.

Lally meanwhile remained the symbol of perfection, albeit acknowledged as a highly immature one, with 'no conception of worldly matters and things which need to be discussed'. These were of course the continuing arguments over money and his prospects. *Odysseus* was doing well with performances pending in Aachen, Cologne, Hamburg, Zürich, Mannheim and Münster. The post in Rotterdam, on the other hand, and much to his relief, was not offered to him. 'That would have been something for me, to go off to the miserable Dutch, leaving the Rhineland where I have status, where I am so lovely and free, influential yet not tied down, all that an artist could wish for himself.' By now he was beginning to experience sour moods in the Heydweiller saga, and was losing his appetite for the fight over Lally. 'For me it would be neither an honour nor a pleasure to become related to such a strait-laced family', he concluded to Simrock at the end of the year.[4]

A few days later, on his own birthday, Max seemed to have had an infusion of renewed vigour and determination to take up the fight once again on her behalf. 'The matter now stands thus: we love one another more than ever, and no obstacles can nor will prevent me from possessing this sweet, simple and completely lovable girl.'[5] After a conference of the girl's relatives in Crefeld, it was agreed that they could announce their engagement, subject to the continuation of the prevailing conditions concerning Max's prospects. 'The long and short of it is that I shall get the girl as soon as I present proof of a secure post with a fixed income. Now I must see what I can do.'

The matter of performing *Odysseus* in Cologne at the end of January 1874 was also proposed at this time. In spite of Hiller's tardiness in mounting the work, the refusal to engage Amalie Joachim for the part of Penelope, and the poor musical preparation of the chorus, Bruch eventually agreed to conduct it. Simrock's comment survives in a note appended to a letter he received from Bruch. 'I have written to Bruch,' he wrote, 'advising him under any circumstances to accept the engagement, for Hiller only exploits Bruch's sensitivity by preventing him from conducting and showing the people of Cologne what a miserable conductor they have in

Hiller. Bruch could not play a more annoying trick if he prepares the work well and conducts it now!'[6]

Hiller left for a trip to Czechoslovakia (where he visited Smetana in Prague) and was not present in Cologne on 27 January to witness Bruch's triumph with *Odysseus*. Four days later Max had 'definitely decided not to leave the Rhineland, and not to take a post which cripples my creative work. From now on let everything take its course accordingly. I have no desire to commit spiritual suicide.' He struggled to keep his creative powers going throughout the difficult months of early 1874. By 11 February the first movement of his projected second violin concerto was completed, and there was 'a glimmer of ideas for the second and third movements'. But his heart was not in it, and as he was both pleased with the first movement, and encouraged by the positive response of friends who heard it, Bruch decided to leave the work as a one-movement *Romanze*.[7]

The work is based on two typically lyrical and melodic themes (Exs. 22 and 23), the second of which is marked by the double-stopping of the solo violin part, and the elegiac and surging orchestral accompaniment. The harmonic language of the *Romanze* is less interesting, and the work is only saved from dullness by its melodic strength.

Ex. 22

Ex. 23

Wilhelm Altmann wrote that (according to the composer himself) the *Romanze* Op. 42 was based on Bruch's preoccupation with Nordic sagas and specifically on Gudrun's Lament by the Sea.[8] Given Bruch's aversion to programmatic music, it is far more likely that its inspirational source was Max's Lament by the Rhine over his troubled love affair with Amalie Heydweiller. More interesting is the assumption that this projected violin concerto would have begun unusually (as the real Second Concerto actually did) with a slow movement. Like so many of Bruch's compositions for the violin, Joachim was soon involved in the practicalities of the solo part. In spite of being in London at the time, the score was sent to him for bowing and fingering. The dedication however is to the Konzertmeister, Robert Heckmann, who was also involved in advising Bruch during its composition.

His other musical preoccupation at this time was with the orchestration of his *Dithyrambe* and 'Rheinsage' (to be published as one of the *Five Lieder* for *a cappella* chorus Op. 38). In a letter to Simrock, he complained that cellists had plagued him for years to write a cello concerto. 'They can wait a long while. I have more important things to do than write stupid cello concertos!'[9] This same letter contained a reference to the man who was virtually to equal Joachim's role in Bruch's life as adviser on compositions for the violin, the Spanish violinist, Pablo de Sarasate. 'The Spaniard Sarasate recently played [the First Violin Concerto] in a Paris Conservatoire concert with "great success" according to Durand & Co., also in Lyons and Brussels. This work is "now popular in France" (although written by a German!!).' *Odysseus* meanwhile continued on its triumphant journey. On 17 February he reported condescendingly on excerpts given in an American performance. '*Odysseus* was given in New York on 25 January by the "Deutscher Liederkranz", but only eight scenes, [without] the Underworld Scene (which probably went far too far over the Yankee horizon, and is not so easy to understand as "Yankee doodle") and one of the scenes for Penelope.'[10]

'For a long time now,' he told Simrock, 'there has been no talk of marriage. I only want to take up a post (if I am to do so at all) which gives me time to compose, for in my 36th year I cannot change my nature. There are no signs of prospects anywhere, and I have had enough to bear with this matter which has now been slowly dragging on since September, and has been accompanied almost always by trouble and worry, with neither joy nor happiness.'[11] During March 1874 his mood slumped so severely that he eventually plucked up courage to write to Frau Heydweiller, and ask for the engagement to be put in abeyance for a while, though without in any way implying a lessening of his love for her daughter. Her nine page reply, which Max received on 20 March, was understanding and sensitive to his feelings, and fully appreciated the reasons for his artistic resistance to the question of a permanent post. However Frau Heydweiller, whilst maintaining her 'high regard' for him, suggested that as an artist, he might bring problems into a marriage with her daughter, and therefore it might be more prudent for him to live 'a single life' in spite of the sorrow this decision would bring Amalie. This only served to revive Max's emotional ardour, and he now found that he depended 'more strongly on this faithful young girl' than he had hitherto believed. He then promptly replied to Lally's mother that he could not 'give up his life's happiness, and would hold on fast to Lally'.

As proof of his sincerity, he also sent her a financial statement of his annual returns for the past eight years, which (at a total of about 8,500 thalers) averaged at an annual income of about 1,000 thalers, and that he could give his word that he would never earn less than 800 thalers a year in the future. Over Easter 1874 his letters to both Simrock and von Beckerath detailed his finances again. Since November 1873, his sister Mathilde had been living in Bonn, and raising the children of the Bruchs' late cousin, Emmi, at the home of her widowed husband, Professor Adolf Kamphausen. Mathilde now assured Max that he would need 1,800 thalers a year to live as a married couple in Bonn, and after doing his sums on the basis of his own income and the dowry Lally would bring with her from her father's inheritance, he was still 450 thalers short of his goal. He now found himself exactly back where he had started six months earlier. The prospect of filling the post in Düsseldorf faded when the incumbent Tausch decided not to leave. Lally meanwhile had turned down an offer of marriage from a certain Emil von Beckerath who 'had loved her since last summer'. Max wrote to Rudolf von Beckerath, 'It is a semi-miracle that love has not been struck dead by all these never-ending difficulties. But in my thoughts I hold fast to this girl.'

'Nothing is going to come of this matter,' he told Simrock on Easter Monday 1874, 'for her mother will not give way, although she is in a most favourable position to do so.' This pessimism finally came to a head on 16 April when the whole edifice fell apart. Max had the support of his relatives in sending Frau Heydweiller an ultimatum. It also contained a thinly veiled reprimand over what Max considered to be the less than generous allowance from Lally's inheritance. He complained bitterly to von Beckerath that other Crefeld families had more beneficent parents, and that Lally's uncle had persuaded Frau Heydweiller to withhold 3,000 thalers from her daughter. Another relative (Dr Märklin) had disappointed Max by suggesting that 'any calm and objectively thinking person must admit that you and Amalie are not suited to one another'. At the age of thirty-six, Bruch resented being 'treated like a 22-year-old'. He decided 'better the shock of an end to it now, than a later shock without end. I write as if the matter is already over — officially it is not.' In a postscript to this letter he reported that he and Lally had exchanged and burned their letters to one another, although 'the heart still quivered'.

Not only his letters, but also his boats were burnt. 'The wretched Crefeld episode makes me unable to do any daily work,' he told Simrock at the end of April. 'It is nearly over; I have told the truth to the family.' On 13 May, in just three words as a postscript, he wrote 'Crefeld is off!' On 15 June he asked Rudolf von Beckerath to obtain the return of his letters to Frau Heydweiller, as he now regretted his candour in detailing his financial affairs. A cruel twist of irony awaited the unfortunate mother. Max had unwittingly and prophetically written as a reason for wanting his letters back, that should Frau Heydweiller 'die tomorrow' another relative could make mischief with the information contained in them.[12] Poor Frau Heydweiller had indeed only six months to live; along with the shock of reading on his own birthday (6 January 1875) an announcement of Lally's engagement to the fortunate Emil von Beckerath, Max had another blow a week later when he saw a report in the paper of her mother's death. Amalie Heydweiller had now joined Emma Landau and Anna Strauss in the small gallery of past loves in the life of Max Bruch.

The immediate aftermath stimulated him to compose again. He began work on *Das Feuerkreuz* (The Fiery Cross) based on Sir Walter Scott's *Lady of the Lake*, though he soon laid it aside for some fourteen years. What he turned to next was another secular oratorio in the mould of *Odysseus*, namely *Arminius* Op. 43.

Bruch's second secular oratorio was a product of the period in Bismarck's Germany immediately after the Franco-Prussian War, and of the subsequent unification of the country. Its theme is Freedom and the Fatherland as seen during Germany in AD 9 when the Cherusci tribe (which inhabited the area between the rivers Weser and Elbe) led by their chief Arminius (18 BC – AD 19) defeated Varus, leader of the Romans, in the Teutoburger Forest. Arminius' German name was Hermann, and Bruch's original title for the oratorio was *Die Hermannsschlacht* (Hermann's Battle), and the year of its composition (1875) was when the dedication took place of Ernst von Bandel's 57-metre-high memorial to the ancient warrior on the Grotenburg in the Teutoburger Forest. Bruch considered the creation of this work to be a 'patriotic and national task', and was well pleased with the author with whom he now collaborated, a 24-year-old teacher named Friedrich Hellmuth, who used the pseudonym J. Küppers. Bruch offered it to Anton Krause, chorus master in Barmen, as an alternative to *Das Feuerkreuz* which was now temporarily abandoned. As with *Odysseus*, Barmen gratefully accepted the première, and asked Bruch to conduct it on 4 December 1875. The three soloists (alto, tenor and baritone) included the dedicatee George Henschel, who sang the *Helden*-baritone title role. Bruch was not happy with the version performed in Barmen, nor with subsequent performances in Bonn and Bergisch Gladbach. He therefore made several revisions of the work over the next two years, ending with the first performance from manuscript parts on 21 January 1877 in Zürich (again with Henschel, who also took on the role of Siegmund for the sick tenor soloist). The initial success of the work in Barmen ('the public were friendly throughout, and at times enthusiastic')[13] was largely attributable to the mood of the day and the celebrations surrounding the dedication of the Hermann monument, but as the years passed so also did moods and memories. Bruch was adamant that *Arminius* was no *Gelegenheitswerk* (a work written for an occasion) and regretted that it failed in later years.

*Arminius* is written in four parts (the work is relatively short at 90 minutes) and comprises nineteen numbers. The four sections are entitled 'Introduction', 'In the Sacred Forest', 'The Insurrection', and 'The Battle'. The Introduction presents the protagonists of the drama, Arminius, Siegmund (a German warrior), and the German and Roman armies. In order to allay the fears of his tribe at the advance of the Romans, Arminius tries to reassure his men with talk of peaceful co-existence. Siegmund on the other hand is more alarmist, and warns of the threat that faces the German tribes. The Roman horde then introduces itself as 'the sons of mighty Mars' and conquerors of the 'unconquered tribes of the earth who lie prostrate' before them. Arminius sees no further point in pacificism, so he joins with Siegmund in encouraging their tribe to resist with force of arms.

In Part II the Cherusci tribe (referred to in the text as the 'free Sons of Woden') has assembled in the Sacred Forest in order to consult with the Priestess. Having called upon Woden, she foretells the battle but is able to reassure the Germans that the gods will be on their side. The tribe then gratefully offers prayers to their gods in Valhalla.

Tension rises in Part III, as Arminius first urges his people to take stock of their own plight. He is followed by Siegmund, who reveals that he has killed a Roman who had insulted his wife. His father has been imprisoned as a reprisal for his son's flight into exile, and Siegmund is powerless to return home to help him. Arminius' call for unity in vengeance upon the Romans is taken up by all in a Battle Song for Freedom.

Part IV begins with a narration of the battle by the Priestess, during which she calls upon Woden to aid his followers. The Germans successfully ambush the advancing Romans and crush them mercilessly. The battle has taken its toll, and the Priestess now entreats Freia to receive the souls of the dying and dead into Valhalla. Among these is Siegmund, who begs with his dying breath to be taken to the Sacred Grove. As he dies, victorious shouts by his fellow tribesmen are heard, and Arminius is acknowledged as leader of the Germans and conqueror of the Romans. Arminius reminds his followers, however, that it is the gods who deserve the praise and gratitude of the victors, and not himself. Arminius and the Priestess join with the chorus in a Finale in praise of 'the renown of the Sons of Germany'.

In contrast to *Odysseus*, Bruch's *Arminius* has a far larger role for the chorus, which is involved in twelve of the nineteen numbers, and is almost entirely used as a mixed chorus. Even the Roman army is scored in this way (there are only two instances of separate male and female choruses in the entire work). But for an introduction of 70 bars to Part II ('The Sacred Forest'), the orchestra's role is entirely subservient to the vocal forces. Bruch had now established a formula of writing in which the woodwinds shadowed the vocal lines, the brass (and the organ in the case of *Arminius*) functioned in block chords to underline the essentially diatonic harmony, and the strings (apart from when accompanying recitative) interwove the texture with rhythmically energetic scales and arpeggios for dramatic effect. Such effects now threatened to blur and even swamp the vocal parts, when depicting storm and battle, by the use of *tremolando* and rushing passage work.

Reaction to the work was initially positive, particularly in post-unification Germany. Such phrases as 'goldene süsse Freiheit' (golden sweet freedom) were appropriate to the prevailing mood, though, considering current operatic activities further south in Bayreuth, the use of such characters as Wotan, Siegmund, Freia and the Valkyrie was perhaps misjudged. Mrs Natalie Macfarren was once again entrusted with the English translation, but it was in America that the work received several performances between 1883 and 1912. It is interesting to savour critical opinion over this 30-year period and see how the work eventually fell from favour. Bruch himself conducted the first American performance in Boston on 5 May 1883, and the following day it was reviewed in the *Boston Herald*:

It is difficult to convey an accurate idea of the instantaneous and overwhelming success which attended the presentation of the work last evening, as no such demonstration of approval has been known in Music Hall for years, the audience for once throwing off the calm self-possession which so often astonishes strangers and for once astonished its own members by an exhibition of enthusiasm that would have been creditable to a public under the sunny skies of Italy . . . the oratorio is a constant source of pleasure to the hearer.

Three years later the *Herald* reported a performance given in September 1886, calling it 'a fresh, bright and tuneful composition, strong in dramatic effects, full of well arranged contrasts and well suited to call out the best work of soloists and chorus singers.'

In May 1892 it was given in the second half of a concert (the first consisted of Beethoven's third Leonore overture and Liszt's First Piano Concerto) and reviewed as follows:

The composer impresses the hearer with a sense of fine talent rather than of positive genius. His choruses are sonorous, his solos are carefully put together, his orchestration is judicious. But all the time you feel that were good workmanship sometimes sacrificed to effect, were finish in construction occasionally neglected for the sake of picturesqueness, and were there a little more boldness in the selection and use of color, we should have something that would give evidence of individuality. As it is, Bruch serves as an illustration of the theories enunciated by Wagner in his famous pamphlet 'Judaism in Music'. It is all very nice, and is entirely unobjectionable, but any one of a hundred composers might have done it.

In 1898 it was given again by the Handel and Haydn Society in their triennial festival in Boston, and was still referred to as 'a grandly impressive work', but by February 1912 critical opinion had changed:

Bruch composed at a time when melody was believed to be effective, as well as satisfying. At that time it had not become the fashion to suppress a tune as soon as that delightful artifice was emerging from a nebulous state to a crystallized thing of beauty.

Its idiom is not a pronouncedly modern one, but it abounds in effective passages for a large body of singers; it is grateful and not over difficult to sing.

Bruch's music is what one might be expected of a respectable German composer writing in the 70's, a man who knew his trade, but was not burdened with imagination; music of thick, solid and four-square polyphony, in which lusty German choruses could roar themselves the evening long, with much sweating and a loud noise.

For *Arminius* was not worth reviving. Much of the music is dull, almost all of it is monotonous. It lacks intrinsic interest; it displays neither chorus nor solo singers . . . Praise ye also the Germans who are a free people — when they are not held in the bonds of such routine and monotonous music. On it goes — thick, solid, heavy, four-square as a stone wall, firmly built by one of the best musical masons, as musical masonry went in the seventies . . . There is hardly a stroke of imagination, hardly a touch of individuality, scarcely a contrast in it — the conventional choral thing in the conventional choral way . . . Of course *Arminius* is 'grateful' music. It has been the concern of Bruch all his life to write 'grateful' music — for the violin, the chorus, the orchestra, whatever medium he happened to choose.

The second half of 1875 was taken up with the composition and preparation of *Arminius*. Much of September was spent working on it at the Igeler Hof, 'on the lonely hilltop, among beautiful trees', which helped to fire his enthusiasm and inspiration. He went on in 1876 to put together more folksongs extracted from James Johnson's *Scotch Musical Museum*, as he had done during his time in Mannheim in 1864. Bruch hoped Simrock would publish a volume of folksongs each year for five years, to make a substantial collection. He actually published three volumes under the agreed title of *Denkmale des Volksgesanges* (Monuments to the Folksong), the first of which comprised Scottish songs, and the other two Welsh songs. Throughout 1876 he revised and reshaped *Arminius*, offering it to Breitkopf & Härtel before Simrock took it in August. Bruch considered dedicating it to either the Kaiser or Bismarck, but not wishing to be regarded as an ambitious medal hunter, he thought better of the idea. A month after the Zürich performance in January 1877, Bruch was making further changes, throwing out two 'weak numbers' and substituting two new ones. *Arminius* was eventually published in 1878.

In 1877, on the journey home from his trip to Zürich, Bruch stopped in Frankfurt and Wiesbaden for performances of his First Violin Concerto. He now had the opportunity to meet and get to know his soloist, the violinist Pablo de Sarasate. According to the 1899 edition of *Grove's Dictionary of Music*, 'Sarasate's distinguishing characteristics are not so much fire, force and passion, though of these he has an ample store, as purity of style, charm, flexibility, and extraordinary facility. He *sings* on his instrument with taste and expression, and without that exaggeration or affectation of sentiment which disfigures the playing of many violinists.' Harriet, wife of the violinist Fritz Kreisler, described him as 'the greatest *grand seigneur* in musical history. He looked like a grand duke. He had a mass of grey hair, but his moustache was dyed pitch black. He played with the greatest nonchalance. When he had already placed his violin under his chin and everybody thought he was about to start, he would drop it again, clamp a monocle into his eye and survey his audience. He had a way of seeming to drop his fiddle that would take the audience's breath away. That is, he would let it slide down his slender figure, only to catch it by the scroll of the neck just in time. It was a regular showman's trick of his.'[14]

During 1876 Sarasate was performing Bruch's First Violin Concerto in Pasdeloup's Paris concerts, and also in Belgium, with splendid results. Bruch was naturally grateful for the violinist's interest in his composition, and held a very high regard for Sarasate's incredible talent and superb musicianship. He instructed Simrock to send the Spaniard a copy of the newest work for violin, the *Romanze*. In February 1877 Bruch wrote ecstatically to Simrock about Sarasate's performances in Frankfurt and Wiesbaden on 2 and 8 February respectively, when together they performed the Violin Concerto with the Court orchestras of the two cities '. . . he playing, I conducting. The public went mad everywhere, I have never experienced anything like it. If I am permitted to use the expression "to rave about", then I say I rave about this Pablo. An extraordinary violinist and a charming man. I shall write something for him — that is quite certain.'[15]

In March his idea to write something specifically for Sarasate had become a decision. A second concerto was now envisaged, and the intention was for it to be ready for the soloist's next European tour, scheduled for the autumn of that year. 'It is definite . . . the main ideas are there — a product of the inspiration aroused in me by his indescribably perfect performance of the first concerto. If the Muse is well-disposed towards me, this concerto should in no way be overshadowed by the first, which is actually now played by all the world's violinists. Everyone expects and wants a second one from me.'[16]

At the beginning of May, Bruch and Sarasate, together with the French violinist Émile Sauret, were dining together in a Leipzig hotel:

> . . . it pleased me to see how well-behaved and nice the two rivals were to one another. As far as technique goes, there are some in Vienna and Leipzig who rate Sauret above Sarasate, but the latter's playing is more soulful, and in any case his technique is so faultless, it's hardly possible to imagine better. From time to time he plays stupid things; I hope by the winter to have weaned him off that! Sarasate prefers my new concerto (which, apart from details to be written, is virtually finished) to the first concerto. After he heard the

first movement (a big Adagio) for the first time, he said: '*Eh bien voulez-vous, que je vous embrasse? Tout cela est superbe!*'

A shadow was cast over this period (February 1877) by Bruch's decision to break off contact with Rudolf von Beckerath. He had hoped that his friend would attend the Sarasate concert in Wiesbaden on 8 February, but when von Beckerath failed to arrive, Bruch wrote the next day to rebuke him. It irked him that von Beckerath was able to travel 'to Carlsruhe and Mannheim to hear the symphonies of Brahms', but that he had stayed away from concerts of Bruch's music. Perhaps the Heydweiller affair had also taken its toll of their friendship, particularly with the involvement of Emil von Beckerath, when possibly sides were taken. On the other hand if, for any reason, a choice was made by Beckerath between the music of Bruch and Brahms, history has vindicated his decision. There was no further contact between the two men, and it was seventeen years later (in 1894) before a tentative approach was made by a remorseful Bruch, who wrote two or three letters to the widowed Laura. Maria Zanders had mediated by passing good wishes from the widow to the composer, but it was a hopeless attempt as Frau von Beckerath had no genuine inclination to heal the rift. The damage had been done years before, and it is clear from Bruch's letters to them how his volatile personality and tactless behaviour must have frequently tested their patience. Perhaps the answer lay in choosing between the personalities of two composers, for Brahms had an equally difficult temperament, and could be exasperatingly rude in public. There is no doubt that Bruch had enormous respect for Brahms the musician, for he was generous in his praise, and was always eager to receive new compositions from Simrock as soon as Brahms had completed them. There was, however, no love lost between the two men, and after another of their occasional meetings, Bruch wrote to Simrock from Ludwigshafen:

On Sunday *Francesca da Rimini* by Goetz (who is dead as you know) was played. Brahms came too. He is and remains a horrible fellow, and if I am to maintain an interest in his works, I must meet with him personally as seldom as possible. No one stands so high that he has a right to maintain that intellectual incognito in which Brahms excels with everyone without exception; and anyway that singular Teutonic boorish behaviour which he still has not shaken off in his 44th year, repels foreigners even more than Germans, as you can well imagine. Sarasate was quite appalled by it! He had been with Brahms, Bülow and Pohl, and now believed himself to be in a den of thieves. If I meet with Brahms in Heaven, I shall have myself transferred to Hell! As far as I am concerned, Joachim can be kicked around by him as much as he wants; I think otherwise, and if anyone does not wish to behave himself as a gentleman with me, then the Devil may take him![17]

By the middle of October, Bruch was in England for the first time. He and Sarasate crossed from Calais to Dover in inclement weather, which caused the violinist much distress and dreadful sea-sickness. Max does not appear to have suffered, on the contrary he took much pleasure in nursing the Spaniard. His first engagement was to conduct the second concert of the season on 13 October 1877, for August Manns at the Crystal Palace, and Sarasate played the First Violin Concerto. The *Musical Times* reported:

. . . Herr Max Bruch, a composer who occupies a high position on the Continent, made, we believe, his first appearance in England to conduct two of his own compositions, the Prelude to his opera *Loreley* and his tolerably well-known Violin Concerto in G minor. Though not of the highest order of genius, Herr Bruch's works show real musical feeling, a thorough command of technical resources and considerable individuality of style . . . [Sarasate] must undoubtedly be ranked as a player of the first order; and his success at Sydenham was as undeniable as it was well deserved. Herr Bruch's conducting of both his pieces was excellent.

Bruch then went on to Liverpool, where he had been invited by Sir Julius Benedict to conduct *Odysseus* on 23 October with the Liverpool Philharmonic Society, and George Henschel took on the title role once again. The *Liverpool Daily Post* reported the performance:

Last night the long talked of performance of Herr Max Bruch's *Odysseus* under the composer's own supervision took place, forming the second concert of the present season, and proved in every respect an unqualified success. . . . Both band and chorus acquitted themselves admirably under the able composer's baton, and it was satisfactory to note that the coldness which was apparent early in the evening gradually gave way to enthusiasm, Herr Max Bruch being loudly cheered at the conclusion of the performance.

The *Musical Times* was no less flattering to Bruch, though it was dreadfully patronizing to music making in the provincial North-west, with phrases such as 'running the metropolis hard for the palm of musical enterprise', and cities such as Liverpool, Manchester and Glasgow 'very nearly rival the mother city in the spirit with which musical operations are carried on'. Bruch, however, 'shows the great gift of melodic inspiration' and has 'a remarkable power of employing the modern orchestra to advantage'. Having recommended the work highly to London, where it had not yet received a performance, the review concluded:

> The Liverpool performance must be spoken of in high terms. . . . Herr Bruch, who had a flattering reception, conducted with as much skill as *connaissance de cause*, and contributed no little to the success achieved. The band played unusually well, nor did the choir fail to meet the exceptional demands upon its powers, one or two instances excepted. . . . The attendance was large; the reception of the work hearty, and the whole affair gave Liverpool reason to boast that its new musical season has already accomplished no mean thing.

From Liverpool Max proceeded to London, where he conducted the first performance of his Violin Concerto No. 2 in D minor Op. 44 at the Crystal Palace on 4 November 1877 with Pablo de Sarasate as soloist. The performance was from manuscript parts and, as a result, it was possible to make changes to the work. This also happened after the Berlin performance in January 1878. Joachim joined the 'team of violinist advisers' (Sarasate and Heckmann) in February, when he met Bruch in Barmen and Coblenz, and the composer reported to Simrock that his old friend had 'played the whole concerto from sight like the Devil, and appeared to get pleasure from it. He says: "The concerto is much easier than the first". Pablo says: "I assure you this concerto is much harder than the first". He [Joachim] also wants to perform it in public.'

In contrast to the lyrical first concerto, the second is conceived in dramatic terms. According to Wilhelm Altmann, and in spite of the composer's oft professed aversion to programme music, Bruch was impressed by a scenario offered by Sarasate himself suggesting the aftermath of a battle in the Carlist War. In the first movement (Adagio), the battlefield is littered with the dead and the dying, among whom a young woman searches for the man she loves, and a funeral march accompanies a burial procession. The second movement is entitled 'Recitative', in which the solo violin conducts a wordless monologue with orchestral interjections, leading directly into the long, fully developed Finale (*allegro molto*) which, with its lively scherzo rhythm, allegedly depicts the tumult of a cavalry regiment. The form of the concerto is certainly unusual, and provoked another sneering comment from Brahms in a letter to Simrock when he wrote that 'we all liked the last movement of his concerto, but hopefully a law will not be necessary to prevent any more first movements being written as Adagio. That is intolerable for normal people.'[18]

Brahms had second thoughts in another letter two months later: 'I was mistaken with the effect of the Bruch concerto. I considered the first movement impractical — somewhat boring.'[19] Bruch, on the other hand, thought it the best, and only Sarasate prevented him from scrapping the other two and issuing it alone. In 1891 he mentioned to Simrock that he had heard the first movement played by itself, and that it worked well. Bruch considered it to be better than anything in the first concerto, but conceded that there was no continuing intensification in the rest of the work. Hans von Bülow, still reeling from the impact of the new First Symphony of Brahms, was also critical of the concerto:

> Clumsy instrumentation, slovenly form, extremely paltry and cool fundamental ideas — on the other hand a good violin part and a clever product. In all technical matters one can consider Herr Bruch as say, a new version of Hiller . . . Ever since my introduction to the Tenth Symphony, alias the First Symphony of Johannes Brahms (in other words for the past six weeks) I have become very unamenable and resistant towards Bruch's works and the like.

The response to the inclusion of the Concerto in a concert in Bonn on 15 November (in a programme which also contained Brahms' Symphony No. 1) inflamed Bruch's sensitivities beyond measure. He reacted strongly to a report in the Bonner Zeitung, which virtually ignored his work and concentrated its attention on the new Symphony. He smarted at the public snub, the more so as the future Kaiser Wilhelm II was present in the audience (he was a student in Bonn at the time). In a letter to his friend Joseph von Wasielewski (then the city's Music Director) he alluded to the existence of a clique in the city, which was bent on elevating Brahms to the status of an idol. Bruch complained that the recognition he was afforded throughout Germany, and now also in England, was denied him in the Bonn report. He continued:

> We are dealing with a knowing and deliberate distortion of the truth, on the part of an exclusive clique, which even the single mindedness and fanaticism of the Wagnerians cannot equal. The

truth is very simple: this *clique* has taken amiss, that on the occasion of the first performance of this new Brahms Symphony, which was intended to be celebrated as a family affair, the public responded very enthusiastically to another work by someone who did not have the good fortune to be called Johannes Brahms. . . . They kill off with childish pleasure all those who also create successfully by their talent, and on the corpses they build a tall pedestal on which to place the idol of Johannes Brahms. . . . Must one continually remind them of Goethe's words 'One should love Art, and not the Artist'? . . . Can an artist not be praised without having to run down, or even kill off another? . . . The whole article is directed against me, this infamous *clique* wants to hound me out of Bonn. I am hurt to the quick, and I ask for satisfaction. If I do not receive it, no further works of mine will be performed in Bonn.

*Anch' io sono pittore*, and many thousands in many lands take the view that *Odysseus*, *Frithjof*, *Schön Ellen* and the two concertos have no reason to crawl off into a mousehole on account of Brahms' works. I have always acknowledged the extraordinary talent of Brahms, even at the time when he was universally derided, I have always defended him. Now I must leave it once and for all to those thoughtless, half-educated and stupid people, the undoubting believers, to elevate him to the position of an infallible Pope.

It is interesting to record Bruch's criticisms of Brahms' First Symphony:

The symphony is to a large part beautiful, in part also reflex music, the Finale most powerful and excellent in its simplicity and magnificence. As I have no desire, however, to grovel at his feet and then permit myself to be trodden on, like our friend Joachim, I say quite openly (and others say so too) that the first movements are in part too thickly, disadvantageously orchestrated. He singles out the winds too little, and doubles far too often, so that it sounds like music subsequently orchestrated from four-hand [piano] music. It is not a naturally born orchestral sound by, for example Beethoven, Mozart, Haydn or even the schoolboy Mendelssohn. He always orchestrates as one who only from time to time has anything to do with the orchestra. Given an opportunity, I shall tell him so in a friendly way, because he's **a cheeky fellow**, so once in a while one can be cheeky to him, **and give him one** on the nose![20]

Bruch also observed of Brahms: 'I have not written Lieder, piano music or chamber music like him, but he has written no *Frithjof* nor

*Odysseus* and will never do so.' Later he wrote, 'People like Mozart and Raphael enjoyed both Life and Love, they never resorted to the element of Meanness as [Brahms] always unceasingly does. *Il se moque de tout*, says Sarasate.'[21] It was therefore a difficult birth for Bruch's new violin concerto, and left an indelible scar on his already tenuous professional and personal relationship with Brahms, a man who from now on was to be universally acknowledged to be the great composer he undoubtedly was.

The Second Violin Concerto has never cast off the shadow of the First, in spite of Bruch's opinion of it and his efforts on its behalf. It certainly enjoyed limited popularity during Bruch's lifetime, and was played by all the famous violinists of the age (although Bruch discovered during the final preparations of the *Scottish Fantasy* that Joachim avoided works not dedicated to him — 'He has played neither my *Romanze* nor the Second Violin Concerto', he wrote in June 1880). Shortly before the Second World War, the composer's son Ewald made strenuous efforts on behalf of the concerto, and succeeded in obtaining a few broadcast performances in Germany. He continued this work after 1945, and with the help of some gramophone recordings, the concerto has become more familiar.

On 1 July 1877, Bruch told Simrock that he had received an approach from Mr Richard Peyton, President of the 1876 Birmingham Triennial Festival. The two men then met in the Hotel du Nord in Cologne at the end of June, and Peyton invited Bruch to come to Birmingham for the Festival in 1879, and conduct one of his own oratorios. The composer decided that this would be the occasion to perform his newest project, a setting of Schiller's poem *Das Lied von der Glocke*. He had started it in Bonn during the early months of 1877, the second part was written whilst staying in Bergisch Gladbach in June and July of the same year, a fair copy of the score was finished on 8 January 1878, and the full score completed on Easter Monday 1878. The first performance took place in Cologne from manuscript parts under Bruch's direction in the famous Gürzenich Hall on 12 May 1878. Barmen was the place selected for performances of the definitive version in January and February 1879, largely on account of the town's organ, which Bruch greatly admired. Simrock was reluctant to take the work at first, on account of his lack of success with *Arminius*, so Bruch paid the initial printing costs himself, and the episode caused a temporary strain in their relationship. Meanwhile his conducting activities had continued apace. At the end of May 1878 he went to England for a performance of the First Violin Concerto (with Sarasate) and *Frithjof*, both given in a concert at the Crystal Palace on 8 June. Prior to this he had conducted a performance of Bach's *St*

*Matthew Passion* in Barmen, taking the place of his indisposed friend Anton Krause, the resident Music Director. But it was the resignation of another friend, Julius Stockhausen, from the Music Directorship of the Stern'schen Gesangvereins (the Stern Choral Society) in Berlin that prepared the way for his next move. He received an official invitation, accepted the post in August 1878, and at once made preparations to return to the city he both loved and hated.

## Chapter Eleven

### RETURN TO BERLIN
### 1878–80

MAX BRUCH'S CANTATA *Das Lied von der Glocke* (The Song of the Bell) is dedicated to the memory of the poem's author, Schiller. A musical setting of the poem had previously been made by Andreas Romberg, and this work was a popular favourite with the Choral Harmonists' Society in its early days in England, retaining an occasional position in concert programmes to the end of the nineteenth century. After the first performance in England of Bruch's version (at the Birmingham Triennial Festival of 1879, where it commenced the Miscellaneous Concert on the evening of the opening day, 26 August), the critic of the *Musical Times* wrote: 'In Romberg's treatment of the text we could scarcely cite a movement which shows high dramatic power, yet there is a charming freshness pervading the entire composition. . . Max Bruch, on the contrary, has endeavoured to give almost a massive grandeur to the choral portions of his work.'

Schiller's poem is an allegory, using the processes involved in the casting of a new bell to portray the many episodes in the life of a human being, from birth to death. The selection of Schiller's poem poses the question of the suitability of such a work for a musical setting. It is a poem of power and strength, much of which eludes or even defies musical composition. The *Boston Evening Transcript* described it as one which 'dwells for the most part in an exalted poetic, spiritual and emotional atmosphere, and gives, moreover, abundant opportunities for picturesque musical treatment. Yet, with all this, a large part of the poem is of the sort which repels the aid of music, rather than invites it.' Bruch is at his most impressive when at his most melodious, and in this work his inspiration is fired by certain concepts. They can be identified as a Wagnerian-style *leitmotif* of three Fs — *Friede, Freude* and *Freiheit* (Peace, Joy and Freedom), although *Sehnsucht* and *Heimat* (Longing and the Homeland) produced a similarly ardent reaction.

The Cantata is in two parts and consists of 27 numbers. It is written for a quartet of soloists and mixed four-part chorus with full orchestral and organ accompaniment. Although numbers often end with the instruction *attacca*, each is nevertheless a self-contained section, whether recitative, *arioso*, ensemble or chorus. The stentorian opening quotes the Latin inscription to be found on the bell at Schaffhausen (though it was from the bells of Cologne Cathedral that Bruch derived as much inspiration for this work as he did from Schiller) — *Vivos voco, Mortuous plango, Fulgura frango* (I call the living, I mourn the dead, I shatter lightning). This is followed by the first statement of a motif intoned by the bass soloist, and recurring throughout the work.

Ex. 24

The critic in the *Liverpool Daily Post* described this solo after the performance in the city on 18 November 1879, quoting Natalia Macfarren's translated text: 'The Bass solo "Fast immured in earthly hollow" is a charming specimen of the composer's style, and with an organ-like accompaniment seems to breathe forth the spirit of the text . . . Herr Henschel gave a fine rendering of this solo.'

There are some excellent moments of orchestral word-painting to be found in the work. In the opening scene Bruch depicts the processing of the molten metal with effervescent writing in a dialogue between flutes and violins. Quite what Herr Henschel (or the audience) made of Mrs Macfarren's English translation of his native German is hard to imagine:

> Bubbles white the surface cresting,
> Lo, the metals glow and fuse,
> Caustic alkalis incasting,
> Not a virtue shall they lose,
> Clear the mass from scum.
> Pure it must become,
> If no flaw or taint be clinging,
> Pure and clear shall be its ringing.

A short orchestral prelude with its sequential harmonies over a D pedal-point now follows. This 18-bar interlude recalls Mendelssohn, in particular the G major organ Prelude Op. 37 No. 2, and the chorus from *St Paul* 'How lovely are the messengers'. It leads directly to a chorus, full of graceful and expressive melody inspired by the word *Freude* ('Joy shall its solemn chime betoken'), and containing another of Bruch's favourite devices, the harmonic sidestep to a key either a third above or below the tonic (in this case from D to B flat). More orchestral word-painting is found with the first appearance of the tenor soloist, as he describes the impetuousness of youth. Bruch obliges with a short orchestral interlude in which the strings play energetically up and down the stave, 'roaming the world and tarrying never'. The tenor sings of Man's first love in an aria ('O could ye linger') leading to an ensemble for the quartet of soloists and chorus, which was described in the Liverpool paper as 'replete with the most dreamy and fascinating melodies conceivable'. This accolade was understandable, for once again Bruch had responded to another of his poetic catalysts, *Sehnsucht* (Longing). In contrast to the tenor's fiery youth, the soprano soloist now intones a sweet and pastoral aria ('Sweetly in the maiden's tresses'). This peaceful mood is rudely interrupted by the trumpet call to battle (the men's chorus 'The man must afield') as the men go off to war, leaving their women behind ('The gentlest of matrons as wife and as mother') to restore a tenderness and tranquillity to the music.

A series of short recitatives now takes the action forward. The warring youth is now husband, father and landowner, determined to protect his property against the power of the elements, but the chorus declares its wariness of this defiance by Man against Nature. Meanwhile, as another age of Man has been reached, so another stage in the casting of the Bell has occurred, and a prayer of dedication is offered over the casting mould. Phrases such as 'Drive the spigot forth' or 'Down the arching ears' recesses, red the molten torrent presses' must have caused some bewilderment amongst its listeners. The Storm chorus ('Hark the signal of alarm') now erupts, 'the tempestuous fury of which almost excels in dramatic and descriptive power anything in choral writing we have previously heard', according to the Liverpool critic. It is full of both polyphonic and homophonic choral writing of great strength, even if the harmonic devices Bruch used are not as imaginative or innovative as the dramatic situation demands (he makes excessive use of both the diminished seventh and the arpeggio). Part I ends with a recitative followed by a solo quartet and chorus in which Man has survived the ravages of the storm, and gives thanks that in spite of losing all material possessions, he still has his loved ones. This quartet is introduced by the soprano ('One blest assurance yet is granted') singing one of the finest melodies in the work.

The bass soloist introduces Part II with the same motif used at the

Ex. 25

beginning of Part I. The farming analogy of reaping is deftly switched to introduce Death, the Great Reaper. The Bell now has a sombre purpose to fulfil. 'From the steeple, sad and slow, peals the bell its summons low', chants the chorus, taking the altos down to low F. The Bell has tolled for Wife and Mother, but in the alto aria ('Ah, the wife beloved is summoned') it is the orchestra which surges up in two passionate outbursts. Under the surface of all those diatonic harmonies, passing notes, suspensions and endless plagal cadences, is there an adventurous chromaticist, struggling to break free of Mendelssohn, Hiller and the like? Rarely does Bruch shake himself free of the trappings of the organ loft, show himself capable of expressing depths of feeling other than by melodic means, and dispel dullness by attracting and retaining the attention of his listener. This is one of those moments, a brief glimpse of what might have made him a great composer instead of a respected craftsman.

It also caught the attention of the Liverpool music critic, who described it as 'a glowing and fervent example of music written from the heart, and appealing directly to the soul', though the moment was obviously too fleeting for the Birmingham critic, who described the aria as 'somewhat commonplace' and overlooked the orchestral passage. At the second outburst (the first, at letter B, lasts only three bars) in the coda of No. 17 (letter E), Bruch withdraws after five bars into a bolthole of conventionalism and meekly concludes with a plagal cadence. (See Ex. 25)

Bruch's favourite element, folk-music, is now introduced in a bass solo ('while the seething metal cooleth, all may rest from labour free') followed by an Intermezzo for a trio of soloists, which also contains passages of rustic dance music. A short recitative by the bass leads to a rousing, climactic chorus to the Fatherland ('Hallowed Order, child of Heaven') full of complex polyphony and counterpoint. The next trio is a hymn to Peace (*Friede*) and is another moment of melodic inspiration, with its emotional, wide *tessitura* of the vocal line (a falling octave followed by a rising seventh). In the middle (letter C), and in the coda, Bruch introduces orchestrally the opening four bars of the Christmas carol 'Silent Night' as an evocation to Peace. (See Ex. 26)

The casting of the Bell is now almost complete, and the mould is about to be broken, though Mrs Macfarren might have considered something less prosaic than:

> Break we now the mould asunder,
> It has served its purpose well!
> Let us gaze in joy and wonder
> At our fair, well-shapen Bell.

Ex. 26

The mould can only be broken by the Master (the bass soloist); anyone else, and the release of the white-hot liquid metal would spread like an insurrection, and anarchy would reign supreme ('The mob in maddened fury enters, when Law and Order it defies'). This is the text for alto, tenor and bass soloists, leading to a substantial orchestral march depicting the rampaging mob. After the chorus has reprimanded the people for their lawlessness, attention is turned to the Master as he breaks the mould of the Bell and christens it 'Concordia'. Its duty (as outlined in the final two numbers for soloists and chorus) is to ring its message far and wide, that of Peace (*Friede*) and Joy (*Freude*), the inspiration for the last of Bruch's melodic outbursts.

'On the whole we are inclined to pronounce a favourable verdict upon the Cantata,' wrote the *Musical Times* after the Birmingham performance.[1] The critic of the *Liverpool Post* was far more enthusiastic, not only about the work, but also about Bruch as conductor and choir trainer. This positive critical response may well have played an important part in obtaining for him the post of Musical Director in the city six months later; his admiring reviewer wrote of the performance:

We cannot hesitate to affirm that Tuesday night's performance was one of the grandest achievements of choral singing ever heard within the walls of the Philharmonic Hall. Mr Sudlow [Secretary to the Philharmonic Society], by his judicious and well-directed efforts to secure adequate rehearsals for Max Bruch's work, has undoubtedly given a stimulus to his choristers, which will . . . eventually place the choir in a position of second to none in England. Mr W. T. Best was an all-powerful aid on the organ . . . and showed a mastery, even over the wretched instrument he had to perform upon, unsurpassable by any living player!

The unsolicited invitation from Cologne to mount the first performance of *Das Lied von der Glocke* pleased Bruch very much, evident in a letter to Simrock. He concluded by breaking out into English:

Mr and Mrs Simrock and the whole family are invited to come to Cologne Sunday Mai [*sic*] 12th, to ring the bell, — bum, bum, bien, bien, klingling. First Performance of Mr Max Bruch's new work: The lay of the bell. Orchestra: 2,000. Chorus: 10,000. The soli sung by Gatschakoff, Andrassy, Bismarck, Disraeli! 'Concord! concord!' . . .

Yours very truly

M. Bruch<br>(Glöckner) [Bell-ringer]

The Stern'schen Gesangvereins in Berlin, to which Max Bruch was appointed as Musical Director in August 1878, was named after its founder Julius Stern. After studies in Dresden and Paris, Stern returned to Berlin in 1846. He formed his choral society the following year, and it soon rose to prominence with the first performance in Germany of Mendelssohn's *Elijah* in October 1847. In 1872 he celebrated his 25th anniversary as its founder/conductor, but two years later was forced through ill health to make way for Julius Stockhausen. When the virtually unanimous vote went in favour of Bruch in selecting Stockhausen's successor, the offer became too tempting to refuse. Wishing Stockhausen well ('Frankfurt and its Conservatoire can congratulate themselves on having you and Frau Schumann'), Bruch also expressed his own surprise that he had been chosen: ' . . . it is to date the only German society, which has taken not the slightest bit of notice of all my works for mixed chorus, neither in former days nor in your time.'[2]

During the period spent in Berlin (1 September 1878–20 June 1880), Bruch wrote just two works, the *Scottish Fantasy* Op. 46 and *Kol Nidrei*

Op. 47. In common with virtually all his works, these new compositions were tried out on several occasions before appearing in print. Although committed to conducting duties in Berlin, he travelled extensively throughout Europe at this time, in particular to promote the Violin Concerto No. 2 and *Das Lied von der Glocke*. The latter received a warm reception in Barmen on 1 February 1879; '. . . herein lies the hope that Bruch's *Glocke*, which had a sensational success here, will again give ever richer pleasure to its listeners,' wrote the *Barmer Anzeiger*. Bruch made some tart comments on the soloists for this performance,[3] and went on to reiterate his antipathy to Berlin and express hopes of a post in England, remarkably accurate in view of events to come:

> Henschel, of course, was splendid. Fräulein Scheel (soprano), whom I recommended here, pleased very much with her strong, clear and not sharp-edged top. Mühlen [tenor] is not adequate, still has not learned to count six quavers in a bar (Trio No. 22). (In fact it is very pedantic to count six quavers in a bar in 6/8 rhythm!!) I shall not do anything more for him. Assmann [alto] at any rate went further than any artist by using her beautiful voice to sing absolutely without expression. It is and remains true (and you may name who you wish), that all other alto voices compare to Frau Joachim's as a molehill does to Cologne Cathedral. Yesterday Assmann committed so many bloomers, there was a veritable flower show among the orchestra! Yesterday's Dress Rehearsal was attended as no other ever before; the Hall and ante-chamber were sold out, and almost 200 people were turned away. This rehearsal alone brought in almost 1300 marks, let the Berlin scoundrels say what they want — the way that people everywhere take to my greatest works, is and remains their insurance, and no one can deny this fact. I am sorry to have to say that the experiences in Berlin with orchestras, press, etc. that I had to go through, have been awakened once again, together with all my former bitterness against the city which is the centre of all wickedness and meanness. I shall take the first opportunity to go to England, if a good post is offered me there.

Berliners fared no better in an observation he made regarding the current success and progress of the Violin Concerto No. 2: '. . . ]it] quickly conquered the hearts of the Russians. They surely have more music in their bodies than the people who inhabit the Imperial Capital.'[4] Having arrived in Berlin, however, and taken up residence at Rauchstrasse 27, he set to work on the *Scottish Fantasy*.

The *Fantasia for the Violin and Orchestra with Harp, freely using Scottish Folk Melodies* (for such is its full title) was composed during the winter of 1879–80. Wilhelm Altmann recalled in later years that Bruch credited the inspiration of the piece to the works of Walter Scott. The Scotsman had been in the forefront of Bruch's mind during his preoccupation with *Das Feuerkreuz*, based on Scott's 'Lady of the Lake', but work on it was currently suspended. The sombre opening of the *Scottish Fantasy* was said to depict 'an old bard, who contemplates a ruined castle, and laments the glorious times of old'. At the conclusion of this Introduction in E flat minor, with interjected recitatives by the solo violin (the same relationship between soloist and orchestra as that found in the second movement of the recent Violin Concerto No. 2), the first of the folk tunes appears, 'Auld Rob Morris' (Ex. 27). This is a richly scored melody, giving prominence both to the violin and the harp, instruments Bruch considered indigenous to the folk music of northern England and Scotland.

Ex. 27

The composer described the ensuing Scherzo as a Dance, its Scottishness to be found not only in the ebullient air 'The Dusty Miller' (Ex. 28), but also in the pedal-point open fifths in the bass, which imitate bagpipes.

Ex. 28

Bruch's lyricism burgeons in the third movement, using the song 'I'm Down for Lack of Johnnie':

Ex. 29

The work ends with a brisk Finale, its tempo indication (like the last movement of Mendelssohn's Symphony No. 3 'Scottish') is *Allegro guerriero*, and the spirit of the movement is indeed warlike. According to legend the text of the song forming the subject of this Finale 'Scots wha hae' was sounded by Robert the Bruce at the Battle of Bannockburn in 1314:

Ex. 30

It has a free style (hence the rejection of the title *Concerto* in favour of *Fantasy*), and the virtuosity of the solo part, in particular its double stopping, equals if not exceeds the technical demands of the concertos. Rich in melody, lush in orchestration, alternately lyrical and rhythmically energetic, it serves as a model of Bruch's work at the peak of his creative power. In spite of its title the composer himself often referred to it as a concerto, and instances of the title *Scotch Concerto* can be found in concert programmes. At the Philharmonic Society

Concert in St James's Hall on 15 March 1883 (the first half of which was dedicated to the memory of Wagner, who had died a month earlier), Bruch conducted the work with Sarasate as soloist. On this occasion it was not only described as *Concerto for violin (Scotch)*, but was also erroneously billed as the first performance in England. At one of his own concerts in Breslau on 28 February 1888, again with Sarasate as soloist, it was billed as *Third Violin Concerto (with free use of Scottish folk-melodies Op. 46)*. In spite of these and other aberrations (Bruch did later agree with Sarasate that 'Concerto' was more appropriate), he eventually took Joachim's advice that the work should be called a *Fantasy*. He also suggested that the four movements should always be listed, so that the word *Fantasy* would not be misunderstood to mean a short piece, 'which only lasts ten minutes'.

The *Scottish Fantasy* was dedicated to Sarasate, but Joachim was involved in the usual fingering and bowing of the solo part before the work went to press. Despite his reluctance (according to Bruch) to play works not dedicated to him, Joachim so admired the *Scottish Fantasy* that he came to play it. This was a difficult time for Bruch and his relationship with the two men. Sarasate was becoming more egotistical than ever, and frustrated Bruch beyond measure both with his laziness in correspondence and by his choice of repertoire, which, together with ignoring 'Beethoven, Bach and Spohr', was beginning to ignore his own works too.[5] Brahms' own Violin Concerto had appeared just a year earlier (in 1878) and it was now incumbent upon Joachim to play this work everywhere, initially at the expense of all others. Bruch's opinion of the Brahms Concerto was high, though qualified. He 'heard it at Radecke's played by Joachim; I like the Andante very much, I did not understand the Allegro movements, because the excess of figuration in the solo part impedes a general view of the work. Now that I have a score, I shall get to the heart of the matter.'[6]

Joachim was beginning the unpleasant episode with his wife Amalie, which led to their separation and eventual divorce. He developed an obsession that his wife was unfaithful, and that the man she was involved with was none other than Fritz Simrock. Bruch, together with many others (including Brahms), completely disbelieved Joachim's suspicions and had no hesitation in telling him as much. His friendship towards Joachim cooled perceptibly at this time, and the domestic problems facing the violinist may well have affected his playing. Bruch implied as much when he described the première of the *Scottish Fantasy*, which took place in Liverpool on 22 February 1881:

Joachim played the *Scottish Fantasy* here on the 22 February, carelessly, with no modesty, very nervously, and with quite insufficient technique — and ruined it. On the one hand he praises it all over the place, and yet, given this opportunity, he proves himself to be the old enemy and the old hypocrite. He calls Sarasate a clown, and makes fun of our relationship. It was exactly Joachim's untrustworthiness and partisanship which drove me directly into Sarasate's arms. Sarasate cares about modern works, because he has respect for them, and loves them more than the yellow-aged Spohr etc., Joachim takes no interest in them (apart from Brahms' works), plays them half-heartedly, and with inadequate technique, doing them more harm than good.

These were surprisingly harsh words about his friend and colleague. Even a year earlier he wrote that 'Joachim's jealousy of Sarasate is now a reality with which I must reckon.'[7] Sarasate 'is now mad,' he wrote, 'and openly considers himself a demi-god, and because they have treated him like one for so long in Spain, he has become one.'[8] A year later Bruch was still as harsh in his opinion of Joachim. This time it concerned his forthcoming appearance which was due in the next concert season 'on 21 February, unfortunately. I am quite guiltless in the matter of this last engagement. The Committee booked him last summer, whilst I was in Germany.'[9] This concert was preceded two weeks earlier by a performance of the other work which Bruch conceived during his stay in Berlin, though most of its composition, and the first performances together with its publication, belong to the Liverpool period: *Kol Nidrei* for cello and orchestra.

In a letter to Emil Kamphausen, Bruch described how he came upon the material for the work:

> The two melodies are first-class — the first is an age-old Hebrew song of atonement, the second (D major) is the middle section of a moving and truly magnificent song 'O weep for those that wept on Babel's stream' (Byron), equally very old. I got to know both melodies in Berlin, where I had much to do with the children of Israel in the Choral Society. The success of *Kol Nidrei* is assured, because all the Jews in the world are for it *eo ipso*.[10]

The melody of Kol Nidrei is a haunting traditional one, and has long exerted a great emotional impact on Jews. It is traditionally sung on the eve of Yom Kippur, during the service of Atonement, and its elements of remorse, resolve and triumph, corresponding to the three stages of repentance, are mirrored in the way Bruch breaks up the long-breathed Jewish melody into groups of three notes, interrupting each group with an emotional sigh by the insertion of a quaver rest.

Ex. 31

The second of the two themes referred to by Bruch ('O weep for those'), recurs as the first of the *Three Hebrew Melodies*, a choral composition with which he was also preoccupied at this time. The passage common to both works occurs at letter E in the cello piece, and at the words 'Wo badet Israel den wunden Fuss?' (Where shall Israel bathe her wounded feet?), letter A in the first of Byron's melodies.

Bruch had long been requested by cellists for a work to match those he was writing for violin. One who asked was Robert Hausmann, and it was he who was rewarded with the dedication of *Kol Nidrei*. From Liverpool Bruch wrote to Simrock, 'I have written a cello work with orchestra for Hausmann, on the finest Hebrew melody, "Kol Nidrei" (Adagio). I shall hear it for the first time here on 2 November with Hollmann, and can then send it to you immediately . . . [Hausmann] has plagued me for so long, until at last I wrote this work. It also sounds very well as a violin piece; I have already arranged it and tried it out with Schiever, and everyone says it works well.'[11]

Not only did Bruch arrange *Kol Nidrei* for violin, it also appeared in versions for viola and piano, piano and harmonium, solo piano, cello and organ, and solo organ. First he had to suffer the frustrations of hearing from afar how Hausmann was coping with the work in Berlin, where it received the customary private hearings (usually using the facilities of the Musikhochschule) that Bruch organized before entrusting any new work to the publisher. Eventually news arrived from Germany: 'Hausmann wrote to me today about *Kol Nidrei*. There is no doubt that they killed the Adagio artistically stone dead in the orchestral sessions with an insanely slow tempo. It is the old story — if you are not present yourself, they have no idea how to do a new work . . . I shall be in Berlin from the 23 December until 3 January, and I shall do the work myself in an orchestral session.'[12]

The reason Max returned from Liverpool to Berlin for Christmas and the New Year was for his own wedding on 3 January 1881. On the one hand he may have been in danger of damaging his friendship with Sarasate and Joachim at this time, but on the other he made one now which lasted until death separated them nearly 40 years later. On 22 August 1880 he became engaged to the 16-year-old Clara Tuczek. She was born in Berlin on 15 February 1864 into an Austrian family of musicians. Her aunt was the famous singer, Leopoldine Herrenburg-Tuczek, seen by the young Max in her farewell performance many years earlier in December 1861 at the Berlin Opera. Max met Clara whilst on a concert tour in the summer of 1880, and in spite of her extreme youth and the disparity of their ages, there was none of the protracted on-off theatricals of his earlier liaisons. He wrote exultantly to Simrock from Marburg on the note carrying the official announcement of his engagement (which he signed 'Max Bruch, Director of the Philharmonic Society in Liverpool'): 'What do you say now? Late, oh so very late this abundance of happiness comes to me, but not too late. You cannot imagine how much Clara loves me, and how much I depend upon the darling, perfect child. She will no longer sing in public, I want her only for myself.'[13]

He was just as ecstatic when he wrote to Hiller (with whom he was now on better terms), 'As you see, Odysseus has found his Penelope at last — late, but not too late.'[14] Four days after his engagement, Max had to leave his fiancée and travel to England to take up his new appointment in Liverpool. He had to endure three months without her (which did not help him to settle in his strange and new surroundings), and he often voiced his frustrations at the enforced separation: 'When I have my good little Clara here (I am fetching her at Christmas), everything will be the better to endure. She is such a loving, simple, modest and gifted girl! And she loves me almost too much.'[15]

He felt the need to justify his decision to marry, probably because as recently as two months earlier he was still very much the impecunious bachelor with a roving eye. He was also aware of his frankness and candour in describing his former *affaires du coeur* to his close friends. This was a postscript to a letter to Simrock in which he anticipated the joys of Liverpool by declaring, 'I shall have a really untroubled position there, and financially it will amount to much. There is no lack of friendly, alluring glances by blonde Misses, with their pretty blue or pink bonnets and pounds sterling. Whether, on the other hand, I (as a 42-year-old) should bring myself to such madness . . . who knows?'[16]

His plans for Clara were quite plainly stated: she had no future as a singer, but was destined for a career as a housewife. She must have had a strong will, even at her young age, for she went on to sing (usually with her husband on the rostrum or at the keyboard) and to win public esteem. Max wrote relatively little about Clara over the years, but he was forthcoming to Simrock when he wrote from Liverpool:

> There will be no lack of people saying that this engagement is madness; for she has no wealth, and I have as good as none, and am generally dependent on what I earn . . . anyway it would be a greater madness to marry a rich Miss on account of money, and little or no love (which would have been possible here). . . . She loves me passionately and was consumed by pain and worry when I left Berlin in June; I had always liked her, and did things for her to encourage her modest musical beginnings, but until then there had never been a word of love spoken between us; but I felt then, as I was separated from her, that her unassuming, perfectly lovely being had impressed itself deeper upon me than I myself had thought. I hesitated a few weeks, for at 42 one understands Life, and knows what the consequences are today to stand alone, and anyway I had not seriously considered marriage any more. However I felt that I loved the good, darling child very seriously and sincerely; I went to Marburg at the beginning of August, and soon everything was decided. No one knows the future, but measured in human terms, we shall be very happy together. She is better than her background, and through me she is worth introducing into the best circles. I hardly considered her musical qualities when we became engaged. I became engaged to a girl, not to a budding musician. The uncertain career (rich in disappointments) for an average concert singer (for geniuses like Frau Joachim occur relatively rarely) and that little thing one calls genius are both spared the dear child — and that is good. Protected in the house, she will pursue the best career as my loving and beloved wife. Her truly beautiful voice will give much pleasure within private circles, and she can give lessons here at a good price (as I do; I get a guinea or 21 marks for a lesson).[17]

Clara had an alto voice (hence the comparison with Amalie Joachim), and she was not quite seventeen years old when she arrived in Liverpool in January 1881. Two months later, as well as cooking the dinner and making the beds, she was singing Verdi's *Requiem* in a

Philharmonic Society concert, so it must in fact have been a remarkable voice. She was also very persuasive in overcoming her husband's attitude to the 'proper' place for his wife. Max's letter from Germany to Mr Henry Sudlow, Secretary of the Liverpool Philharmonic Society, clearly shows that he was besotted with her, and that his English, together with his emotions, had been affected:

> I have the pleasure to communicate to you, that I am engaged since a few days to a young Berlin lady, Fräulein Clara Tuczek. Between Christmas and the New Year our marriage will be celebrated in Berlin. Would you be kind enough to communicate this to the gentlemen of our Committee? You can scarcely imagine how happy I feel. In this moment, Fräulein Tuczek is staying with friends. As we are engaged only since a few days, and as I must be such a long time far from her, she would be so very sorry, when I should be obliged to leave this week for England, that I think it impossible to conduct the first Chorus rehearsal on the 23th Aug. I trust that the Committee will not be cruel enough to ask that under such extraordinary circumstances, the date of the first rehearsal might be fixed on the 23th, but I promise to leave Marburg for England on the 24th or 25th of August, and to conduct the first rehearsal on the 30th Aug. . . . I am studying English with zele, and I hope that I can speak about all musical and technical things to the Chorus without any difficulty.

His request was granted, and he enjoyed the four extra days with his bride-to-be, but on 30 August 1880 he was in Liverpool to fulfil his duties as Director of the Philharmonic Society, the contract for which he had signed just four months earlier. Rather than leave Berlin for his beloved Rhineland, he had decided to cut his ties with Germany (where he felt himself to be a prophet without honour), and reap the benefit of his fame and popularity in England — *Das Land ohne Musik.*

# Chapter Twelve

## LIVERPOOL
### 1880–83

THE LIVERPOOL PHILHARMONIC Society, currently Europe's fifth oldest surviving concert organization, was founded in 1840, and gave its first concert in a dancing academy, Mr Lassell's Saloon, on 19 March of that year. By the 1870s, the chorus numbers stood at about 100, and the orchestra comprised more professional than amateur players, many being called in from Manchester and London for the fortnightly concerts. The season's twelve concerts ran from October to April. Tickets were sold by subscription, other than those for the under-privileged classes who sat in a segregated area.

In 1867 Julius Benedict was appointed Musical Director to the Society at an annual salary of £200. Born in 1804 in Stuttgart, he was considered one of the most eminent foreign musicians to have settled in England since Handel. He studied with Hummel, saw Beethoven at Weimar in March 1827, and, after an introduction to Weber, was treated for three years by the composer 'not only as a pupil, but as a son'. After time spent in Vienna, Naples and Stuttgart, the young *maestro* went to Paris, where he was introduced into the circle of musicians which included Rossini, Meyerbeer, Halévy, Donizetti, Bellini, Auber, Hérold, Adam and David. He then journeyed on to London, where he lived (at No. 2 Manchester Square, W1) for the rest of his life. Benedict (knighted in 1871) was a prolific composer, writing symphonies, operas (the most famous of which is *The Lily of Killarney* 1863), oratorios, cantatas, ballads, piano works and orchestral pieces, in addition to his many conducting engagements. Two years after his appointment to Liverpool, he introduced extra Monday concerts, modelled on, and styled 'London Monday Popular Concerts'. The programmes of both these and the Tuesday Subscription Concerts comprised a regular diet of mixed orchestral, choral and miscellaneous solo items, generally with two contrasting soloists in each programme. Some concerts were devoted to one choral work, and it was for such a concert that Max Bruch was first invited to the city, in October 1877, to conduct *Odysseus*. Bruch's secular oratorio was the most unusual suggestion on the list submitted by Benedict for the 1877–78 season. The rest was staple fare of Bach, Handel, Hiller, Mendelssohn, Spohr, Macfarren and Sterndale Bennett — though the Musical Director was enterprising enough to propose that Mendelssohn's music to *A Midsummer Night's Dream* should be performed in a reading of the work by Sir Henry Irving or 'some other leading man', and that Wagner should come to conduct one of the orchestral arrangements of the 'Niebelungen Rings'.

Benedict's invitation to Bruch was confirmed by the Committee at its meeting on 7 June 1877, and they also agreed to reimburse the composer's travelling expenses of ten guineas. In 1879 Bruch returned for his triumphant account of *Das Lied von der Glocke* and he left the city with two auspicious successes behind him. In 1880 events began to take shape which were to culminate in his permanent appointment. Sir Julius Benedict, then aged seventy-six and in his thirteenth year with the Society, had been in indifferent health. In 1879 he had undergone an eye operation, which had proved only partially successful, but the old man had no plans to give up the post, nor any of the other activities which he undertook from his London base. Matters came to a head on 27 January 1880 during a performance of Mendelssohn's *Athalie*, described in the *Liverpool Mercury*:

> . . . the work of those he conducted was continually jeopardized in consequence of the failure of his sight. An extraordinary pair of lamps had been rigged up for him at the rostrum, but they proved of only partial assistance and rendered more vivid with their glaring light the final episode of the regular career of the antique conductor of the Philharmonic Society . . . The whole went unsteadily, and more than once utter collapse seemed imminent. Matters grew worse apace towards the close of the performance, and the suspense at one portion was almost unbearable. It seemed there could be nothing less than a positive breakdown, but the veteran knew of a haven not far ahead, and heedless of the beats or bars he skipped, he gave an appealing look at the trumpets and trombones, which they were not slow to interpret, the chorus took up the cue, and with a triumphant shout at the words 'Heaven and Earth', one of the most painful recollections of half a century of music in Liverpool was brought to as painless a conclusion as might be.

The very next day Benedict wrote his letter of resignation from London, and the three remaining concerts of the season were apportioned to Alberto Randegger and W. G. Cusins. Benedict died in 1885 at the age of eighty. The Committee met on 23 February 1880, and drew up new conditions for his successor. There was to be no more commuting from far-off London; the new Musical Director would have to reside in Liverpool. It was resolved that '£400 would be appropriated for the joint offices of Conductor and Chorus Master', and an advertisement was placed in the *Musical World*, the *Choir*, the *Era*, *Academy*, the *Athenaeum*, *The Times* and the *Londoner Zeitung*. A sub-committee was formed to consider applications from 33 musicians, among whom were Frederic Cowen, Dr Swinnerton Heap, George Henschel and Ebenezer Prout. The 'names of the following Gentlemen, who had not made any application' were added to the list: Charles Hallé, Alberto Randegger, Hans Richter and Max Bruch. This list of 37 was shortened, first to fifteen names, then to four (Hallé, Richter and Randegger were eliminated as they were unwilling to reside in Liverpool). The final choice was between Cowen and Bruch, and the sub-committee went on to recommend Bruch to the Selection Committee by nine votes to two. An exchange of confirmatory letters took place in April 1880, after which Max Bruch became the new Director of the Philharmonic Society in Liverpool.

One of the reasons given for Bruch's eventual departure, under a cloud, is that he insisted on accompanying choir rehearsals from the piano, and thus made it difficult for himself to communicate directly with the members of the chorus (or 'the Practicals' as they were known). It was, however, the Committee who insisted on combining the post of Conductor with that of Chorus Master, and it was Bruch himself who persuaded them to accede to his request for a rehearsal pianist (Horatio Branscombe was appointed at a 'salary not to exceed thirty guineas a year'). His other resident keyboard player was the famous organist W. T. Best who had been with the Society intermittently since 1848. A man of strong personality, he could be prickly in mood, and was given to an acerbic style in his notes to Sudlow. Asked to play in a certain chorus, in *Das Lied von der Glocke*, he replied: 'I shall be glad to co-operate in the cause of "Hallowed Order", and will produce myself at Rehearsal on Monday.'[1] A note of disapproval underlies his request to Sudlow for details of the extent to which Bruch wanted to use the organ (presumably to help the chorus in maintaining pitch) in Verdi's *Requiem* (or *Burial Service* as Best called it); '. . . it would, I think, be well to ascertain from Herr Bruch how far the co-operation of the organ is desirable . . . as Mr Verdi does not include the organ in any part of the score.'[2] It is doubtful if Bruch appreciated his dry English sense of humour: 'I think the "Piano" will be most useful for rehearsal,' he wrote, 'and I will tickle it up.'[3]

Bruch's English was reputedly poor, but apart from the letter excitedly announcing his engagement, the standard of his written English appears very good. His letters in English were fluent, and do not appear to have been dictated. His grammatical and spelling mistakes are no better nor worse than could be expected of a foreigner coping with the vagaries of the English language. Some of his expressions were charming, as for example when he ended a note to Sudlow, 'I hope that you will spend merry holidays in Essex.'[4] His knowledge of the language went back to his early childhood, when he spoke English and French with his father on the post-coach journeys between Cologne and Bergisch Gladbach. Liverpool had long accustomed itself to the linguistic hazards of employing a German Music Director. Benedict, even though 50 of his 80 years were lived in England, was renowned for his execrable grasp of the language. 'O for ze vinks off a duff', he would demonstrate to his choir in an attempt to obtain clear enunciation. Bruch's successor, Charles Hallé, also spent the first 30 years of his life in his native Germany. It is probable that it was purely Bruch's accent that was incomprehensible, and the amateur Liverpudlian chorister, possessing a temperament not noted for its mildness and patience, no doubt gave him short shrift. The fault did not lie on one side alone, however, for it appears that discipline among the choir was not always what was expected. A member called Fanny Bennett wrote a letter of complaint to Henry Sudlow:

> We shall be very grateful if you will kindly do something to put an end to the incessant talking and rude remarks, to which we, in the front row, are at present victims. If anything, the annoyance is worse than last season, one young person — I cannot call her a Lady — appearing to delight in making all the ridicule possible of our Conductor, and that in such a loud and insulting manner, it is quite painful to us to hear. If she is such a paragon that she does not consider Herr Max Bruch capable of conducting such talent, why does she remain in the Society? I believe I do not exaggerate, when I say that there is not a remark made by our Conductor, but she makes some comment on it such as 'What is the soft old thing mumbling about now?' 'What is the soft old thing doing; who is to understand his beat? I can't!' . . . It is simply open defiance of the Conductor and yourself, and ought not to continue.[5]

In the three years he spent in Liverpool, he conducted 35 concerts for which he received consistently good reviews (ironically his results with the chorus were singled out for special praise). 'His beat is clear and decisive,' wrote the *Liverpool Mercury* 'and his manner establishes a bond of sympathy between himself, the players who follow him, and the composer who is being interpreted.'[6] The *Liverpool Post* supported him, after his second concert on 19 October, with encouragement.

'That Herr Max Bruch has some very uphill work before him, and that he is equal to the task which he has undertaken, were alike manifested. . . . The chorus for female voices gave gratifying evidence that an important section of the "Practical Members" are rapidly becoming more tunefully "practical" under the influence of their distinguished conductor and chorus master.'

Bruch showed some restraint in the promotion of his own works during his stay in the city. Both *Odysseus* and *Das Lied von der Glocke* (after their 1877 and 1879 performances) were given once again during his time there, the former on 22 November 1881 with Clara singing Penelope, and the latter earlier the same year on 8 February. Both his latest concerted works for violin and cello (*Scottish Fantasy* and *Kol Nidrei* respectively) received premières in Liverpool, together with his new *Three Hebrew Songs*. The *Romanze* for violin was performed by Ludwig Straus on 19 October 1880, the First Violin Concerto with Sauret on 24 January 1882, and of his shorter choral works he selected *Schön Ellen* (30 November 1880), *Die Flucht nach Aegypten* (11 October 1881), the first of the five choral part-songs Op. 38, 'Waldpsalm' (24 January 1882), and *Die Flucht der heiligen Familie* (6 February 1883) with Clara as soloist. The choral works of other composers which he performed were Verdi's *Requiem*, Mendelssohn's *Elijah* and *St Paul*, Haydn's *The Seasons*, Handel's *Judas Maccabaeus*, *Messiah* and *Joshua*, Sullivan's *Martyr of Antioch* and Gounod's *Redemption*. Among the soloists he engaged were the singers Edward Lloyd, Zelia Trebelli, Joseph Maas, Giovanni Vizzani, Clementine Schuch-Proska, Emma Albani, Charles Santley, and George Henschel. His solo instrumentalists included Joachim, Piatti, Sarasate, Straus, Barth, Sauret, Hausmann, Madame Norman-Neruda (Lady Hallé), and Saint-Saëns. The French composer came on 11 October 1881 as soloist in his own Second (it should have been the Fourth) Piano Concerto and as conductor for his symphonic poem *La Jeunesse d'Hercule*. Bruch's repertoire was largely standard for the day, though an early novelty was the first performance in Liverpool of Mozart's Sinfonia Concertante K.364, which he strongly recommended to Henry Sudlow, having received a letter from two German players in the orchestra. 'Schiever and Straus would like to play a magnificent concert by Mozart (which is very seldom performed) for Violin and Viola (Tenor).'[7]

He gave opportunities to English composers such as Cowen, Stanford, Heap, Benedict and Sullivan, and in spite of his antipathy to Wagner, the composer is surprisingly often to be found in his programmes with orchestral extracts from *Die Meistersinger*, *Tannhäuser*, *Siegfried*, *The Flying Dutchman*, *Rienzi* and *Lohengrin*. Brahms is also among the composers, though only the *Hungarian Dances* and the *Song of Destiny* (which he considered 'very difficult', but was pleased with the result). It is certain that Bruch considered Brahms' new symphonies (only the first two had been written by this time) too difficult for the orchestra, given the extremely limited orchestral rehearsal time. He had plans for one of the two when he wrote to Simrock immediately after his first concert, which had successfully taken place just four days earlier. 'Our orchestra is very good. On 30 November I shall perform either Brahms' First or Second Symphony. Benedict performed the Second already two years ago — only do not ask me how! It is said to have been awful!'[8]

Bruch obviously thought better of it, for Mozart's G minor Symphony was played instead. The concerts were fortnightly, but the orchestra (which largely consisted of members of the Manchester-based orchestra run by Hallé) would appear only on the day prior to the concert, whereas the chorus was resident in the city and available to him for more rehearsal. His opinion of the orchestra remained positive throughout his stay, although he was compelled to write to Henry Sudlow about two members (Bruch's letters are quoted here in his English, complete with spelling errors): 'As to Jollyfe, the Tymbalist . . . it is a shame, really, that a member of our Orchestra does not come to the General Rehearsal, without making any excuse, and that tonight during the first part of the concert he was unable to play — evidently because he had drunk.'[9] 'Did Jollyfe send a letter of excuse to the Committee, or not? I have not received a letter from him, and find that he is a naughty man.'[10] His exasperation grew to include his first horn player. 'It is a very unpleasant thing indeed, that Mr Jollyfe is so deaf, and that evidently the instruments are not good. Very seldom the Kettle-Drums are in tune; the beginning of the Beethoven [Violin] Concerto was really awful . . . Our orchestra is splendid and could not be better than it is, excepted Mr Jollyfe and van Houte, the first horn; his playing gives me the impression that he is suffering from consumption.'[11]

Poor Mr van Houte (or Mr Vanhaute, to use the name which appeared in the printed concert programmes) was indeed terminally ill; the following year, Charles Hallé wrote to Sudlow, 'My first Horn, poor van Houte, died yesterday. I think he was your first Horn also; if I am right, may I ask you what you mean to do, and if you have anybody in view?'[12] The lack of tact that Bruch showed here, was also apparent in his uneasy relationship with Hallé during his stay in Liverpool. Hallé gave some concerts there as well as in Manchester, and there was a certain degree of poaching of players, and even of soloists. Madame Clementine Schuch-Proska was engaged by Hallé for seven concerts in the autumn of 1881, including one in Liverpool. The soprano then asked Bruch for a concert with his orchestra, and was offered and accepted one in October, just prior to her engagement with Hallé and his orchestra. Hallé was annoyed with his soloist for not referring to him during her dealings with Liverpool, but he became more incensed when Bruch defended her actions and threatened to take Hallé's letter to his committee. Henry Sudlow had to intervene and pour oil on troubled waters, to restore peace between the two German conductors.

It was the duty of the Musical Director to engage soloists and plan programmes, which were then submitted to the Committee for approval. His letters to Henry Sudlow are largely confined to matters of detail, such as orchestration, timings of works, requests for scores and parts, discussions of fees for the soloists, rehearsal schedules and duration of concerts ('Our concerts begin too late, and the interval is too long').[13]

He strongly opposed the extortionate fees demanded by some artists (particularly Italian singers) when other high-calibre artists would sing or play for sums ranging from £25 to £50. 'Albani — I am glad that I have not the responsability,' he wrote to Sudlow, 'for this engagement. I never would consent to give 150 guineas to a singer.'[14]

He was also very unimpressed by the selection of songs for the Miscellaneous Concert (in which he often accompanied the vocalist at the piano), proposed by Albani and Maas:

> . . . of course I know perfectly all good music in the world, but I don't know all this fearfully bad music, which the Italian singers are accustomed to perform in the Philharmonic concerts, I am sorry to say. I hope and expect that in the future we will not depend entirely from the Italian singers, and that we will have better programmes than now sometimes.[14]

> As to Maas' second song, I believe that 'Blumenthal' would spoil our programme, that's the wrong music, I know. Would you kindly ask him to sing something else, and adding that the Liverpool public does not like 'Blumenthal'. Perhaps that's not true, but that is all the same. I don't accompani 'Blumenthal'.[15]

He may have taken the side of the Liverpool public in making his point about the selection of repertoire, but he also had no hesitation in asking the Committee to reprimand them on the subject of talking during the performance. 'I recommend the Committee,' his memo advised, 'to take in consideration very seriously the insolence of a small minority of our public who are always talking awfully during the performance of instrumental works. . . . I have been in the whole of Germany, in France, in Belgium, Holland, Switzerland, and in the different parts of England, but I never saw that the minority offended in this way the large majority of the honest public, the artists, the conductor and the art itself.'[16] In response the Committee passed a resolution: 'that Commissionaires be placed at each of the box corridors at the next concert, and that a printed slip be placed in each of the book of words. The following form was adopted for the slip: The Committee urge the support of the proprietors in maintaining silence in the Hall and Corridors during the performance. The Refreshment Rooms will remain open the whole evening where conversation can be carried on without disturbing the audience.'[17]

He came to the defence of his chorus when necessary. The Committee wanted more part-songs in the programmes, and also a work by Macfarren, but Bruch was very reluctant to expose them or himself to risks:

As to part songs generally, allow me to suggest that *a cappella* music . . . is considered everywhere in the world to be the most difficult thing for a large mass of performers. It wants plenty of time to train a mass of about 200 performers by and by for *a cappella* music . . . the Chorus as it is now, is not able to sing in tune without sinking, 3–5 bars without accompaniment; the single voices and the whole mass are always too flat; the rule is, when part songs are to be performed, that they begin in G and end in F or in E, or that they begin in C, and end in B or in B flat. Part songs performed in this way may be a treat perhaps for some amateurs, who never did seriously occupied themselves with artistic things; but I venture to say that it is not a treat at all for the Conductor, who is responsable for all performances, and for the true amateurs of art, and for the celebrated foreign artists who come here to play and to sing etc. . . . I hope you will excuse my bad English; it is very difficult to give such a long but necessary explanation in a foreign language.[18]

I most earnestly entreat the Committee to reconsider their decision with regard to the Macfarren Chorus. The accompaniment of this piece consists of occasional orchestral chords and passages, and as the Chorus sinks in tone, the difference between chorus and orchestra when they join together is painfully apparent to musical ears. Surely the Committee do not wish to act unfairly towards me in forgetting that I have a musical reputation to lose and that, whatever may be their considerations in putting together a programme before the world, I am responsable for it.[19]

On the other hand, when the sopranos led the chorus astray in a straightforward Mendelssohn part-song ('The Lark'), he wrote to the Chairman:

> The ladies of the Sopranos committed the mistake . . . of over-looking some small rests, so that the Male and the Female parts got half a bar apart . . . although I endeavoured to set them right in good time. I can only explain their want of attentions to my signs from their looking at their music, and not looking to my baton . . . The result was particularly and seriously unpleasant to myself, as I was compelled to do what I have never done during the whole of my career as a Conductor, i.e. to stop the singing and make the Chorus begin afresh.[20]

Some of his notes to Sudlow were concerned only with practical matters: 'For the next Monday rehearsal (27 Feb.) we want the man for the bellows (Bellow-treader), as I propose to try the Funeral Anthem with Organ.'[21] Another asked for Clara to be released from her participation in Mendelssohn's *St Paul* on 21 March 1882. She was now expecting their first child and Max was 'obliged to request you to inform the Committee that the health of Mrs Bruch is just now not to be depended upon, and that it would therefore not be safe for her to sing the Contralto part in *St Paul*.'[22]

Max had returned to Berlin for Christmas in December 1880, and married Clara on 3 January 1881. The newly-weds returned to Liverpool and took lodgings at 18 Brompton Avenue, Sefton Park, a substantial three-storey building in a residential part of the city. His first concert, a week after his marriage, produced a compliment in the *Liverpool Mercury*. 'Mr Bruch conducted, and the greater warmth of the greeting he experienced must be regarded as conveying to him congratulations on his marriage, an event which took place at Berlin on Monday last week.'

Clara also received good press notices. In a review of a performance of *Odysseus* with the Bach Choir in London in March 1883, her vocal ability did not go unnoticed by the *Musical Times*. 'Of [the soloists], though all did well, Madame Bruch demanded most attention. She was suffering from a cold, but indisposition could not conceal the fact that she possesses a fine contralto voice, with almost the upward range of a mezzo-soprano, and that she uses it like a true artist. Her delivery of Penelope's music was really fine. It struck home to the audience, and secured for the singer a repute which will make her welcome when next she comes. Herr Bruch conducted skilfully.'

Two months later she sang Penelope in *Odysseus* once again, though this time under Dr Swinnerton Heap in Birmingham. The orchestra's brass section was described as 'occasionally obstreperous', but 'Frau Max Bruch, the wife of the composer, displayed a contralto voice of considerable range and power, allied to earnest dramatic feeling in the music of Penelope.'

When Bruch first arrived in Liverpool he was insecure and lonely. Soon after he had accepted the appointment, and whilst still in Germany, he had somehow heard of criticisms made in a 'penny dreadful' of the selection of a foreigner to the post. Even after his friend Henry Rensburg had sent his telegram ('Congratulations, you have been elected unanimously on printed terms you received. Secretary writes tonight. Please telegraph me your acceptance') it took a long, patient letter of reassurance, together with those from the Deputy Chairman and Chairman of the Philharmonic Society, before Bruch would believe that the knives were not out for him. Leaving Clara behind for three months could not have been easy, and it is no surprise that by the end of September 1880, even before his first concert had taken place, he was writing to Simrock, 'Liverpool is a desert . . . one should not wish to be buried here, let alone live here. You all advised me badly; if only I had stayed where I was! I miss Germany by the day and by the hour.'[23]

By the following February, however, he could write from Sefton Park in the first person plural, 'we are living very peacefully and happily in our new circumstances'. Although enjoying his own marital bliss, he was also very upset by the rapidly worsening relationship between Joseph and Amalie Joachim. The violinist came to Liverpool and played the *Scottish Fantasy*. Frau Joachim was to have sung on 7 January 1882, but cancelled one week before. The decision to divorce had been taken a few months earlier (October 1881), and it was some time before Amalie recovered enough self-confidence to sing in public. Bruch and Brahms remained loyal to her and to Simrock, and Bruch's own estimation of Brahms' character rose accordingly. The friendship between Brahms and Joachim never fully recovered from the whole sorry affair.

As the collapse of the Joachims' musical and marital partnership began, Max and Clara began their married life with a musical collaboration in Verdi's *Requiem* on 15 March 1881. In a letter to Clara's aunt Adolfine in Berlin, Max revealed the extent of the role he played in this relationship:

In purely musical respects I could be thoroughly useful to her. At the start she took everything too literally, but as I put matters in perspective for her (which is especially necessary for this type of music) her expressiveness was freed. Musically she was quite secure, and in the evening she did not make a single mistake. The middle register and the notes from D upwards rang powerfully and clearly through the hall. In my opinion she uses her chest register too cautiously—though a minus in this regard is better than a plus—. . . knowledgeable friends report only the best about the effect of her voice in the huge hall (2,500 people). The excellent acoustics favour singers. Joachim told me recently that our hall is the best that he knows anywhere, not just in England. I cannot praise too highly Clara's manner, reliability and accuracy in the ensembles. The *Requiem* has many places (also *a cappella* sections) which totally rely on vocal effects and are only attainable with very good singers. Further, in these *a cappella* parts there are very dubious modulations, discordant and confusing, in short all sorts of difficulties. However as all four soloists were excellent, there was not the slightest deviation of pitch; it was a real pleasure, when, after 20 or 24 bars of *a cappella* singing, the orchestra came in again, and the soloists had not gone flat by one iota. Our soprano was Miss Anna Williams, one of the best singers in England . . . Mr [Edward] Lloyd was the tenor, first class in every way . . . I told him in Birmingham, in 1879, 'You are the Bismarck of English tenors!' I have not heard a better tenor in my time. It is very gratifying that Clara carried herself among these people with full honours, and she has earned full recognition . . . she was received with lively and continuous applause and, to my joy, excellent artists from the orchestra (Straus, Schiever, Vieuxtemps the cellist [brother of the famous violinist] and Jacobi) enthusiastically joined in. . . . She also sang Mendelssohn's Psalm 13 (not a distinguished work) in English; it went quite well as she had studied it with English ladies whom she had befriended. To sing English in its pureness (i.e. horribly) is a nasty matter. Lisping is never beautiful, on the contrary, but this ugly, unmelodious language encourages the lisp. 'TH' sounds horrible. I advised Clara to put all emphasis on the musical effect, and that way she coped well. They pronounce Latin here like Italian, with some laughable results. Consider for example, instead of *Ag-nus Dei*, they sing *Ang-jus Dei*, or *detschet* instead of *decet*, which anyway is only an arbitrary, corrupt version of the Italian.

The experience of conducting Verdi's *Requiem* made a very strong impact on Bruch. He admired the work enormously:

It had the same powerful and magical effect upon me when I first heard it in 1877. The *Requiem* contains not places, but whole movements of the highest beauty. True music gushes and sparkles from it, a truly overpowering, melodious abundance enchants and makes me so happy. Even the most peevish German philistines cannot fail to recognize that parts of it, like the first *Requiem aeternam* and the frightening *Dies irae*, the humble, entreating, exquisite, strangely mysterious *Hostias et preces*, the wonderful trio *Quid sum miser tunc dicturus*, the magnificent *Lacrymosa*, the *Agnus Dei*, which is unique in its brilliant intensity, and several other places are seriously, deeply and truly products of genius, and effected with consummate mastery. Hiller thinks as I do, and it also made a deep impression upon Brahms.[24]

Bruch met Verdi just once, in Cologne during the Music Festival in 1877. He was very proud of a letter, which he subsequently received from Verdi (written in French from Bussetto), in praise of the *Messensätze* (which Verdi called *Messe Solennelle*).

Dear *Maestro*, you will be justly astonished that I gave no sign of life, after you were so extremely kind to send me your beautiful pieces of music. But there were many reasons. The first is that I received them very late, and I had such a lot of dull business to attend to upon my return from Cologne, one thing after another, that I was left no time to attend to pleasant artistic matters. However, I did not wish to write to you, dear master, without being able to tell you of all the pleasure I received in reading your music, truly done by the hand of a master! Everything pleased me, but above all the fragments of the *Messe Solennelle*, which are very beautiful! As modest as it is, I hope, dear master, that you will accept the sincere expression of my admiration for your learning and your talent. Thank you, dear master, and believe me your devoted G. Verdi[25]

The letter to aunt Adolfine then turned to the subject of Mozart, another composer greatly admired by Bruch:

Your news about *Idomeneo* interested us very much. In 1869 I travelled from Sondershausen to hear and see *Idomeneo* in Leipzig, where Laube began his Theatre Directorship with it. I had the same impression as you, in other words in spite of all the splendour of the work, the opera is no longer viable on the stage today. After we received your letter, we found O. Jahn's *Mozart* and read the history of the work's genesis and the first performance in Munich (January 1781). Mozart never again used the chorus in such a great and truly original way. The opera's orchestration excites me all over again, and arouses my greatest admiration. This man, with his 24 years, knew everything, and already then was virtually infallible in the domain and essence of sound.[24]

Max went on to describe Joachim's disappointing rendition of the *Scottish Fantasy*: 'in the Scherzo, he lacked Sarasate's incomparable charm and grace, the *cantilena* in the first and third movements were too restless, the series of trills in the Finale were slow, and the top notes were completely missed. He played from the music (which I never like), and one had the impression that this normally great violinist was not in command of the situation. The disappointment was universal. I cannot explain the cause other than his psychological state.' Max reported that Hausmann and Hollmann had now played *Kol Nidrei* in London (Crystal Palace) and in Russia, and Delsart was due to play it in Paris. That week (mid-October 1881) he would send it to Simrock for printing.

It was the year of the assassination of Tsar Alexander II, torn apart by an anarchist's bomb thrown into his carriage on 13 March 1881. 'The dreadful death of the Emperor Alexander,' Max continued in his survey of current events, 'has shocked us deeply. Much will change now in politics. We are surrounded by enemies, and we shall experience sadder and more terrible things in the future.' But for the present, their lives were domestically blissful and secure.

Clara told her aunt that they were often at home, and preferred it that way ('we are both domestic animals'), though that night they were invited to a reception given by Lord Derby ('one of the top aristocrats here'). They travelled to friends in the country near Birmingham and in Cheshire, and found themselves among a thriving expatriate German community based around the Union Club. But although Liverpool itself had culturally little else to offer, Clara had occasion to describe a visit by a travelling theatre and opera company.

> Liverpool is somewhat monotonous, and it was a change to have a visiting company. We saw *Othello* and heard *Lohengrin*. It was my first time. Much was lost on me in the play, as I could not follow the language so fast. I was entertained from time to time by *Lohengrin*, though even in this most melodic of the Wagner operas, I longed for a coherent melody. It is almost always RECITATIVE, that is tiring. The performance and décor were brilliant, wonderful costumes and effects; my ear will still not yet get used to singing in English, but at present it simply must. The Greek Penelope must sing in English. It is a pity! We are doing *Odysseus* on 22 November, but I still have time to patch up the English.[26]

Clara did her best to make Max feel at home, 'I try with all my might, as far as possible to preserve a German way of life in our house, and I cook German meals to keep the dear composer in a good mood, that is my sole interest.'[26] Two weeks later Max wrote to 'Tante Fine' that 'Saint-Saëns was here for a week, played and conducted for us on 11 Oct. Then he gave two very well-attended organ recitals, and took £120 away with him (not bad!). As we had to invite him, Clara rose to the occasion with her first real dinner. The table looked charming, and what was on it was not to be sneezed at. Everything went brilliantly, and the little housewife was accorded full honours.'[27]

Bruch seems to have considered aunt Adolfine able to understand the most detailed musical facts and figures.

. . . on 7 March the eleventh concert is *The Martyr of Antioch* by Sullivan (one must throw a bone now and again for English chauvinism to gnaw) . . . our chorus has improved, and the orchestra is still first class. We play symphonies with 26 violins (14 firsts and 12 seconds), 8 violas [8 cellos] and 7 double-basses etc. . . . Hausmann and Barth have no doubt told you the news. It was a real pleasure to have those two good German friends here. They both were a success. Their opinion of Bülow's orchestra was generally the same as yours. We do not need such conducting virtuosos to tell us how to perform Beethoven's symphonies. Like you, I heard all these works performed excellently by such masters as Hiller and Rietz (my memory does not go as far back as Mendelssohn).[28]

It was not long before Clara became a mother as well as housewife. Their daughter Margarethe was born on 29 August 1882, and Simrock was one of the first to receive the news from the proud father: 'I am delighted to inform you and your dear wife of the happy birth of a healthy, strong girl. At present all is well.' Two months later he was still full of fatherly pride, 'be prepared to receive at least 372 cradle songs.'[29] The summer of 1882 was domestically perfect. Aunt Adolfine arrived from Germany to be present at the baby's birth and attend to mother and child, but the restless Max was beginning to consider a change from Liverpool. His thoughts were not, however, directed towards Germany, but further north in Britain, to Edinburgh.

Henry Sudlow, Secretary to the Philharmonic Society, was holidaying in Harrogate, when he received an enquiry from Frederick Corder, a young composer and conductor. He had heard a rumour that Bruch 'had resigned, or was about to resign his post', and sought to put his name forward for consideration in the event of a vacancy. He was 'desirous of leaving my present post as Musical Director at the Brighton Aquarium, because the place is becoming disreputable and there is no support to be given to good music.'[30] Sudlow, no doubt irritated at having his holiday disturbed by the letter, replied abruptly that 'any rumour you may have heard on the matter referred to is without foundation'. Whether Corder did in fact know that Bruch had been approached by the authorities in Edinburgh, with a proposal to move to the city, is not known. Corder had been a pupil of Hiller, and was grateful to his German teacher for the recommendation which secured his 'Capellmeistership at Brighton', in May 1880 (six hours' conducting a day for £400 a year). He could well have been informed by Hiller that Bruch was unhappy in Liverpool and might be moving. Bruch had written to Hiller to obtain advice on the subject of administration in Conservatoires, in which Hiller had gained experience in Cologne:

> . . . Yesterday I received the official offer from Edinburgh, the Directorship of a Conservatoire yet to be established, and the Directorship of Concerts in Edinburgh and Glasgow. I am offered £700 for the work at the Conservatoire, and £300 for directing the Concerts, a total of £1000. Here I receive only £400, plus virtually meaningless perquisites . . . £700 is guaranteed, and one for the outstanding £300 is expected. All in all, everything is now up to the Committee in Edinburgh to ascertain by what means they can put the project together. When the matter is further advanced in its planning, I shall be asked for details of organization. It would be very valuable if I could be privy to the organization of the Cologne Conservatoire. The Edinburgh institution will, as in Cologne, be privately funded; there is no hope of State support, on the other hand it is possible that the City Council may do something . . . As a rule one can assume that when such projects are undertaken in this country, given that the means may be there, or may soon prove to be there, it will be successfully followed through.[31]

The letter had started with Max's disappointment at not being able to convey to Hiller an official invitation to play at the opening concert of the 1882–83 season. Max wanted him to play a Mozart piano concerto, and there was also talk of performing Hiller's own *Loreley* Op. 77. Max was unfortunately frustrated by the members of the Selection Committee, absent and holidaying 'on their Welsh and Scottish estates'. He had already agreed a fee with Hiller ('I think we can offer you £50 (1000 marks), but more would not be possible because the mad expenditure on Albani and other *prima donnas* has created a deficit'), and now was forced to withdraw the offer much to his extreme embarrassment. A month later he wrote again, in the meantime having tried fruitlessly to get the Committee to accept his advice:

. . . Now it has been shown that these people (who generally understand as much about music as a donkey does about lute playing) had something else planned for 10 October, and no power in Heaven or Hell will compel them to change their plans and adopt ours . . . we have suffered a defeat, which has so vexed the President of the Selection Committee, that he told me he wanted to submit his resignation. There are too many cooks on the Committee, and I do not have to tell you that they very often over-salt the porridge. Regarding Edinburgh, were the matter farther advanced than it is, I also would have responded with my resignation. As it is, however, two very necessary things are still lacking, money and agreement; a speedy end to the matter is not expected, meanwhile I must submit myself to the decisions of the asses here! The 10 October is definitely impossible. I really do not know what is to be done now. We must shelve the lovely plan. I am so annoyed by the stupidity of these wretched cotton-merchants, that it was some days after the Committee meeting before I could write to you. Please do not take it amiss![32]

Max was very disappointed when the authorities in Scotland finally abandoned the scheme for lack of funds. He had already drawn up a detailed scenario of what he hoped to do there, particularly regarding the Conservatoire. He had plans for teachers listed in his notebook for 1882, requiring 'two for violin, one for cello, two singing teachers and one organ teacher, and one for harmony and counterpoint. I shall teach score-reading and playing. Teachers for form, advanced composition, orchestra and song classes, teachers for wind instruments.' He proposed a library to serve both the music school and the orchestra, and he drafted details of concerts (twelve fortnightly in Edinburgh and Glasgow between October and March; six each in Aberdeen and Dundee, and two in Inverness). He wanted to find out how many towns had choral societies, the distances between places where concerts might be given, the names of freelance players in Edinburgh and Glasgow, the need for an Edinburgh-based assistant conductor for concerts in the smaller towns, and a paid secretary. He also listed questions regarding other musical organizations which might already have commitments to the area. He was very interested in the cost of living, prices of houses, and the opportunities for private teaching not only for himself, but also for members of the orchestra. All these plans foundered, as he explained to Hiller:

> I soon got over the failure of the Edinburgh project, for quite early on I realized that nothing would come of it; the one wanted too much, the other too little, and too few wanted what was right. When things went wrong from the outset, the Edinburgh Committee demanded permission from me for them to use my name as matters developed. I must have been a fool to allow that to happen. It did not occur to me (seen against my own Committee here), that I would be hopelessly compromised as a result. Further, I made it a *conditio sine qua non* from the outset that my going there was subject to the simultaneous establishment of a permanent orchestra and a Conservatoire, in as far as I made it clear to the people in Edinburgh that there was no question of a musical life there without an orchestra. Edinburgh agreed with this, but not Glasgow, but because Edinburgh has the intelligence and Glasgow the money, once again the latter was victorious. In the end a very modest Music College has been created in Edinburgh, a ludicrous mouse of a thing to which Frederick Cowen was called as Director after my withdrawal. Scotland still has no orchestra; it makes do with the occasional guest appearance of the orchestra of Hallé or Manns. The main point is that everything stays as it was.[33]

In November 1913 Sir James Donaldson (then Principal of St Andrews University) wrote an article in the *Dunedin Magazine* entitled 'A Scottish Academy of Music for Scotland'. By the omission of Bruch's name from the account of events around 1880, it would appear that Max might perhaps have overestimated his role in the drama. Hans von Bülow and Alexander Mackenzie had been ardent supporters of the scheme, which was promoted by the Scottish Musical Society; but the Reid Professor of Music at Edinburgh University (Sir Herbert Oakeley) strongly opposed it, especially when it appeared that he was unlikely to be offered the post of Director. According to Donaldson, Alexander Mackenzie was the only suitable candidate to head the new institution. Unfortunately Mackenzie had fallen foul of the music critic of the *Scotsman*, and his nervous disposition was unable to endure the attacks on him in the press. In 1881 he left Scotland for London, becoming Principal of the Royal Academy of Music in 1888 and remaining in that post for 36 years. His departure sealed the fate of Donaldson's plans for a Music College because the financial backers immediately withdrew their support. In Bruch's notebook, written during his days in Liverpool, all the detailed questions he wished to put to the Scottish authorities are listed, and mention is made of a Dr Donaldson in the draft of a covering letter. This is dated 11 July 1882, so it would appear that Donaldson made another attempt to launch the scheme, but without the necessary financial backing. In Donaldson's 1913 account, he takes events no further than Mackenzie's departure, nor is there any mention of the creation of a smaller College under Frederic Cowen.

Bruch's association with Scotland was therefore to remain purely in the musical inspiration he derived from its folk music. A misunderstanding prevails concerning an incident in 1899 on the subject of Elgar's new *Enigma Variations*, which the Scottish Orchestra in Glasgow were considering for performance. In a letter to A. J. Jaeger, Elgar wrote, 'When will those Vars. (score) be ready? I think my MS must have frightened poor Bruch at Glasgow — so they have put off the performance and probably I shall have to thank your firm for another entire loss of performance.'[34] The Bruch to whom Elgar referred was not Max, but a German conductor and composer called Wilhelm Bruch. He was born in Mainz, studied law in Leipzig but began his conducting career as a Kapellmeister in Strasburg. After a guest appearance, he held the appointment as Musical Director of the Scottish Orchestra for an unhappy two years (1898–1900). He pined for Germany and became utterly miserable during his stay in Glasgow. The poor man's problems were made worse by bad English, which never improved owing to his total inability to comprehend the Glaswegian accent. He returned to Germany and became conductor of the Philharmonic Orchestra in Nuremberg until 1918. He wrote two operas (*Hirlanda*, Mainz 1886, and *Das Winzerfest am Rhein*, Nuremberg 1903), Lieder, works for violin, symphonic poems and chamber music.

Sir Henry Wood wrote about Wilhelm Bruch ' . . . it occurs to me that the Scots' temperament inclines towards a foreign name. On one occasion, when a permanent conductor was sought, [Hans] Richter recommended a certain Wilhelm Bruch. He could not speak a word of English, and hated the cramped life of Glasgow — no cafés, no lager, everything closed at night, and deadly dull on Sundays! The band nicknamed him Sleepy Billy, as he evinced excessive boredom. After the first month, the first English he spoke was to express a longing to go home. Home he went after a season in Scotland.'[35]

Max Bruch referred to Wilhelm Bruch just once in a letter to Simrock from Breslau probably after the publisher had received a copy of *Hirlanda* from Wilhelm. This may have prompted an enquiry

to Max to see if the two were related, but the response he got must
have left Simrock in no doubt.

> This Wilhelm Bruch's relationship to me is questionable, as you
> suppose. He is only a terribly distant cousin; the relationship cannot
> be exactly established, but our great-grandparents are the common
> denominator — that is quite enough! In short, this exceedingly
> arrogant Wilhelm who has written to 'wretched' publishers is
> primarily an ass. Ten years ago (1876) his mother asked me if I
> would advise him to become a musician; I replied 'No', his talent
> was insufficient. The fool discovered this, and was so angry that he
> avoided me for years (which suited me very well). Eventually he
> overcame his hatred and visited me in Berlin on his way to Posen (at
> that time he was a 'Kapellmeister' in the summer season in Posen —
> another fine career!) Now he is appointed to the theatre in Mainz
> and writes operas. The basic purpose of the letter of the high and
> mighty simpleton is as follows: 'I have written an opera, which is
> splendid. I now place it at the disposal of miserable publishers and
> others, and to a certain Simrock in Berlin who unfortunately
> usually publishes the dreadful stuff of my cousin, the phony M.B.
> This Simrock is now obliged to hurry *ventre à terre* to Mainz to hear,
> praise, buy and print the opera' . . .[36]

Max Bruch's disappointment concerning Scotland was consoled
by the confirmation of plans for a visit to America, scheduled for
the following spring of 1883. He had already been approached a
year earlier regarding a possible visit in 1882, but matters had been
left too late to organize sufficient concerts to make the trip
worthwhile. Bruch had already turned down the offer of a post in
New York, and the tour was salvaged from the abortive negotiations. His arrival in New York was planned for 1 April, and
twenty concerts were scheduled for the tour. He was to return to
Europe in mid-July and resume his duties in Liverpool during
August. Although his American trip followed the plans of October
1882 described to Simrock, his destination upon leaving America
was to be Germany rather than Liverpool. In November 1882 he
reported to Simrock:

> I have curious news to report to you, and I would find your opinion
> valuable. Scholz is leaving Breslau and is going to Frankfurt. Thirty
> people, mainly young, have applied to Breslau, but the Committee
> of the Orchestral Concerts have approached me, through Joachim,
> with an enquiry as to whether I might take the post. Joachim did not

Max as a child

In his thirties

At the time of his
American tour in 1883

Clara Bruch

*Left:* Christian Gottlieb Bruch, Max's grandfather

*Right:* Maria Zanders at the time of her marriage

Max Bruch and Joseph Joachim

Bruch's three sons: *l. to r.* Hans, Max Felix and Ewald

Max Bruch in his Berlin study, *c.* 1911, photographed especially for
the American journal *The Musical Courier*

*Left:*
Igeler Hof
1908:
Max at a
window

*Right:*
Igeler Hof
1908:
Max and his
sister
Mathilde

*Above:* Bruch in 1919, aged 81

*Left:* Margarethe Bruch in 1930

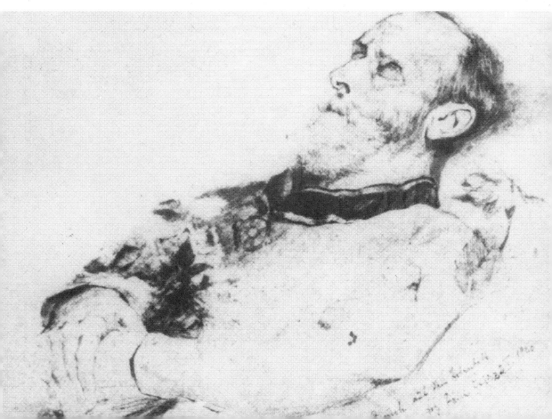

Bruch's handwriting

Bruch on his deathbed: 2 October 1920

write to me, but used the intermediary of my wife's aunt. He said that the post is so wonderful, that, were he free, he would take it himself, a manner of speaking on which I lay little value. Only five or six months' work (end of October till the end of March), almost seven months quite free (here it is five), about 6000 marks salary. Ten to twelve orchestral concerts, but no choir. Do you think I should seriously consider it? It appears to me that it would be a step back rather than forward, as if I would be stepping down in the world. It does not appear to me to be a first-class post, like the one here. And Germany above all else! I am already frightened to return to that world of pettiness, meanness, envy and wretchedness. The English are often stupid, but not mean or nasty. On the other hand I do not want to stay here for ever. Life is terribly expensive, and you get nowhere if you are not also a businessman like Hallé and Benedict etc. One day I want to go back to Germany, but not at any price. I have asked for time to consider, but you may well say there is nothing to consider, just reject it. Anyway tell me what you think.[37]

Both Max and Clara deliberated for some while before taking the decision to leave Liverpool and accept Breslau. At the end of November Clara reported to Maria Zanders' daughter, Margaretha:

. . . we are naturally unsettled by the Breslau business, as Max cannot make up his mind whether to accept it or turn it down; I think we shall never know the feeling of being at home, for it would do us both good to be settled once and for all, especially now that the family is larger by one. I wish so much for our own home, whereas here we live in lodgings, and this is now becoming more disagreeable. At first I was so enthusiastic at the thought of returning to Germany, that I was all for accepting the job, but on closer examination this is no longer the case. As Max is torn from day to day between being for and against, we shall only be at peace once again when a decision has been made, whatever it may be! You know yourself how domesticated my husband is, despite all the artistic trappings, and how he loves stability; I do not wish to break up the home so soon after establishing it, so I think we will stay here in the end.[38]

Max wrote to aunt Adolfine two days later:

. . . meanwhile I am in a dreadful dilemma over the 'Breslau Affair', for it is not so easy to make a decision. A number of people have expressed their opinion, in fact each one says 'I will give you good advice on condition that you do not follow it!' Hiller says 'Everything speaks against Breslau', Reinecke says 'Everything speaks for Breslau, come back to Germany!' Clärchen and I considered it all for a long time last night, without being able to reach a decision. I wish an angel would come down from Heaven and tell me what I should do! In many ways Liverpool is not good, but Breslau does not appeal to me either. One must accept the lesser of two evils, and in the end that is probably Liverpool. But my Committee here is so stupid, too much happens here which is contrary to my wishes, and I have to publicly put my name to wrong resolutions passed by twenty blockheads — in other words I must account myself publicly responsible for matters which I neither wish nor can be responsible for, but which I am powerless to oppose — because in this country with its crass democratic attitudes, no one has any power. Perhaps matters will improve because of this business. In any case the thought of returning to the petty and hateful musical faction fighting of our dear Fatherland is not an agreeable one. God knows what will happen, but Germany is once again the land of petty grumblers, and in this respect England is better.[39]

In spite of what appeared to be a decision in favour of Liverpool, he changed his mind after Christmas 1882, and accepted the Breslau position on 3 January 1883, just three days before his 45th birthday. There is no doubt that, by this time, Bruch's relationship with his Committee was not a happy one. His friend, Henry Rensburg, who was so influential in getting Bruch elected in the first place, had moved from Liverpool to London, and with his departure Bruch lost an invaluable ally. The embarrassment of having to withdraw his invitation to Hiller was deeply felt, and matters were made worse by the inclusion of Gounod's oratorio *The Redemption* against Bruch's advice. He neither considered the work to be very good nor suitable for the Philharmonic Chorus. Nevertheless he fulfilled his duty by conducting it on 20 March 1883. He finally decided it was now or never if he was to get back to Germany, and so, from Winnington Hall, Northwich, Cheshire, where he spent New Year with friends, he wrote to Henry Sudlow:

You will oblige me by communicating to your Committee, that in December I have received the offer of the position as conductor of the concerts in Breslau, the capital of Silesia and the largest provincial town in Germany, and that, after very careful consideration, I have come to the decision to accept this honorable offer. In consequence of this decision I am now compelled hereby to give formal notice to the Committee of the Liverpool Philharmonic Society of my intention to terminate my present engagement on the 1st May next, in accordance with my agreement with your Society.

Allow me, my dear Sir, to express through you to the Committee the sincere regret with which I leave my present position as conductor of such distinguished a Society, but my intention having always been to return sooner or later to my native land, I could not refuse so favorable an opportunity, which might not have offered [sic] again for many years. I intend and hope to visit England frequently in the future, and I trust it may be my good fortune to keep up those friendly relations with the Liverpool Philharmonic Society which I value very highly.[40]

Alfred Castellaine (Chairman of the Liverpool Philharmonic Society) replied most courteously expressing the Committee's regret at Bruch's departure, but offering congratulations on the new appointment and wishing him well. 'The Committee,' he continued, 'desire to acknowledge the talent, care and attention which you have bestowed upon the production of the different works which have been given in Liverpool under your direction.'[41] Castellaine was also moved to send Max a personal letter, expressing his congratulations and good wishes. Max was also especially pleased to receive a letter of good wishes from the Chairman of the Chorus Committee, William Roberts:

> . . . I may say that I shall always have a kindly recollection of the great courtesy you have always evinced towards myself and colleagues as representatives of the Chorus of the Society, of which you have become during the past three years its able and esteemed conductor. I need not tell you that I shall look forward with much interest on your future career and doubt not that, God giving you health and strength, you will be enabled through your great talent and ability, to still further advance the art of music by the production of new works that will add new laurels upon your head, and place the Divine Art under still further obligations to you.

Arrangements for the American tour were now finalized, and Bruch was required to ask for a release from his contract immediately after the penultimate concert of the season (Gounod's *Redemption* on 20 March 1883). This was granted by the Committee, though his request for the loan of scores and parts of his own works for the

duration of the trip was declined. The last concert of the season was
given to Alberto Randegger, and in due course Hallé succeeded
Bruch in the post.

His conducting commitments of the period 1880–83 in Liverpool
had virtually brought the production of new works to a standstill.
He completed the *Scottish Fantasy* and *Kol Nidrei*, and then worked
on the *Three Hebrew Songs*, which (like the other two works) had
been started in Berlin. They are subtitled 'after Lord Byron's Hebrew Melodies', and are for mixed chorus and full orchestra. The
melodies are not original, but the work of Isaac Nathan. He published them in 1815, having first attracted Lord Byron's interest and
then persuaded the poet to compose a text. According to Nathan's
letter to Byron he had 'with great trouble selected a considerable
number of very beautiful Hebrew melodies of undoubted antiquity,
some of which are proved to have been sung by the Hebrews before
the destruction of the Temple of Jerusalem.'[42] The duo of Nathan
and Byron set 26 poems, which were an immediate success and
brought the composer instant fame. Nathan went on to lead a life full
of adventure and misfortune. He was a compulsive writer of letters
to newspaper editors, a duellist and a litigant. His varied careers
included music teacher to Princess Charlotte (daughter of the future
King George IV), author of a *History of Music*, and even a spy on
behalf of Queen Caroline, and a secret agent on behalf of King
William IV (though only on Nathan's word). By December 1840
Nathan's fortunes were at a low ebb, and he emigrated with his
family to Australia, where he became the 'Father of Australian
Music'. His eventful life ended bizarrely, even considering some
of the experiences of this colourful character. At the age of seventy-
four he was crushed to death beneath the wheels of the first horse-
drawn tram in Sydney.

The popularity of his *Hebrew Melodies* had declined by the time
Max Bruch encountered them. They were out of print by 1861, but
it is possible that a member of the Stern'schen Gesangvereins in Berlin
showed them to him during his two year tenure of office there. A
manuscript score of Bruch's orchestrated version still exists in the
Liverpool Public Library, given as a birthday present to his sponsor
and close friend, Henry Rensburg, and dated 1880. The second page
of this manuscript bears the inscription, 'Philharmonic Society,
Liverpool' in Bruch's handwriting. The third Melody appears to
have been added slightly later (it is dated 16 December 1880 and also
dedicated to Rensburg). Bruch arrived in Liverpool at the end of
August, so it is fair to assume that he orchestrated the first two
Melodies between September and November 1880.

In the manuscript score, the order of the three choruses is 1. 'She walks in beauty', 2. 'On Jordan's banks', and 3. 'O weep for those'. When the work was published (with no opus number) by Breitkopf & Härtel in 1888, the order was completely changed to 1. 'O weep for those', 2. 'She walks in beauty', and 3. 'On Jordan's banks'. Each is a hymn-like homophonic chorus of several verses, with the only variation at each repetition being a slightly more florid line for the inner parts or the bass. The middle chorus is scored for strings, solo flute and solo clarinet until the last eight bars, when full wind, horns, trumpets and organ join, but the remaining choruses require full orchestra with organ. Though appearing today to be no more than three simple hymns of no striking interest, they were well received at no less than three Philharmonic Society concerts (2 and 30 November 1880 and 21 November 1882). Curiously only two of the three were ever performed at any one concert, though 'On Jordan's banks' was sung at all three, having scored an immediate success with the public and being recalled 'by desire' according to the programmes.

The *Hebrew Songs* were followed by *Four Choruses* for unaccompanied male voice choir Op. 48, which once again used texts by Eichendorff, Uhland and von Scheffel, though the poetry of Freiligrath as a source was a new departure. They were also arranged for mixed chorus, and are typical examples of Bruch's expressive, declamatory style of chorus writing. They are more varied and contrasting than the *Hebrew Songs*, ranging from the tranquil mood of No. 1 'Morgenständchen' and No. 3 'Friede den Schlummernden' (Peace to the Slumberers) to the boisterous drinking song 'Trinklied'. Bruch considered the fourth chorus 'Media Vita' to be 'one of the best which I have written for male voice choir'. The text, like that of his *Normannenzug*, is taken from *Ekkehard* by von Scheffel. 'Media vita' is a six-part chorus subtitled 'The Battlesong of the Monks', and is divided into a three-part tenor chorus (the Monks of Reichenau) and a three part-bass chorus (the Monks of St Gallen), both groups combining at the richly textured D major conclusion, taking the second basses down to D below the bass stave.

Clara was the dedicatee of Bruch's other completed work of the Liverpool period, the *Lieder und Gesänge* Op. 49. The seven songs (in two volumes) use authors familiar from previous works, and as the title suggests, are a mixture of Lieder and folksong. They are 1. 'Lied des Rugentino' (Goethe), 2. 'Der Einsiedler' (Eichendorff), 3. 'Ungarisch' (Folksong), 4. 'Serenade' (Kruse), 5. 'Weg der Liebe' (From the English by Herder) part one, 6. 'Weg der Liebe' part two, 7. 'Kleonike's letzter Wille' (Kruse). Bruch wrote to Simrock and asked £40 for them. He continued:

*Der Einsiedler* [The Hermit] (Eichendorff) has made a deep impression on all deeply sensitive and seriously minded people; the accompaniment must be played very well, tenderly and legato — the songs do not lie high, mostly in the [Amalie] Joachim range. *Das Lied des Rugentino* (Vol. 1 No. 1) was originally for baritone, and notated in the bass clef. I would like you to publish it separately in this form. The verse from H[einrich] Kruse's *Marino Faliero* is funny, Italian and charming. A real tenor song. Look out for the delightful words in the middle section . . . I know the song *Frage* (Liebliches Kind) by Brahms, but it has remained quite unknown, and is not one of his most beautiful works; I therefore had no reservations in composing it. I also know the Duet *Weg der Liebe*. *Kleonike's letzter Wille* (an excellent poem from Kruse's *Mädchen aus Byzanz*) must be whispered softly and eerily. I have orchestrated it, as well as the *Romanze des Rugentino* but only for my private purposes.[43]

The *Lieder und Gesänge* did not have the initial success Bruch wished for, and provoked another outburst to Simrock. 'I do not wonder that the collection of blockheads called the public have not meanwhile taken note of my Lieder Op. 49, for I no longer wonder about anything.'[44] This bitterness was largely provoked by the critical response to the *Scottish Fantasy*, which had nevertheless found favour with musicians and public alike. Bruch even declared to Simrock that he would stop composing when he had reached his Op. 50, and continued:

The *Scottish Fantasy*, which even gives pleasure to people like Brahms and Joachim, is torn apart everywhere by the mob of critics. One can bear all this for many years, but there comes a time when disgust and bitterness overpowers a creator, and one says to oneself, 'how much longer do I cast pearls before swine?' I shall withdraw into myself, my house, my loved ones, and my daily duty, and only now and then will I dream that there was once a time when I fought with Good and Evil in the dust of the arena. This is more than a passing mood, I have for a long time had no other desire than to withdraw from this miserable commotion. Since I now love and am loved, and have at last found the simplest and deepest happiness, it has lost the last of its charm for me.

I saw the latest published works of Brahms with my usual interest. As far as Dvořák is concerned, I tell you this as a well-meaning friend: be a bit choosy, in spite of Joachim and Brahms. He is a talented man, but is quite a bit overrated in certain quarters.[45]

Happily, his creative spirits for composition lifted towards the end of his stay in Liverpool. Walter Damrosch commissioned a new symphony during 1882 for performance the following year by the Symphony Society of New York. The singer Hermine Spies, who took up the *Lieder und Gesänge* in 1886 and often promoted them, also asked for a work. Bruch began immediately on what was to become the *Szene der Marfa*. The success of the Liverpool performance of *Odysseus* on 22 November 1881 (no doubt helped by Clara's presence as Penelope) stimulated him to resume work on what was to become his next large-scale oratorio, *Achilleus*. For a while he considered entering a competition for composers in Vienna in February 1882, and sketched *Das Lied der Deutschen in Oesterreich*, but finally changed his mind, largely because he felt that a quotation from *Arminius* in the work would infringe Simrock's copyright.

After travelling to London to conduct *Odysseus* with the Bach Choir at St James's Hall on 8 March 1883 (again with Clara singing the role of Penelope), Bruch returned to Liverpool for his final concert on 20 March to conduct Gounod's *Redemption*. It was then time to pack his trunks for the trip to America, though Clara and daughter Margarethe were left behind in Liverpool. Perhaps the essence of the uneasy relationship between Bruch and Liverpool lies in a letter to Hiller written in November 1881, a year after his work there had begun: 'As far as I am concerned, I live well and sufficiently and I am very happy at home, but, all in all, I regret almost every day that I came to England. I am too much a German, and my whole being and feelings are too deeply rooted in German soil for me ever to consider myself to be at home among the driest, most boring, most unmusical race on earth. Yet one must recognize that in musical matters they are merely stupid, and not malicious or narrow-minded, like our dear country-men.'[46]

His arrival in Liverpool had been heralded in the Press, but his departure hardly received a mention. His reputation has remained: an autocratic perfectionist, impatient and cynical, a man of impulse, but a highly talented and respected musician. Liverpool had had in its midst one of the foremost and eminent of contemporary musicians, sensitive to the insensitivity of committees, misunderstood by those who could never have understood, but held in awe and respect by those who did.

On 18 and 19 December 1917, as part of the celebrations for his forthcoming 80th birthday, the supplement to the *Täglichen Rundschau* published a two-part article by Bruch entitled 'England'. It looked back 40 years to his first visit in 1877, and gave a detailed assessment of his association with the country thereafter. It had the benefit of hindsight, but it was also written at a time when anti-English passions were running high in the final year of the First World War. It makes interesting reading to juxtapose some of the complaints he made in the article with letters written during his stay in Liverpool. It is also worth noting that the memory of his attitude to Berlin has undergone a change:

. . . In the autumn of 1877, Sarasate and I travelled to England for the first time, and everything there went very well and satisfactorily. By and by, the first performance of my Second Violin Concerto (written for Sarasate) followed in London (Crystal Palace, November 1877), my own concert at the Crystal Palace (June 1878), and performances of *Glocke* in Birmingham (1879 Festival) and Liverpool (1879).

Now that I was universally well known in England, and Benedict had given up his post in Liverpool for reasons of old age, the enquiry came in the spring of 1880 whether I would be interested in becoming his successor. The contract came as a surprise, for it was not generally the case to offer fixed posts to German musicians; probably I had cause to be grateful to Benedict's recommendation, and to the success of *Odysseus*.

I would have liked to remain in Berlin, for I was beginning to settle in there; the Stern'schen Gesangvereins, which I had directed since 1878, was dear to me, and I enjoyed moving in the pleasant artistic and literary circles of the intensely inspiring capital city. But it was a matter of financial subsistence . . . I would much improve my circumstances by answering the call to England, and could once and for all set up a home. It also appeared that there would be more opportunities to promote my choral music in England . . . I went in the autumn of 1880, full of hope, and with the happy uncritical preconceptions of England which were bestowed upon it by Germany at that time . . . one loved and admired everything English, and we were naïve enough to be almost convinced by the reciprocated love offered us by our 'cousins' across the Channel. Only a few realized that the truth over there was quite different, and that throughout the whole of the 19th century, England was never on our side in all the important crises of our development, on the contrary they were always against us.

. . . The Committee consisted of rich and esteemed merchants, who on the whole understood little or nothing about Art, and who let themselves be led by anything and everything done by London. The diamond-wearing public of this glittering commercial city was generally entirely unmusical, and much preferred to hear a yellow-with-age artful aria by Madame Trebelli than the most perfect symphony. The chorus consisted almost exclusively of very plebeian elements, was difficult to handle and achieved less than most other English choruses. Liverpool did not have its own orchestra at the time; the first-rate orchestra of the anglicized German Karl Hallé (Sir Charles Hallé) came over from Manchester for our concerts ten times during the winter. It contained foreigners of all nationalities, and gave me much pleasure and joy.

. . . The English families among whom we moved were, it is true, friendly and polite, but the social life of the commercial city was generally depressing and dispiriting. This has apparently improved meanwhile since the founding of the University.

Contact with the German community in Liverpool was very pleasant, for at the time there were very capable, all-round cultured men and charming, true German women there. In the years 1880–83 we always celebrated the birthday of our old Kaiser with a concert and a feast.

It was not possible to get close to the leading English musicians, for one continually met everywhere a much greater reserve and stiffness than in any other country. Already, at that time, the Germans were loved no longer, and no one wanted to see a permanent post in their hands.

Bruch then gave details of an incident which occurred after his March 1883 London performance of *Odysseus*. This had been attended by Princess Helena, a daughter of Queen Victoria. The Princess enjoyed it so much that she suggested that excerpts should be performed before the Queen at Windsor. The conductor was to be W. G. Cusins (described as 'Kapellmeister to the Court of the Queen'), and, according to Bruch, it was he who cancelled the performance which was to have taken place while the composer was away in America. This was considered an act of petty chauvinism and anti-German feeling, which was rife at the time. Bruch went on to describe how a committee had been formed to set up a new Music College under the chairmanship of the Duke of Edinburgh. One of the members of the committee was supposed to have said 'Ladies and Gentlemen, it is high time that England had its own Mozart and Beethoven!' In spite of this, Bruch complained, England was happy to send its young musicians to study in Germany, and reap the benefits of that country's heritage. 'England had the biggest fleet of ships, the best livestock, the most money, the strongest commerce. Why should it not now produce the best composers?' But in the intervening 35 years the only composer of note was Sullivan, 'whose *Mikado* was known in Germany', and he was unfortunately no Englishman. He came from 'unhappy Ireland, the Emerald Isle which over the centuries has been so shamefully treated by England'. Only Purcell and Dowland escaped Bruch's savagery towards English composers.

The second part of his article described a happy association with the impresario Otto Goldschmidt (Director of the London Bach Choir) and his wife, the 'Swedish nightingale' Jenny Lind. The mood then changed again when he attacked England's anti-German sentiments, which he considered to be predominantly anti-Prussian. 'I was once seated next to the Mayor of Liverpool at a banquet,' he related. 'As I considered, during the course of conversation, that the honourable Gentleman had an extremely vague knowledge of recent German history, I asked him "But Mr Mayor, who, other than the Prussians, could have united Germany?" He smiled at me and said "Austria!" Englishmen had simply no idea of Prussia's singularity and its historical mission.'

Bruch then continued this political theme by turning to the English view of Bismarck, and acknowledging the respect afforded to the Prussian 'Grand Old Man' by the 'Gentlemen of the West End and Piccadilly clubs'. To emphasize his point, he described an encounter in Birmingham with Joseph Chamberlain, during which the politician questioned the composer on the subject of Bismarck's recent change of economic policy from a free market economy to one of protectionism. '[Chamberlain],' he wrote, 'was annoyed because England now earned less money from Germany. I answered that, as an artist, I understood little about such matters. Mr Chamberlain could, however, rest assured that Count Bismarck had acted (as in all circumstances) in the interests of Germany. He had no cause to concern himself with the financial problems of others. At that the honourable gentleman smiled and said nothing.'

Bruch's article concluded:

After I had lived for a time in England, it became clearer to me that in one important matter I had made a mistake when I took the post. If you live there and you wish to achieve something, then you must become anglicized. To many German nationals that was not especially difficult, but for me it was quite out of the question. I was already over forty years old, and was no longer malleable as wax like the young 20-year-old businessmen and musicians who went there, only to fall prey to any strong, new influences. My spiritual direction and my whole conception of life was already formed, and was German through and through; I loved the Fatherland too much ever to be able to feel at home for any length of time abroad. I was also utterly lacking in any business or commercial sense which several German artists there gradually brought to bear, and even worked their way up to becoming a 'Sir'. Although the musical circumstances abroad were always very interesting, and although I made many life-long international musical contacts, which were both valuable and gratifying, nevertheless I resolved never again to take up a permanent post abroad. I gave up my post in Liverpool amicably, and took up the offer in Breslau. At least I was back in the Fatherland, even if too far to the east.

## Chapter Thirteen

### BRESLAU
1883–90

ON 31 MARCH 1883, Max Bruch boarded the Cunard steamer *Gallia* in Liverpool bound for New York. His tour brochure, prepared by the agents Wolfson and Lavine, listed his engagements with various choral societies in the cities of Boston, New York, Milwaukee, Cleveland, Newark, Philadelphia, Chicago and Cincinnati. It stated that 'Herr Bruch is a comparatively young man, but he has already made so marked an impress and exercised so widespread an influence among the musicians and the young composers of the Fatherland, that his admirers have every reason to feel proud of his achievements, and if his future may be indicated by his past, a still more brilliant career lies before him.'

The profile then gave a biographical outline of Bruch's life until his time in Liverpool (though his resignation was not mentioned), after which it turned to his music. Detailed descriptions of *Die Loreley* and *Frithjof* were followed by accounts of his smaller-scale choral works, and only then by the first Violin Concerto.

> . . . two of Bruch's works have not been mentioned that ought to be more particularly commented upon. They are the Violin Concerto in G minor (No. 5) [*sic*], and the first Symphony in E flat major. His success in these compositions entitles Max Bruch to an honorable place among the great instrumental composers of the day. The Violin Concerto was almost as agreeable a surprise for the violin virtuosi as was *Frithjof* in its day for the male chorus. It may well be said that since Mendelssohn's Violin Concerto no other work of this kind has found and merited such a general friendly recognition.

It concluded that 'Max Bruch holds a high position today among the great composers of the world', reiterating his pre-eminence as a choral conductor. Bruch's agent offered five 'Festival Programmes', including two movements from the First Symphony, the First Violin Concerto, excerpts from *Frithjof* (also offered as a complete work), *Das*

*Lied von der Glocke, Odysseus,* choral songs and shorter choral works such as *Schön Ellen, Die Flucht nach Aegypten* and the *Römische Leichenfeier.* During his trip he also conducted complete performances of *Arminius, Das Lied von der Glocke* and (at his second concert in New York with the Oratorio Society on 19 April) the *Jubilate.*

When Bruch's visit was confirmed, a press release appeared in the *Boston Evening Transcript:*

> . . . Max Bruch is still in the prime of life, and for many years has stood in the foremost rank of modern German composers . . . In person Max Bruch is a German blonde, rather stout with a mild, amiable, serene, expressive countenance . . . one would single him out as a kind, genial philanthropist, rather than as a great composer. Max Bruch's visit to America is partly social, partly professional; i.e. the first motive suggested the visit, which was looked for last year, and will insure him a personal welcome apart from questions of business; while the flattering and liberal proposals from the people who manage foreign artists have induced the distinguished German to combine pleasure with profit, and perhaps advance a little the musical education of this young Western world that has already received so eagerly his fresh, vigorous work.[1]

Bruch arrived in New York on 10 April, and the *New York Times* had a reporter awaiting him at the Belvedere House Hotel:

> He is a man of medium height, but his thick-set figure makes him appear somewhat short. His head is large and his face broad. He is bald on the top of his head, but a long fringe of wavy brown hair falls upon his neck. A short brown beard surrounds his typical German face. The eyes are small and gray, and in conversation twinkle with good humor. . . . He appears to be genial and good-humored in talking, and speaks English very intelligently. 'I had a pleasant trip altogether,' he said; 'I was sea-sick about a day and a half, for we had dreadful weather at first and made a slow passage of 11 days. You need not be surprised at my speaking English, because I have been conductor for the Liverpool Philharmonic Society for the last three years. My music has been known in this country, thanks to Mr [Theodore] Thomas and Dr [Leopold] Damrosch for about 10 years. My special line of work is choral, though I have written symphonies, two operas, violin concertos and some string quartets and trios.
> . . . I learned English enough in England to talk to my orchestra, but here I find I can return to my native tongue. In looking over a list of 100 musicians of the Philharmonic Society I find that 94 or 95 of

them are Germans. I look forward with great pleasure to my tour in America, for I am told that there is a large music-loving public here'.[2]

There is only one letter to Simrock. It was written from Beverly Farms, a small town twenty miles to the north-east of Boston, shortly before he began the journey home:

Before I leave, I must send you a greeting from the 'New World'. On the whole I can be very satisfied with my success. My name and works had long been known here, and so I found the best and most enthusiastic of welcomes among Germans and Americans everywhere. As far as Mammon is concerned, I took the greatest trouble to restore to you all that the American gentlemen have stolen from you, and yet meanwhile I am still not overburdened by the weight of my money bags. I do not fetch as much as Madame Patti does in an evening's singing. I will come again, however, for America is newly discovered territory, and under certain circumstances is for you too. We will talk more of this. My new Symphony (No. 3 in E major) was played by the Music Festival orchestra in Boston under Henschel on 4 May. Adagio and Scherzo were all right; I must do more to the first and last movements. The first movement was a bit too long, but the last was too short. But as Henschel and Dr Damrosch, together with the best orchestral musicians in New York, strongly urge me to publish the Symphony soon, I shall do so. As soon as I have made the changes, I shall have it played again somewhere in Germany (though where, during the summer, I do not know), and then give it to you.[3]

Bruch had been commissioned by Damrosch during the summer of 1882 to write a symphony, with the rights of the first performance to be given to the Symphony Society of New York. He had sketches for a new work 'lying about' (in fact these date back to 1870 in Sondershausen), and the financial rewards seemed propitious enough, so he sent off the completed manuscript on 1 October 1882. The first performance took place on 17 December 1882 in New York, and Henschel paid him $75 for a performance in Boston in February 1883. Bruch himself conducted a performance in New York in April, and from June he had the score again in order to effect the changes upon which he had decided. These were made during the years 1884–86, after which it was published by Breitkopf & Härtel. Bruch had tried to get Simrock to take it, but the publisher's poor sales of the Second Symphony left him reluctant to take another in spite of Bruch's persuasive efforts. 'Much water has flowed down the Rhine since 1870; I have shed several layers of skin since then, and because I had somewhat bad luck with the Second Symphony then, it does not mean that I will have again.'[4] Mention of the river was pertinent, for Bruch considered subtitling the symphony 'On the Rhine'. The material came from his 'freshest and happiest youth' and not only shared the tonic key of the prelude to *Die Loreley*, but recalled, in the second subject of the first movement, a similarity of mood and rhythm with Lenore's theme in the opera.

The Symphony No. 3 is in four movements. The first movement is preceded by a slow introduction of a stately *tutti* interjected with solos from the first horn and the first clarinet, both of which play important roles throughout the work. The movement proper is marked *allegro molto vivace*, and is in classical sonata form with broad melodic themes developing to an imposing climax. Like the last movement of Schumann's Third Symphony (the *Rhenish*), the second movement has a religious feel with its chorale-like introduction, followed by variations and a return to the opening chorale character. This slow movement and the ensuing scherzo were sometimes interchanged. Hans von Bülow did so with Bruch's permission at a concert in Bremen on 5 November 1888 ('The Adagio requires concentrated listening . . . and the Finale sounds fresher after it than after the Scherzo'). Following the concert, Bruch's friend, the conductor Carl Reinthaler from Bonn, described the change as 'a happy inspiration'.[5] The C major Scherzo is happy and boisterous, and is the most effective and successful movement in any of the three symphonies by Bruch, who expressed a special love for it. The movement is unconventionally in rondo form, melodically simple in its foundation on the common arpeggio, but with a strength derived from syncopated rhythm and orchestration of immaculate clarity. The *Boston Daily Advertiser* (after Henschel's performance) described the Scherzo as having 'the flavor of a minuet in which the dancers have forgotten their courtly manners in the exhilaration of the sport. The movement is ingeniously humorous and entertaining.'[6] The *New York Times* called it 'bright and original, with a dash about it that is irresistible' when Damrosch gave the première two months earlier.[7] After Bülow's performance in Bremen, a friend wrote to Bruch 'the Scherzo was a success, and you could witness Bülow's joy in repeating it'. Unfortunately the Finale is not of the standard of the earlier movements, and seems to lack a creative spark. With its firmly anchored pedal of E major and a paucity of melodic ideas, it is also encumbered with cloying textures of thick orchestration and doublings.

In spite of these successful American performances, Bruch's symphonic music was by now receiving no more than a polite reception. 'It manifestly does not aspire to the highest rank of symphonic composition,' wrote the *Boston Daily Advertiser*, 'but it accomplishes all it sets out to do, and, if we are not greatly mistaken, rather rises above its standard than otherwise. It is a fine example of what may be accomplished by a composer with a good, but not extraordinary gift of inspiration, with exquisite musical sensibility, refined taste, great learning, and masterly command of his orchestral sources.'

Bruch returned to Europe at the beginning of June 1883, sailing on the Cunard liner, R.M.S. *Bothnia*. On the evening of 6 June he took part in a concert held in the saloon of the ship. His contributions to the programme were performances on the piano of Bach's Prelude and Fugue in G minor, the Scherzo from his own new Third Symphony and the Romanze and Scherzo from Schumann's Fourth Symphony. He also took part in a piano-duet performance of two movements from Beethoven's Septet. The programme included contributions from other passengers, and ended with '"Stump Speech" by E. Garrety (sailor)'. Clara and Margarethe, meanwhile, had remained behind in Liverpool to prepare for the journey to Breslau. Clara had a few engagements during Max's absence, ranging from Penelope in *Odysseus*, in Birmingham on 7 May, to solo arias (Gluck's 'Che faro', Taubert's 'In der Fremde' and Schumann's 'Widmung') in a charity concert, on 12 April in aid of All Saint's Church Sunday Schools in Stoneycroft, at St George's Hall, Liverpool. When the couple were reunited, they travelled on 26 June to Bonn where Max was laid low with neuralgia, reporting to Hiller that he was 'confined to his bed and *chaise longue*.'[8]

The summer of 1883 was spent in Bergisch Gladbach and at Friedrichsroda in Thuringia, and on 14 September the couple finally took up residence on the third floor of Museumplatz 9, Breslau. Although Max felt distinctly uncomfortable living close to the Polish border, it was not long before they were enjoying themselves setting up their own proper home for the first time. There were comparatively few possessions to bring with them from Liverpool, as they had rented furnished accommodation in England, so they could now enjoy purchasing the basic household goods of their own choice. Their pleasure was enhanced by the news that Clara was now expecting their second child. 'I have my safe stronghold,' he told Simrock, 'my house, my dear wife, my child, and good friends in all parts of the world — in Germany as well as in England and America. The longer I have false or semi-friends and opponents, the less I bother about them. I let them get on with it and laugh at their monkey-business.' He had 'a splendid orchestra,' he wrote at the beginning of November, 'an agreeable Committee (who bother about nothing), a lot of freedom, light duties and no choral hack-work. What more could I want?'⁹

Bruch began his duties in Breslau at a salary of 7000 marks. He was fortunate in having a seven-man Committee that left him alone to run the musical life of the city as he thought fit. Together with Dr Kaufmann (who assisted him in artistic matters) he began confidently preparing his programmes, and expressed himself content with his lot. His orchestral strings consisted of 14 first violins, 14 seconds, 8 violas, 8 cellos and 6 double-basses. He had fortnightly concerts, each of which was allocated three orchestral rehearsals. Though he had no chorus of his own, those in the city, occasionally participated in his concerts and often sang his music. A successful performance of *Arminius* by the Singakademie took place on 18 March 1884 under their conductor Stapel. Max reported: 'the success was not just good, it was brilliant; Breslau presented me with a triumph which I had not expected in the least from this somewhat cool city. . . . The chorus of the Singakademie was splendid: 130 sopranos, 200 altos etc. It was just like a Music Festival . . . The large hall, which holds 2,000 people, was completely sold out . . . it was one of the most brilliant evenings of my life, and its resounding success has completely consolidated my present position.' In 1889 the first performance of *Das Feuerkreuz* took place in the city after fifteen years' work on the composition. Shorter pieces such as *Frithjof* and *Schön Ellen* were also performed, together with choral excerpts and scenes from *Odysseus* and *Die Loreley*. Of his other compositions, he conducted *Kol Nidrei*, the First Violin Concerto, the first movement of the Second Concerto, the *Romanze*, the *Scottish Fantasy*, and the First Symphony. His Lieder, together with other smaller works, also appeared in his programmes.

He offered a broad spectrum of composers in his seven seasons in Breslau. Most of Beethoven's symphonies, the piano concertos, the violin concerto, and excerpts from *Fidelio* were included. The symphonies of Haydn and Mozart appeared, and the pre-classical period was represented by Bach, Handel and Rameau. Predictably, however, it was the Romantics who predominated. Weber, Schubert, Mendelssohn, Schumann and Brahms were most often to be found, but Wagner, Liszt and even the young Richard Strauss were surprisingly included. In spite of his antipathy to the New German School, which often bordered on fanatical hatred, he was fond of performing the orchestral overtures, preludes and scenes from Wagner's operas and music dramas. A chorus from *Prometheus* and the Second Piano Concerto were all that he could bring himself to conduct of works by Liszt, whilst the 25-year-old Strauss had to content himself with a performance of one work, his *Aus Italien* in December 1889.

After the performance of *Aus Italien*, Bruch reported the outcome to Richard Strauss. The reply Bruch received from Strauss in Weimar thanked the composer sincerely for 'the great deal of trouble you took over my *[Aus] Italien*'. 'I am only heartily sorry,' Strauss continued, 'that your apparently still very conservative public did not better reward your great deal of work, and that your struggle met with opposition. Here [Weimar] our trusting public, as with the works of Liszt, Berlioz and Wagner, would not find anything especially surprising in my last movement.'[10] The mention of those three composers was like a red rag to a bull for Bruch, who was not guilty of neglecting the last two named. Among his personal papers is a copy of the reply to Strauss, in which he defended both his personal record and the reputation of the Breslau public.[11]

> I told him . . . his supposition was incorrect. For example, during my régime 13–14 Wagner works have been given (and some of those two or three times), so that the name of Wagner appears on average four or five times on the programmes each season. Equally the sins of omission of my predecessor Scholz regarding Hector Berlioz have been strenuously made good; under my direction the *Harold Symphony*, the love scene and Capulet's feast from *Romeo and Juliet*, *Lear* overture, *Carnival Roman* [*sic*] etc. have been performed. It is true that the public has not exactly been richly provided with Liszt by Damrosch, but frankly overfed etc. etc. The reason for the cold reception of the second movement and the rejection of the Finale cannot be found in the 'conservative' inclinations of our public . . .

The performance of the programmatic music of Berlioz, Saint-Saëns, Glinka, Grieg, Dvořák and Tchaikovsky brought many works to the audiences of Breslau for the first time, plus a host of works from many other minor composers. In his 1887 season he celebrated the 25th anniversary of the Breslau Concert-Verein performing music by the three conductors of the organization: Damrosch (1862–71), Scholz (1871–83) and himself.

Bruch invited many eminent soloists to Breslau, some of them composers playing their own works. Grieg played his Piano Concerto in Bruch's first season (on 27 November 1883), and afterwards ungraciously described his host as 'a frightful bore'. Brahms played

Beethoven's Fourth Piano Concerto on 30 March 1886, and in the same concert accompanied Clara in three of his own Lieder, as well as conducting his new Fourth Symphony from manuscript parts. Bruch's friendship with Saint-Saëns, which had developed during the years in Liverpool, now brought the French composer and pianist to Silesia. In Bruch's first programme (16 October 1883), he conducted Saint-Saëns' symphonic poem *La Jeunesse d'Hercule*, and the piano or violin concertos appeared regularly. Saint-Saëns himself played his own Fourth Piano Concerto in the 1885–86 season. There were three seasons in which Eugen d'Albert appeared. He asked Bruch to write a piano concerto, but was considered too strongly associated with the Liszt school to be trusted, and the request was refused.

Bruch's instrumentalists and solo singers were often friends and colleagues: the Joachims, Sarasate, von Bülow, Heckmann, Barth, Scharwenka, Hausmann, Henschel, Sembrich, Schauseil, Spies, von Sicherer, and Sauret were among them. Clara also took her turn, and appeared in each of the first four seasons. Although her name does not appear in the programmes of Bruch's last three seasons in Breslau, she sang in a concert put on by the Singakademie on 28 February 1888, in which Sarasate also took part and her husband conducted. The combined choral participants numbered 250 male voices, whose contribution consisted of a chorus from Mendelssohn's *Antigone*, Bruch's *Hebrew Songs*, *Media Vita* (one of the four choruses Op. 48), some arrangements by Kremser of old Dutch folksongs, and the final chorus from *Frithjof*. Clara sang 'Parto, parto' from Mozart's *La Clemenza di Tito* and the aria 'Erbarme dich' from Bach's *St Matthew Passion*, in which Sarasate played the violin obbligato. The Spaniard also played his own *Muiñera* and the *Scottish Fantasy* (described in the programme as Bruch's Third Violin Concerto).

Between the fortnightly concerts, or when he had engaged a guest conductor, he was at liberty to travel elsewhere. On 20 November 1883 he conducted *Odysseus* in Cologne and again in Coblenz three days later. Clara sang Penelope in both performances. They then returned to Breslau for his concert with Grieg, after which he set off for Moscow to give two with Sarasate for the Philharmonic Society on 4 and 11 December, and one at St Petersburg on the 6th. He described his trip to Simrock when he returned on 15 December:

> The Russians treated me very well, it is true there were explosions, but only of enthusiasm, not dynamite! . . . On 2 and 10 December I was the guest of the German Union in Moscow; on the 6th I went to [St] Petersburg and conducted my First Violin Concerto in Sarasate's concert, together with my *Loreley* prelude. With the Russians you

never get away with less than three curtain calls! After deducting all
expenses, I have about 180 marks left over, not bad for a devilishly
poor German Kapellmeister. They want me back, and I do not see
why I should not take more money from our dear 'enemies' on the
other side of the [river] Niemen. Pablito played *superb*, [*sic*] but is
not in *high spirits* . . . I visited Grand Duke Constantine, who
turned out to be an *Odysseus* enthusiast and had some scenes played
for me by his Court musicians. I stayed on to dine. I also met with
Davidoff, Auer, Brassin, Madame Rubinstein etc. Otherwise
conditions in this country are horrifying. It could not have been
much worse during the decadent times in ancient Rome.

In a letter to Hiller, soon after his return to Breslau, he reflected on
the breadth of his travels during 1883. On 25 April he had been
conducting on the shores of Lake Erie in Cleveland (Ohio) and on 4
December he would be standing on the podium in Moscow. His
relationship with Hiller had healed. He now held an important post in
Germany, and Hiller no doubt hoped to get some of his own works
performed in Breslau in exchange for the promotion of Max's works
in Cologne. Sure enough Hiller's *Idyll* for orchestra was performed on
25 March 1884. It was however, an unfortunate coincidence that at the
very time that Bruch was beginning his work in Breslau, Hiller was
now on the verge of retiring from his post in Cologne, one which
Bruch had always coveted.

On 6 April 1884 Ferdinand Hiller conducted Handel's *Messiah* in the
Gürzenich in Cologne. It was the last concert of the season, and during
an official supper after the performance he announced his resignation
from the post of Kapellmeister to the city and Director of the
Conservatoire. He was seventy-two years old and forced to spend a
lot of time at home. He was physically frail with a heart complaint,
but in every other way he was in total command of his faculties. On
the day before the concert he wrote to Brahms, and on the day after to
Bruch, announcing his decision to both men before they could read it
in the press. Hiller then wrote again to Brahms, this time directly
stating his desire that the composer should succeed him in his post. He
reminded Brahms that 34 years earlier he had asked Schumann to take
over his post in Düsseldorf when he moved to Cologne. Now he was
asking Brahms to do the same thing in Cologne. Unfortunately
Brahms' reply rejecting the request is lost, though Hiller's response
to it survives. He turns to the question of a second choice: 'What now?
After you I would wish most to see Bruch here — he is from Cologne
etc., but precisely that means he will have a lot of opposition.'[12]

Hiller then wrote to Max.[13] He began by asking him to burn the letter after reading it. This Bruch did, but not before first making a copy. The talk in musical circles, Hiller continued, was his own forthcoming vacant post in Cologne and the common knowledge that it had been officially offered to Brahms, who had turned it down. Hiller had therefore recommended Bruch to the Committee, but they could not come to an agreement. At that point Hiller did not know which other names were under consideration. He knew that Dr Becker (the Mayor) had accepted the suggestion in principle, but now it was time to ascertain Bruch's own interest in the post. Hiller acknowledged that Max had only just arrived in Breslau ('would that you had remained in Liverpool!'), but an interregnum of guest conductors in Cologne for a season would do no harm until he could take up the post, and there were enough competent people within the Conservatoire to keep it running. He also wondered whether Breslau would release him and concluded, 'for years I have always thought that you would be my successor here, it would be so natural! I still hope that this will be the case.'

Without revealing that he had made a copy of Hiller's letter, Max replied that he had predicted the course of events now under way. He had been told four months earlier that a change was imminent, but had concluded at the time that 'Brahms will most probably turn it down. Then they will think of me among others. Some will be for me, others against, perhaps a majority will decide for me in the end, but perhaps not. That is exactly what has happened, for at this moment it is by no means certain that I am wanted in Cologne.'[4] He could never have turned down Breslau and remained in 'that desert' Liverpool in the hope that he would have been offered Cologne at such time as it became vacant. So it was with a heavy heart after seven weeks deliberation that he exchanged 'the Atlantic ocean for the Polish border'. Having then described the advantages of Breslau, with which he was genuinely satisfied, he turned to his feelings for the situation in Cologne, 'my mother city, the centre of my Rhenish homeland, which becomes ever dearer to me the longer I must be away from her, and the old friends there who can never be replaced by new ones.' In short, he wanted the job but there were problems. He did not consider himself at liberty to leave Breslau so soon after his arrival, neither did he know whether it would even be legally possible for him to do so. He did not consider himself trained in directing the Conservatoire, many of whose teachers were either much older and more experienced than he, or were his friends. He feared creating a situation in which he would be either embarrassed by being their superior, or impotent in establishing a credible authority. Max also rejected any possibility of a move during 1884, for the birth of their second child was expected in the middle of the year, and Clara could not endure the additional upheaval. Max was aware that he 'was not the one that Cologne wanted to have', and also feared that he would be open to attack from the *Kölner Zeitung*, one of whose staff he had offended in 1876 by putting together a dossier of complaints and sending it to the editorial board.

Enclosed with his long letter to Hiller was a copy of one to Michael Du Mont. This member of the Committee had made a covert approach via Mathilde Bruch to sound out her brother's interest in the post. Max's reply more or less reiterated the contents of his letter to Hiller, but also asked for specific details of the duties of the Cologne post. Matters became acute during May 1884, though unfortunately all documentation of events was destroyed during the Second World War. It is clear that Hiller wanted Bruch as his successor, but that the Committee were about to decide on appointing Franz Wüllner (at that time Hofkapellmeister in Dresden). A letter to Hiller from the Chairman of the Committee, Robert Schnitzler, reveals that Bruch's personality and his knack of alienating people were once again the cause of his undoing. 'I always shared your view,' wrote Schnitzler, 'that Bruch should be the one to take in the first place.' (Presumably Schnitzler meant that Bruch was his first choice once Brahms had declined.) 'However he revealed a well-known fault in his personality. Instead of stating above all else how proud he would be to become your successor, he asked questions about whether the post would leave him free time for artistic work. Through his correspondence with you he must have known the answer. I thought it right that Bruch's name was passed over on the agenda.'[15]

Max was indignant at this treatment. On 24 May he told Hiller that he was aware of the impending decision to take Wüllner, 'not without painful regret, for I knew how much you wanted me, and also the thought of having to relinquish my homeland has caused me a few unpleasant hours'. However he did not take the possibility of defeat lying down. He complained that, having asked Du Mont for more details, Cologne neither acknowledged receipt of his letter nor replied to it. He had been kept in the dark for three weeks. He had also been informed of malicious rumours circulating in Cologne that he was going blind, and that he had to be led to the podium to conduct. He had now sent another letter to Cologne setting out his conditions for leaving Breslau, among which was a stipulation that he could not start before 1885 and that he must be given a period of time to consider an offer. It was small wonder that at its meeting on 29 May 1884 the Committee unanimously selected Wüllner as Hiller's successor. Another Committee member, Robert Heuser, informed Hiller the next day of the appointment. He also criticized Bruch's behaviour: 'Now to "poor" Bruch. I do not know if you are aware of the letter which he sent to De Lange to get himself known. I advised De Lange in Bruch's interest not to reveal it, and if anything can console me that I was overruled, it is that the letter is the product of an unbalanced temperament.'[16] The episode fuelled Bruch's resentment and hatred of the powerful committee men who ran the musical life of Cologne. Although his artistic qualities and abilities were never called into question, they regarded him as ambitious, egotistical, scheming and paranoid.

Wüllner could not match the growing international reputation of his defeated rival. In May 1885 Max received a letter from a conductor in Constantinople reporting successful performances of excerpts from *Das Lied von der Glocke* and *Schön Ellen* for the German community in the city. Musikdirektor Dethier went on to ask for advice from Bruch on the composer's other choral works (he possessed scores of *Frithjof* and *Salamis*) which he might perform in spite of a heavy bias by the Italian community towards their country's music, and the primitive music library facilities in Turkey. 'The earth is somewhat virgin here,' Dethier continued, 'and we have taken on the role of pioneers, who step by step must bring a better culture to this wilderness of Italian taste. We do not often lack battles and crises.'[17] The choral society was only eighteen months old but had 60 voices, and soloists were also on hand.

A less exotic international success had taken place a year earlier when *Frithjof* was performed on 17 April 1884 in Paris to great acclaim. The concert was one of six festival concerts organized by the *Union Internationale des Compositeurs*. Bruch's work was the sole representative of current German composers, and he shared a platform along with such eminent colleagues as Tchaikovsky, Smetana, Gounod, Massenet, Saint-Saëns and César Franck.

The Cologne affair was temporarily forgotten with the telegram from Sarasate in Paris telling of *Frithjof*'s success, but the final decision to appoint Wüllner must have reached him on the very day that his second child was born; Clara gave birth to their first son, Max Felix, on 31 May 1884. The birth was straightforward but the child was weak and sickly, suffering from rickets. A nanny was brought into the household; Bruch's daughter Margarethe described this nursemaid, whose name was Lene. 'She had hard hands, a good-natured ugly face, she waddled like a duck, on deformed feet, and spoke pure Breslau dialect.' The young Max Felix moved uncertainly between life and death. By the age of eighteen months he was showing no signs of crawling or walking; his only reaction was to Max's piano playing or

Clara's singing. In spite of holidays in Thuringia and Bergisch Gladbach, it was a full three years before the boy began to walk and talk. Margarethe herself also came close to death when she contracted diphtheria in Breslau. She was fortunate to survive, and so were her family to remain uninfected: a little boy in the flat below, with whom she played, became infected and died from the disease.

Max was a doting father, strict but fair. He always brought home a doll for his 'Gretel' when he returned from his travels. The regular joke as he unpacked his suitcase would be, 'now this time I really have brought back only dirty washing', after which he would root deep into it and produce a doll for the excited child. At six each evening he would take the two young children into the music room and they would sing nursery rhymes around the piano. He appeared to them as ancient as Methuselah with his long scraggly beard that scratched when he kissed them. The young Gretel was convinced that it was an extension of the hair on his head, and grew right through him. 'Poor Papa,' she would say, 'it must hurt you dreadfully to have your hair grow through your throat.'

After the summer holidays of 1884, which included his annual visit to Maria Zanders and her family, Max began his second season in Breslau. He wrote to Simrock, 'Yesterday we had Brahms' third symphony. On the whole it is very beautiful, it would be still more beautiful, however, if the first and last movements were better orchestrated. Meanwhile a leopard cannot change his spots, nor I!'[18] Bruch had invited Brahms to conduct the work himself, but the offer had been politely refused owing to other commitments. Brahms did eventually appear with Bruch and his wife on the concert platform (30 March 1886). Margarethe Bruch recalled Brahms' visit, even though she was barely four years old at the time.

One day we returned from a walk to hear music coming from the music room. I noticed that it was not my father's music, although my mother was singing. Carefully I opened the door. A man, with a long white beard, thick-set and shorter than my father, sat at the piano. They stopped the music and my mother said, 'Come Gretel, shake hands with Uncle Brahms.' Quite contrary to my habit, I ran happily to him, unresisting and unembarrassed, and fell into his arms. Two inscrutable, deep blue eyes looked penetratingly through me, searching but lovingly. As was his habit (often according to how his heart was moved) Brahms liked to make an ironic or comic remark. He said to me, 'Will you be my little wife one day?' My father was indignant. How could anyone talk to such a little girl like that! With a child's instinct, I sensed that Brahms and my father did not care for each other. And so it was.

Margarethe's childlike view of Sarasate was coloured more by his collection of walking sticks than by his virtuoso violin playing. 'The fiery southerner was never without a walking stick. He was supposed to own some with gold or silver handles, which were set with diamonds and other precious stones. One day he came to eat, and we had pheasant with sauerkraut. Sarasate, who liked children, pulled a medal (probably a Bavarian one) from his pocket to amuse us.'

Margarethe also had some childhood memories of her father as a conductor, having been taken with Max Felix to the final rehearsal for one of the Breslau concerts. His manner with the baton was confident and calm, it all looked so easy that the children wondered why the orchestra could not play on their own without him. After the rehearsal they visited their father in the artists' room. To their surprise they met, not their 'happy, bubbling and childish father but a broken man, streaming with perspiration from his forehead, and from time to time having to take a gulp of red wine to regain his senses'.

Bruch had a well-stocked cellar. His taste for wine was something he shared with Rudolf von Beckerath, who often used to buy on his behalf. When Max was in Bonn, he placed an order with von Beckerath for '12 bottles of Bordeaux à 10 Sgr, 24 bottles of Ockenheimer à 6½ Sgr, and 18 bottles of Hochheimer à 8 Sgr. My sister would like half the Bordeaux to be in half-bottles, all the rest in full bottles. I look forward very much to having this good wine at home.'[19]

Margarethe recalled her father's mixed feelings of pleasure and pain when working with singers. Pauline Lucca was scheduled to sing with him in Moscow, in the presence of a music-loving Grand Duchess. Lucca decided at the dress rehearsal that she would reorganize a Mozart aria in order to avoid a top C. Bruch would have none of this, and warned the *diva* that he would not conduct unless she sang what the composer had written. Neither would give way, and consequently it was not Bruch who took his place on the rostrum that evening. Others, like Wally Schauseil, Hermine Spies, Amalie Joachim and Maria Schmidt-Koehne enjoyed a happy and fulfilling professional relationship with him.

On 18 March 1887 Clara gave birth to their third child, a son who was christened Hans. He was his father's favourite, with a sunny disposition and blonde curly locks. Unlike Max Felix, who appeared to have inherited his father's musical talent, Hans developed an early gift for drawing. Their fourth and last child was also a son, Ewald, born on 19 May 1890. His birth took place a few months before the family left Breslau for Berlin, which was to be the last move of Max Bruch's life. His move from Breslau was prompted by disagreements with political factions in the city. It was from about 1885 that Bruch encountered opposition to his choice of soloists and conservative programming, but the root of the rising antagonism was political, and lay in his ardent support for Bismarck. The years 1888–90 were momentous ones for Germany.

On 9 March 1888 Kaiser Wilhelm I died just days short of his 91st birthday. He was succeeded by his 56-year-old son, Friedrich III, who had already lost his voice owing to an operation for cancer of the throat. The poor man reigned for just 100 days, and was succeeded by his son, Wilhelm II, on 15 June. The new Kaiser, like his father before him, had inherited his grandfather's powerful Chancellor, Count Otto von Bismarck. The 'Iron Chancellor' was now an old man of 73, but he was in excellent health and led a relaxed life on his country estate, Friedrichsruh near Hamburg. The young Kaiser was initially respectful of the man he had admired and hero-worshipped from childhood. Bismarck felt secure, for his hands firmly gripped the reins of power. His son Herbert was in the Foreign Office, and he had numerous spies in the new Kaiser's entourage. But opposition was growing, first in the military, then amongst those close to the young Kaiser. The Chancellor's friendly attitude to Russia and his long absences from Berlin gradually eroded his influence in Germany's political life and encouraged his enemies at court. During 1889 the Kaiser came to believe that Bismarck was showing signs of age and losing his ability in foreign affairs. Wilhelm was also beginning to see himself as another Frederick the Great or even Julius Caesar, and he had no wish to be overshadowed by his famous Chancellor.

It was at the beginning of 1890 that relations between the two men swiftly deteriorated. The Kaiser decided to improve the lot of the working man by mitigating anti-Socialist laws. He proposed to cut working hours, abolish child labour and Sunday working. The Crown Council had been summoned to hear the Emperor's proposals without prior consultation with Bismarck. This piqued the Chancellor, who anyway had his own plans to abolish universal suffrage and harden rather than soften the anti-Socialist laws. The other ministers, all of whom owed their political careers to Bismarck, wavered initially to see which way the wind would blow. At the next Council meeting they came down on the side of the Kaiser and his reforms. On 15 March a stormy meeting took place between Bismarck and the Kaiser, and afterwards Bismarck invoked an Order of 1852 forbidding ministers to advise the Emperor unless the Chancellor was present.

Eventually Wilhelm commanded Bismarck to withdraw the Order or resign, and the 'Iron Chancellor' chose the latter course. The nation was gripped by the power struggle between the new Emperor and the old Chancellor, and public opinion was divided in support of the two men. Kaiser Wilhelm often visited the estate of Count Eberhard Dohna at Prokelwitz in Silesia, so it was perhaps unfortunate that Bruch chose to show his support for Bismarck in that part of Germany where the general mood favoured the Kaiser.

The intrigue in Breslau against Bruch for his pro-Bismarck sentiments was centred around Ernst Flügel, a composer and director of one of the choirs in the city. In 1884 Bruch had been on good terms with Flügel, even recommending him to Simrock as 'a really good musician' after performing a Concert Overture in one of his concerts. 'It is no better or worse,' he wrote, 'than x similar works written every day in Germany.'[20] Matters came to a head in the autumn of 1889, when, after their friendship had soured, the combinations of Flügel's campaign against him, together with a boycott by sections of the public and by business interests, threatened the Concert-Verein. Max wrote to Simrock, 'I am leading a dog's life here, it is no longer bearable. Our organization can expect a deficit of not less than 7000–9000 marks. In short I am being led a merry dance, and have long lost my enthusiasm to take part.'[21] By the middle of December matters had deteriorated so much, that the management was forced to give notice to the orchestra's leader and other salaried members. Bruch tendered his resignation on 11 December, and it was accepted by the Committee. In an effort to soften the blow, he was assured that the post would not be filled after his departure, which effectively meant the dissolution of the Concert Society. It later transpired that this was a ruse to soft-soap him, for by May 1890 his successor in Coblenz (Maszkowski) had been called to Breslau. Bruch was understandably furious. 'They let a German artist like me go,' he wrote to Simrock, 'and call in an ageing Pole as saviour of this German organization.'[22]

The running of the Breslau Concert-Verein had been taken over from Dr Kaufmann by a Herr Rosenbaum, and he had a few pertinent comments to make to Simrock about Max Bruch. 'I am in the know about the "Bruch affair". I feel sorry for our friend. From time to time one encounters people of indisputably good character, and all possible attributes which nevertheless do not help. Bruch must find himself a position in which, with his basically idealistic outlook, he has nothing more to do than compose.'[23] Bruch, by now weary of the problems of being a Music Director in any city, had independently come to the same conclusion, and told Simrock, 'everything will be fine if I do not need to take on the martyrdom of a Music Director's post again.'[24] It was a brave decision to take, for he now had four children and a wife to support. It was a 'leap in the dark,' wrote Margarethe Bruch, 'and perhaps it meant serious deprivation for us all.' The post of Musical Director, held by Friedrich Gernsheim in Rotterdam, became vacant at this time, when he was appointed to the Stern'sche Gesangverein in Berlin. Bruch did not apply, but allowed his name to go forward for consideration. It was a matter of protocol that he was prepared to allow approaches to be made to him, but was too proud to submit an application himself. The Dutch, as it happened, were not interested. 'The die is cast: I have not been selected — my lot from now on will be freedom and worry . . . for the first time in my life I have totally failed.'[25] The successful applicant was a protégé of Brahms from Vienna, von Perger, 'a young man who has never conducted', complained Bruch. Max now took a long hard look at the choices facing him, and decided that the best place to be without a job was back in the German capital. On 9 September 1890 the Bruch family moved from Breslau to take up residence in Albestrasse 3 in the Berlin suburb of Friedenau. This was to become Max Bruch's home for the rest of his life.

When Bruch was Music Director in Liverpool, he wrote just a handful of compositions. His tenure of the English post was only three years, whereas in Breslau he remained for seven, writing comparatively little music during his stay. The major task was the completion of his secular oratorio *Achilleus*. Having written *Odysseus* in 1873, it was a logical step to turn to Homer's *Iliad* as a source for another work, but the idea did not produce any immediate results. It was the Liverpool performance of *Odysseus* on 22 November 1881 that rekindled his enthusiasm for the project. Finding a librettist proved no easy matter, but eventually his Bremen friend, the conductor Carl Reinthaler, recommended Heinrich Bulthaupt, a librarian from that city. The collaboration began in the spring of 1882, and Bruch was working on the full score during his trip to America in the spring of 1883. His move from Liverpool to Breslau in the late summer of 1883 was followed by a period of settling in to his new post. Throughout 1884 he worked between concerts on his new oratorio, and it was finished in early 1885. Its first performance was from manuscript parts at the Bonn Music Festival on 28 June 1885 under Bruch's direction. A year later Bruch conducted *Achilleus* in Breslau. 'Breslau is standing on its head with joy, I have not encountered such a storm of rapture — I cannot express it any other way.'

*Achilleus* was considered by Bruch to be the sequel to *Odysseus*, first performed twelve years earlier. The scenario for the oratorio is the closing stages of the Trojan Wars, from which Bulthaupt selected three events involving the Greek warrior Achilles. These were the death of his close friend Patroclus, his revenge by killing Hector, and his meeting with Hector's father, King Priam. A choral Prologue sets the background to the origins of the Trojan Wars. In the first scene, Agamemnon releases his tired soldiers from the long and arduous campaign and agrees to take them back to Greece. Odysseus intervenes and reminds them all that the gods are on their side, and that victory is eventually assured. The soldiers' mood changes and the battle is resumed. The Trojans gain the upper hand over the Greeks, who have been weakened by the absence of Achilles' men. He has quarrelled with Agamemnon and withdrawn his troops from the battle. His close friend Patroclus, sensing imminent defeat, has disguised himself in Achilles' armour and led the Greek army into battle. The soldiers, believing themselves led by Achilles, are inspired to victory, but the valiant Patroclus is killed by Hector's lance. In Scene 2 of the oratorio, the news of the death of his friend is brought to the remorseful Achilles. He curses Hector and calls upon Thetis (his mother, the sea-goddess) for help. She promises him blazing armour from the god of fire to protect him in battle, and, in the final chorus of the first part of the oratorio, ascends with her goddesses to fetch it from on high.

The second part views the conflict from the Trojan perspective and introduces Hector, his wife Andromache, sister Polyxena and father King Priam. After the assembled Trojan company has offered up prayers for victory and peace, Andromache pleads with her husband not to return to battle. He takes no heed of her, and leads his men to the fight. In an ensuing chase and duel Hector is killed by the divinely protected Achilles.

Part III opens with the full burial honours and rites accorded to the fallen Patroclus by his friend Achilles. When King Priam arrives from Troy to plead for the broken body of his son, Hector, Achilles at first hardens his heart to the old man's pleas, but then relents when Priam asks Achilles to imagine his own father pleading for the body of his beloved son. The oratorio ends with Trojan grief at the death of Hector, a choral epilogue describing the death of Achilles, the fall of Troy and a eulogy in praise of the dead hero.

The three parts of the oratorio comprise seventeen scenes, most of which involve the chorus. Although named after one of its eight characters, the oratorio is far from centred on Achilles. He appears in only four numbers, but is the pivot around which all three parts of the oratorio move. His emotional response to the death of his friend in the

first part, his actual vengeance in the second and his eventual display of
compassion for the father of his enemy in the third, are all the focus of
attention at any one moment in the drama. The chorus is prominent in
narrative and dramatic moments: it is often left to them to propel the
drama through events which were not included in the setting (such as
the duel with Hector, and Achilles' own death). Of the soloists,
Achilles (*Heldentenor*), Priam (bass), Hector (baritone) and Andromache (alto) are the main protagonists singing in a variety of
styles, though mainly *arioso* and recitative. Unlike *Odysseus*, there are
few self-contained arias or extractable sections suitable for separate
performance, though Bruch did have the 'Wettspiele zu Ehren des
Patroklus' (The games in honour of Patroclus) published separately as
an orchestral work for the concert hall. Each of the three numbers is
preceded by a brass fanfare, and they are followed by 'Ringkämpfer'
(The wrestlers) for strings, 'Wagenrennen' (The chariot race) for
strings and woodwinds, and 'Die Sieger' (The victors) for full
orchestra.

*Achilleus* did not eventually enjoy the success of *Odysseus*, with
which it stands comparison. Even Bruch's melodic inspiration rarely
surfaces above its unimaginative, uninventive harmony and counterpoint. One such rare moment occurs at the end of the second part
('Traget die Kunde') sung by the chorus of Greeks, and another is
Hector's tender blessing on his child before leaving for his fateful duel
with Achilles ('Wachs' und gedeihe'). The orchestration has none of
the subtle colours and tender beauties of *Odysseus*. It is overburdened
with instrumental doublings and overwhelmed by a thickened texture
(twelve of the 21 numbers use the full orchestra). Clarity is lost in the
frenetic string passages at melodramatic moments, and too many
punctuating *sforzandi* followed by *tremolando* make the recitatives
tedious. Dramatic impact is predictably and unsubtly enhanced by the
use of the brass. The choruses, as so often in Bruch's music, are the
most effective and successful, and that which follows the Prologue is
particularly so. His mastery of polyphony was assured, and his use of
choral recitative now extended to unison, homophonic or imitative
writing. Where he does succeed is at the emotional high points in the
drama, when various protagonists react to the death of a loved one,
Achilles to Patroclus, Andromache to Hector, and Priam seeking the
return of Hector's body from Achilles.

Bruch took great time and trouble on the text for *Achilleus*, often
consulting with Amalie Joachim on matters of diction and style.
Sometimes his correspondence with Bulthaupt frustrated him, even
to the point of envying Wagner ('who did everything himself' and
avoided the need for a librettist). The issue of the work's length was a

matter of contention between them, and even for the first performance Bruch was still being forced to make cuts. Critical reaction
included an attack on its duration, to which Bruch responded that 'the
philistines can sit in the theatre for five hours through one of Wagner's
completely inorganic, formless tootlings which is all too seldom
interrupted by flashes of genius.' The *Neue Musikzeitung* was effusive
in its praise after the première during the Bonn Music Festival on 28
June.[26] Amalie Joachim and George Henschel performed the roles of
Andromache and Hector with great success. *Achilleus* was extremely
well received, and a repeat of the 'Ringkämpfer' movement from the
orchestral interludes at the beginning of the third part was demanded.
The *Kölnische Zeitung* carped about its length: 'The new composition
*Achilleus* by Bruch received a brilliant performance yesterday in Bonn,
despite lasting three hours on a day of tropical heat.' The Festival
seems to have been a particularly successful one. It was interesting for
the performance of the recently discovered *Cantata on the Death of
Joseph II* by the city's most famous son, Beethoven. This took place on
the day after *Achilleus*. Clara sang 'Parto, parto' from Mozart's *La
Clemenza di Tito* on the same occasion. Her voice was considered too
small for the concert hall by the reviewer in the *Neue Musikzeitung*, but
just right for a salon ('very soft, very nice and infinitely lovely, but
unfortunately weak and quite colourless on some notes'). On the third
and final day of the Festival, Max conducted a lengthy programme
consisting of Schumann's Second Symphony ('which suffered from
too fast *tempi* under his restless conducting'), the aria 'Ocean, thou
mighty monster' from Weber's *Oberon* (with Marie Schroeder-
Hanfstängl), Brahms' *Academic Festival Overture* and the Second Piano
Concerto with the Glasgow-born composer and virtuoso pianist
Eugen d'Albert as soloist ('with a *bravura*, expression and delicacy
which no other artist can imitate. A pity Brahms did not come to hear
his work!'). The concert concluded with a chorus from *Achilleus*.
Interspersed among the orchestral items were vocal contributions by
Henschel (who accompanied himself in a ballad by Loewe) and Clara,
who sang two of her husband's songs Op. 49. Two Schumann songs
were sung by Emil Götze and finally Frau Joachim contributed Lieder
by Schubert and Brahms ('pure sunshine' enthused the critic), whilst
d'Albert played works by Chopin and Rubinstein.

*Achilleus* had made an auspicious impact, but Bruch was drained by
the effort it involved when he composed it. 'My brain is empty after
completing *Achilleus*,' he wrote to Simrock. 'If it were up to me I
would end my public career as a composer with *Achilleus*.'[27] He
reflected that for 28 years he had been in a publication war with the
'New Germans', and now he was tired. Until he left Breslau in 1890,

his career was to be largely confined to that of a conductor. He was nevertheless encouraged by *Achilleus* being requested in Barmen, Cologne, Berlin, Hamburg and Breslau, where in each place the work was scheduled for performance within nine months of its première. It was translated into English by the American Mrs John P. Morgan but, like *Das Lied von der Glocke*, was ill-served by such phrases as 'Go in peace, thou hoary Sire'. Its performance in Cologne took place under Franz Wüllner on 15 December 1885. Amalie Joachim sang Andromache once again, and reported Wüllner's negative approach to rehearsing the work. Bruch was furious once again with his mother city. The *Kölnische Zeitung*'s report by Dr Guckeisen which began '*Achilleus* was the short title of this long concert' hardly endeared itself to the prickly Bruch. Wüllner insisted on using a string complement of 72 players, though Bruch thought 32 sufficient. The resultant balance between singers and orchestra was decidedly one-sided in favour of the latter, so varying the shades of dynamics was impossible. This all proved grist to the mill in another series of tirades against Cologne, and again Bruch concluded that he would have no more to do with the city that never seemed to acknowledge him as its own son. 'That is my mother city,' he complained to Simrock, 'and I, like a fool, have maintained a special attachment to this city. Fine! I will now tear it from my heart.'[28]

Another major work written by Bruch during his period in Breslau was the dramatic Cantata *Das Feuerkreuz* Op. 52. Like *Achilleus*, this was a work that had preoccupied Bruch for some time. He first considered it in the autumn of 1874, and began collaborating with Wilhelm Graff, his librettist for *Odysseus*. This was immediately after the unification of Germany, and Bruch was euphoric, like all devotees of Bismarck and his policies. It was also the time of his love affair with 'Lally' Heydweiller. The Scottish setting of *Das Feuerkreuz* (and its themes of love and patriotism) was always a ready source of inspiration for the composer, yet in spite of these ingredients for creative work, he shelved the idea and wrote *Arminius* instead. He was not satisfied with Graff's attitude to the project, and his relationship with 'Lally' was also beginning to founder. References to *Das Feuerkreuz* occur in letters to Simrock in 1876 and 1878 but it was not until 1888 that he finally composed it.[29] In a letter to Simrock from Bergisch Gladbach, where he was on holiday, Bruch recalled his first encounter with *Das Feuerkreuz* and his enthusiasm for setting it.[30] In the autumn of 1874 Graff had recently married a rich, young Russian widow and moved to Wiesbaden. By 1888 Bruch had lost touch with him. 'I think', he wrote, 'that he lives in the country in Mecklenburg and now occupies himself solely with raising oxen, cows and pigs. I have not heard of him for ten years.' Bruch had by now decided on Heinrich Bulthaupt (his librettist for *Achilleus*). 'He needs the money.'[31]

*Das Feuerkreuz* is based on Sir Walter Scott's 'Lady of the Lake', and it carries the following preface (by Caroline Holland) in the English version of the score:

> During the Middle Ages, in the Highlands of Scotland a curious custom prevailed. Whenever a quarrel arose between the clans (a circumstance of no unfrequent occurrence), the Head of the Clan would summon the priest and a rude altar would be erected. Then with weird rites and solemn imprecations, a bull was sacrificed thereon; and a rough Cross, made from the wood of a yew tree, was dipped in the blood of the victim and set on fire. This Cross was then entrusted to some youth of noble lineage, whose duty it was to start at full speed across country and deliver it into the hands of the nearest Chieftain, who in his turn had to carry it on. By this means the news of the outbreak of war was spread with inconceivable rapidity throughout the countryside, and every clansman seized his arms and hurried off at once to the place of meeting. This custom is described in Sir Walter Scott's 'Lady of the Lake', and it is upon an incident which occurs in that poem that the following Cantata is founded.

The Cantata comprises eight scenes, the first of which (two choruses framing a love duet) is set at sunrise on the wedding day. The bridal boat is seen crossing the quiet lake, and Norman (baritone) and his bride Mary (soprano) are enthusiastically hailed by the friends who await them on shore. The second scene follows without a break, This is a wedding hymn set in a woodland chapel — a bell on the note G sounds in the orchestra virtually throughout the movement. The marriage is barely over when Angus (bass) appears, dusty and travel-stained. Waving aloft the Fiery Cross, he thrusts it into Norman's hands and bids him bear it on. Confusion now breaks out as Norman is torn between love and duty, with Mary and the women imploring him to stay, the men maintaining that he is honour-bound to depart. Duty prevails, and Norman bids farewell to the weeping Mary before hurrying off bearing the Fiery Cross. At the end of the third scene, the ladies remain to comfort the forsaken bride. The fourth scene (which had already been used by Schubert in his 'Normans Gesang') is a lengthy solo for Norman, now alone among the hills and alternately overcome with grief at parting so soon from his bride, yet elated at the prospect of victory in war. The narrative passes to the chorus in the fifth scene, as Norman's progress carrying the Fiery Cross is observed on his journey through raging torrent, over towering rocks and from crag to crag, all accompanied by a fearsome storm. Eventually he encounters the men of Clan Alpine, who leave their work to arm themselves and gather around the Cross. Mary meanwhile appeals to the Holy Virgin in Scene 6 with an Ave Maria. The seventh scene is entitled War Song, in which Norman exhorts his men to heroic deeds by recalling the past triumphs of Clan Alpine. The final scene is the battle itself. From a hillside, Mary and her friends anxiously watch the progress of the conflict, which is depicted in extended orchestral passages. Bad news of defeat is brought to the women, but this proves incorrect, for the battle has indeed been won by Norman and his men. The lovers are reunited and the work ends with joyful and triumphant acclamations of the clan.

The plan to dedicate *Das Feuerkreuz* to the young Kaiser was abandoned by Bruch in 1889, when he concluded that the Emperor's taste in music was satisfied either 'by the blarings of massed trumpets' or the stupor induced by Wagner's 'hypnotic music'. Bruch observed that the Kaiser even 'attended rehearsals of Wagner's operas, and displayed an unhealthy appetite for this world of dragons, dwarfs, giants and supermen.' Instead the Cantata was dedicated to the Breslau Sing-Akademie, and received its first performance on 26 February 1889 in the city. There had been a possibility of the première being given in Cologne in June 1889, but plans appear to have foundered when Wüllner rejected the idea of sharing the podium with Bruch (who would have conducted it). The composer was mollified by the thought that, for the autumn of 1889, *Das Feuerkreuz* was to be performed in seven cities (Rotterdam, Leipzig, Magdeburg, Barmen, Bonn and Riga, with Zürich also considering it). He was nevertheless encouraged that Cologne had made an approach to him for the première. After the troubles surrounding the appointment of Wüllner, and Bruch's failure in securing the post for himself, it seemed that without Hiller (who had died in May 1885) his music would rarely be heard in his mother city. The letter to Simrock announcing these plans for the Cantata concluded with Bruch's reaction to the death two days earlier at Mayerling of the Austrian Crown Prince Rudolph. 'So he did shoot himself,' observed the composer. 'He became the victim of his own debauchery, and in despair he took his own life. A dreadful story.'[32]

The matter of an English translation of *Das Feuerkreuz* caused much trouble for the next fifteen years. In a letter to Simrock, Bruch assumed that it would be done by Mrs John P. Morgan (who had translated *Achilleus*). 'She can have absolute freedom,' wrote Bruch, 'except for Norman's scene (No. 4). Here she must use Walter Scott's poetry, and lay it out under the text. I think that Bulthaupt translated this poem metrically. Please ask Mrs Morgan in my name to compare Scott.'[33] This particular number (and the Ave Maria) is subtitled 'adapted from Sir Walter Scott'. By November 1904 Bruch was becoming very indignant at the way *Das Feuerkreuz* was being translated by Caroline Holland, and complained bitterly to Hans Simrock, who had taken over the publishing firm from his late uncle Fritz:

> Now I must bring to your attention a highly absurd matter. A Miss Holland in London wishes to make my *Feuerkreuz* more Scottish than it is, and through you wishes to purify and improve it for an English version. To enliven the work with a bit of local colour, I used echoes of Scottish melodies at certain points. My source for these melodies was a quite trustworthy collection: *The Scotch Musical Museum, Popular Songs of Scotland*, published in 1787 by James Johnson. What I undertook with careful limitations and great care, is not enough for this strange female; she obviously has the Scottish disease, she has put the work under a Scottish magnifying glass from A to Z and corrected it as one would correct the bad exercises of a music student. She has hung a Scottish tail on anything and everything, changed my melodic form hideously in many places, changed the vocal lines of the choruses, removed repeats, in short she has bowdlerized the whole work in such a way that makes me see red. As well as sending me her improved vocal score, I received a letter in which at one point she goes so far as to say 'this and that is not worthy of you'. This person would be prepared to make the music of Mozart's *Don Giovanni* or *Marriage of Figaro* more Spanish because both operas are set in Spain. Neither would she refrain from smothering Handel's *Judas Maccabaeus* with Hebrew embellishments from top to bottom, or changing his melodies and adapting it in the fashion of old synagogue songs to make it all sound really Jewish!

This incident not only hastened the disintegration of his relationship with Hans Simrock (for Bruch there was no one to replace Fritz after his death in 1904), it also revived his anglophobia.

> Perhaps English musicians are behind her. Ignoramuses, members of that envious group who knowingly prevented the private performance of *Odysseus* before Queen Victoria at Windsor in 1883,

and later prevented performances of *Glocke* etc. anywhere they
could. I say it again, that England is no country for my choral
works, because there they hate us Germans too much, and because
they seek at every turn to suppress and harm German musicians in
particular. There would be much more to be done in America, also
with *Feuerkreuz* which is not so well known there as *Frithjof, Die
Glocke* etc. Were the translator a North American citizen, at least the
translation would be respected there. You know that![34]

*Das Feuerkreuz* is not comparable to *Frithjof* or *Schön Ellen*, for
Bruch does not succeed in maintaining dramatic tension in the work.
A surfeit of meandering passages based on the common arpeggio, the
overused device of the chord of the diminished seventh for melodramatic moments, and a dearth of inventive chromaticism help little in
holding its audience's attention. It nevertheless enjoyed much success
in Germany, and Bruch extracted the Ave Maria as a separate
publication (Op. 52 No. 6) for concert performance. This acquired its
own deserved popularity for many years, and was recorded as recently
as 1953 by Joan Hammond. It consists of the finest of Bruch's
melodious inspirations in *Das Feuerkreuz*, enclosing a dramatic
recitative. The orchestration is well crafted, particularly in its use of
horns, cellos and harp, all instruments which brought out the best in
the composer. In 1892 Bruch adapted the movement for solo cello and
orchestra, and it was published as *Ave Maria* Op. 61.

When Max Bruch left Liverpool in 1883, he left behind him several
friends with whom he kept in touch (not all of these friends were expatriate Germans, indeed, in spite of his fast developing anglophobia,
some were English). One of these was Andrew Kurtz of Grove
House, Wavertree. He was head of a chemical factory in St Helens, a
Committee member of the Liverpool Philharmonic Society, and an
amateur pianist. In 1881 Bruch began a Piano Quintet in G minor for
Kurtz, which was partially complete by 1886. It remained incomplete
until he was urged by a letter from Liverpool in January 1888,
containing a plea from the amateur musicians, 'We are all anxious for
the completion of the work — which of course we rarely play because
of its incompleteness, and because we have been anticipating every
week to receive the conclusion of the last movement.'[35] Bruch did
complete it, and the manuscript score carries his dedication in English,
'Composed for and dedicated to Mr A. G. Kurtz in Liverpool, Breslau
1886.' It remains unpublished. Bruch was aware of the abilities of
Kurtz and his associates, so he cut his cloth accordingly and placed no
complex technical demands upon them. This considerate approach
also manifested itself in the structure of the work with its occasional

textures of unison writing in the strings above a chordal piano accompaniment, little filigree work and a simply structured form in each of its four movements. As well as its *cantilena*, the slow movement shares both key and time signature of 3/8 with the slow movement of its famous predecessor, the First Violin Concerto. The manuscript of the work is in Bruch's handwriting (including an instruction placed under the first bar of the work to his English friends that *allegro molto moderato e tranquillo* should be 'not too fast! M.B.') until the end of the fourth page of the Finale. Then follows a version of the whole Finale in a copyist's hand.

During the last two years of Max Bruch's period in Breslau, he was far more productive as a composer. He was beginning to experience disillusion from extra-musical pressures, in particular his politics which did not find him many sympathizers in the city. Flügel was harassing him with intrigues and attacks in the newspapers, and Bruch lowered his public profile to resume work as a composer. On holiday in Johannaberg in the summer of 1889, he wrote 'Two Choruses' for four-part male voice choir Op. 53 and the *Siechentrost Lieder* Op. 54. Dedicated to the University Choir of St Pauli in Leipzig, the 'Two Choruses' once again use an ancient historical setting for their texts. The first, is 'Auf die bei Thermopylae Gefallenen' ('To the Fallen at Thermopylae'), in honour of the Spartans who defended Greece. Bruch later wrote a short Cantata entitled *Leonidas*, giving a fuller account of this historic event. It is a funeral dirge, and (apart from the middle section mourning the loss of Leonidas) its mood is introspective. Not so the second, which is a translation by Emanuel Geibel of 'Schlachtgesang' ('Battle Song') by Tyrtaeus of Athens. The turbulent and restless orchestral figuration strikes a contrasting mood with the first chorus, until a short choral recitative accompanied by the brass is reached. A brief homophonic passage for chorus with a rhythmic *ostinato* in the strings leads to a change of metre and a contrapuntal, two-part antiphonal chorus. The conclusion of the work builds from a mood of prayer in remembrance to praise in honour of the immortal name of the fallen hero. Though the contrast between the two choruses (which are accompanied by full orchestra) is striking, their common theme is *dulce et decorum est pro patria mori.*

The form of Bruch's *Siechentrost* Lieder ('Solace in affliction' in the English translation by Mrs John P. Morgan) illustrates the importance he placed on the suitability of his chosen text. Dedicated to the poet Paul Heyse, the five songs were written for one or more voices, with violin and piano accompaniment and published by Breitkopf & Härtel in 1891. In Heyse he found common cause against the modernists of the

Liszt-Wagner school. From his home in Munich, heartland of the
Wagnerites, Heyse wrote on Christmas Eve 1891 to thank Bruch for
sending the songs, though he also expressed his doubts that he would
ever hear them played in his neighbourhood. Each of the songs is
prefaced by a short text that sets the scene.

> Suddenly strains of most wondrous music resounded; the tones of
> muffled strings, as though from a violin but softer, purer, clearer
> than ever fell from a fiddle at a village church festival. The sound
> seemed to float from on high above them, and its more than earthly
> loveliness took possession of all its listeners so irresistibly, that
> suddenly the many hundred voices, even the murmur of softest
> whispering was stilled, and all eyes turned to the source of the sweet
> sounds. They discovered that the fiddler sat on the topmost boughs
> of a linden tree, whose fresh bright green foliage could not entirely
> conceal his form.

The first song, a folksong for bass, follows. The piano and violin
play a lengthy introduction, beginning with the quiet calm of
arpeggiated chords over a pedal bass and the addition of the violin,
which now takes over the piano's arpeggios until the singer begins.
His song is a very short and simple folksong expressing feelings of
love and happiness for his beloved, its first six lines divided and
followed by a short phrase for the violin. All three players combine for
the second verse in the two varieties of style: voice and piano in simple                          ·
homophony, and the violin above with a more elaborate *cantilena*. The
narrative continues: 'Even as the host had finished speaking, the
playing and singing from the top of the linden tree began again, this
time in more sorrowful tone.'

The singer's love and trust have been misplaced. Where others can
enjoy the delights of love in spring, he can only reflect that solace is in
vain, that hate is born of trust and disdain of love. He is now named as
Siechentrost (baritone). Voice and piano start together (without
instrumental introduction) and have moved from the first song's
bright key of E major to sombre F minor. They remain alone together
in a sad duo until the violin's entry. At this point the piano
accompaniment changes to a more agitated and dramatic mood.

> They appeared one afternoon in a little community of wine-
> growers near St Goar, before a house from which that morning the
> body of a young dead girl had been borne away; the only child of
> good parents whose wealth was now worthless, and to whom the
> consolation of their friends and neighbours could give little solace.
> As they observed the mourners, the player stroked his strings

gently and began to sing, and his companion sang with him in a softer, higher voice.

A tenor (Gerhard) joins Siechentrost in the third song, which is an expressive and tender duet in two sections. The first is in A minor, and after a short instrumental introduction, the tenor echoes in refrain the verse sung by the baritone. Later the violin joins, interweaving arpeggios around each voice in turn. The voices briefly combine before piano and violin pause before the second section in the tonic key of A major. From here to the conclusion, the text exhorts the heart to raise its spirit and seek goodness. A short coda in A minor for piano and violin brings the duet to a calm close, the quaver figuration of the violin part now giving way to a slower pulse.

They still needed to take care and frequently change their place of refuge, which they sought in the decaying huts of hunters, deserted ruins of castles, and in gloomy woods. They carried with them such household materials as they needed, and travelled long distances by night until they could rest again in the morning. They had a song that strengthened their hearts on their nocturnal journeying.

Another duet follows, contrasting in style and mood with the first duet just as the second song had contrasted with the first song in the work. The voices sing mostly together in harmony throughout, accompanied constantly by simple piano writing and by the violin, which shadows and interweaves the vocal lines from mid-way through the song.

There is no written text between this duet and the final song for a quartet of voices, piano and violin. It is subtitled 'Spring in the Mosel Valley' and 'Siechentrost's Death'. Its introduction takes material from the beginning of the first song, giving the work a cyclical form. Then follow a number of chorale-like homophonic choruses which are either unaccompanied or are joined by the solo violin. The short instrumental coda again uses material from the end of the introduction to the first song to bring the work to a peaceful close. In the *Siechentrost Lieder*, Bruch revealed himself to be a musician sensitive to the poetry, and in accord with his poet's romanticism.

The other compositions completed before he left Breslau for Berlin were purely instrumental. The first two were the closely related *Canzone* for cello and orchestra Op. 55 and the *Adagio on Celtic Themes* Op. 56, also for cello and orchestra. Together with the *Adagio appassionato* Op. 57 for violin and orchestra, they all three led to the

Third Violin Concerto Op. 58, on which Bruch was also working in his final year in Breslau.

Like *Kol Nidrei*, the *Canzone* for cello and orchestra was also arranged by Bruch for other instruments: violin, viola or clarinet with piano accompaniment. He was insistent that it could and should be played with piano accompaniment as an integrated work in its own right, and that this should not be considered as an arrangement of the orchestral version. From the sketches to both this piece and the *Adagio on Celtic Themes* it is clear that Bruch conceived his work exclusively in melodic terms. Harmonic underlay is implied here and there at crucial structural points where modulation or form becomes important. Both works could have been vocal compositions, indeed (as its title implies) the *Canzone* was intended to include a vocal melody. It was to be from his early setting of Goethe's *Claudine von Villabella* (since lost). Both works are in clearly defined form, the *Canzone* in a simple ternary structure with its middle section modulating to the third of the principal key (B flat major — D major — B flat major), a specially favoured relationship of keys. The melodies of the outer and middle sections are:

Ex. 32a

Ex. 32b

Both these melodies were Bruch's. Not so those of the *Adagio on Celtic Melodies* which followed. This work and the *Canzone* were

written in July 1890 on holiday in Bergisch Gladbach, whilst Bruch was
working at his beloved Igeler Hof. He had known both melodies used in
the *Adagio* for 25 years, though he had not considered setting them in
this manner. When Amalie Joachim endorsed Bruch's tentative
suggestion of a cut in Andromache's second scene in *Achilleus*, he
concurred 'with regret', but considered retaining the excised music as
material for a cello piece. Though this idea came to nothing, it
nevertheless awakened in him the memory of melodies he always
intended to set from James Johnson's *Scots Musical Museum* once again.
In a letter to Simrock he wrote that 'the first melody is Scottish, the
second (in E major) is Irish.[36] As it was not possible to call the work
"Adagio on Scottish and Irish melodies", the idea occurred to me when
I was playing the work to Rensburg [the cellist Jacques Rensburg] in
Bonn to use the collective word "Celtic". But now I believe the Scots
are not in fact Celts—do you know for certain?' Rather cynically Bruch
decided that he would 'throw all his scruples overboard. No ordinary
cellist . . . would give the word "Celtic" another thought. It sounds
somewhat foreign and strange to the ear, and that is good enough!'[37]

Ex. 33a

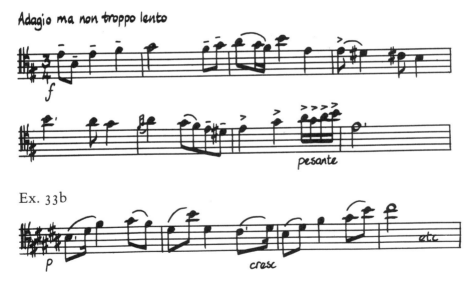

Ex. 33b

Breitkopf & Härtel eagerly accepted the *Canzone* for 1,500 marks in
November 1890, having remembered the success of *Kol Nidrei*.
Simrock was offended and had to be placated by Bruch, who
reminded him that, until now, he had always enjoyed first refusal on
the composer's works. This meant that he naturally chose those that

were most viable in commercial terms, leaving others to pick up the rest. Bruch, looking ahead to the day when he might be forced to go elsewhere, decided on a more pragmatic approach and now began to court new publishing houses or revive relationships with those with whom he had dealt in the past.

The case of the *Adagio appassionato* complicated matters. Joachim had participated in Bruch's farewell concert in Breslau in April 1890, for which Bruch was very grateful. The *Adagio* was then written and promised to Joachim, but since his divorce from Amalie, there was great ill-feeling towards Simrock, who was wrongly suspected by the violinist of an involvement with his wife. There was therefore no question of Joachim's name appearing on any work published by Simrock. Since November 1889 the composer had begun to sense a reluctance on Simrock's part to exercise his rights of exclusivity on new compositions (in fact the partnership had already been unsettled three years earlier with the Third Symphony and the *Hebrew Songs*, both of which were subsequently taken by Breitkopf & Härtel). Bruch therefore suggested that the publisher should relinquish his option, and release him to make approaches elsewhere. Simrock was initially indignant, but eventually came to an arrangement for first rights on any work which the composer produced for solo violin. The troubles Bruch encountered with the *Adagio appassionato* were resolved when Simrock took it and published it without its dedication to Joachim. Simrock seems to have swallowed his pride by the time of the appearance of the Third Violin Concerto the following year, for this was published complete with Bruch's dedication to Joachim.

The *Adagio appassionato* Op. 57 in F minor for violin and orchestra is a single movement in sonata form. It was thought by Wilhelm Altmann to have been a projected movement for the following Third Violin Concerto Op. 58, but this is untrue. There is certainly a superficial similarity between the first-subject theme of Op. 57 and the latter part of the main theme in the first movement of Op. 58, but the comparison can be taken no further than this. (See Exs. 34a and 34b)

'It is one of my best works,' Bruch wrote to Simrock, 'and pleased Joachim, the orchestra and the artists at a rehearsal in the College exceedingly well. You can have it for 2,000 marks.'[38] It is a showcase for the violin — the orchestra has hardly any part of it to itself, and from the soloist's first entry in the fifth bar it demands a continual virtuosic display in both passage work and arpeggios. It is full of sweet melody, has a cushioning orchestral texture on which the violin can alternately sit, plunge into or soar above. It also bears the fingerprint of its composer's harmonic suspensions, his predilection for the mellow sounds of horns and violas, the combined funereal sounds

Ex. 34a

Op. 57 bars 17–20

Ex. 34b

Op. 58 bars 23–26

of muffled timpani, soft trombone chords and *pizzicato* string chords. This latter effect is also achieved at the opening of the *Scottish Fantasy*, though the *pizzicato* string chords were replaced by the harp.

Bruch's letter describing Op. 57 in such glowing terms was written from the Estonian capital of Reval (now Tallinn) on the Gulf of Finland. Bruch visited the German community of this Hanseatic port for three weeks, beginning on 17 November 1890. His time there was hectic. 'In haste,' he wrote, 'a couple of words between rehearsals and concerts, and terrible 24-hour winter journeys in temperatures of 15–16 degrees below zero . . . A very tiring journey, but the enthusiasm of the Russian–Germans refreshes me, and something always results. On Monday 1 December I am doing *Feuerkreuz* and *Frithjof* here. Next winter *Feuerkreuz* will be done in Riga; recently it was done in Speyer; in January it will be done in Carlsruhe.'[38] Upon his return he wrote to Simrock: 'My Russian trip was very successful, and apart from the tiring long journeys, very pleasant. Everywhere in the Baltic lands I felt myself borne along by a wave of pure, beautiful enthusiasm; the people live and breathe the melodies of *Odysseus*, *Glocke* etc., and recently *Feuerkreuz* has been added to their enthusiasm, which I cannot describe in words. "They threw garlands and shouted for joy", and the people, musicians and press were quite unanimous.'[39]

On 9 September 1890 Max Bruch left Breslau with his family for the uncertain life which lay ahead in Berlin. By now he had adopted a

philosophy akin to Mr Micawber's. 'Until further notice,' he told
Simrock, 'I shall work quietly here. From time to time I shall undertake
big tours from which something will turn up.'[40]

*Chapter Fourteen*

BERLIN I

1891–97

MAX AND CLARA Bruch with their four children Margarethe, Max
Felix, Hans and Ewald, and their faithful Breslau maid Lene, all
moved to the then rural Berlin suburb of Friedenau at the beginning of
September 1890. Family finances had to be closely watched so Max
selected a cheap upstairs flat for rent at Albestrasse 3. Although it
was considered by the family to be only a temporary residence, it was
to be the final home for Max and Clara. Their daughter Margarethe
recalled (in an unpublished memoir) that there was no longer a library
or music room, and that her father's rented grand piano now stood in
the dining room. 'His beloved books, his four Bismarcks, the bust of
Homer and a picture of the old Kaiser were consigned to a garden
room,' she recalled. The children slept in two little rooms, but at least
they had the run of a garden before the city encroached upon them,
spreading its suburbs and finally surrounding them. They were
initially still able to sit in the spring sunshine among the cherry trees,
the lilac and the jasmin in their garden, and to enjoy the first fruits of
their vegetable plot — radishes!

During the weeks of November and December 1890 Bruch was
having to placate Fritz Simrock over matters other than the dedication
to Joachim in the *Adagio appassionato*.

Simrock became convinced that the composer was deserting him
for Joachim and his circle. It is unusual to see Bruch in the position of
soothing someone else's ruffled feathers. 'You see ghosts where there
are none,' he wrote in another attempt to calm his publisher.[1] Bruch
justified his renewed association with Joachim, not only on musical
grounds but also because the violinist had helped him through his
difficulties in Breslau (another ally, to his surprise and pleasure, was
Hans von Bülow). Ingratitude was not a vice which could be laid at
the door of the composer, and Bruch was grateful to these two
eminent musicians in his fight against those 'bad, miserable, petty,
two-faced and treacherous' people in Breslau for whom he would
feel the 'bitterest hate for the rest of my life.'[1] Simrock also suspected
him of a renewed association with Hermann Levi, but this too was

refuted. Levi was the Chairman of the Committee running the Stern'sche Gesangverein and inevitably came into contact with Bruch, though their meetings were purely formal. Bruch had conducted the chorus in the New Year of 1890 and was once again offered the post which had been his twelve years earlier. He did not consider the salary commensurate with the work involved, nor did he consider that he would have been given the artistic freedom that he had enjoyed in his earlier tenure. A letter to Anton Krause in Barmen also complained of the 'American-style star system' which now prevailed in Berlin in order to ensure the survival of organizations such as the Stern'sche Gesangverein.[2] Concluding his pacifying letter to Simrock, he wrote: 'One must also add that we [Joachim and Bruch] are both getting older and more reasonable. Formerly he was often unreliable and generally dismissive of me. Now he recognizes and values the fact that I have my place in the world, that neither stupidity nor wickedness can rob me of it, and he is too great a musician not to see clearly that I belong to the few who now, along with Brahms, maintain the true, organic essence of music.'[1]

Bruch then tempted Simrock by telling him that news of his latest Violin Concerto was spreading, and publishers were fighting over it like the Greeks 'over the body of Hector'. They were all thinking of the world-wide fame of the first concerto, and were now lined up to make Bruch an offer, 'all first rank people, apart from Härtel's who on the whole are unmusical and behave like a mule in the mist'. He asked Simrock to release the work from his exclusive hold, but the publisher decided to take a chance, exercise his right to all new violin pieces by Bruch, and accept that it would appear complete with its dedication to Joachim.

Unlike its two predecessors, the Violin Concerto No. 3 in D minor Op. 58, begun in the summer of 1890 and completed in February 1891, is written in the classical mould. Bruch described the genesis of the work. 'I returned from my summer rest with, among other things, a *Concert Allegro* in D minor . . . and thought of dedicating it to Joachim. Immediately before my departure for Russia, I was with Joachim to talk the work through with him, and it was decided to expand the piece to a complete concerto.'[1] This *Concert Allegro* became the long first movement of the concerto. The work begins with an extensive orchestral introduction based on a strong rhythmic motif:

Ex. 35

This acerbic figure gives way, in true sonata form, to the second subject, the contrasting, passionately lyrical theme which closely resembles the principal melody of the *Adagio appassionato*. Another reminder of this earlier work is the soloist's flamboyant, virtuosic entry which follows. The style of the opening movement of the Third Concerto is broad and heroic, departing from the more lyrical first movements of its two predecessors for a robust *concertante* form. The slow movement, however, is more reminiscent of its famous ancestor of 22 years earlier, with its expansive *cantilena*. It is a *romanze*, which unusually is not in the conventional key of the relative major (F), but takes a step of a major third in the other direction, down to B flat major. The structure of this second movement is simple, with the soloist developing the main theme by figurations and variations against the background of a subdued orchestral accompaniment.

Ex. 36

The final movement is dominated both by its strong rhythmic motive and accented accompaniment, each in contrasting simple and compound triple beats. It is a conventional rondo, with the *perpetuum mobile* of the principal material (Ex. 37) interrupted by more lyrical passages (Ex. 38), often using the favourite device of double-stopping. Bruch's friend Otto Goldschmidt reported to him from

London that *The Times* described this last movement as possessing a
'Hungarian character'. 'Rubbish,' said the composer, 'this is only
because Joachim is Hungarian. Utter nonsense!'[3]

Ex. 37

Ex. 38

Bruch was anxious for Joachim's advice on the bowing of the
figuration of the motto theme in this Finale as it appears in the
orchestral first violin part at bar 69. He put three alternatives
to Joachim.[4] (See Ex. 39)

The final version appears with all the notes played staccato, so
presumably Joachim rejected all Bruch's ideas.

In spite of Bruch's appreciation of Joachim's interest and enthusiasm for the work, his opinion of the violinist's performance of
the piece was mixed.

Joachim certainly grasps the first movement with immense energy,
and plays much of it very well, but he rushes the figuration,
especially in the development and as a result the movement loses its
style.

Ex. 39

Violin I letter D/bar 69

In the Adagio, I consider certain figurations purely as a tender, whispered melisma — he plays them too quickly and too ardently, somewhat nervously. We could never agree on the interpretation of this middle part. Sarasate will be able to play it more as I wish it. His [Joachim's] playing of the Finale is splendid throughout; the end unfortunately did not go well this time, which had never happened to him before. One must however take account of his present indisposition.[5]

Joachim organized a play-through of the first two movements in February 1891 at the Hochschule in Berlin. Bruch was then able to make corrections. The Finale was delayed by Joachim's concert engagements elsewhere (his heavy schedule also precluded him from giving the first performance of the *Adagio appassionato* in England. He had no time to memorize it, refused to play from the copy, and so the honour went to Sarasate in June 1891). Eventually the rehearsal of the completed concerto took place on 21 April in the Berlin Hochschule, and the work received its public première on 31 May 1891 in Düsseldorf. According to Bruch it was 'not a success, but a triumph.'[6] Joachim was tireless in performing the third Violin Concerto. Bruch listed eight performances within five months in the cities of Hamburg, Berlin, Frankfurt, Strasburg, Breslau, Leipzig, Cologne and London.[7] This last performance was scheduled for a Philharmonic Society concert under W. G. Cusins in March 1892. Hans von Bülow (who also thought highly of the work) conducted the Hamburg and Berlin performances (on 2 and 9 November 1891). In spite of Bruch's protests to the contrary to Simrock, the creation of the concerto healed the rift between Joachim and the composer over the former's divorce. When Bruch saw Joachim on the concert platform beside him, giving the première of a violin concerto exactly as he had done 23 years earlier, he could not resist succumbing to sentiment and nostalgia. 'You have interceded for me on the Rhine as in Berlin with the full power of your personality, and if the sunshine of happiness is now upon me instead of the experience of much trouble, then that is largely through your good offices.'[8]

The Düsseldorf Music Festival was a great success for Bruch. Nearly 800 voices from ten choral societies combined to perform excerpts from *Das Feuerkreuz*, *Achilleus* and *Das Lied von der Glocke*. 'One hears with justification of the fickleness of the masses,' he told Joachim, 'but the singing masses of the Rhineland have remained true to me for twenty years, and it is the case wherever my choral works are sung. There must be something in the music which strikes their hearts and gives them something which I arouse and continually please. . . . Of one thing I am absolutely clear; in spite of everything that the radical parties have done over the years, music based on the principle of Melody and possessing the purity and definitiveness of Form still has its public, and a very large one at that.'[8]

Max Bruch had scored a triumph with his first attempt at the violin concerto *oeuvre* in 1868 (also his first successful full-scale orchestral work). The time was ripe for such a success after those of Beethoven and Mendelssohn, and in turn it was superseded by that of Brahms. However Bruch was unable to follow it up with his next two. He always extolled the virtues of the Second and Third Concertos and exhorted all violinists to play them, but none of his works for violin consistently matches Op. 26, a fact which Bruch only grudgingly conceded.

One of Joachim's innovations at the Berlin Königliche Akademie der Künste (Royal Academy of Arts) was to create a Meisterschule for composition, and to staff it with eminent pedagogues. One of these was Heinrich von Herzogenberg, formerly conductor of the Bachverein in Leipzig and (from 1886) professor of composition in Berlin in succession to Friedrich Kiel. In the summer of 1891 von Herzogenberg's wife became ill, and doctors advised a move further south. Herzogenberg resigned his post at the Berlin Akademie, and through the good offices of Joachim and Philipp Spitta, Bruch was offered the Directorship of the Masterclass for Composition on 26

November 1891, by the Minister of Culture, with effect from 1 April 1892. With the post went the automatic membership of the Senate of the Akademie and the title of Professor. For Bruch it was 'a happy good fortune that I am now, after a lifetime, free of public opinion, the misery of the daily newspapers and the ordinary orchestral player', and it also provided a much needed regular income. Once again he had good reason to be thankful to Joachim.

A step towards securing the post had been the commissioning by the Akademie of a festive cantata for the Kaiser's birthday in 1892. This work for soloists, chorus, orchestra and organ was first performed at the Königliche Akademie on 17 January 1892 and, after making revisions during the autumn, it was published in the following year by the Magdeburg publisher, Heinrichshofen, under the title of *Hymne* Op. 64. Bruch had been reluctant to write it (as an unsympathetic subject of his Kaiser), but he was pragmatic enough to appreciate the significance of accepting the commission with an eye on his long-term security. Although it was requested for a specific event, he and others (such as Joachim) considered it to be 'above the standard of an occasional piece'.[9] After the celebration, it was published for general use. He described the work (which takes Psalm 91 as its text) as a 'broadly laid-out, architectural and effective choral work, divided into four sections'.

Bruch was now free to dedicate as much time as he wished to composing and, in a flurry of activity, he produced several vocal and instrumental works. In 1892 Schott published *Five Lieder* for baritone, Op. 59, which consisted of 'Um Mitternacht' (Mörike), two 'Kophtische Lieder' (Goethe) and the two-part 'Die Auswanderer' (Stieler). These songs were first written during Bruch's time in Liverpool, but reworked in 1891. In the same year Heinrichshofen published *Nine Songs* for *a cappella* mixed chorus Op. 60, which included texts by Mörike, Scheffel, Karl Simrock and Geibel, as well as an Irish and a Scottish folksong. The remaining three had not previously been used by Bruch, and were from the thirteenth-century Minnesänger Hugo von Singenberg, J. Nachtenhöfer and Paul Gerhardt. The various subjects of the texts range from the seasons and prayers, to folksongs and a knight's song of farewell before a tournament. The last of this current output of vocal or choral compositions was written for Clara Bruch, and was a Christmas hymn entitled *Gruss an die heilige Nacht* Op. 62 to a text by the literary historian Robert Prutz. It is for 'high alto solo, mixed chorus, orchestra and organ, and lasts 17–20 minutes. My wife will sing the solo at the first performance.'[9] This took place on 16 January 1893, husband and wife together on the concert platform in Berlin with the

Philharmonic Chorus. Performances followed in Bonn, Essen, Elberfeld and New York within a year. 'It belongs quite definitely to the
best I have produced, including the *Messensätze*.'[10] 'The work contains all the ingredients for a truly popular work in the noblest sense,'
he concluded in a successful effort to interest Simrock in the work.[11]

These vocal compositions were followed by the completion of
another for cello, the *Ave Maria* Op. 61. This was virtually a
transcription of the aria from *Das Feuerkreuz* (No. 6), though
modifications had to be made to the middle recitative section and the
instrumentation. It was also transposed from D minor to A minor.
Bruch's cellist friend, Robert Hausman (the driving force behind *Kol
Nidrei*), was helpful to him in much the same way as Joachim gave
advice on the phrasing and fingering of the violin works. It is
especially interesting because a comparison between the original vocal
concept and the instrumental arrangement highlights Bruch's deploy-
ment of accompanying instruments. Whereas the voice was often
doubled by woodwinds, the emphasis in the version for solo cello is
placed on instruments with a lower *tessitura*. The middle section of the
vocal work, a recitative, now becomes a cadenza for the cellist, and is
limited solely to recreating the mood of the original. (See Exs. 40
and 41)

Ex. 40

On 19 June 1892 Bruch sent Joachim a new composition for
appraisal and advice on fingering and phrasing. The work was the
*Swedish Dances* Op. 63, which appeared in various guises, initially for
violin and piano, but later also for piano (2 hands), piano duet (4
hands), for military band and for full orchestra. The orchestration of
the Dances was originally for 'my private pleasure', and because he
'was unable to think of them without [orchestral] colour'. They
comprise an orchestral introduction leading to fifteen arrangements of
loosely connected folksongs (though the last arrangement is a repeat
of the first). Their model was Brahms' *Hungarian Dances*. There are
some beautiful variations for solo instruments among the collection
(clarinet and French horn in No. 2, cor anglais and French horn in No.
6, and solo violin in No. 12), and the mood of most is tuneful and
simple (humorous in the case of Nos. 5, 7 and 13). The work loses

Ex. 41

impetus, however, in the ponderous and thick orchestrations of Nos.
9 (the middle section) and 10.

Bruch had an optimistic opinion of their popularity: 'There is
no question that these pieces will be quickly boiled, baked and roasted,
and easily spread about on foot and on horseback. Just like the
*Hungarian Dances.*'[12] Discussion of the financial arrangements with
Simrock led Bruch to make some spurious assessments of his self-
importance. 'As I am really recognized everywhere,' Simrock read in
Bruch's letter 'as having no competition at the present time in writing
for the violin, and holding an exceptional position; and furthermore
after the very great and quick success of the Third Violin Concerto in
various countries, the expectations of my new works for violin will be
as great as those initially enjoyed by the *Hungarian Dances.*'[13] Simrock
agreed to Bruch's demands for 3000 marks for the violin and piano
version and a further 1000 marks for the orchestration. He also agreed
to a request from Inspector Rossberg of the Prussian Army Band for
an arrangement for military band (Bruch took advantage of this new
outlet by suggesting to Simrock that the orchestral 'Games in honour
of Patroclus' from *Achilleus* might also be arranged for military band).
The various guises of the *Swedish Dances* appeared in two volumes,
containing seven and eight Dances respectively, but it is the version
for violin and piano which has endured.

Another composition for violin entitled *In Memoriam* Op. 65 soon followed. It is one of the deepest felt of Bruch's works, and he considered it to be his finest. He rejected a suggestion from Simrock to add further movements to the work:[14]

> *In Memoriam* is in itself so complete that nothing can follow it. If it had been my original intention to write a little *Concerto* or a *Konzertstück* consisting of an Adagio and a Finale, I would have composed the Adagio as if something were to follow it. But I never had such an intention, and were I to do so now (albeit for viable commercial reasons which I am quite able to understand) I would be bowdlerizing the work and going against its inner impulse. At the beginning of the year I carefully went over all this by myself and together with Joachim, and he thinks as I do. Now we both know what is not good about Joachim, but all the same he remains a great musician and in artistic matters he has significantly more of an opinion than Sarasate, however high the latter stands as a soloist.

Simrock accepted Bruch's decision and bought Op. 65 for 2000 marks. Bruch wrote to Joachim regarding its title and the programmatic implications it carried. 'The piece actually is a lamentation, or a type of instrumental elegy; I could not say however that it was written for specific persons or those of the past. If I say 'In Memoriam 1888', this title reminds one of the two dead German Kaisers; but they should be honoured through vocal works for large forces. A piece for violin strikes me as inadequate, and anyway the occasion is in the past.'[15]

*In Memoriam* is substantially scored for two each of flutes, clarinets and bassoons, one oboe, a cor anglais and a contra-bassoon; four horns, two trumpets and three trombones, three timpani and cymbals. In the unusual key of C sharp minor, *In Memoriam* is the largest of Bruch's single-movement works for solo violin, and has effective moments of orchestral colour in its use of cor anglais, contra-bassoon and cymbals (which, as in the *Scottish Fantasy*, are never clashed, but occasionally and quietly brushed). Its structure is an extended sonata movement in which themes are substantially developed in a *concertante* style between soloist and certain orchestral instruments. Prominent is the first horn, which is given a recurring high-lying triplet figuration in repeated dialogue with the soloist. Bruch's use of varied rhythms played simultaneously as an accompaniment, which developed from the First Symphony (Ex. 20), is used again to great effect. The melodies are typical of the sweetness and lyricism in his writing, though surprisingly the second subject's more surging and passionate outburst is hardly developed.

In another letter to Joachim, Bruch again emphasized his indebtedness to the great violinist for furthering his career by propagating the First Violin Concerto, and by reminding him that it was 25 years earlier that this had occurred. He repeated his deep regret that he had sold the work outright to Cranz, and received no royalties from this 'terribly popular work'.[16] In his reply Joachim modestly thanked Bruch for the accolade and expressed his pride at having made his own contribution to the composer's success. Their friendship was now firmly re-established. Joachim performed *Rorate coeli* at the Hochschule on 17 June 1893, having asked Bruch to play it at the piano for his benefit. 'Your *tempi* are not easy to grasp,' he observed. Once again they were able to take an interest in one another's families, with the shadow of the Joachim divorce distanced through time (though Bruch always felt Amalie to have been the injured party). Joachim related how his daughter Marie 'is travelling to Bayreuth to study a few roles with Frau Cosima; for like all opera singers, she is under the influence of the Wagner cult — these days there is nothing one can do against it. I must bear with it, and reassure myself that one day a greater artistic seriousness will prevail.'

Bruch's character, now that he was settled in Berlin as a Professor, was perceptibly changing. He was mellowing with age in some ways, though he was still capable of extremely bitter outbursts. His attitude to Brahms, for example, was uncompromising:

I will hear Brahms, but not speak to him. Last year I experienced such an uncouth and arrogant snub from him when I had made a friendly approach, that I have lost all inclination to repeat the experiment once again. The time is now gone when I conduct myself *en canaille* in honour of him and his many works. He has every reason to respect my position in the artistic world alongside him and not under him (if he is not prevented from doing so by his arrogance and envy). If he does not wish to do so, then I for my part do not wish to have any further personal dealings with him. No single artist has ever possessed Art, and he too cannot monopolize it. I am sorry, but it really will not do.[17]

Bruch was sensitive to encroaching old age, particularly with the deaths of his friends and colleagues, which began in the 1890s. Apart from a bout of influenza in May 1893 (all four children going down with scarlet fever the following month), he was generally in good health, though Clara suffered from asthma and Simrock from gout. His entry into middle-age may have begun to affect his personality, but it also coincided with the beginning of official recognition both at

home and abroad. In 1890 the Beethovenhaus–Verein in Bonn had
made him an honorary member, an accolade he had also received in
the same year from the Singakademie upon his departure from
Breslau. He was awarded the Maximilian Order for Arts and Sciences
by the Prince Regent of Bavaria, 'a Bavarian "Pour le Mérite" as I
hear.'[18] The irony of the situation did not escape him that this honour
came from the heartland of Wagner territory, where 'I have as good as
no connections at all.'

In 1893 Cambridge University Musical Society (CUMS) celebrated
its golden jubilee by organizing a concert during which five eminent
composers each conducted one of his own works. On the following
day these same eminences received honorary degrees of Doctor of
Music from the University. The occasion was the brainchild of
Professor Charles Villiers Stanford of Trinity College, who was retiring after 21 years as conductor of CUMS (Schumann's Piano Concerto and Brahms' *Alto Rhapsody* together with his First Symphony
were some of the many works to receive first British performances
under their auspices). The composers originally chosen were Brahms,
Verdi, Gounod, Rubinstein and Grieg. Brahms refused the invitation
because he loathed travel and Verdi declined on account of his age;
consequently Stanford proposed Bruch and Boïto as representatives
of Germany and Italy. Saint-Saëns and Tchaikovsky became substitutes for Gounod and Rubinstein, leaving Grieg as the only survivor
of the original plan. Invitations were sent out by the University's
Vice-Chancellor on 12 December 1892 to the five men and Bruch
replied immediately with his acceptance, declaring it 'a great distinction for me to receive the title of Doctor of Music hon. causa from
your highly esteemed University.' Bruch did not object to being
second choice to Brahms, who on the other hand told Simrock in a
typically marked display of sour grapes: 'May one congratulate Bruch
as Doctor!? The hat has been turned inside out! (Between ourselves: it
was originally offered to me and to Verdi; neither of us could
undertake the journey, he on account of his age and I because of the
inferior title.)'[19] As it happens Grieg became unwell and did not attend
the celebrations (he received his Doctorate in May 1894).

The concert took place on Monday 12 June 1893 in the Cambridge
Guildhall at 2.30 p.m. The programme was:

| | |
|---|---|
| The Banquet with the Phaeacians from<br>*Odysseus* Op. 41 | Max Bruch |
| Fantasia for Piano and Orchestra *Africa* | Saint-Saëns |
| Prologue to *Mefistofele* | Boïto |
| Symphonic Poem: *Francesca da Rimini* Op. 32 | Tchaikovsky |

Suite: *Peer Gynt* Op. 46            Grieg
Ode: *East to West* Op. 52         Stanford

Stanford conducted his own work together with that of the absent Grieg and also *Africa*, in which Saint-Saëns appeared as soloist. Both *Africa* and *Francesca da Rimini* were receiving their first performances in Britain on this occasion. The excerpt from *Odysseus* went well and Bruch was repeatedly recalled to acknowledge the applause. He kept a copy of the programme containing a short biography among his personal papers, and indicated with a pair of exclamation marks a printing error which misspelt *Römischer Triumphgesang* as *Komischer Triumfgesang*. Another souvenir was a plan of the Dinner (tickets cost a guinea a head) in the Hall of King's College, which took place that night. Bruch sat at the top table between Lord Kelvin and the Provost of King's, and at seat 15 table D was the young first-year Trinity man, Ralph Vaughan Williams (himself four years away from a period of study with Bruch in Berlin). The dinner was followed by a *conversazione* beginning at 10 p.m. in the Fitzwilliam Museum, specially installed for the occasion with electric lighting. 'The soft glow of the incandescent lights, which were absolutely steady, produced a most pleasing effect upon the beautiful building, the dresses and the pictures, and gave general satisfaction.'[20]

In a temperature of nearly 80°F at midday the following day, the four composers together with General Lord Roberts, Lord Herschell and the colourful figure of the Maharajah of Bhaonagar (by dispensation wearing a turban rather than a doctor's cap) processed across the Green to Senate House to receive their degrees. The crowd of attending students regaled Lord Roberts with a rendition of 'For he's a jolly good fellow' ('sung with more vigour than musical ability').[21] It was a performance which caused 'M. Saint-Saëns to twist his fingers, Herr Max Bruch to look pensive, Signor Boïto to smile, and M. Tchaikovsky to sink into ineffable meditations.'[22] When Tchaikovsky appeared, the shout of a single student voice crying 'Good old Shakemoffski' and attendant 'roars of laughter' were heard.[23] Quite what the painfully shy Tchaikovsky and the stiffly correct Bruch made of such high jinks and English eccentricity is not hard to imagine. The oration for Bruch, delivered by the Public Orator (the eminent Classicist Dr John Sandys), was translated from the Latin into German by the composer and sent to Simrock upon his return.[24] It contains references to several of his compositions:

Now follows a praiseworthy son and heir of the Rhineland, who once set to glorious song the story of the death-dealing nymphs of the river in his homeland. Whether he dedicates his songs to a hero of his Fatherland like Arminius, liberator of the Germans, or creates his material from the national poetry of Schiller (the honour of Germany), whether he interprets the sagas of Scandinavia and the warlike virtues of the Normans, or if he turns to Greece and depicts for us anew the Battle of Salamis or the Wanderings of Odysseus — we happily recognize the great minstrel in him everywhere. In praise of such men, the poets of Greece and Germany unite with one voice. What did Homer once say? 'Minstrels will be worthy of attention and respect by all mortals because the Muse has taught them song, thus the minstrel benevolently has power.' And Schiller? 'Painting breathes Life, I demand the Spirit from Poetry, but only Polyhymnia [the Greek Muse of Music] expresses the Soul.'

The ceremony over, the Doctors now made their way to Christ's College, where they were entertained to luncheon by the Vice-Chancellor and Master of Christ's, John Peile. Bruch found himself seated between two ladies (Miss Day and Miss Sieveking) and opposite Boïto and Stanford. He had found an unlikely admirer in Boïto, who expressed both a very favourable opinion of the extract from *Odysseus* and an intention to study the complete work. Boïto gave his opinion of the Banquet Music to a friend: 'I cannot deny that it is somewhat heavy, but the structure and treatment are marvellous, and it is inexhaustible in its changing ideas, which are sometimes harmonic, sometimes rhythmic, sometimes contrapuntal, sometimes instrumental.'[25] Saint-Saëns wrote of the Bruch piece that it was not 'spiced enough; one should go to a concert as to a firework display, with the hope of being surprised and dazzled; now M. Max Bruch never lets off rockets.'[26] The luncheon concluded with a large antique loving-cup being passed around the tables in celebration of the new Doctors, after which they were invited to inspect the gardens of Christ's College and join a tea-party organized by the Vice-Chancellor's wife. Farewells were then said (though not before the indefatigable Saint-Saëns had rushed off to Trinity College chapel to give an organ recital) and the four composers departed from Cambridge. Bruch was last seen 'philosophically standing by a lamp-post of the station, leaving frivolous colleagues to travel by another line, and preserving a magnificent solitude.'[27] Juxtaposed with the elegant nobleman Tchaikovsky, the handsome Boïto and the charismatic Saint-Saëns, Max Bruch appeared dull and stuffy. After the first orchestral rehearsal (held in the Royal College of Music in London, now the Royal College of Organists) on 9 June,

Stanford held a soirée at his home. 'The evening was none too cold for any of the performers,' wrote Stanford, 'but even so was rather trying to the draught-fearing Bruch, who looked like an Arctic explorer, having armed himself with goloshes, a waterproof wideawake and a thick mackintosh to combat the rigours of an English June.'[28] Joachim had sent commiserations at the end of May to Bruch, who was recovering from influenza.[29] Another impression of his unprepossessing physical appearance is gained from the tenor soloist at the jubilee concert, Harry Plunket Greene. A guest commented to him that Tchaikovsky and Bruch looked respectively like 'an ambassador and the other like a store-keeper from the Middle West'.

Alexander Mackenzie's view of Bruch when he met the composer in Sondershausen (where Mackenzie was a young orchestral musician) was of his 'great ability as a conductor', but 'the impression created by Bruch's personality on me was that of a highly cultured, musically gifted man, somewhat cynical of speech and brusque of manner.'[30] Accounts of Bruch's physical appearance nearly always referred to his myopia and the thick glasses he was forced to wear. When he completed the form for his file at the Königliche Akademie der Künste, he had to describe his military service. He wrote, 'I did not serve, on account of serious short-sightedness.' Edward Speyer (writing over 40 years after meeting him in Berlin in 1878) described Bruch as 'appallingly ugly. He had an unusually large forehead with a marked backward slant and protruding fishy eyes. Although one could not help being impressed by his intelligence and sensibility, and his prominent gifts as a conversationalist, his personality was unattractive.'[31] This description of Bruch's physical appearance is scarcely borne out by contemporary photographs. Louis Elson was more tactful and accurate. Having acknowledged the composer's 'right to admission to the ranks of the masters', Elson wrote: 'In personal appearance Bruch is by no means as majestic as one would suppose from his works. He is small of stature, and his dark eyes peer through his spectacles with the sharp glance of a teacher rather than of a creator of heroic cantatas. He is quick and nervous in motion and, when directing an orchestra or chorus, his gestures are spontaneous and expressive.' Elson went on, 'In the latter part of the nineteenth century probably no composer has done more for the development of the chorus, and especially for the *Männerchor*, than Max Bruch.'[32]

In spite of Stanford's invitation to Cambridge, the Irish professor of music was reported to have answered Edward Dent's enquiry if it would benefit him to travel to Germany to study with the composer: 'I wouldn't wish me worst enemy to go to Max Bruch.' Stanford also advised Vaughan Williams to choose Italy rather than Germany as a place for further study. Speyer entertained his reader with anecdotes about Bruch and Brahms, the first of which concerned the unconventional Adagio first movement of the Second Violin Concerto. These accounts must be treated as apocryphal, for in the second, Speyer goes on to relate a tale about *Arminius*, yet Jeffrey Pulver tells the same story in which the composition described is *Odysseus*. According to Speyer, Bruch told him:

> The work had a great success, and at the end of the performance I was warmly congratulated by all present with the exception of Brahms, who only exclaimed, 'My dear Bruch, how can one commence a violin concerto with an Adagio?' Not content with this, he followed me round during the afternoon and kept on tugging at my coat-tails and repeating the words, 'How can one commence a violin concerto with an Adagio?' An unsupportable fellow.[31]

> Brahms chanced to visit Bruch in Cologne, and Bruch put into his hands a manuscript score of considerable dimensions with a request for his opinion and a solemn admonition to secrecy. It was the score of an oratorio entitled *Arminius*, founded on an episode in early German history, which eventually enjoyed a short-lived popularity. Bruch waited anxiously for the verdict, but all Brahms said after a seemingly close scrutiny was: 'I say, what splendid music-paper this is! Where did you get it?' A few days later Brahms and Bruch met again at a large dinner-party as the guests of a wealthy patron of music. When the sound of a barrel-organ in the street reached the ears of the company, Brahms called across the dinner-table in stentorian tones: 'Listen, Bruch. The fellow has got hold of *Arminius*.'[33]

When the Secretary of the Philharmonic Society, Francesco Berger, heard, in the New Year of 1893, of the visit of five (albeit four in the end) eminent composer/conductors scheduled for the following summer, he at once offered them engagements. Bruch, Tchaikovsky and Saint-Saëns all accepted the offer of an appearance at a Philharmonic concert for a fee of 25 guineas. Boïto refused on account of prior commitments in Italy after the degree ceremony, and Grieg's non–negotiable demand for a fee of £50 was rejected. Tchaikovsky and Saint-Saëns appeared together in the same programme on 1 June, the Russian conducting his Fourth Symphony and the Frenchman playing his Second Piano Concerto and conducting the symphonic poem *Le Rouet d'Omphale*. Bruch appeared two weeks later on 15 June together with Melba and Paderewski. The concert was conducted by

Alexander Mackenzie, but Bruch conducted his First Violin Concerto (with the Polish violinist Ladislas Gorski) and the three orchestral pieces from *Achilleus* (the games in honour of Patroclus). He insisted on including these in the programme, because to perform the famous Violin Concerto alone was no incentive, 'anyone can do that equally well'. According to Bruch, his conducting received 'great ovations'.[34] On the following day (16 June) Bruch was guest of honour at a dinner given by the Philharmonic Society. On 19 June he fulfilled a similar engagement, this time in Liverpool as guest of the German Club, and on 21 June his hosts were the German Club in the London Athenaeum.

Back in Germany Max took Clara to Bad Pyrmont for August 1893. He himself had sciatic pains in the leg, for which he took mud-baths and long walks in the wooded hills, while Clara 'bathes and drinks'. Bruch also reported observations, made during his trip to England, on the progress of his violin works in that country. It was proving to be a rich hunting ground. 'The Third Concerto,' he wrote, 'is played by all the best pupils at both the London Music Colleges; the *Romanze* Op. 42 was played by five girls in different places in London during June and July. The *Swedish Dances* are also beginning to be known and liked. The best two violin teachers at the Conservatoires (Sauret and Gompertz) are devoted to me and are continually having all my violin works studied; this in itself ensures a greater dissemination throughout England, for London is England (but Berlin is no longer Germany). Later I will send *In Memoriam* to both of them.'[35]

At the beginning of September 1893 Max and Clara returned to Berlin, and later in the month both travelled to Baden near Vienna. Whilst Clara remained there to visit relatives (her sister Helene was suffering from tuberculosis and died a year later), Max travelled to the Austrian capital on 1 October to begin rehearsals for the first performance of *Leonidas* Op. 66 a week later in the presence of the Austrian Kaiser, Franz Josef, and the King of Saxony. It had been requested by the Wiener Männergesangverein (Vienna male-voice Choir) for their golden jubilee, and Bruch worked once again with his librettist for *Achilleus*, Heinrich Bulthaupt. He described it as a work 'for baritone solo (a significant role), male-voice choir and orchestra. It lasts 24–25 minutes (35 minutes if Dr Wüllner drags all the *tempi*). The contents are naturally heroic, a development in an ascending line from the hopeless sadness of the beginning to the unselfish impetus of idealism in the face of death at the end.'[35] It was Bruch's first substantial work for male-voice choir since *Frithjof* nearly 30 years earlier. The performance promised to be excellent, with the young baritone Josef Ritter (described by Hanslick as 'the best Don Giovanni') in the title role, and singing 'quite splendidly'.

The chorus is the best in our time, and so too is the Royal Opera orchestra. The Society is enraptured and basks in its own glory (which only male-voice choral societies can!). Representatives of no less than 170 European and American societies are announced, even the gentlemen from Cologne are coming and will see me on the rostrum, whilst last year I was expected to let Wüllner conduct *Frithjof* for me at their festival celebrations. The Kaiser and all the Archdukes are coming, and the Committee has asked for all those lucky owners of decorations to adorn themselves with their crosses and ribbons. . . .

We have decided to go and visit Brahms tomorrow in Vienna; perhaps he will not be back there yet, in which case we will leave our card. We will also both definitely visit Hanslick; he is the only critic proven worthy of attention, and above all he is an old acquaintance, who would probably notice if I did not come. Above all I expect and want nothing from him, he can write what he wants. He has asked Kemser [the chorus master] for both an orchestral and a vocal score of *Leonidas* for a few days.[36]

The occasion brought Bruch another honour, this time honorary membership of the Wiener Männergesang-Verein. After the performance he told Simrock: 'As expected, *Leonidas* was brilliantly launched the day before yesterday . . . as far as I can see Bremen, Cologne, Königsberg, Minden and Stuttgart will perform the work . . . we got on happily with Brahms. On the whole he was quite human. Hanslick too was very nice.'[37]

In November 1893 Bruch warmly thanked Simrock for a volume of folksongs the publisher had sent him. 'It contains a veritable treasure trove of the most beautiful folk music. The very latest Schools can learn from this what Melody is, and everyone should drink from this fountain . . . only those melodic thoughts endure which possess the simplicity, beauty, greatness and tenderness of the true folksong . . . the folksong is my old love and as you see, it never fades.'[38] Nothing had ever come of the suggestion that Simrock should regularly publish a collection of folksongs to follow up the *Twelve Scottish Folksongs* that were brought out by Leuckart in Breslau during 1864. The Scot, Alexander Mackenzie, whom Bruch had met again on his recent trip to Cambridge and London, recalled that 'when he assured me of his interest in Scottish folksong, saying "it really inspired me to compose", I hardly realized how much truth the statement contained until I heard the once popular prelude to his own *Loreley*.' (See Exs. 42 and 43)

Ex. 42

Act III No. 14 'Gesang der Loreley'

Ex. 43

'Lochaber no more'

'A prominent subject in that piece consists of four bars of the second part of "Lochaber no more" . . . and the opening bars of the often sung Ave Maria in *Das Feuerkreuz* are clearly recognizable as our old song "Will ye gang to the ewebucts, Marion".'[39]

Ex.44

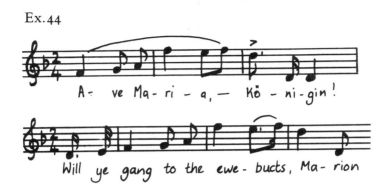

The year 1894 seemed propitious both for new works and performances of music already written. On 1 March Bruch conducted the concert to celebrate the 50th anniversary of the Bremer Künstlerverein in Bremen. The programme was devoted entirely to his own music, consisting of *Leonidas*, the *Romanze*, the *Swedish Dances*, and extracts from *Achilleus* and *Das Feuerkreuz*. His presence on the staff of the Musikhochschule produced further performances. 'Yesterday evening during a recital at the Hochschule,' he told Simrock, 'a young Russian played the Adagio from the Second [Violin Concerto] very well.'[40] In addition to his duties as a teacher, Bruch began work on his next oratorio in December 1893. '*Leonidas*', he wrote to his old friend and now colleague at the Akademie, Dr Philipp Spitta, 'is just an interlude; I can only use my whole powers by putting them into a large work.' What he had selected represented a departure from his former preoccupation with the myths of ancient Greece. His new source was the Old Testament and the new oratorio was to be *Moses* Op.67.

In spite of his assertion made to Hermann Deiters in January 1873 (see page 131) that the sacred oratorio had no future after Mendelssohn, Bruch opted for a work that would (in dramatic terms) continue directly on from Handel's *Israel in Egypt* of 1739. He knew several works on the subject of Moses written by C. P. E. Bach (1775), Kreutzer (1814), Lachner (1833), Grell (1838), Drobisch (1839), Marx (1841), Schmitt (1841), Berlijn (1844), and Thoma (1855). Since 1870

Blumner, Kiel, Wilsing and Meinardus had composed cantatas or oratorios on related events, whilst Anton Rubinstein's *Moses* (1894) belonged more to the domain of spiritual opera than oratorio. Bruch first conceived the idea of his oratorio in 1889, but only began work after he was fully established in Berlin.

'Spitta,' wrote Bruch to Simrock, 'who was preoccupied with oratorio matters throughout his life, was a true and all too invaluable adviser in the whole affair . . . it is one of the greatest undertakings of my life and I have laid down the totality of my ability in this work.'[41] Bruch saw Moses as the 'only great representative and preserver of monotheism'. That was how he delineated the character to Spitta.[42] By early January 1894 Ludwig Spitta (the Hanover theologian and brother of Philipp) had accepted the task of forging a libretto for Bruch's oratorio. The character of Moses was to be depicted as a caring but prophetic leader of the Israelites, a heroic warrior and a disciple of God for whom his followers had the greatest respect. Many of these characteristics were in common with the heroes of the earlier secular works, Odysseus, Achilles and Arminius.

*Moses* was begun in the early months of 1894, and produced a constant flow of correspondence between the brothers Spitta and Bruch. The first occasion upon which Bruch met his librettist, Ludwig Spitta, was at the graveside of his brother, for at midday on 13 April Philipp suddenly died only a day after writing again to Bruch on the subject of *Moses*. Bruch was devastated by Spitta's death. 'I cannot tell you,' he wrote to Simrock, 'how much I have lost in him.'[43] In time Bruch and Ludwig Spitta continued work on the oratorio, and it was first performed under the composer's direction in Barmen on 19 January 1895. It received five performances in the following year (Bonn January, Düsseldorf March, Schwerin May, at the Berlin Akademie on 7 May under Joachim, and Gotha in December), whereupon the work virtually disappeared from the repertory in spite of the composer's frequently expressed high opinion of it. The oratorio reached America (in an English translation by Paul England), where it was performed in Baltimore on 6 February 1896.

Four chronological events from the life of Moses form the four parts of the oratorio. It begins with Moses as the spiritual leader of his people receiving the ten commandments on Mount Sinai. The second part deals with the worship of the golden calf by Aaron, depicting Moses in angry mood as the rebuker of his renegade people. Having arrived at Canaan's borders, the third narrates the report of the scouts sent out to reconnoitre the lie of the land, and after a further confrontation with Aaron and his followers, the warrior Moses leads his people into battle against the Amalekites. In the final part of the oratorio, Moses has led the Israelites into the Promised Land and is now the respected leader of his people. It ends with his final blessing of his followers and his death.

There are three soloists; Moses (bass), Aaron (tenor) and the Angel of the Lord (soprano). The libretto is a mixture of paraphrase from the Old Testament and quotations from the Psalms. Although divided into nineteen numbers, Bruch used his established mixture of both connected and separate numbers. Each soloist sings in a variety of styles (recitative, arioso and aria), with the chorus as the People of Israel (in four, five or six-part homophonic or polyphonic writing and choral recitative). The orchestra's role is solely to accompany, and it does so largely in instrumental family groups. The function of the woodwind, for example, is often to double the choral parts, leaving the strings to provide the various styles of accompaniment to create a mood befitting the text, and the brass to reinforce the dramatic impact.

No orchestral sections or complete numbers are extractable although the *Lobgesang* (Hymn of Praise No.4) was performed by itself at the Cologne Music Festival in the summer of 1895. The scoring is conventional, with instrumental colour (provided by percussion, harp, cor anglais or piccolo) added where appropriate. The organ plays a prominent part, either as a solo instrument for recitative or in the orchestral texture, but Bruch (consistent with his other compositions which include the organ) made provision for any absence of the instrument in the concert hall by scoring the part as an *ossia* for wind instruments.

*Moses* is another product of Bruch's conservative and unimaginative mind. His concepts were often original, but he carried his ideas through in an entirely unoriginal manner. Taken together with contemporary events in the world of music (Mahler's *Resurrection* Symphony, Strauss's *Don Juan* and *Tod und Verklärung*, and Debussy's *Prélude à l'après midi d'un faune*) it is no wonder that such works as *Moses* had only a few performances before fading into obscurity. Contemporary criticism and reviews of his music were now beginning to repeat the point that it was Bruch's lack of imagination and dearth of innovation that hampered him. *Frithjof*, *Odysseus* and *Schön Ellen* were the works to which his later creations were often unfavourably compared. A lack of structural power and freshness of invention were the inherent weaknesses and uneven qualities of *Moses*, yet there are strong moments. These include the death of Moses, related by the unison choral basses in a hushed recitative to an accompaniment of three trombones and organ, the fearful heartbeats of the Israelites (20 bars of timpani triplets accompanying short and impassioned triadic string phrases) as they await the return of Moses, and the three scenes depicting the Adoration of the Golden Calf. These last are largely dominated by chorus and orchestra, and excite, in their dramatic flow, complex rhythmic and melodic textures, and strong articulation in the choral confrontation with Moses.

Simrock bought *Moses* for 15,000 marks (Bruch had asked for 20,000 on account of that 'very bad work' *The Redemption* by Gounod having earned more, but he was reminded by his friend that Mendelssohn had received only 600 friedrichs d'or for *Elijah*). Bruch anticipated a success for the first performance in Barmen on 19 January 1895. 'Everything is going very well,' he wrote. 'The choir is very large (280 voices), secure and imposing and very well in tune. Organ excellent. Orchestra naturally not first class, but fully adequate. The whole world is looking forward to the performance; I think we shall be happy.'[44] A reviewer acknowledged Bruch's total inability and unwillingness to join the 'modern, free way of writing', yet he also declared that 'without the declamatory style and rich colours of Wagner's orchestra, absolutely nothing can be composed today. Art lies solely in not losing the ability to gather splendid material, in a clear flow and healthy naturalness of expression, the beauty of sound and a talent to write for the voice. Just a detail perhaps, but one which many composers never learn and for which Bruch seeks his equal.'[45] Perhaps this was the 'stupid stuff' Bruch described to Ludwig Spitta as having appeared in the daily press, but 'on the whole the work seems to have made a good and strong impression'.[46] Among the subsequent performances of *Moses* was one conducted by Joachim on 7 May 1896 to celebrate the bicentenary of the Berlin Königliche Akademie der Künste. Bruch went so far as to attribute the disappearance of *Moses* from the repertory to this performance, owing to Joachim's 'unbelievable inability as a conductor of large choral forces'.[47]

The death of Philipp Spitta had the effect of bringing Brahms and Bruch together again. Brahms wrote offering 500 marks as his contribution to the memorial to Spitta organized by Bruch, Joachim and Herzogenberg to be erected by Adolf von Hildebrand. 'It is a beautiful letter,' Bruch told Simrock, 'so warm and deeply felt — one sees once again that when it comes to it, this strange and significant human being has his heart in the right place.'[48] Unbeknown to poor Bruch, Brahms wrote in 1895 to Clara Schumann 'Bruch has just published a *Moses*, and Herzogenberg . . . a sort of "Birth of Christ". If only one could feel a spark of joy at all these things! They are in every way weaker and worse than their earlier works. The only pleasant fact about it all is if one can, as I think I can, thank God for having preserved me from the sin, the vice, or the bad habit of mere note writing.'[49] There are no further letters between Brahms and Bruch after the short correspondence at the beginning of June 1894. Three years later Brahms was dead, and by a strange twist was himself the subject of the same sculptor when his own memorial was erected in Meiningen.

'I could never have written *Moses*, if a strong and deep feeling for God were not alive in me,' wrote Bruch just after its first performance. 'Once in the lifetime of every deeply concerned artist it will happen that the best and innermost emotions of his soul can be announced to the world using the medium of his Art. I am little or nothing — I obey the spirit which is in me, and moreover I seek seriously and conscientiously with the gifts which are loaned to me to develop them in any way possible. And thus *Moses* has proved to the world that I have not remained standing — for that is the greatest danger in old age.'[50] Whatever Bruch himself might have felt were the developments in his compositional style in his latest oratorio, they were not keeping pace with those elsewhere. From now on battle was to be joined with a greater ferocity and intense bitterness, though it was a fight which provoked little or no response from the other side. The 'Modernists' (Strauss, Wolf, Reger and Pfitzner at their head), successors to the 'New Germans' (Wagner and Liszt), felt sure of their high ground. After Hans von Bülow's death in 1894 (he died on 12 February far from home, in Cairo, where he had gone to seek recovery of his health), Richard Strauss was engaged by the powerful and influential impresario Hermann Wolff as conductor of the 1894–95 season of the Berlin Philharmonic concerts. At the beginning of 1896 he was invited to conduct a performance given by the Berlin Wagner-Verein at which, as well as compositions of his own, he conducted works by Liszt, Wagner and Hugo Wolf. 'Although until now I have avoided that great artists' pigsty established by Messrs H. Wolff and R. Strauss at the Philharmonic,' wrote Bruch, 'I would have liked for Sarasate's sake to come to the rehearsal yesterday, but Wolff would not even send me rehearsal tickets. What do you say to that? . . . We shall both come tonight, although it is a veritable torture for me to hear one of my works performed by such a rogue as Str[auss], and just as embarrassing to hear the Finale rushed again.'[51] Bruch was referring to a performance of the Third Violin Concerto, which he now felt was not at all suited to Sarasate, but belonged to Joachim's temperament. Sure enough he wrote to Simrock on the day after the concert that much had gone wrong. The letter provides a fascinating critique of the performer by the composer, their relationship now not quite what it was in earlier years when Sarasate could do no wrong.

Sarasate began the Finale too fast, and at the tuttis Strauss drove it faster so that by the end it was a real Witches' Sabbath, and I had to ask myself if I had written such madness. Almost worse was the middle movement, instead of Adagio they took it Andante con moto whereby the melody was completely destroyed. In this way they could also kill any of those by Beethoven or Schumann. Breadth and pathos were totally lacking, and for me the beautiful delivery of separate *cantilena* could not make up for it. Especially distressing for me was that the semiquaver in the main theme of the first movement was played as a quaver throughout [see Ex. 34b, page 235]. As a result it made the rhythm, which is developed through the movement, weak and meaningless. Overall he is lacking in the passion, power and stature to realize my intentions through his playing of this movement, in spite of the perfection in the technical details and the constant pleasure of his sound. The accompaniment was the sloppiest I have ever heard, because Herr Strauss did not understand the thematic work at all, and all the filigree work of the Finale was completely destroyed by the mad *tempo*. . . . If I am not up there on the podium, the most stupid things happen. I wrote the Second Concerto and the *Scottish Fantasy* for Sarasate, body and soul, and no one can touch him in playing them. We were both so annoyed that we left immediately after the concerto.[52]

Following *Moses*, Bruch produced a series of small choral works and a group of pieces for cello. He told Anton Krause in Barmen: 'My mood after the completion of a large work, which has concentrated all my spiritual strength powerfully for a long time on one place, is quite unbearable. Smaller undertakings do not satisfy me, and larger ones are not easy to come by. It follows that as I am only alive when I am creating, I am now not at all alive but purely vegetating.'[53]

A surprising revival of *Die Loreley* was staged in the New Year of 1896 in Cologne, and Bruch was asked to add some ballet music. After considering the idea he refused, and turned his attention instead to composing three *Neue Männerchöre* Op.68 for the Arion Society in New York. Written for four-part male voice choir and full orchestra, the three choruses are 'Seeräuberlied' (Song of the Pirates) from 8heinrich Kruse's play 'Die Gräfin' (The Countess), 'Psalm 23', and 'Kriegsgesang' from Goethe's 'Des Epimenides Erwachen' (Epimenides Awakened). They appeared with an English translation, once again by the American, Paul England who, in Bruch's opinion of his work on *Moses*, had produced a natural English rather than one which was stilted and obviously a translation (an accusation he now saw fit to throw at Mrs Macfarren's previously lauded work). Bruch also produced a final version of the five-part mixed chorus *Sei getreu bis an den Tod* (Be thou faithful unto death) Op.69, a work originally written in 1885 for Krause's jubilee in Barmen. At that time an attempt was made by Kapellmeister Buths in Elberfeld to orchestrate it, but the result was unsatisfactory. Of the earlier alternatives of piano or organ accompaniment, Bruch selected the latter to ensure an ecclesiastical venue for performance.

The Four Pieces for cello with piano accompaniment, Op.70, were composed in the late summer of 1896, and dedicated to Robert Hausmann. Bruch had known the famous German cellist since they appeared together in a Liverpool concert on 7 February 1882 (Hausmann played *Kol Nidrei* on that occasion together with Carl Eckert's cello concerto). Born in 1852, he completed his studies at the Berlin Hochschule and left for London to become a pupil of Alfredo Piatti. After working in Dresden he joined the staff of the Berlin Hochschule and remained there until his death in 1909. Throughout his life he followed a performing career, working closely with and advising both Bruch and Brahms. He received the dedication of *Kol Nidrei* from Bruch and that of the F major Sonata Op.99 from Brahms. Hausmann was the cellist in Joachim's famous quartet, and was the cello soloist in the first performance of Brahms' Double Concerto in the Gürzenich in Cologne on 18 October 1887 with Joachim as violinist and Brahms conducting.

The Bruch family spent much of the summer of 1896 at the spa of Bad Pyrmont, because Clara's asthma (together with recurring migraine) was taking its toll of her strength. During the summer holidays their eldest son, Max Felix (now aged 12 and known as 'Maxel'), wrote a piece for flute with piano accompaniment. The boy was later to take up the clarinet and become an accomplished player. His Pyrmont composition was played for him by the flautist of the wind band in the spa (the Kurkapelle), and impressed Father Bruch so much that he plagiarized the work and adapted it as the first of the Four Pieces for cello. Like the original piano and violin version of the *Swedish Dances*, these cello pieces are in ternary form, but unlike the *Dances* they are not interrelated movements, nor does the piano perform the purely accompanying role but rather takes its fair share of melodic importance. Its harmonic role is simplistic, the chordal accompaniment when used is invariably triadic chords. After the first piece, based on Max Felix's melody, the remaining three use melodies of various nations. The rustic rhythm and dynamic energy of the folk movements is achieved through the use of staccato, portato and sforzato. The four movements are entitled 'Aria', 'Finnländisch', 'Tanz (Schwedisch)' and 'Schottisch'. Although Bruch made plans for a further three or four pieces for cello and piano, these came to nothing, but on 13 March 1899 Bruch and Hausmann played through the 'Aria' and 'Tanz (Schwedisch)' (at the Hochschule afternoon orchestral rehearsal), for the cellist had requested the instrumentation of these two pieces.

Heinrichshofen in Magdeburg published the *Seven Choral Songs* Op. 71 for mixed chorus, and the male-voice chorus *In der Nacht* Op. 72, in 1897. The former can be seen as following the Mendelssohn choral style but with a simplistic folk element as the dominant feature. The songs are 'Sommerlust' (Summer delights), 'Der fröhliche Musicus' (The happy musician), 'An die Musik' (To Music), 'Narrenfahrt' (A parcel of fools), 'Musicaklang' (The sound of Music), 'Lenz komm herbei!' (Spring come again) and 'Morgengesang' (Morning song). The fifth and seventh songs are in six parts, the rest are in four. Some of these part-songs (such as 'An die Musik') are simple and homophonic, others have a *scherzando* and *giocoso* quality ('Der fröhliche Musikus' and 'Narrenfahrt') in a more polyphonic style. The first song ('Sommerlust') places the melodic emphasis upon the sopranos accompanied by the other three voice parts, whilst the last ('Morgengesang') is a loosely structured counterpoint interweaving the setting for double chorus. *In der Nacht* (text by Tersteegen) is written for four-part chorus of altos, two tenor parts and basses. This short but expressive hymn comprises just three verses of 22 bars. Though these works were briefly successful, Bruch was on the hunt for another major choral work. His friend Anton Krause resigned his post in Barmen through ill-health in 1897, and consequently Bruch lost a centre of loyal support. Ever since the triumph of *Odysseus*, nearly a quarter of a century earlier, Barmen was a bastion for his choral works. But the city was to provide him with one more triumphant première.

In January 1897 Bruch wrote to Krause's daughter Susanne, 'There is not much awaiting me in 1897, but perhaps there is in 1898, because for some time now I have been carrying about with me great and daring thoughts. I will tell you and your parents in confidence what they are: "Gustav Adolf, an Evangelical Oratorio"! What do you say? The plan (on which I have been busily working these past two months) is ready, but the poet is lacking.' After providing a sketch of the synopsis of the oratorio, Bruch concluded, 'I have never been an especially devout person, but I am filled through and through with Protestant convictions. Before I can no longer work, I want to perform a great service to the cause of Protestantism, and through it set down an illuminating distinctive sign for all who are not Catholic and who love Gustav Adolf.'[54] His fifth and final oratorio was to be

*Gustav Adolf* Op.73, but as he began work on the oratorio in April
1897, news came to him of the impending death of the man whose
personality he alternately despised and liked, yet for whose music and
musicianship he had profound respect.

As Johannes Brahms lay dying from cancer of the liver, Bruch
wrote to Simrock:

> Your sad news about Brahms has shocked us very much. It truly is a
> pity that such a great artist and an exceptional man must go in such a
> distressing way before his time. One sees Fate creeping up step by
> step, getting nearer and nearer — and one can do nothing to avert
> the disaster. The only thing one can do is to show him our concern
> from time to time, that is what we meant by our New Year
> telegram of 1897. . . . Perhaps my wife will still send him some
> spring flowers. What is Man — what are we all — only shadows and
> phantoms. . . . So the Great depart and on their glorious deeds one
> seeks to build and elevate in the midst of the madness of these
> uncultured changing times; and what results is not worth men-
> tioning. . . . If I could not always reconcile myself to his character,
> I have always most clearly recognized what the totality of his
> distinguished achievements meant for the present and for the
> future. A true and mighty guardian of pure Art will depart with
> him.[55]

At 9.30 am on the morning of 3 April Brahms died peacefully, and
two days later Bruch wrote to Anton Krause:

> Brahms is dead! A very great loss to Art. Posterity has less to do in
> making good towards him than it has had to do when those before
> him have passed on, because for years he already stood at the
> pinnacle of public recognition and glory, and no more can be
> achieved after his death than was during his lifetime. I could write a
> book about my highly strange experiences with this unique and
> very prickly man during the course of 32 years' acquaintanceship —
> I shall however keep quiet.[56]

For the first ten years of their virtually parallel careers (from about
1863 to 1873) Bruch, through *Die Loreley*, *Frithjof*, the First Violin
Concerto and *Odysseus*, had been the dominant partner in their joint
opposition to the ideals of Wagner and Liszt (though Bruch was far
more uncompromising in his opposition to the New-Germans than the
more respectful and less aggressive Brahms). Through the composition of his *Requiem*, the Piano Concerto No.1, the Violin Concerto

and the First Symphony, Brahms' star soared ever upward in the public's eyes, whilst Bruch tenuously held a position through choral works which fulfilled a rapidly dwindling need, and violin works which the public constantly compared to his First Concerto. The greater Brahms became, the less he had to struggle against the pressures inflicted by the 'opposition'. He remained buoyant whilst Bruch (in danger of fading into obscurity) ranted and raved to make his presence felt. Without Brahms, Bruch lost a peg on which to hang his own coat. He was becoming more and more isolated in his politically and musically conservative ideology. The extremes now acquired the labels of Academicism (Bruch) on one side and Art on the other (Strauss, Reger and Pfitzner). Wagner enshrined his music in mythology, but Bruch was embalming his in political nationalism against 'the musical social-democrats' as he called his opponents. He ended a letter to Leo Schrattenholz about Brahms' death with the words: 'The important people with whom I have lived are going one after the other. Only the gods know what will happen to Art in the twentieth century.'[57]

# Chapter Fifteen

## BERLIN II
### 1898–1911

ON 4 NOVEMBER 1897 Max Bruch read a speech to family and friends in praise of Mendelssohn who had died exactly 50 years ealier. In it he spoke in highly emotive and eulogistic language in praise of his idol, and of his own musical philosophy at a time when he was beginning to be more and more isolated. Form, melody, beauty of sound and classical structure were all enshrined in the achievements of the man 'we Germans can say with joyful pride "He was ours!"' These were also ideals Bruch himself strove for but inconsistently achieved. As the old century gave way to the new, Bruch saw Mendelssohn's greatness and achievements ('harmonic personality, Greek sense of Beauty, all-round glorious works') thrown into starker relief, and with them his own. Johannes Brahms, his closest musical ally, was now dead, so Bruch considered himself to be the torch-bearer of conservatism. His ideals were still based on the glories of 1872 Bismarckian unification and nationalism, with the overriding philosophy of Prussian Protestantism. He saw his foes as the destroyers of cultural ideals, the developers of social democracy in Art, the denigrators of Bismarck (who died in July 1898) and the disseminators of the musical philosophy of Wagner, Liszt and their successors in Germany and elsewhere. It proved to be an uneven fight.

Honours and official recognition still continued to be awarded to Max Bruch. On 6 January 1896 he celebrated his sixtieth birthday. An international committee was formed to organize a benefit fund — one of the donations came from Fritz Simrock:

> I find your name among the list of the international committee and their 600 contributors, whose wonderful gift of honour (at present standing at 57,000 marks) reached me on 5 January. I do not need to tell you what heartfelt joy this has given me! My close connection with you for many years has secured the present — this beautiful gift will ensure the future for my family. That is the greatest and most beautiful pleasure which can be granted me in these times. A thousand thanks! . . . On 22 January I travel to Hanover for three

days (*Frithjof* — as it were a post celebration of the 6 January) . . .
283 telegrams and letters from every country arrived here on 6
January, and stragglers are still coming in!'

At the end of the year he was afforded further honour, from a
foreign country. 'The Permanent Secretary of the "Académie des
Beaux Arts" in Paris (Institut de France) officially informed me of my
nomination as a member the day before yesterday, short and
businesslike, but with his *félicitations personnelles*.'² He replaced the late
Théodore Gouvy. In the following year Bruch was made a member of
the Directory of the Königliche Hochschule für Musik, and before he
retired from the Königliche Akademie der Künste in Berlin, in 1910,
he became Chairman of its Senate (1907) and Vice-President in
succession to Joachim. The Stockholm Academy, the Swiss
Musikgesellschaft, the Dutch Society for the Promotion of Music and
the Philharmonic Society in London all honoured the composer
during the last twenty years of his life. He was also to become *persona
grata* with the Kaiser and his wife through the composition of *Gustav
Adolf* Op.73, in 1898.

Germany, Austria-Hungary and Italy, led by Bismarck, the Haps-
burgs and Cavour respectively, imbued Europe with a strong sense of
nationalism in the second half of the nineteenth century. With it
(especially in the colonization or efforts in controlling Africa, Asia and
eastern Europe) came a widening of the schism between Germany's
Protestant north and Catholic south. Germany had three dominant
figures in its history to represent the ideals of Protestantism or
Nationalism. They were Arminius (or Hermann), Martin Luther and
Gustav Adolf. Following *Arminius* in 1875, Bruch rejected the idea of
an oratorio on Martin Luther in 1883 (the tercentenary of his birth),
and elected instead to commemorate the tercentenary celebrations, in
1894, of the birth of Gustav Adolf. Several new books on the king also
inspired him to write the oratorio, which appeared four years later in
1898. At the suggestion of Ludwig Spitta, Bruch chose the Lutheran
Pastor Albert Hackenberg as his librettist. 'My wishes and hopes',
Bruch wrote, 'transcend aesthetic purposes this time. Through this
work I want to serve the cause of Protestantism as much as I have it in
me so to do.'³ He sent Hackenberg folksongs and religious songs of
the period, and demanded total subordination of the drama and text to
these folksongs and religious chorales. 'Amongst a collection of
unprepossessing ballads,' he wrote, 'from the period of the Thirty
Years War, I recently found some poetical pearls from the purest
water — beautiful folksongs which, together with the evangelical
chorales, must build the corner-stone and foundation of the work.'⁴

*Encyclopaedia Britannica* (1971) describes the Swedish King Gustav Adolf as 'a brilliant orator and natural stylist, a keen musician with an insatiable curiosity'. He brought Sweden into the Thirty Years War on Germany's side against Russia and Poland, not only in his country's own interests but also in defence of Protestantism. He fought against the Catholic armies led by Wallenstein, and though he failed at Magdeburg, his victory at Breitenfeld was seen as 'a landmark in the art of war and in the history of Europe. It ensured the survival of German Protestantism.' Although once again defeated (this time at Nuremberg), he led his troops to battle at Lützen on 16 November 1632. His death aroused and enraged his troops under Duke Bernard to defeat Wallenstein once and for all, and secured the ultimate safety of Protestism.

In Bruch's oratorio three historical characters from the drama are portrayed. They are Gustav Adolf (baritone), Duke Bernard of Weimar (tenor) and the page and minstrel Leubelfing (alto). Gustav Adolf's death is not in the work, and Leubelfing (who actually perished with his King at the Battle of Lützen) survives to mourn him in the oratorio. The chorus is used in various roles as German people, Lutheran clergy, Swedish or German warriors, Women, Priests and Monks. This represented a return to the use of the chorus in earlier oratorios, such as *Odysseus* (where it also took several roles), rather than in *Moses*, in which it was simply cast as 'The People'. Similarly the soloists' music tends towards dramatic *arioso* rather than set-piece arias. An exception is the page Leubelfing whose music is for the most part through-composed and strophic. The other two protagonists are invariably used with either each other or with the chorus. Bruch makes use of four traditional Lutheran chorales during its course, and thus provides the oratorio with a unifying element. The music (with new text) of *Kommt her zu mir, spricht Gottes Sohn* (a popular song at the time of the Thirty Years War) appears at the end of the first and second scenes, the first time sung in unison by nine male choristers (Lutheran clergyman) and harmonized at the repeat in the second scene by the full chorus. *Nun danket alle Gott* with its original text is sung by chorus and soloists at the end of Scene 11, and the work ends with a setting of *Ein' feste Burg*.[5] A brass ensemble (behind the scenes) plays *Wie schön leucht' uns der Morgenstern* as an accompaniment to Gustav Adolf's *arioso* in Scene 12. The religious atmosphere of the opening of the final scene revealing Gustav Adolf's lying-in-state in the castle chapel is enhanced by a substantial introduction for solo organ. This device is used at exactly the same point in *Moses*, when his impending death is revealed to him by the Angel of the Lord in the final scene, and the music used in *Gustav Adolf* is an extended version of that used in the earlier work. The orchestra's function is once again purely to accompany and to colour the text, as for example by imitating period instruments or rhythms in the accompaniment of *arioso* (the psaltery in *Moses* and the woodwinds to accompany the Swedish folk songs of the minstrel in *Gustav Adolf*).

Bruch's five oratorios were composed over a period of 27 years (between 1871 and 1898) and represent conservatism at a time when music was embarking upon one of the most innovative periods in its history. His innovation was to return the oratorio to the secular and historical literature and away from the sacred tradition of Handel and Mendelssohn. They embody his musical philosophy of academic correctness, classical form, beauty of melody and sparing use of chromaticism, and they exactly cover the central period of his life. Bruch's view of harmony and tonality were as a means to an end as well as expression, whereas his particular emphasis was upon the simple musical concepts of motives, phrases and themes.

The first performance of *Gustav Adolf* was given on 22 May 1898 under Bruch's direction in Barmen, the heartland of evangelical Protestantism, 'because there they will go through fire for me and for my music'.[6] The success of the work was immediate and fulfilled the needs of the prevailing public sentiment at that time (as *Arminius* had also done). A year later it had been performed in eleven cities, with another dozen committed to performances. When Berlin performed the work for the first time (not until the 400th anniversary Reformation festival celebrations of Luther's 95 Theses on 31 October 1917), Karl Schurzmann reported performances in '65–70 German cities since the work was first performed 20 years earlier'. Bruch told Krause that 'the impression was universally the same — and it has provided something for the members of the Anti-music and Unmusical parties to think about — it is a success; one which has spread far and wide in the face of the prevailing current of the times — perhaps it is a last glimmer of the old, great and honoured Art which is supported by melody, strict form, beauty in key structure, knowledge of song, temperate orchestration — before complete barbarism breaks out in the 20th century.'[7] It is the ultimate irony that the 'complete barbarism' which broke out in 1914 was not the fault of music, but of the very patriotism that a work such as *Gustav Adolf* engendered. Prussian ideology seized upon the work as a manifestation of the current Protestant nationalism of the time and used it to broaden its message. It was a work, the success of which both increased its composer's self-confidence and secured him a firm place at the head of conservative circles in music.

★

*Gustav Adolf* was the last major choral composition by Max Bruch but, caught up in the excited aftermath of its success, he pursued the Protestant-national theme in two short choral works. These were *Herzog Moritz* Op.74 (published by Heinrichshofen in 1899) and *Der letzte Abschied des Volkes* (1888) Op.76 (published by Bock in 1901). *Herzog Moritz* (an historical Saxon Duke 1521–53) is for *a cappella* four-part male voice choir and subtitled 'Warsong of the Magdeburgers against Duke Moritz of Saxony' (from a poem by Karl Storch). According to an autograph dedication of thanks in the score to Richard and Anna Zanders for a holiday at the Igeler Hof in the spring of 1902, Bruch conceived *Der letzte Abschied des Volkes* (The Last Farewell of the People) in 1888, wrote it in 1900 and orchestrated it at the Igeler Hof in September. Written for male voice choir (with occasional passages for four choral soloists), organ and orchestra, the subject of the work (with text by Baron von Grotthus) is the lying-in-state of Kaiser Wilhelm I in Berlin Cathedral, a scenario similar to the Finale of *Gustav Adolf.* It was dedicated to the famous Cologne Male Voice Choral Society.

The decade between his 60th and 70th birthdays was largely spent teaching at the Hochschule, conducting his compositions and composing smaller-scale vocal works together with several orchestral pieces. Among his pupils were Oskar Straus, Ottorino Respighi and Ralph Vaughan Williams. In October 1897 Bruch sent the young Englishman a short note in English: 'My dear Sir, I have arranged to give you the first lesson on Saturday 6th of November at 12 o'clock. Yours truly, Dr. Max Bruch.'[8] When Vaughan Williams left Berlin (after just three months), Bruch wrote him a reference (in German):

Herr Ralph Vaughan Williams, who attended classes of the Academic Masterclass for Composition under my direction during the winter of 1897/1898, is a very good musician and a talented composer. He is worthy of warm recommendation to all musical organizations and church choirs etc.[9]

The next day young Ralph reported to his cousin Ralph Wedgwood:

You will be glad to know that Max Bruch considers I am a 'guter Musiker und ein talentvoller Componist' and that I have 've-ry o-riginaal ideeas' but that my harmonies are 'rather too originell'. In fact I meet with much more encouragement . . . all the living Germans I have heard in Berlin are most feeble folk — it seems to me that the future of music lies between England and Russia, but first the Russians must try to give up being original and the English being imitators. I very much believe in the folk tune theory — by which I don't mean that modern composing is done by sandwiching an occasional national tune — not your own invention — between lumps of '2d the pound' stuff, which seems to be Dvořák's latest method. But that to get the spirit of his national tunes into his work must be good for a composer if it comes natural to him, in which case it doesn't matter if what he writes occasionally corresponds with some real 'folktune'. All this because in the last thing I wrote for Bruch I used a bit of Welsh tune as my 'Haupt Thema' — unacknowledged of course, but then 'I made it my own'. . . .

We went to a most wonderful dinner party the other day — all professors — the two 'Hauptsaches' were (a) the food and drink which kept on going after dinner in this order 9.30–11.30: Cigars, coffee, liqueurs (Have you ever made a practice of liqueurs? If not you have neglected your opportunities like I have. This must be rectified at our next *festlichkeit* together), *belegtes Brot*, caviar, sweets, beer, tea. (b) The subjects which I discussed with the most brilliant professors of the Berlin University in this order 9.00–11.00: In German — Bach, Wagner, Classical/Romantic, Shelley, Keats, the Puritans, the influence of religion on art, Browning, Rossetti, Swinburne, lodgings. In English — The Riviera, Coleridge, Wordsworth, Oxford, prigs, German art galleries, Fra Angelico.[10]

Later Vaughan Williams described his studies with Max Bruch:

I had an introduction to Herzogenberg, who looked at my work and said it reminded him of Mascagni, and advised me to study with Max Bruch. It is difficult to say what it is one learns from a teacher. I only know that I worked hard and enthusiastically and that Max Bruch encouraged me, and I had never had much encouragement before. . . . When I was under Stanford I used to vex him much with my flattened sevenths . . . Max Bruch was equally worried by this idiosyncracy of mine: he said, *Sie haben eine Leidenschaft für die kleine Septime.* [You have a passion for the flattened seventh.] He also warned me against writing *Augenmusik* as opposed to *Ohrenmusik.* . . . My old teacher, Max Bruch, used to say to me, 'You must not write eye music, you must write ear music.' He, at all events, had got hold of the truth.[11]

Bruch's obsession with folk music continued with the *Serenade* Op.75 for violin and orchestra, which was written at the Igeler Hof during August 1899. He told his friend Carl Hopfe that it was originally intended as a fourth violin concerto, [12] and to Simrock he revealed that 'at the insistence of Sarasate, I have written a large new work for violin and orchestra for him — a Concerto in the form of a Serenade . . . Joachim has edited the solo part and will play the work for the first time on 19 December at the Hochschule in the orchestral session under my direction.'[13] The *Serenade* is in four movements, opening with a lyrical Andante con moto whose main motif is a free adaptation of a Nordic melody in a loose sonata form. The *scherzando* quality of the second movement, a strongly rhythmic if rather lumpy Teutonic *alla Marcia*, provides an effective and contrasting Rondo with exquisite writing for woodwinds in Mendelssohn vein. Tension flags somewhat in the ensuing *Notturno* (the only one of the four movements designated by a title) whose tender melody (occasionally reminiscent of 'Auld Rob Morris' in the first movement of the *Scottish Fantasy*) is often accompanied in *recitativo* style by the soloist. This is a feature of the second movement of the Second Violin Concerto, and a further similarity between these two works occurs in the 3/8 rhythmic ostinato of their last movements. In the *Serenade*, inspired by the Spaniard Sarasate, it has the hallmarks of the Seguidilla (it was entitled *Tanz* or Dance in the manuscript sketch), and through frequent use of pizzicato in the orchestral strings, it evokes the Mediterranean flavour of a chorus of accompanying guitars. A cyclical conclusion to the work is effected by a return in the Coda to the lyrical opening of the first movement and its wistful Scandinavian folk melody. The *Serenade* is scored for full orchestra without trombones, and the solo part is full of the virtuosic double-stops and passage work associated with Bruch's violin music. Simrock, who bought it for 6000 marks, was still hoping for a repeat of the success of the First Violin Concerto.

Sarasate was enthusiastic when Bruch played it to him at the beginning of February 1900, but the Spaniard did not take it up, much to Bruch's disappointment and displeasure. At the time, Joachim was infatuated by Nellie Melba (to whom Max sent his 'Ave Maria' from *Das Feuerkreuz* at her request when she visited Berlin). Amalie Joachim had died in the spring of 1899, while still estranged from her husband. Bruch, who was wryly amused at the violinist's passion for the singer (whom he mistakenly assumed was English), told Simrock with a generous helping of gossip: 'Joachim now lies in the bonds of the English singer Melba (the divorced Mrs Armstrong), a very good interpreter of the Italian *bel canto* who is at present in Berlin, and who is a very pretty woman of 34 years — in other words of a tempting age. Joachim is not going to England, but to Italy with Melba. She is wild about him and he is quite mad for her.'[14] The dedication of the *Serenade* created a dilemma for Bruch. Joachim had declined the honour because two concertos were already dedicated to him, so instead he made the startling suggestion that Bruch should honour him by dedicating the *Serenade* to his friend Nellie Melba. Whilst full of the utmost admiration for her abilities as a singer, and whilst liking her as a person ('a very charming woman . . . and not at all the prima donna'), Max nevertheless baulked at Joachim's suggestion.

> After all it is well known (and Joachim himself told me with a sorrowful shrug) that she was the lover of the young Prince of Orleans (son of the Comte de Paris and nephew to Louis Philippe). She lived with him too — as Joachim told me. I was naïve enough to suggest that the Prince might have wanted to marry her, but I think that it belongs beyond the bounds of probability that Princes marry their mistresses! Now I do not wish to follow the profession of guardian of the virtues of English singers, and it is of no concern to me how many 'connections' she has with princes or violinists — but there is no question of dedicating a great work to such a person, and in the process making a fool of myself in England (like the great Joachim) . . . On the other hand there is Pablo who, I believe, expects the dedication (although I have already dedicated two concertos to him as well). The matter therefore stands so: Joachim did all the work, and Sarasate wants all the glory . . . So I agree with you: no dedication! It is the only way out, and the best under the circumstances.[15]

A year later when Sarasate's indifference to performing the *Serenade* was apparent (and Bruch had been neglected in the distribution of complimentary tickets for a Sarasate concert in Berlin), the composer became enraged and decided to sever any association that remained. He wrote to Hans Simrock (now playing a more active role in running the business than his ailing uncle Fritz), describing the Spanish virtuoso as 'an enemy rather than a friend . . . One can call his conduct lazy, but it is far more, it is a betrayal of an old friendship. I expect nothing from my opponents, but when old friends let me down so completely, as Sarasate in this instance, then I am done with them. . . . Ultimately the *Serenade* will make its way without Sarasate; but he should have set it on its course, that was his d—— duty and obligation. But I did not want to run after him.'[16]

The *Serenade* received its first performance on 15 May 1901 in Paris with the Belgian violinist, Joseph Débroux, and Camille Chevillard conducting the Orchestre Lamoureux. Bruch himself then conducted the work with Débroux in Berlin and with Willy Hess in Cologne. Interest came from abroad (Madame Norman-Neruda, wife of

Charles Hallé, wanted it for performance in England in May 1900) and
on 11 February 1903 it was performed in Boston. Hess (now resident
in Boston) vacated the leader's chair to conduct the *Serenade* with
Marie Nichols as soloist. The reviewer's response was mixed, the
work being doomed the moment a comparison was made with the G
minor Violin Concerto. 'His 2nd and 3rd Violin Concertos show a
decided falling off,' wrote the correspondent, 'and we fear this
*Serenade* must also be classed with his second-rate compositions.'
Reminding his readers that the G minor Concerto and the *Scottish
Fantasy* had been heard in Boston just recently, 'the contrast shrivels
up the *Serenade*.' A 'sweetness' was acceptable in the eighteenth-
century serenade, but that quality in Bruch's work was 'very cloying
to the auditor of the twentieth. We change and music changes with
us . . . We were uneasy under his more saccharine spell . . . Miss
Nichols played no better than a half-dozen violinists who sat behind
her could have done. [This must have been a highly gifted section of
first violins, for the *Serenade* is no easy work.] . . . Strauss's *Don Juan*
after this . . . was like brandy after vanilla soda.'[17]

A year later Hess was more successful in Bruch's cause. He played
the First Violin Concerto and provoked enthusiasm and wit from the
critic. 'The audience was thoroughly aroused', he wrote, 'by the time
the end was reached and the brilliant violinist was recalled four times
in the midst of considerable excitement — a great Hessian victory over
the Americans, even if a century or so belated.'[18]

At the end of 1899 Bruch re–negotiated his timetable with the
Hochschule. On two days in the week he taught at the School, 'in the
second half of the week I have five master-class students, and on
Tuesdays and Fridays I am often conducting the orchestra for Joachim.'

His conducting activities were many — 'Cologne has invited me to
conduct *Feuerkreuz* in the Gürzenich on 22 January [1901]. Wüllner
himself wrote charmingly to me. You can yet experience the most
wonderful things if you do not die too soon!'[19] He was also asked by
Simrock for opinions of works submitted by others for publication.
The Czech composer Vitezslav Novák wrote some chamber music
which Bruch appraised for Simrock with some pertinent remarks.
Novák was 'a very talented person who has ideas and has learnt
much'. He criticized the music as being too Brahmsian, but on the
whole considered it worthy of a publishing house with Simrock's
reputation. But for a publisher to earn money from chamber music
was impossible, 'for the days of chamber music are long past and the
last one to achieve anything significant in this area, Brahms, is
gone.'[20] Bruch considered Dvořák to be a *Deutschfresser* (a devourer
and copier of German style).

In spite of Brahms' death four years earlier, and the respect Bruch had for him, he was jealous of the greater man's power with audiences and concert managements. In October 1901 the Meiningen orchestra gave several concerts in Berlin, largely devoted to the works of Brahms, who had had a special association with the orchestra. Bruch refused to attend any of the concerts (Clara and Margarethe went instead), complaining bitterly to Simrock that the conductor Steinbach had ignored 'my effective *Achilles* pieces, the melodic, world-renowned *Loreley* Prelude, my violin concertos . . . I expect this from my principal enemies like Richard Strauss, Nikisch, Weingartner etc.' If *Odysseus* could be performed as far apart as Leeds (The Banquet with the Phaeacians, autumn 1901) and Milwaukee (March 1902), Bruch expected performances in Germany — currently true of *Gustav Adolf*, though Meiningen had unfortunately ignored this work too!

Joachim might have caused all sorts of problems regarding the dedication of the *Serenade*, but none appears to have arisen when Bruch's *Damajanti*, for soprano, chorus and orchestra, appeared with his name at the head of the title page. The work carries the opus number 78 (inexplicably there is no Op.77 in his published output). When Bruch turned from ancient history to the Bible for composition of *Moses*, it was a temporary change of direction. In 1894 he considered the subject of Alexander in India, the following year Themistocles, and in 1897 The Death of Themistocles. Not satisfied with any of these projects, Bruch decided upon scenes from the Indian epic poem *Nala and Damajanti* in 1899, the ideas for which had first occurred to him as far back as 1886 in Breslau.

The work begins with a short *pianissimo* orchestral introduction leading directly into the first scene for solo soprano. Separated from her husband King Nala, the Princess Damajanti (daughter of King Bima) is in despair and decides to seek help from the Penitents in their Grove. Fearlessly she sets out through the tiger-infested jungle, over hills and across rivers, strengthened by love and resolve which will light her way. The second scene, for chorus alone, is a description of the flora and fauna of the Grove of the Penitents, followed without a break by the third and final scene. A four-part male chorus of the Penitents introduces the Grove as a place of peace and tranquillity for man and beast. Damajanti arrives and greets the Penitents, who are overcome by her radiant beauty, and desire to worship her at their altar. She assures them she is only mortal and asks for their aid in seeking her missing husband. They reassure her that she will find him, and after a journey of penitence they will both regain their homeland once more. The Penitents suddenly vanish together with their Grove, and Damajanti questions whether they were merely images of her distraught mind. Her doubts are dispelled when a (mixed) chorus of unseen protecting Genies urges her on her way to seek out her missing husband, and she sets off full of confidence and hope.

Bruch arranged two sets of four-part Welsh folksongs in 1901 to add to the collection which, in Simrock's catalogue, was called *Denkmale des Volkesgesanges* (Memorial to the Folksong). This was part of his ambition to include 'all nations', but there were no more than these two to add to the earlier Scottish set (Simrock also published separately a selection taken from all three sets, consisting of six folksongs of Scottish and Welsh origins).

His close study of Swedish folksong in connection with *Gustav Adolf* resulted in the *Lieder und Tänze* (Songs and Dances) Op.79 for Violin and Piano (dedicated to Joseph Débroux). This collection of nine short pieces, based on Russian and Swedish popular airs, was published by Simrock in two volumes in 1903. Six of the collection of nine pieces are Russian, and were taken from Balakirev's *Recueil de chants populaires russes* (published in Leipzig in 1898), the remaining three Swedish pieces came from *Svenska folkvisor* (Stockholm 1880) by Gejer and Afzelius, and were adapted for Bruch by Svante Sjöberg (a pupil between 1900 and 1902). The five pieces in the first book consist of 'Prisoner's Song', 'Muschik's Song', 'Dance', 'Funeral March' and 'Song and Dance'. Of these works the third is Swedish, the rest are all Russian. The second book consists of 'Song', 'Dance', 'Song' and 'Dance', the first two are Swedish, the third bears the title *Kleinrussisch* (Ukranian) and the last is Russian. Other than their countries of origin, there is no common theme linking any of the nine pieces. The range of difficulty of the set is considerable, often quite simple one moment and becoming highly virtuosic the next, particularly in the varied repeat of the movements in ternary form. The piano accompaniment is often orchestral in colour and texture (No.2 could have been written for harp and violin), and the full range of piano style is used. Polyphonic elements are abundant throughout the work (mainly free canonic imitation in Nos.2, 6, 8 and 9) and a predilection for the folksong-like dominant minor chord (No.2 bar 5 (Ex.45), No.4 bar 7 and No.7 bar 1 (Exs.46, 47)) had already occurred in the *Serenade* (second movement bar 44 (Ex.48)) just two years earlier. Was this a case of the teacher plagiarizing the favourite flattened sevenths of his young English student Ralph Vaughan Williams, whom he had reprimanded for 'having a passion' for exactly that harmonic device?

Four of the *Lieder und Tänze* were orchestrated, and together with new material formed into the *Suite für grosses Orchester nach russischen Volksmelodien* Op.79b in the summer of 1903. They were performed

Ex. 45

Op. 79 No. 2 bars 4–6

Ex. 46

Op. 79 No. 4 bars 6 and 7

Ex. 47

Op. 79 No. 7 bars 1–3

Ex.48

Op.75, second movement, bar 44

from manuscript parts for the first time in Barmen in November that year and published by Simrock in 1905. The four dances taken from Op.79 were Nos.2, 5, 9 and 4, which became respectively the first four movements of the five-movement Op.79b. The original keys and harmonization of these four dances were not disturbed in the process of transition, but introductions were added as well as other minor details. A Finale was added to Op.79b using new material (the 'Song of the Volga Boatman'), and the fourth movement is in two parts, the first of which (serving as an introduction) is also original and not from the earlier Op.79. A comparison of the two works gives a vivid insight into Bruch's abilities and craftsmanship as an orchestrator. From among the many instruments (including piccolo and contra-bassoon) used in the orchestration, it was once again his favourite alto register instruments that were fully exploited (the cor anglais in the first movement and the violas in the second) together with the solo violin (in No.4b) and the harp (Nos.1, 4a and 4b).

Bruch wrote a total of five orchestral suites beginning with Op.79b in 1903, but only three are extant. The whereabouts of the other two remains a mystery, for they were listed among those placed, for safekeeping, by the composer's surviving children, with the publishing firm of Rudolf Eichmann in Berlin during the Second World War. The firm no longer exists, and various attempts by German scholars and the present author to ascertain whether or not the manuscripts survived the war have proved fruitless. In 1956 Eichmann published Bruch's orchestral *Suite No.2* and called it the *Nordland Suite*. This was in all probability the *Second Suite* for large orchestra with free use of Swedish folk melodies Op.80, performed from the manuscript in Barmen in November 1906. This opus number was later assigned elsewhere. The titles of the five movements of this Suite were provided by Eichmann, and bear neither authentic proof of the composer's intentions nor conform to his dislike of programmatic titles.

Although the Suite was written and performed in 1906, it will be dealt with at this point because (like Op.79b) it too draws some of its material from the *Lieder und Tänze* Op.79 (Nos.7 and 6 from the earlier work become the third and fourth movements respectively of the *Second Suite*). The final movement is a Swedish March which, together with the Funeral March from the *Lieder und Tänze* Op.79 No.4, was later arranged for military band at the request of Army Superintendent Grawert and performed on 22 June 1909 by a large military band in an afternoon concert at the Hochschule under Grawert's direction. The complicated story of these compositions now takes a further twist. The first two movements of the *Second Suite* are new creations, but they recur in later works. The second theme in the first movement reappears as the second theme in the second movement of the Concerto for Clarinet and Viola Op.88 (composed in 1911). The Serenade for String Orchestra Op.posth. (1916) is a taut reworking of the *Second Suite*: its last movement becomes the first and last movements of the Serenade, while the inner three movements of both works are identical. On 4 April 1903 Bruch was made an honorary member of the Royal Swedish Academy in Stockholm. His interest in and dissemination of Scandinavian folk music and history, from *Frithjof* to *Gustav Adolf*, including all the instrumental works, was recognized and rewarded.

The years 1902–04 were unproductive for Bruch because his health broke down. In spite of annual visits to Bergisch Gladbach or Johannaberg, or even to spas such as Bad Pyrmont or Baden-Baden, he seemed unable to cope with the harsh winters of northern Germany through which he maintained a rigorous schedule. His nerves began to be affected by his medical condition, and he worried endlessly about his financial responsibilities towards his family. Margarethe was eking out a living as a poetess and writer, Max Felix was a pupil at the Berlin Musikhochschule (where he studied clarinet and composition, the latter under his father), Hans was about to become an art student and Ewald was still at school (and having to receive extra private coaching to maintain academic standards). Clara too was unwell with frequent migraines.

On 20 August 1901 Fritz Simrock had died, and his nephew Hans took over the running of the publishing house. After an association with Fritz of over 30 years, Bruch now found himself dealing with a man of a totally different generation, and without the close personal friendship that he had enjoyed alongside the professional one. A series of letters written to Maria Zanders in Bergisch Gladbach between 1902 and 1904 illustrates his troubles and how he dealt with them.

In June 1902 he had intended to be at the Igeler Hof, but was unwell and postponed his trip until September. As a result a performance of the *Messensätze* on 3 June 1902 was conducted by Joachim instead of

Bruch. On 7 September 1902 Franz Wüllner died in Cologne and Bruch
was sent to the funeral as representative of the Berlin Hochschule. He
then began deeply involving himself in intrigues surrounding the
selection of a successor to the post he had coveted all his life. He was in
contact with influential members of the Kölner Concertgesellschaft
such as Viktor Schnitzler (its chairman from 1897 to 1931) and Otto
Deichmann, who entertained Schumann and Brahms as well as Bruch
at his villa in Bad Godesberg, and whose Cologne house was used
between rehearsal and concert by many illustrious musicians such as the
Joachims and Rubinstein. These patrons were from other professions
(Schnitzler was a lawyer) but their wealth and influence supported the
music-making of the city through the Society.

The Society's first concert had taken place on 16 July 1827, and on
14 November 1857 its first concert was given in the Gürzenich hall,
which became its home until its destruction in a bombing raid during
1943. Three days before Bruch returned to Berlin after Wüllner's
funeral, he wrote to Schnitzler the first of several letters canvassing
support for the Music Director in Meiningen, Fritz Steinbach — this
within a year of vituperative complaints to Hans Simrock about
Steinbach, whose Berlin concerts with the Meiningen orchestra Bruch
boycotted on account of the neglect of his compositions in their
programmes. The letter to Schnitzler contains his usual abuse of the
'Social Democrats of music', but also attacks the conducting of
Weingartner, Mottl, Richard Strauss, Nikisch, Hausegger and
D'Albert.

All these men conduct Wagner, Liszt and R. Strauss very well, and
the classics very badly . . . Strauss has conducted the Coriolan
overture and the C minor Symphony out of recognition, Nikisch
continually makes so many fundamental errors in conducting
Beethoven, Schumann, Mendelssohn etc., that I no longer attend
his Berlin concerts, Weingartner bowdlerized the Ninth Symphony
so much with impossible *tempi* at the start of his activities in Berlin,
that the leader went to him and told him openly that it was
impossible. To which he replied 'Well, you see, I hardly know the
symphony yet — I have never conducted it before' . . . they all
have the technique of conducting but they have no tradition and
wish only to promote themselves, and not present a work
objectively in its purity and truth (as we old ones always wanted), as
the master conceived it. . . . The only young conductor of
moderate standpoint is Steinbach . . . a very good conductor, a
Brahmsian through and through. . . . I have heard very good
Beethoven, Schumann, Haydn etc. under Hans Richter . . . but he

will be difficult to get. Eugen D'Albert is not to be taken seriously. He is a brilliant pianist, but a very average conductor (who cannot even conduct his own works), and he has no personality to impose on a large choir or orchestra.[21]

At the beginning of October 1902, Steinbach was selected as Wüllner's successor (he held the post until 1914), and Bruch immediately hoped for a revival of his own works in Cologne (the new *Damajanti* in particular) as a reciprocal favour. The new piece was performed on 20 October 1903 in Cologne, but in due course, as Steinbach inevitably programmed works which either did not meet with Bruch's approval or replaced his own compositions, their association became strained.

Bruch was housebound for the first three months of 1903 when the doctors diagnosed severe anaemia. At the end of March he had recovered, but could hardly walk and suffered badly from asthma. His daily regimen permitted no more than short periods of morning exercise, usually supported by one of his children (he was quite unable to walk up or down steps). He complained bitterly to Maria Zanders that he had not heard a note of music 'since the concert at the Hochschule given before Kaiser Wilhelm II on 2 November 1902'.[22] He had written a *Hymne*, at royal demand, to celebrate the inauguration of the Charlottenburg Palace at the end of October. On the advice of his doctors he was given sick-leave by both the Hochschule and the Akademie which was to last from the winter of 1902–03 until May 1904. He described his ailments to Maria Zanders.

The cough which has plagued me (as it always does at this time of the year) since the beginning of November, appears at last to have gone — touch wood! On 21 March (the beginning of spring on the calendar) I went out for the first time after 2½ months' house arrest, sick-bed etc., but walking was and still is only creeping because my movements are hampered by badly swollen feet (the doctor says this is only because of lying down for a long time, nothing worse) and asthma (which I never had before). Supported by Cläre or my daughter, I need 20 minutes to walk a distance others do in 5. *It is a shame!* No symptoms indicate a skin disease more than the often unbearable itching, burning and pinching which has plagued me for a fortnight, yet it seems to be a benign crisis in the blood; as a result of all possible medications, it seems to have revived itself and now rages somewhat rebelliously around my body. It will pass! But it is very unpleasant and sometimes very painful. On the other hand I have completely lost the nervous depression from which I suffered during the worst time (January and the first half of February) . . .

P.S. Last night I did not once close my eyes; neither powders nor morphine nor carbolic washes worked — everything is helpless against the power of the disease. Think of the famous flea in *Faust* and multiply by 1000, imagine that company in an uninterrupted affectionate study of my body, and you have my condition at night when the warmth of the bed increases the torment. There is no end to the matter!

Some further news to conclude with — I am made an honorary member of the Royal Swedish Music Academy in Stockholm . . . Ah, would that the Swedes had sent me a remedy for the itching instead of a Diploma![23]

The letter also outlined possible plans for travel to health resorts and complained at the costs to be incurred ('I must keep my post and work to my last breath, otherwise we cannot live'). It concluded with news of his daughter Margarethe. She was now twenty-one, intellectual and reserved by nature. She was beginning to attract suitors, one of which, 'a refined and cultured man, but sickly and weak', soon disappeared to be followed by a Government building advisor of considerable private means. Bruch and his wife privately approved, hoping something would come of the friendship, but Margarethe took fright at the man's advances (away on business, he sent a friend *in sui loco*) and she broke off all contact. He was no more 'than uncle' to her, she 'hardly knew him' and he was 40 years old. The disparity in ages between the couple must have given a sense of *déjà vu* to the parents, but Max regretted that 'the child did not know what she was doing, it would have been a nice insurance for her and Clara's future.' Margarethe remained unmarried for the rest of her life.

In May 1903 Bruch reminded Maria Zanders that '25 years ago today, on 12 May 1878, was the first performance of *Das Lied von der Glocke* in Cologne'. Frau Zanders had a performance planned in Bergisch Gladbach for the next day by her Cäcelienchor, for which Bruch expressed his gratitude. He continued, 'About 1000 singers are singing *Frithjof* in Frankfurt am Main on 3 June for the Kaiser (at the opening of the singing competition). I am sure that great lover of Art, the Kaiser, and all his music-loving (?) courtiers will consider this strong 40-year-old lad (first performance 1864 in Aachen) to be a new work! But hush — high treason!'[24] Bruch had to withdraw from conducting a performance of *Das Lied von der Glocke* in Kiel on 8 May on account of his poor health.

By the middle of June 1903 Max and Clara had left Berlin for Bad Pyrmont, travelling on to the Harz mountains in August. Upon his return, at the beginning of September, he hoped to take up his duties at the Hochschule, but the doctors thought otherwise. Finding signs that the anaemia was still present, and that 'noises around the heart' were causing concern, it was decided that he would winter in Italy from the beginning of October 1903 until May 1904. He therefore made plans to visit Maria Zanders in Bergisch Gladbach on 7 October (where he also saw his sister Mathilde, now 63 years old and still living in Bonn) and five days later to travel on to Frankfurt, where he would meet his sister-in-law Marie Tuczek. She too had health reasons to travel to Italy, and so it was decided that Clara would remain behind in Berlin, leaving her sister to take care of Max.

Bruch sent a series of letters from Italy to Maria Zanders, the first from Rapallo, which began 'I am feeling well!' He went on:

> Objectively speaking I find everything here very beautiful, the sea, the chestnut groves, the old, dusky widespread olive plantations, the well-built villas, the blue distance, the palms, oaks and laurels etc. etc., but subjectively and to tell the truth, every wooded vale of the Bergisches Land is preferable to me, for I am and remain a man of the woods, who in time cannot live without his German forests. There is no substitute for them, not even in the South. On top of that we have had almost unbroken bad weather this past week — pouring rain, howling storms, boiling sea, nocturnal thunderstorms, thoroughly dirty under foot, and I am vainly searching for the 'ever blue skies of Italy' which play such an important part in letters from German friends! . . . So I think that soon we shall leave for the South, straight to Rome from here (stay two weeks if the weather is good), then Naples, Sorrento, Capri — and in the New Year back *via* Rome, Florence, Bologna, Venice and Vienna.[25]

In Rome he was limited by his frail condition to morning excursions to places where steps did not impede him. He managed to visit St Peter's, the Sistine Chapel, part of the Vatican, the Forum Romanum, the Colosseum, Monte Picino and the Villa Borghese. For the rest of the day he rested, read and wrote letters. Art galleries were, to his immense disappointment, out of the question on account of tiring him out by straining his poor eyesight, and by climbing too many steps to reach them. He missed the sounds of orchestral and choral music, and began to see his separation from Germany as an exile rather than a cure. By the middle of February 1904 he was in Naples, where his health began to improve, though not his mood. He was beginning to

worry more and more about the costs he was incurring in travel,
living and doctors' fees. He envied Mendelssohn who was 'luckier
when carried off at 38, whereas I must bear all the bitterness of old
age'. 'Italy', he decided, 'is a country one must see when young,
when one has no worries.' The last week in February found him in
Sorrento, Amalfi, Salerno and Paestum before embarking for Capri
where he arrived on 1 March and stayed until 7 April. His journey
back (changed slightly from earlier plans) took him to Rome,
Florence, Milan, Lucerne, Baden-Baden (where Clara met him for a
fortnight's stay) and back to Berlin, where he arrived on 4 May and
resumed his duties at the Hochschule the next day.

One of Bruch's pupils at this time, Hans Joseph Vieth, wrote an
account of his studies under Bruch from 1901 to 1905. Vieth had
befriended Max Felix, who showed his father one of Vieth's compositions, and effected an introduction for the shy young man who
hero-worshipped the old master. Bruch accepted him on to his
course, and the new student soon became a family friend, often
visiting the Bruch household. Every Sunday afternoon between 4pm
and 7pm was open house at the Bruch home, when anyone from
Joachim to the newest music student might come unannounced to
the house for tea, cakes and conversation, though music was not
performed. Bruch's youngest son Ewald wrote in 1970 of the
eminent musicians who attended these informal 'at homes'. Engel-
bert Humperdinck and Camille Saint-Saëns were two of the composers he remembered, while performers such as Artur Rubinstein,
Wilhelm Furtwängler, Georg Kulenkampff, Willy Hess and Joseph
Débroux, and musicologists such as Wilhelm Altmann and Max
Friedländer were either occasional or frequent guests. A select few
(invariably his music students such as Vieth, Eduard Künnecke or
Leo Schrattenholz) were invited to remain behind for a simple supper
with the Bruch family, 'each guest receiving a bottle of beer, whilst
my father drank a glass of Bordeaux'. On these occasions the
evenings often developed into the playing of chamber music and
Bruch's own works.

Vieth's studies with Bruch initially involved orchestrating extracts
from classical piano compositions such as Mozart's *Fantasia* in C
minor or the slow movement from Beethoven's *Pathétique* Sonata,
before producing works of his own. These ranged from the composition of a string quartet to songs for mixed chorus and orchestra.
At first Bruch was critical of the texts Vieth chose, until the young
man used poems by the composer's own daughter Margarethe to
forestall further criticism. He progressed to an orchestral suite and a

symphony at the end of his studies in 1905. Classes in analysis were also taken, but in groups.

'What', asked Bruch, 'should inspire a composer to work? First a beautiful painting, second a beautiful landscape, and third a beautiful woman.' His analysis classes were given from the keyboard, where he would score-read a Beethoven symphony to his assembled students. Only rarely would he use his own works as an example (Vieth quotes the G minor Violin Concerto and the *Scottish Fantasy*). He also analysed contemporary works of his hated opponents, the *Sinfonia Domestica* by Richard Strauss for example, which he played effortlessly at the keyboard from the full score. He had no inhibitions in giving his opinions of such compositions. 'That is how you do not write a symphony,' he exclaimed to his disappointed accolytes who also admired the opposition.

Vieth praised Bruch's abilities with large choral and orchestral forces, which he observed by taking part in a concert on 9 May 1905 in celebration of Schiller. The programme included the opening chorus from *Das Lied von der Glocke*. Later he watched the composer performing the orchestral arrangement of his *Swedish Dances*. Bruch taught conducting technique from the piano where he would sit playing opera scores whilst being conducted by a student. His favourite 'fire and water' test was (appropriately) the scene between Tamino and Der Sprecher in Mozart's *Die Zauberflöte*, with its complex alternating *recitativo* and *arioso* to confound any apprentice Kapellmeister. Perhaps this work was either already used by all German teachers of conducting, or it subsequently became the traditional hurdle to jump, for the present author was subjected to it 70 years later at the Hochschule in Bruch's native Cologne.

He was much loved by his pupils, who bore his intolerance with a forgiving nature and thought him a kind and considerate man. They had high regard for him as teacher and conductor, and kept in touch with him long after completing their studies. Bruch, for his part, duly helped his pupils in pursuing their careers as composers or conductors, always assuming that they did not join the opposition camp of the 'New Germans' or the 'Modernists'. His demands for loyalty extended to performers of his music and to those holding posts where they could play his music. Many fell from favour, even some, such as Siegfried Ochs or George Henschel, whose association with Bruch went back many years. In the case of Henschel, Bruch's growing anti-semitism seems to have influenced his opinion of the singer/conductor. The correspondence with Simrock over the years often contains unpleasant and insulting remarks about the Jews but, from the troubles in Breslau onwards, there were often instances of vicious

and bigoted comments which do the composer no credit (a letter to
Maria Zanders also contains equally disturbing views on the Jesuits).
As a virtual worshipper of Mendelssohn and close friend of Joachim,
this anti-semitism might be thought paradoxical, but Bruch was
obviously a man who attacked groups he considered to be conspiring
against him.

Clara Bruch wrote to Maria Zanders in November 1904 to commiser-
ate with her on their shared suffering from migraines: 'I had hoped to
lose them when I turned 50.' She went on to report Max's return to full
health, though 'we have not been out in the evenings for two years'.[26]
Her letter continued with news of their children. Margarethe had now
had some poems published (some had even earned her money), Max
Felix had conducted his own Motet in the Hochschule, and his Op. 1
was ready for printing (a Romance for Clarinet and Orchestra). Hans
was now at art school and taking drawing classes. This was the last
news that Maria Zanders was to receive of the children of her close
friend, for during the night of 6 December 1904 she died of a heart
attack.

Bruch was devastated by the loss of his trusted *confidante*, with
whom he had been on the closest terms for more than 40 years. He
wrote to Olga Zanders (a daughter-in-law to Maria): 'Every child and
every worker in Gladbach knows how I stood with Mama and the
Zanders family for half a century . . . much could be said about the
strong influence her friendly nature had on creative artists, especially
mine.'[27] Bruch had not only conceived or developed many of his
compositions at the Igeler Hof, but he had written occasional pieces
for the Zanders family such as the orchestration for brass of the chorale
*Ach bleib mit deiner Gnade*, the orchestral movement to another
chorale, *Geistlich gesinnt sein*, a *Präludium* for organ or harmonium
(written for the baptism of his godchild, Maria's grandchild Hildegard
('Hilla') on 25 October 1897), and the *Mindener Fantasie* for the
marriage of Margaretha Zanders. This was a work possibly sketched
much earlier in his life. It was written in two versions in 1881, for
small orchestra or for two pianos, and its style suggests that Bruch
may have written it for amateurs, such as members of the Zanders
circle or Andrew Kurtz in Liverpool, who commissioned the Piano
Quintet. Margaretha Zanders was again in Bruch's mind (this time as
first pianist) when he made the four-hand arrangement of the sixth
*Hungarian Dance* by Brahms. Also included in the Zanders archive is a
song written for a concert in the factory on 22 March 1897 to celebrate
the centenary of the birth of Kaiser Wilhelm I (Maria Zanders herself
wrote the words and the melody, Bruch then harmonized it and also

wrote a choral version), and a *Wächterlied* (Song of Vigil) for the death of the same Emperor on 9 March 1888.

In 1906 Simrock published the *Szene der Marfa* Op.80, taken from Schiller's unfinished work *Demetrius*. Written for solo mezzo-soprano and full orchestra, this short dramatic *scena* is a series of *arioso* interspersed with recitative, culminating in an extended lyrical passage at the words 'Du ew'ge Sonne'. The singer, Hermine Spies, had suggested the work to Bruch in 1883, when he was in Liverpool, and he made a sketch for it in February of that year in spite of being hard at work on the Third Symphony. He then moved to Breslau and in October 1884 agreed with Simrock on terms for the composition, but it was twelve years before it appeared. Ernestine Schumann-Heink, who had earned ten curtain calls singing Penelope's scene from *Odysseus* in New York (and with it Bruch's approval), in July 1906 proceeded to use the extract 'as a showpiece'. Bruch urged Hans Simrock to send the *Szene der Marfa* to her at Bayreuth, and also to the young Dutch singer, Julia Culp, whose voice he considered to be suited to the work.

On 1 August 1907 Joseph Joachim suffered a stroke which paralysed his left side and left him unconscious, though he rallied from time to time. On 6 August, Bruch was on holiday in Thuringia when the violinist's daughter, Marie, broke the news that her father was dying. He rushed back to Berlin, but Joachim was too ill to see him and Bruch and his family resumed their holiday. When Joachim died on 15 August they returned again, this time to accompany a large crowd of mourners bearing his old friend from his home to the Berlin Hochschule for a lying-in-state on 18 August. Bruch's doctors forbade him to attend at the graveside, but he gave a speech at the funeral service. He told Anna Zanders:

On 24 July, on my journey from Minden to Oberhof, I sat for the last time at his bedside and held his hand in mine for a long time. He was feeling better at that time, a small operation had helped him much — his mood was very much better than at the beginning of July, and he had hopes. How we others also hoped that this dear, invaluable life would be spared for us! But it was not to be — on 15 August it was all over and we, who were so close to him and loved him so much, asked ourselves 'How are we to live on without Joachim?' . . . What the death of Joachim means for me and the world! This man reigned so powerfully over us all, like Cologne Cathedral over a molehill. And to me he meant very much![28]

His feelings for Joachim did not prevent him, however, from a bitter complaint to Arthur Abell about the strange exclusion of any of his violin compositions from Joachim and Moser's published *Violin School*, and the letter went on:

A few years ago (after Joachim's death) at the Hochschule concert to celebrate my 70th birthday [1908], my First Violin Concerto Op.26 was supposed to be played, but the work was missing from the library. Joachim had never bought it![29]

It was not long before the question of a successor to the late Director embroiled the composer in internal intrigues. What may have been wishful thinking was his assumption that he was under consideration. 'In public,' he told Francis Kruse (Maria Zander's son-in-law), 'I am being named everywhere as his successor.' He did in fact succeed to one of Joachim's posts when, on 4 October 1907, he was appointed Vice-President of the Akademie. He was prepared to submit to his doctors' wishes that he should give up the various seats he held on committees (Chairman of the Performing Rights Association, first Chairman of the Senate of the Akademie, and membership of the Mendelssohn and Meyerbeer Foundations) provided he could retain his position as Director of the Masterclass in Composition. He tried to influence developments as Chairman of the Senate and get the Ministry of Culture to appoint a suitable successor to Joachim's post of Director. 'It appears to me,' he told Kruse, 'the danger that they might appoint a modern rostrum virtuoso to the head of the Hochschule is past. Weingartner is staying in Vienna as a Kapellmeister, Mahler (who writes destructive rubbish) is going to America for four years and will dance the "King Dollar" around the Golden Calf, Steinbach in Cologne is out of the question . . . the Senate under my influence is opposed to Richard Strauss with such energy and keenness . . . that the Ministry will not dare to plague us with him. Also he looks down upon the Hochschule too much, and knows us all as his enemies.'[30]

The Ministry seemed to take advice from no one, and appointed the writer on music Hermann Kretschmar as Joachim's successor from 1 October 1909. With his arrival came a change in personnel and in the system of running the institution. Bruch found it difficult to cope with the changes without 'betraying my whole artistic past and the tradition of my whole life'. Provided his pension would remain unaffected, he resolved to resign from the Hochschule but maintain his Masterclass in Composition at the Akademie.[31] He was persuaded (by a rise in salary as well as genuine interest in keeping him) to stay a further year, and it was decided that he would retire on 1 January 1911.

Henri Marteau, the violinist, succeeded Joachim in his capacity as violin teacher, and brought new methods and ideas with him. This together with the untimely death of the cellist Robert Hausmann (on 18 January 1909 while on a concert tour in Vienna) caused Bruch to feel isolated, especially as he had nothing in common with Hausmann's successor, Hugo Becker. Bruch felt able to serve only under someone who could combine the crafts of pedagogue and conductor, and recoiled in horror at the suggestion that Max Reger might have been appointed to the post. He expressed his opinion of Kretschmar in a letter to the violinist Willy Hess:

You will get on very well with Kretschmar, he is quite a good-natured, polite and well-meaning Saxon, more a musicologist than artist, quite modern with a very decided but innocuous preference for antediluvian little masters from the pre-Bach period; this hobby horse, which he rides with a special liking, disturbs us little. Until now I have prevented the worst modern abominations, but I am old and will not stay long in the Hochschule; one cannot know what will come later.[32]

Simrock, Joachim, Hausmann, Anton Krause (31 January 1907), Sarasate (20 September 1908), Hans Simrock (26 July 1910) and Maria Zanders all died between 1901 and 1910, but Maria's eldest son Richard was also a victim in this first decade of the new century. He died in 1906 and was sorely missed by Bruch, particularly on his summer visits to the Igeler Hof. Bergisch Gladbach was among the many who honoured Bruch on his seventieth birthday, which occurred on 6 January 1908. On the previous day he had attended a celebration concert by the Cäcilienchor, which began with the Cologne critic Otto Neitzel reading a speech in honour of the composer. The programme included scenes from *Frithjof*, the *Loreley* Prelude, the First Violin Concerto and *Schön Ellen*. Hans Zanders then concluded the celebrations with birthday greetings to 'Uncle Max'. From Bergisch Gladbach, Bruch travelled to Cologne at the invitation of the Kölner Concertgesellschaft to conduct a Gürzenich concert of his own works on 7 January (Clara was unwell and had remained in Berlin). The *Messensätze* (a particular favourite with the composer, and a work which had been revived the year before on 21 January 1907 by the Berlin Philharmonic Orchestra and Choir under Siegfried Ochs) and *Schön Ellen* were among the choral works on the programme. On Christmas Eve 1907 he confided to his friend Arnold Kroegel (who had conducted the Cäcilienchor concert in Bergisch

Gladbach and rehearsed the Cologne choir for Bruch's concert the following day):

> I lay this trustingly in your hands, my dear friend! On the whole I do not doubt that we shall have an impressive performance. As a 22-year-old young man (1860), and still a wholly starry-eyed Parsifal full of secret ideals, I conceived the opening of the Sanctus in Cologne Cathedral. On the other hand 40 years ago in 1867, I stood in the Gürzenich on the same spot and conducted *Schön Ellen* for the first time. And I am still alive, and will stand there once again![33]

The celebrations had begun with concerts as far back as November 1906. 'A young Spanish cellist called Pablo Casals has had exceptional success with my *Kol Nidrei* on the Rhine.'[34] In May 1908 he told Anna Zanders that 'the festive performances ended only recently in April. The happy participation of the nation and the whole musical world has shown me that I have not lived quite in vain, and that in spite of all modern madness, my constant efforts to hold aloft the flag of perfect form in Beauty will now be honoured by thousands.'[35] On the occasion of his birthday he received the highest honour in the realm for arts and sciences, the 'Pour le Mérite' medal. At the Court ball on 3 March 1908 he was introduced to Kaiser Wilhelm II, who 'gave me his hand and showered me with words of honour and courtesy'.[36]

By 1908 Bruch had more or less recovered his health, writing to Margaretha Kruse in May that he was 'working much and feeling very well as a result'.[37] A month earlier he told her of the latest composition on which he was working. 'I am writing an Easter Cantata (with wonderful words by Mörike among others) for America (and incidentally for much money).'[38] The *Osterkantate* Op.81 (to texts by Mörike and Geibel) is a five-movement work for solo soprano, chorus, orchestra and organ. The movements are 'Grüss an die Charwoche' (Greeting to Passion Week) for solo soprano and male chorus, 'Passionshymne' for two-part female chorus, 'Am Ostermorgen' (Easter morning) for soprano solo and chorus, 'Osterruf' (Easter call) a chorale for mixed chorus and 'Schlussgesang' (Final chorus) for soprano solo and chorus. Negotiations with the Americans moved so slowly that, still feeling goodwill and gratitude towards Cologne for the seventieth birthday celebrations earlier in the year, Bruch dedicated it to the Kölner Concertgesellschaft, who gave the first performance on 17 November 1908 in the Gürzenich. It was published in the same year by Leuckart in Leipzig. Performances of the work followed in Bonn, Bromberg, Berlin, Magdeburg and

Barmen within a year, with a performance in Baltimore scheduled for March 1909.

The genesis of the *Wessobrunner Gebet* Op.82, written in 1909 and published by Siegel in the following year, is described by the composer on the title page of the work as 'with the free use of a part of the poem and a musical motif from Op.19 Book II No.1'. This earlier version was written for the Concordia chorus in Aachen as Bruch was leaving Mannheim for his first professional post in Coblenz (1864–65), and it was scored for male voice choir accompanied by brass — a pair of horns, trumpets, trombones and timpani. The later version, begun at the Igeler Hof between 22 and 25 July 1909, was completed on 8 August in Oberhof in Thuringia. A comparison between Opp.19 and 82 reveals a slightly extended version of the eighth-century poem and an expansion in instrumentation to full orchestra and organ to accompany a mixed chorus. With repetition of the text, the later Op.82 is a far longer work than its precursor, but common to both is the opening chant motif upon which each is based.

Whereas Bruch had sometimes had his wife Clara in mind when writing vocal works, his son Max Felix, now a gifted clarinettist, was the inspiration for the first of two compositions written specifically for him. The *Eight Trio Pieces* for clarinet, viola and piano Op.83 appeared in 1910, published by Simrock. Bruch had yet again selected instruments of that favoured mellow quality of the alto register. To broaden their appeal, they also appeared in alternative versions for violin, viola and piano or clarinet, cello and piano. The alternative of a violin for clarinet is also a feature of Mozart's *Kegelstatt* Trio K.498 and Schumann's *Märchenerzählungen* (Fairy Tales) Op.132, both of which could have been models for Bruch's Op.83. It seems that two years earlier Bruch had yet another instrument in mind for inclusion in the composition. He wrote to Arnold Kroegel: 'There are now 5 for [clarinet], viola and piano and 3 for the same instruments with harp, but they are not yet printed. My son Max Felix (at present a theory teacher at von Barmuth's Conservatoire in Hamburg), a good clarinettist, is playing the pieces on 20 January in Bonn with Grüters, J. Schwarz and a harpist from Cologne.'[39] Bruch hoped that Steinbach might hear the pieces and perform them. His letter to Kroegel is confusing, first, by not listing the clarinet among the instruments (though he goes on to talk of Max Felix playing (*bläst*) them in Bonn), and also because it is unclear whether the harp joins the piano or substitutes for it. Had he included the clarinet in his list, the sentence (*Es existieren jetzt 5 [Clarinette] Bratsche und Klavier und 3 für dieselben Instrumente mit Harfe*) would favour the conclusion that the piano shared the composition with the harp. Bruch also told Kroegel: 'I hope you received the C sharp minor piece safely. It is one of the most important (a kind of dialogue between clarinet and viola) and must at all costs be played. My son will take special pleasure in staying with you, it is also better as far as rehearsals are concerned than staying with Deichmann. May one definitely depend on a harp? If so, the 'Nachtgesang' and the 'Rumänische Melodie' must be played.'[40] An examination of the piano's arpeggio-style accompaniments to Nos. 3, 5 and 6 would certainly confirm the possibility that the harp was originally intended to join the viola and clarinet in these pieces. There is no further information on the performance in Bonn, nor any mention of a harp in correspondence with Simrock during 1910, so it must therefore be assumed that Bruch changed his mind on its use, perhaps because it would limit sales among amateur music makers.

Max Felix gave successful performances of Op. 83 in Cologne and Hamburg in 1909. Fritz Steinbach reported to the composer that his son's performance in January in Cologne bore favourable comparison with the renowned clarinettist, Richard Mühlfeld, the Meiningen player for whom Brahms wrote his clarinet works. Max Felix possessed 'a tone and sense of phrasing which is pure and free from dross', according to Steinbach. Bruch considered this 'high praise' from a man who, as Musical Director in Meiningen before moving to Cologne, had enjoyed the high standards of Mühlfeld as his principal clarinettist.

The first six pieces are structurally in either binary or ternary form, whereas the last two use sonata form. They reveal an invention and freshness in their colour and structure, an expressiveness in chromaticism using diminished sevenths and key-related thirds, and a contrast in moods. The two soloists take an equal share in the proceedings, whilst the piano performs a largely subsidiary role in accompaniment (sometimes assuming orchestral characteristics such as *tremolando*). The pieces are self-contained units and Bruch advised against the playing of all eight together in a concert programme. Contrary to his appetite for folk music, only one (No. 5) has its roots therein. This 'quite exquisite Rumanian melody' was suggested to him by one of his Sunday open-house visitors, 'the delightful young Princess zu Wied' (to whom Op. 83 was dedicated), and only this piece and the Nocturne No. 6 ('Nachtgesang') carry titles. The *Eight Trio Pieces* Op. 83 represent a successful return to chamber music by the ageing composer, half a century after his Second String Quartet in 1860.

With this work, Max Bruch entered the last phase in his life. From 1 April 1911 he retired from all his official duties at the age of seventy-three. He was still unwell, and by now had developed a bladder complaint. For the years remaining to him, he was to be crushed by personal tragedy, live through the First World War, the immediate aftermath of Germany's defeat, and witness his further remoteness and isolation from events in the world of music. This would in turn lead him to moods of increasing bitterness, resignation and loneliness. For him there was to be little peace in the days of retirement which now lay uncertainly before him.

# Chapter Sixteen

## THE FINAL YEARS
### 1911–20

In the *Musical Courier* (26 May 1915) Arthur Abell cast his mind back to a conversation he had had with Max Bruch in Berlin seven years earlier on the occasion of the composer's seventieth birthday.

> . . . the master declared that his composing days were over. 'I shall write no more,' he said, 'for the source of my inspiration is dried up.' At that time he meant what he said, too, and for a long period he was inactive. But then the spell came upon him again, and during the seven years that have elapsed since he attained the biblical age, Max Bruch has enriched musical literature with several interesting and important works, among them being his Fourth Violin Concerto, which was introduced to America by Maud Powell several seasons ago.

The work referred to by Abell was the *Konzertstück* for violin and orchestra Op. 84, the title of concerto being considered, but eventually rejected by Bruch because the composition consisted of only two linked movements. It was completed at the end of November 1910 and dedicated to Willy Hess, who, with Bruch's help, had returned from his post as leader of the Boston Symphony Orchestra to take a position in the Berlin Musikhochschule as violin teacher and conductor of the School symphony orchestra. While Bruch was informing his publisher, Simrock, that the work was completed, Hess was performing the composer's Third Violin Concerto with the Hallé orchestra in Manchester during Hans Richter's last season as conductor (Hess's association with the Hallé went back many years to the days when he was its leader and Joachim a frequent soloist). Upon his return from England, the *Konzertstück* was tried out, first at the Hochschule with Hess conducting and one of his pupils playing the solo part, and then, on 5 January 1911, Hess played it through with the Berlin Philharmonic Orchestra in a private session for the composer. The matter of the title, *Konzertstück*, was apparently resolved unanimously by members of the orchestra at this rehearsal, and Bruch took their advice. The American violinist, Maud Powell, gave the première at the Norfolk Festival in Connecticut on 8 June 1911. Her association with it brought about the first recording of a composition (albeit only in part) by Max Bruch. Bruch's response was one of disapproval, though probably more of making a cut than opposing the making of gramophone records. He described the episode to Abell: 'I had not expected it of Maud Powell that she makes cuts. At first she cabled me after the first performance on 8 June (Norfolk), 'Great success'. But then she writes to me on 20 June that she cannot play the *Konzertstück* in orchestral concerts next winter, because it ends with an Adagio (*hear hear!!!*). She has also played the Adagio alone, half of it cut, into a machine (!!!) I told her a few truths!'[1] Maud Powell confirmed Bruch's reaction to Abell: 'It is so truly Bruchian, the Adagio, that I was tempted to play a portion of it for the Victor Machine. This has horrified the good Doctor, who seems to feel that it may do him harm!'[2]

The first movement is in sonata form, and dominated by a strong and dramatically coloured main theme in the tonic key of F sharp minor. The mood is reminiscent of Brahms and of Bruch's own third Violin Concerto. The orchestral introduction to this movement is (for Bruch) long and substantial, with both first and second violins given double-stopping and passage work with which the soloist has later to contend. The second subject, which is curiously not in the relative major key of A, but in A minor (underlining Bruch's preference for the mood of minor keys), brings the repeat of this subject back in the tonic F sharp minor during the recapitulation. The Adagio follows without a break in an enharmonic switch to the major key of G flat, and its melody is the Irish folksong 'The Little Red Lark'. Bruch's treatment of it recalls (in mood, melodic beauty and its 3/8 time-signature) the famous slow movement of his First Concerto. This was the first work for violin written after Joachim's death and, coming full circle from the renowned Op.26, was appropriately the last.

Bruch's love of the French horn, clarinet, viola and cello was much in evidence at this period in his life. Following the *Eight Trio Pieces* for clarinet, viola and piano and before the Double Concerto for Clarinet and Viola Op.88, he wrote a short work for solo viola and orchestra. This was the *Romanze* Op.85, written in 1911, dedicated to Maurice Vieux (principal viola player with the Paris Opéra and the Paris Conservatoire Orchestra) and published the following year by Schott. Sharing the key of F with the violin Romances by Beethoven, Dvořák, Lalo and Svendsen (although all these were in the minor key), this single movement has a tightly constructed sonata form, with the melodic *cantilena* of the solo viola guiding its underlying homophonic orchestral accompaniment in a calm andante tempo. Modulating sidesteps to D flat major or (from the dominant key of C major) A flat major are typical fingerprints of Bruch's style; but where the violin *Serenade* ended in a blatant plagal cadence, the *Romanze* at least varies somewhat by preceding the final tonic chord of F major with the chord of the submediant (D minor). Like the following Double Concerto, the instrumentation is almost of chamber orchestra proportions (single flute and oboe, double clarinets and bassoons, three horns, two trumpets, timpani and strings). The eight-bar dialogue between the solo viola and the first clarinet beginning at bars 36 and 95 demonstrates how the *Romanze* could have been a preparatory exercise for the Double Concerto, which appeared later the same year. Willy Hess played the *Romanze* through for Bruch on 25 April 1911 with Leo Schrattenholz (a composition and conducting pupil) conducting his Orchestergesellschaft in Berlin, and Bruch was grateful for the chance to work further on the piece throughout the summer of 1911.

The flurry of activity in the immediate aftermath of Bruch's retirement also produced two choral compositions during 1911. The first of these was the *Six Lieder* for mixed *a cappella* chorus Op.86 published by Heinrichshofen. His daughter Margarethe was the author of the texts of four of them, whereas the remaining two (Nos. 4 and 6) were taken once again from the works of Thomas Moore. The subjects of the songs are a mixture of pastoral and religious verses. 'Ackeley' is a short three-verse pastoral homophonic song. 'Kleine Maria', another strophic three-verse song (though unlike 'Ackeley' there are slight differences in each repetition), is on a religious theme, whose plain and effectively naïve setting culminates in a dramatic and sombre image of Golgotha in the dark key of D flat minor. 'Deutscher Frühling' (German Spring) is a fresh and energetic three-verse song, with a characteristic sidestep in the middle from the tonic key of B flat major to its mediant D major at the word 'Frühling'. 'Geh, wo Ruhm dir winket' (Go, where fame beckons you) has Irish origins, and is the most complex of the six settings. Whereas most of the songs have occasional divisions of one or more parts, this two-verse song is in eight parts throughout and is divided into a main and a semi-chorus. 'Im Moselthal' (In the Mosel valley) reverts to the pastoral theme in a rustic greeting to Whitsuntide, while 'Weit über dem Meere' (Far across the sea) is another two-verse Irish text for five-part chorus.

During the course of the summer 1911, Bruch also set Schiller's poem 'Die Macht des Gesanges' (The Power of Song) for baritone solo, mixed chorus and orchestra, which was published by Simrock as Op.87 in 1912. Bruch described its genesis in a letter to the firm:

'You will know the wonderful poem . . . I still felt myself drawn to
Schiller, and I believe that something of the spirit of *Glocke* can also be
sensed in this new work.'[3] The piece is in five distinct (but untitled)
sections and adopts many characteristics of his dramatic oratorios. A
substantial orchestral introduction precedes the opening chorus and
effectively paints an image of a rushing torrent cascading down a
mountainside and sweeping away all before it. Much passage work for
strings and solid chording for brass create this dramatic scenario.
Through the turmoil comes the power of song to quell the flood,
musically achieved by the turbulence of the writing giving way to an
*espressivo* homophonic chorus followed by an orchestral postlude to
end the first section. The second and third are linked, the first a short
chorus (begun by the basses) questions the ability of any to resist the
power of song. The third introduces the baritone soloist (accompanied by the brass), who compares the power of the gods to that of the
singer. Music can sway the heart, and can even penetrate the realms of
death or (to a string figuration of arpeggios) point heavenwards. The
fourth section personifies song as the truth, which throws out
falsehood and fraudulence. The climax of the work (at the first
mention of truth) is a glorious and pure C major for full orchestra and
(optional) organ, the strands of the choral lines converging soon after
in a hymn to the victory of truth over the evils of deceit. There is no
break before the fifth and final part of the Cantata, a tranquil song of
praise by soloist and chorus to the magical enchantment and power of
song.

The last work of the fruitful year, 1911, was the Double Concerto
for Clarinet, Viola and Orchestra, the second composition written
expressly for his son Max Felix. The first performance from
manuscript parts took place in the seaport of Wilhelmshaven on 5
March 1912 'in front of all the admirals and captains of our navy'. The
soloist was Bruch's friend Willy Hess, who played the G minor Violin
Concerto in the first half, and then exchanged his violin for the viola to
play the new concerto in the second. After revisions, the work
received a second performance on 3 December 1913 with Max Felix
and Werner Schuch accompanied by Leo Schrattenholz's privately run
Orchestergesellschaft. This concert took place in the Berlin Hochschule, which Schrattenholz had to hire for the performance. Bruch
also wrote a version in which the violin substitutes for the clarinet. A
potentially more interesting substitution was proposed by Bruch to
Schrattenholz when he reported that 'Dr Niel Vogel from Amsterdam
showed me his six-stringed viola d'amore, a very lovely-sounding
instrument that interests me very much. He wants to hear the Double
Concerto on 3 December and then transcribe the viola part for his

instrument (which would not be difficult), so he is coming especially to Berlin from Amsterdam on 1 December.'[4] The outcome of Dr Vogel's interest is unfortunately unknown.

The Double Concerto was printed in 1943 by the publisher Eichmann and, though the original manuscript was destroyed during the last stages of the Second World War, it has since been reconstructed and reprinted by the successors to Simrock, Anton Benjamin. The orchestration is curious. It begins with chamber orchestra proportions (1 each of flute and oboe, 2 each of clarinets, bassoons and horns, timpani and strings) but adds other instruments as it proceeds (another flute and oboe, plus cor anglais and 2 trumpets in the second movement, and 2 more horns in the last). This tends to cloy the texture for the viola soloist, already contending in its middle register with the bright, high tones of its solo partner, the clarinet. The viola in this work is afforded a subservient role to the clarinet, whereas in the Trio Pieces they shared an equal status.

The Double Concerto has characteristics of many of Bruch's earlier concertos. The opening declamatory *quasi recitativo* for each soloist is reminiscent of the *Vorspiel* of the First Violin Concerto and the second movement (Recitative) of the Second Concerto. Harmonic sidesteps to the mediant (E minor to G major in the first movement and E major to G major in the last), rigid sonata form in the last movement and phrases in four- or eight-bar periods are typical examples. Melodic *espressivo* is a feature of the elegiac first movement and the second subject of the second movement is lifted bodily from the (so-called) *Nordland Suite*, written five years earlier (where it is also the second subject of the second movement). The principal melody of the first movement is derived from the first four bars of the Swedish folk tune 'Vermelandsvisan'. (It was also set by Percy Grainger in 1902 as part of *La Scandinavie* (Scandinavian Suite) for cello and piano. The following year it was reworked for a five-part *a cappella* mixed chorus entitled *A Song of Vermeland*. Typically for Grainger, this version was credited to the composer Ycrep Regniarg!) The last movement is dominated by *ostinato* triplets (the principal material being no more than ornamented passing notes and scales), and technically more challenging passage work for both instruments. The Double Concerto was described in the *Allgemeine Musikzeitung* as 'harmless, weak, unexciting, first and foremost too restrained, its effect is unoriginal and it shows no master-strokes.'[5] Perhaps, seen in the context of the more lively debate surrounding the controversial première of Stravinsky's *Le Sacre du printemps* which took place in Paris two months later, this criticism is justified; but Bruch seldom, if ever, provoked such controversy, nor should it

have been expected of this 75-year-old conservative whose creative
energies were running low.

With the completion of the Double Concerto, Bruch's musical
output faltered for four years, largely owing to external events almost
crushing his spirits. When he visited the Igeler Hof in the summer of
1909, he did not realize that he would never see it again. This was in
spite of a philosophical approach to life, often voiced with the turn of
each calendar year or birthday. 'At my age,' he wrote to the widowed
Anna Zanders, 'one does not make long-term plans; but I would be
happy if a friendly Fate would lead me once again this coming summer
to the ever beloved Igeler Hof.'[6] After this last visit to Bergisch
Gladbach in 1909, he was forced to decline his annual invitation there.
By the spring of 1910 he had been suffering for four or five months
from a disease of the bladder, and sleeplessness on account of the pain
and discomfort it caused him. It also restricted his ability to travel long
distances. He managed the five-hour journey to Oberhof in Thuringia, from where he wrote to Hans Zanders, refusing an invitation to
the Silver Jubilee concert of the Cäcilienchor on 24 July. His *Waldpsalm*
and other choral songs were to be performed. 'I too am celebrating a
special little jubilee,' he continued, 'for this summer it will be exactly
60 years that, as a 12-year-old child, I went for the first time to
Gladbach and the Igeler Hof (1850). In 1855 I met your blessed father,
and on 6 July 1857 your dear mother on her return from her
honeymoon. Under the circumstances I must for this year unfortunately also refuse my usual visit to the Igeler Hof, which is always so
dear to me. I am not yet dead, nor even half dead, and the complaint is
not dangerous, only very wearisome. My present excellent doctor has
begun a new course of treatment, which he says promises very much,
as demonstrated in many cases.'[7] Bruch was still in Oberhof at the
beginning of September 1910, and reported to Anna Zanders that the
doctor from Hamburg had completely freed him of his complaint. It
was this remission that enabled him to recharge his strength for the
next year (1911) in which Opp.85–88 were written. 'I am quite
healthy,' he wrote to Anna. 'I have no complaints and work with a
complete freshness and joy as of 30 years ago.'[8] The letter went on to
regret the change of direction that the Hochschule was taking under
the leadership of Kretschmar, and to express his lack of joy in his work
since the death of Joachim. He would give up everything by 1 April
1911 and work for himself and his own interests in absolute freedom.

Bruch's spirits were renewed by the end of the year, when the
*Konzertstück* was to receive its first run-through in the Berlin
Musikhochschule (2 December). He still took a vigorous interest in

the way his music was being performed. Steinbach came in for criticism after a performance of *Odysseus* in Cologne, which he nearly ruined by taking the wrong *tempi*. Bruch told Hans Zanders that Steinbach had apparently taken everything 'too slowly, lamely, without fire and strength. The devil take these rostrum virtuosi! Whenever I am not there, stupid things are done, but I cannot be everywhere!'[9] These conductors, Bruch contended, were the victims of pressure from the newspapers to perform the works of certain composers, in spite of rapidly dwindling audiences and poor financial results at the box office. Halls such as those in Düsseldorf were being emptied by the music of Strauss, Reger etc., he told Francis Kruse when the couple announced their plans to move to the city. 'The present conductor, Panzner,' Bruch went on, 'is an Austrian conducting virtuoso who completely boycotted me in Bremen (where he was before). There is nothing more to be done about Steinbach in Cologne either; everyone there (even non-partisans) says that he overfeeds them with Brahms; one has nothing against Brahms, rather against Steinbach's unbearable exclusiveness. And on the other side there is the musical social-democracy and anarchy!'

Blinded by these obsessive opinions, Bruch was quite unable to see his own bigotry and prejudice. Composers fared no better. As well as his continual attacks on Strauss, Reger and Pfitzner, others came in for similar treatment. Debussy was an 'unqualified scribbler, almost as bad as Reger, Strauss, Schillings and their gang, which does not say much . . . the music of Herr Debussy shows throughout that one key does not relate to another; it is of no matter to him to write simultaneously in C major and B major etc. . . . I looked through an opera of his once but, filled with disgust, I soon threw the thing into the corner. And there it is just one of many . . .'[10]

He asked the opinion of Arnold Kroegel about 'the criminal madness that those in Bonn are up to; for their Beethoven Festival in Beethoven's birthplace they are devoting a whole evening to the dreadful concoctions of the greatest destroyer of Art in our time, Herr Max Reger! If Beethoven were to return, he would throw Herr Grüters and his whole committee out of the Temple as Christ did with the moneylenders!' Mahler and Korngold were both 'Jewish rogues', the former was 'a good Wagner conductor but a bad composer', the latter 'writes senseless stuff in the manner of Reger'.[11] He told Arthur Abell with pride that *Frithjof* was celebrating its 50th anniversary. 'Where', he asked, 'will the works of Messrs Richard Strauss, Reger and colleagues be in 50 years time?'[12] Bruch had no talent as a clairvoyant, for *Frithjof* gets even fewer performances than the infrequently performed Reger, and Strauss is now a household name.

When Bruch retired, he did so on an annual pension of 3,000 marks, supplemented by royalties (5,300 marks for the 100 performances his music received in 1911), yet in spite of this he was already considering the sale of the original manuscript of the famous First Violin Concerto, even if it meant selling it abroad. Negotiations with a cartel of Americans and with the Belgian violinist Ysaÿe failed because the sums discussed were insufficient, and it was to be some years before the Sutro sisters swindled the old man out of his most valuable asset.[13]

In spite of spending May and June of 1911 in Bad Wildungen (south-west of Cassel) the remission of his health did not continue into the following year. In May 1912 he wrote to Arnold Kroegel:

> You fantasize about my next 'Rhine journey', my dear chap. But oh, the days are over and they will not return. For my bladder complaint, from which I have been suffering for two years (not life-endangering but troublesome) requires continual daily treatment, and precludes long journeys. At best I can get to Oberhof ($4\frac{1}{2}$ hours). More annoying than anything for me is that I shall not see my beloved Igeler Hof again. But there is nothing to be done — I am too old and live too long in this miserable, thoroughly changed world, which no longer knows what is beautiful or ugly, nor what is good or bad.

The same letter to Kroegel contains an interesting memory of Bruch's childhood studies of the violin and the early history of the Cologne Musical Society:

> [It] was founded in 1812, that is right. Perhaps you do not know that my grandfather Almenräder (a teacher) was in the forefront of the founders of the Society, and also his son (my uncle Jakob Almenräder), who was a member of the Cologne City Orchestra from 1810–60. I had violin lessons from him for five years; when we scratched away at violin duos by Mazas and other venerables, it was so wonderfully horrible that rats and mice hurriedly hid in their holes. He was a grand old man, his old music shop in the Schildergasse (Almenräder Bros.) has been there a long time.[14]

When Maria Zanders died in December 1904, she left unfinished a life-long dream to revive the fortunes of the ruined cathedral in the little town of Altenberg in the Bergisches Land. Her tireless labours finally came to partial fruition in the summer of 1904 (she was too ill to attend the celebrations), but the restoration of the organ was only completed nine years later in the summer of 1913. Maria's sons

Richard (until his death in 1906) and then Hans, in turn chaired the committee to organize the rebuilding of the instrument. It was Hans who asked Max Bruch to write a composition for the celebrations held on 16 July 1913 to mark the completion of the work. Bruch called it the *Altenberger Hymne*. Bruch's association with the Cäcilienchor was still close; he had conducted *Das Lied von der Glocke* in 1896, *Odysseus* for Maria's sixtieth birthday celebrations in 1899, and *Das Lied von der Glocke* had been repeated in 1904, while he was away in Italy.

The manuscript score of the *Altenberger Hymne* is dated 11 May 1913. This short hymn is written for four-part mixed chorus accompanied by two trumpets, three trombones, timpani and organ, and takes as its initial text the Latin *Domine salvum fac regem*. Bruch marked the brass parts *ad libitum* on the manuscript as the organ doubles them throughout. Hans Zanders subsequently asked for the work to be orchestrated, and the same manuscript contains Bruch's sketches for the reworked version (performed on 27 January 1916 at Berlin University, prompting the composer to write that it 'had strongly touched the hearts of the almost desiccated professors, and should from now on be played at the University's imperial celebrations'). It is in three short sections, two homophonic chorales encasing a more contrapuntal section. Bruch was careful that this middle section should not be too complex, for he was familiar with the resonant acoustics of the Altenberger Dom:

> When I wrote the piece, I thought constantly of Mama and of the beautiful church in the lovely wooded valley . . . The principal requisite of the style of choral writing was a noble simplicity; for the lofty building would not tolerate a complicated structure nor any intricate figuration — it would all come out sounding higgelty-piggelty. That is why, in my opinion, the old Catholic church music of Palestrina, Lotti, Gabrieli etc. is far better for large, wide church buildings than, for example, the often very active polyphony and the rich figuration of Bach's Cantatas and other Protestant church music.[15]

Kaiser Wilhelm II was supposed to be present for the celebrations, but after a week in Kiel for the Regatta, he went off on a journey northwards rather than south to the Bergisches Land. Bruch had provided a German alternative text for the Latin (the last section was originally already in German) in the event of the Kaiser cancelling his visit. The Emperor's absence would remove the royal ceremonial element and emphasize the work's 'more religious content'.[16] The Kaiser had taken a genuine interest in the restoration of the Altenberger Dom, having paid a visit there in October 1906. On that occasion Hans Zanders was introduced to him and explained in an audience, lasting half an hour, the details of the complex restoration. Today the fully restored cathedral remains a testimony to Maria Zanders' faith and philanthropy, but the *Altenberger Hymne* (which was never printed) has faded from memory after one further performance in 1977 by the Cäcilienchor to whom it was dedicated.

When Bruch wrote to Arnold Kroegel to warn him not to expect the Kaiser, his letter also included a vitriolic attack on a Cologne priest who had dedicated a Whit Monday service in Wagner's memory. The organist (Professor Franke who, by playing the organ in first performances of such Bruch works as the *Messensätze*, *Osterkantate* and the *Altenberger Hymne* was much in favour) had refused to play the service. 'Next they will be declaring Richard Wagner a god, and hanging his picture up in church!' Bruch concluded to Kroegel. He wrote to Franke directly: 'If my grandfather, who was a pastor of the evangelical church in Cologne for 34 years (1802–36) knew of this, he would turn in his grave.'[17] 'Do you not think it possible,' he wrote again, 'that services in Cologne will next be dedicated to Richard Strauss, Ibsen or Oscar Wilde (who has been in prison)? Is not anything now possible in Cologne?'[18]

Bruch was so preoccupied with these critical attacks, and also with the final details of the *Altenberger Hymne*, that he was totally unprepared for the shock that hit the household a few days later. His 26-year-old son, Hans, was with friends on a study holiday in Thuringia, when a boil he developed turned septic. His friends rushed him to a hospital in Jena, where he lay seriously ill for three days and, on 4 June, died from blood poisoning. He was buried in Jena to where his distraught parents hurried for the funeral.

I am still suffering in the lowest of spirits; there are days when I can do nothing at all — only wrestle with Fate — but I pull myself together again and try to take part in matters of the world. If you saw Clara, you would weep. Yet in spite of everything, she holds herself together admirably. Even at the worst possible moment she never lost control, and soon began to think of everything again, which she still does here with her former conscientiousness and dependability in all matters. This woman was and remains a match for all situations. You know her as such, and she will continue likewise to remain in the minds of her children and all who know her. But during the past five years she has suffered too much over the fate of our three eldest children, and this last and greatest tragedy is too much for her heart. Oberhof (where we journey on

26 June) will not help much, for there we shall realize exactly how much we miss him!![19]

Hans Zanders received a letter from Bruch, in which he described his dead son as the favourite child, not only of the parents, but of all the family. 'For precisely this son was our joy, our sun and our hope.'[20] He had always been a happy-go-lucky child, with blonde curls, a happy disposition and a great talent as an artist (he had already had a successful exhibition in Berlin). His sister Margarethe felt his loss keenly. Being especially close to him, she wrote a long poem in his memory shortly after his death. The tragedy completely broke down Clara's spirit; she never recovered from the shock but lingered in a poor state of health for six more years. Bruch wrote to his pupil and close friend Leo Schrattenholz (it carried the cryptic heading 'All Souls' Day'):

> Last night I saw him in a dream as a child; he said 'Papa, soon I shall be going away from you both, do not forget me, and do not cry too much!' I awoke and realized once again how hard life is after such a loss, and how trivial other matters become if one has to surrender such a beloved child — one who was bound to us with all human bonds. But it will not and cannot last much longer, for we old ones will soon follow him. His mother has placed every picture of him (the sweet childhood pictures too) beside her writing desk amongst white flowers of mourning and forget-me-nots. We live in the memory of this poor dear boy, who has been so cruelly stamped out by such a bitter fate.[21]

The year 1914 dawned heavily for Europe, and for Bruch and his wife there was little satisfaction in celebrating his 76th birthday. It was a year in which he was to write no new compositions. He was resigned to remaining in Berlin and not undertaking long journeys, and saw the melancholy word '"Resignation" written above the gates of old age'. His concern was now for his 73-year-old sister Mathilde in Bonn, who was suffering from arteriosclerosis.

> A few weeks ago she had another fainting fit, and it appeared to be an ominous heart failure as well as a total collapse. Everything points to a development of the hardening of the arteries, which is undeniably present and has persisted for some years, (this between ourselves, for she knows nothing about it); under-nourishment might also have contributed to her breakdown. She has been in bed for the past two weeks, my cousins in Bonn have nursed her well.

The situation has improved, but on doctor's orders, she is to give up all her activities; even the few pupils she still has would be too much for her. As she is in her 74th year, we are continually worried.[22]

Max and Clara had just two more months to worry about Till, who died peacefully on the evening of 25 March, but they were unable to travel to Bonn for the funeral; Max Felix and Margarethe were sent instead. At the beginning of June, Bruch and his wife revisited their son's resting place in Jena, where a tombstone had now been erected.

I do not need to tell you how hard these days have been for us . . . and yet I feel a certain sense of peace from having been there, and from having seen once again the incomparably beautiful resting place of the poor boy among the green hedges and trees. This is possibly the most beautiful cemetery in Germany. It lies on the slopes of the wonderful wooded hills surrounding Jena and is truly a garden of God. It was just like a year ago — the birds sang, the sun shone brightly and the trees rustled over his fresh grave; and, as before, one tearfully asked the question 'Why did it have to happen, why did we have to surrender this beloved gifted person in the full flower of his life?'[23]

Bruch was pleased that, despite the prevalence of anti-music ('as Brahms called it, though he did not have to live through the worst of it'), he was still receiving a fair income from royalties. In 1913, 130–140 performances yielded 5,000 marks. Later in the year (on 20 November) the 50th anniversary took place of the fiirst performance of *Frithjof*, and the First Violin Concerto and *Schön Ellen* soon followed with their jubilees. All three were expected to receive many performances from music societies at home and abroad.

Cologne's music society had its attentions elsewhere at this time and was undergoing yet another change of leadership: Fritz Steinbach had resigned when misdemeanours with a young female student of the Cologne Musikhochschule came to light. The post of Music Director to the city also included the Directorship of the Conservatoire, and Cologne's mayor, Wallraf, was forced to offer the compromised conductor a choice between resignation or an official inquiry. He wisely chose the former and promptly felt the need of an early holiday in Italy. Hans Zanders was on the Committee of the Gürzenich Society and corresponded with Bruch on the Steinbach affair. Bruch wrote commenting on the conductor's behaviour since his appointment to Cologne in 1902. Steinbach (a married man) had apparently brought a girlfriend with him from Meiningen, which was a private matter.

Unfortunately he had then enrolled her as a student at the Cologne Conservatoire, which outraged the professorial staff and broke down discipline at the school. In Bruch's opinion the staff had no alternative but bring the matter to the attention of the authorities. 'The Cologne Conservatoire', he told Hans Zanders, 'should not get into the harem business, which prevailed at the Paris Conservatoire under the famous Auber, and which was also common in all Court Theatres throughout 18th-century Germany.' Tackling the question of a possible successor to Steinbach, Bruch drew attention to the need for someone of repute and talent:

[Karl] Muck in Boston (formerly Music Director at the Imperial Opera in Berlin and very good) has an annual salary of $10,000 or 40,000 marks and another two years of his contract. Richard Strauss lives like a prince, has become rich on royalties, and would not consider a post such as Cologne. Reger (whose music is becoming more and more of a caterwaul) is leaving Meiningen, but he is a bad conductor, a drunkard, a rough fellow without any manners, and until now has not proved himself in any post . . . Weingartner would be very good, but has just concluded an agreement with the Grand Duke of Hessen in Darmstadt. Mahler (a man who accomplished a colossal *nihil* by colossal means) would perhaps have come — but he is dead. Nikisch earns in Leipzig and Berlin at least 40,000 marks. In my opinion there is no one on the Rhine who could be considered a possibility for Cologne.[24]

The post was finally offered to Hermann Abendroth, who began his duties in the city during 1915. He did not prove himself to be a particular devotee of Bruch's music, although he gave the first performance in Cologne of the new composition *Die Stimme der Mutter Erde* Op.91 in celebration of Bruch's eightieth birthday three years later in 1918.

On 1 August 1914 Germany declared war on Russia, two days later on France and by the 4th, Britain had declared war on Germany. The 'lights were going out all over Europe' and the First World War had begun. On the day following German mobilization (31 July), Bruch wrote a long impassioned letter to his daughter Margarethe from Oberhof in Thuringia, where he was to be trapped until the end of September because all trains to the capital were commandeered for troop movements. Whereas so many thought the war 'would be over by Christmas', Bruch's letter was uncannily accurate when he wrote that 'streams of blood will be the price for justifying our cause, for the shocks and horrors of this war will be greater than any other hitherto.'

Although he took this anti-war stance, he was in no way shedding his patriotism. His youngest son, Ewald, having studied forestry for three years, had enlisted voluntarily in 1913 but was now drafted to the front as an infantryman. This became an intense strain for his parents as contact between them and their son became infrequent during the war. When hostilities commenced, Bruch could only guess where his son was: 'Waldi is possibly already with his battalion at the Russian or French border.' Max Felix was drafted into the Territorial Reserve, probably on account of his indifferent health. As the war slowly progressed, Bruch's attitude to Germany's adversaries hardened perceptibly. He believed what he read in the newspapers: that the French manipulated the Belgians into believing the Germans to be a barbaric race of Huns, and that Belgian women were showering advancing German troops with boiling oil from the rooftops. His patriotism was still inspired by the victories of the Franco-Prussian War. He even reminded Hans Zanders of Moltke's words after the victory at Königgrätz in 1866 — 'What we have achieved in a week, we shall have to defend with weapons in our hands for 50 years.'[25]

Bruch's bitterness against England was intense. One of his first acts when war broke out was to renounce his honorary Doctorate from Cambridge University; it gave him great satisfaction 'to throw it at their feet' (though he was offended that no German university thought to honour him with a replacement!). On the other hand he could not understand why his membership of the *Société des auteurs compositeurs* was terminated nor why, along with Humperdinck and Siegfried Wagner, he should be thrown out of the Paris Académie. He had, he argued to Arthur Abell, been a good friend to Saint-Saëns (who 'has lost his reason'), as well as Lalo, Débroux, Maurice Vieux etc.[26]

When war was declared, Bruch was immediately deprived of a considerable portion of his income from royalties on performances abroad. Either his works did not receive them because he was a German, or there was no method of sending the money to him. As the ar progressed and inflation grew, his financial circumstances became more serious; his letters to Olga or Anna Zanders (by 1915 both were widows) for occasional food parcels became more and more grateful.

It was at this time that the American Sutro sisters asked the composer to write them a concerto for two pianos. Ottilie and Rose Sutro were born and raised in Baltimore, later studying piano with Heinrich Barth at the Berlin Musikhochschule (where Bruch may have heard them). They gave a successful début recital in London in 1894, whereupon they returned to America for their first concert, with Anton Seidl conducting the New York Philharmonic Orchestra. In

1911 they returned to Germany, where they played Bruch's *Fantasia* for two pianos to the composer. He was so impressed by the two pianists that he agreed to their request to write a concerto for them. The result was the Concerto for Two Pianos Op.88a, which was not in fact an original work but a reworking of his unpublished Third Suite for orchestra, whose fascinating history began several years earlier.

Bruch had been convalescing on the isle of Capri in the spring of 1904 when, on Good Friday, he witnessed a procession passing his window at the Hotel Royal. He described the event in a vivid account:

> Beautiful weather. In the evening between eight and nine a procession in the narrow streets and alleys of Capri. Leading it was a messenger of sadness with a large tuba on which he played a kind of signal.

Ex.49

Not bad at all; one could make quite a good funeral march out of it!

Next came several large flowered crosses, one carried by a hermit from Mount Tiberio. A few hundred children dressed in white and carrying large burning candles, each of them also holding a small black cross. They sang in unison a kind of lamentation that sounded approximately thus:

Ex. 50

In the procession a frightening Corpus Christi was carried on a stretcher, behind it was a canopy carried by four men and then the clergy. Then towering high (again on a stretcher) was a gigantic, splendidly decorated but quite horrible puppet doll representing the Madonna. When the procession emerged again from the nocturnal darkness of the narrow alleys, it went over the *Piazza* and climbed the high steps to the church (a picturesque sight). Suddenly the loud and dissonant cry of a donkey mingled with the long-drawn-out tones of the song of lament from the hundreds of voices. At once the devout mood of the crowd changed, and everyone laughed loud and heartily.

Soon afterwards the 'holiness itself' appeared, everyone bared their heads, the people knelt down, crossed themselves and followed the procession into the church, where the priests ceremonially adorned themselves with 'burial' clothes. The bells of Capri were silent on Good Friday and Saturday . . . in all the windows lights were burning while the procession passed; it was like an illumination at a feast.[27]

The differences between the original version for orchestra and organ (the Third Suite) and the reworked version as a Concerto for Two Pianos are largely confined to orchestration. The organ plays a more substantial role in the outer movements (where occasionally it is a solo instrument), but is used primarily as a means of colour and texture. After the slow introduction to the second movement, it plays no part in the ensuing Scherzo. The keys of both works are the same throughout, and the instrumentation is identical but for the addition of a contra-bassoon in the Suite. String passage-writing from the earlier work is often allocated to the pianos in the later, and conversely the pianos sometimes embellish what was originally chordal. There are just a few bars in the Suite which do not recur in the later version. Bruch told Leo Schrattenholz that originally he had titles for the four movements in the version as the Third Suite, but that he considered that it should stand without the aid of programmatic headings.[28] It is possible to see some of these titles from the manuscript of the Third Suite, but the handwriting is not Bruch's. The outer movements were based on the ceremonial procession he witnessed on Good Friday 1904, the first movement carrying the title 'Präludium' and the last 'Festliche Ausklang' (Festive Finale); the second has a variety of alternatives mostly concerning spring, and the third is entitled 'Nocturno'.[29] It is possible that the publisher, Eichmann, was responsible for these titles, having treated the second (*Nordland*) Suite in like manner.

The opening unison fanfare by both pianos in the tonic key of A flat minor is the ceremonial tuba melody quoted in Bruch's Capri letter. It resolves on the dominant whereupon the first piano begins a *fugato* on the second Capri melody. The second piano joins, followed by the orchestra in a build-up to the combination of the counter-subject and the opening fanfare. The section subsides to bring the movement to a *fermata* on the tonic major chord. The second movement (linked *attacca* to the first) begins with a reflective passage for violas and cellos, then solo oboe, which modulates to E major by the enharmonic switch of A flat to G sharp. A lively Allegro in sonata form then follows. Strongly galloping triplet rhythms shape the first subject, whilst the second is a calmer *duo* between clarinet and the second piano, both subjects forming material for the ensuing development. The conventional recapitulation precedes a *stringendo* which brings the movement to an abrupt conclusion. The ternary-form Adagio (it has moved to the dominant of B major from the second movement's key of E major) uses the 3/8 time signature common to his slow movements. The tranquil opening soon builds to an impassioned climax rich in melody. This material encases a contrasting section dominated by a repetitive dotted rhythm. The final movement initially reverts to the opening Good Friday fanfare followed by a short fantasia on the material, all by way of introduction to the movement proper. Its loose form (like that of the first, to which it relates) develops material based on the processional themes in the tonic major key of A flat, though Bruch jokingly told his American friend, Arthur Abell, on the occasion of a private run-through that the heroic qualities of this Finale were inspired by Bismarck.[30]

The strong symphonic element of the work created problems for Bruch in naming it when first written as a Suite. The period of composition was long, lasting from 1904 until 1915 before it was declared finished. In May 1909 it was performed by Sir Henry Wood at a Promenade Concert at the Queen's Hall in London, with Frederick Kiddle playing the organ part. On 9 July Bruch played it through with the Gürzenich orchestra in Cologne and referred (in a letter to Hans Zanders) to a performance in the forthcoming winter season.[31] It was reworked in 1912 (two movements were recomposed, but it is unclear to what extent) before Bruch played it through in October with Leo Schrattenholz on two pianos in Blüthner's Berlin showrooms in the Potsdamerstrasse, and he altered it yet again at Oberhof during 1915. It was this final version of the Suite on which the Concerto for Two Pianos was based. The subsequent fate of the unpublished manuscript of the original Suite is complicated by its association with the publisher Eichmann, but the history of the reworked two-piano version for the Sutro sisters is nothing short of bizarre.

The first public performance of the Concerto for Two Pianos took place on 29 December 1916 in Philadelphia, with the Philadelphia Orchestra under Leopold Stokowski and the Sutro sisters as soloists. According to the programme notes, Bruch first conceived the idea of writing the concerto on 6 February 1915. On the 10th he began work, and by 27 March it was completed. On 24 April a private play-through took place with the Berlin Philharmonic Orchestra under Bruch in the main hall at the Philharmonie. Bruch told Arthur Abell (whom he invited to attend) on 20 April that as the work was 'only intended for America', the Press would not be present. Bruch was angry when one or two German journalists managed to get into the closed session and subsequently wrote about the work. His reservation of the piece for America was based on the premise that the original version would be published in Europe in due course as his Third Suite. He told Abell: 'I will neither permit the work to be performed nor printed here in its form as a piano concerto.'[32] It was dedicated to the sisters, 'whom I love and value', though later he stressed to Abell that the ban on performances of the work in Europe included those by the sisters themselves.[33] Nowhere in the programme note for the Philadelphia première is any mention made of Capri or of the inspiration Bruch derived there for this work, nor, more importantly, is there any reference to it as a rescoring of a piece already written by Bruch, namely the Third Suite for organ and orchestra — and this in spite of Arthur Abell's report to an American journal, containing a full and accurate account of the Capri events.[34] But Abell also did not mention the Third Suite and wrongly described the Concerto as being 'based in parts on sketches made in Italy some ten years ago'. W. H. Humiston's programme note for the only other contemporary performance (with the New York Philharmonic Orchestra under Josef Stransky on 30 November 1917 at the Carnegie Hall) was only slightly nearer the mark: 'It was first sketched a dozen years ago at Capri during the Easter season' . . . 'there was a poetic basis for each of the movements'. Humiston incorrectly merges the first and second movements in his programme note, thereby making it a composition in only three movements, but his programmatic description correctly covers all four.

These inconsistencies and incorrect reports in American journals and programmes show that the Sutros had both rewritten the Concerto for Two Pianos, and presented it as a work meant for them by the composer, though quite what their motivation was for doing so remains unclear. To deal with the latter point first, it is possible that they simply wanted the kudos of having received a work from an eminent composer, for their biography in the programme of the

Philadelphia première stated that the concerto 'was written especially for them.' It clearly was not — it was an arrangement of a previously written piece.

On the matter of the Sutros rewriting the work, the history of the Concerto now continues on its curious way. Ottilie and Rose Sutro were either not particularly good pianists or perhaps not very powerful ones (Ottilie injured her hand in 1904 and could not play for six years), for it appears that they proceeded to tear the Concerto to pieces, reorchestrate it, simplify the piano parts and generally restructure the work. They either decided that Bruch had done a poor job in the first place, or they realized that their own piano technique was inadequate. The latter is more likely and more remarkable, because Arthur Abell had reported in his article (which carried the melodramatic headline 'Bruch's Muse Undaunted by Moloch of War'), that the sisters 'played their exacting parts with sovereign mastery'.[35] At the end of 1916, however, the reviewer in the *Public Ledger* of Philadelphia wrote after the première: 'It is not the sort of thing most pianists would choose for a display of their mettle. Their part in it was submerged often, and so it was not easy to tell just what the artistic calibre of the Misses Sutro is. They would appear to be finished and accurate, without a great deal of passionate intensity or vigour of phrasing.'[36] What the reviewer had heard was the simplified version of the concerto, which bore scant resemblance to Bruch's work. When the sisters had cobbled together their version of the work, they copyrighted it and lodged the score with the National Library of Congress. The date for the deposition is 1916; America, therefore, heard only the Sutro version of Bruch's composition. Shortly afterwards the score was mysteriously withdrawn, whereupon it vanished for 50 years.

In 1970 Ottilie Sutro died two years short of her 100th birthday, surviving her sister Rose by some thirteen years. When her effects were auctioned in Baltimore, a trunk remained at the end of the sale containing oddments of music, autographs and newspaper cuttings. These were purchased for $11 by Nathan Twining who, together with the pianist Martin Berkofsky, proceeded to play through the manuscript of what transpired to be Bruch's autograph score of the Concerto for Two Pianos. Having managed to repurchase the bowdlerized Sutro version together with its orchestral parts from buyers who had attended the same auction, they proceeded to reconstitute the work, following the composer's original intentions. Clearly the Sutros had somehow managed to secrete their copyright score out of the Library of Congress. It was also apparent from the effects of the eccentric sisters that they proceeded to make very many changes, and to fashion their version of the Concerto until as recently as 1961, Ottilie persisting with this obsession even after Rose's death. Countless scraps of paper contained amendments to the music. They were even found on envelopes and accounts from the International Nickel Company of Canada, on a circular dated March 1960 from the Baltimore Chapter of the American Goethe Society, or on the 1948 balance sheet of the United Aircraft Corporation. After the 1916 and 1917 Philadelphia and New York performances, the Concerto was never performed again by the sisters. When the reconstruction process was eventually completed by Twining and Berkofsky, history nearly repeated itself when the two men fell out over possession of copyright of the original Bruch version, and it looked as if the work might disappear from public hearing once again. Happily this did not occur, and the work is now in print.

The six remaining works of Max Bruch's output published in his lifetime, were all vocal. The first was completed on 22 January 1915 as a direct consequence of the war, and was called *Heldenfeier* (to a text by Bruch's daughter Margarethe) for six-part chorus with organ accompaniment. The simple, predominantly homophonous movement captured the pathos of the time and was immediately popular among church-based choirs after its first performance in Berlin in October 1915. Though grateful to these small choirs, Bruch resented the lack of interest shown in the work by large city choruses, particularly Cologne, which by 1916 was beginning to play down the emotive, patriotic atmosphere of those early days of the war. The three-verse *Heldenfeier* was published by Leuckart in 1915 as Op.89. In 1962 the piece was virtually recomposed by Hermann Erdlen in a dozen different versions, and to a new text by Ludwig Schuster, perhaps to avoid Margarethe's chauvinistic libretto, which began 'Bedenk es, O deutsche Seele' (Consider, O German soul).[37] The melodic outline is still Bruch's, though Erdlen transposed the work up a tone and added a few bars of introduction. It was published by Leuckart under the title *Totenfeier*.

Bruch reworked his 1863 *Gesang der heiligen drei Könige* at the beginning of 1915 as well as completing the Third Suite and the Concerto for Two Pianos during the course of the same year. The reworking of Op.21 was solely concerned with reorchestration. He added cor anglais, two more horns, trumpets and organ, changed the tempo indication from Adagio to Andante sostenuto and redistributed the orchestral parts in many places. This later version remains unpublished. He also orchestrated songs by Schubert and Beethoven, and was commissioned by the Ministry of Culture to arrange 100

German folksongs for two and three parts for use by the troops in the field. He was proud of this 'war work', particularly as three million copies were being printed. Yet, in spite of this seemingly active period, he felt himself forgotten and neglected. Although his 78th birthday, in 1916, produced some 60–65 telegrams, he ruefully remembered the 700 he had received in 1908 on the occasion of his seventieth birthday.

He had reason to be grateful to Hans Pfitzner for a timely revival of *Die Loreley* in Strasburg on 26 March 1916. Pfitzner belonged to the hated opposition, but while in no way changing his opinion of his music (the opera *Rose vom Liebesgarten* made him 'feel sick and gave Clara stomach cramps'), Bruch was impressed both by Pfitzner's sincerity and by his genuine enthusiasm for *Die Loreley*.[38] 'Even in these unmusical times,' he wrote to Francis Kruse, 'there still appear to be musical souls here and there, who briefly but gladly seek refuge in the melodic spring of *Loreley* from the wretched declamatory desert of modern German opera.'[39]

One of the church choirs that took up Bruch's *Heldenfeier* (the Kreuzkirchenchor in Dresden) received the dedication of the *Five Lieder* Op. 90 for four-part *a cappella* chorus, which were published by Leuckart in 1917. 'Im Himmelreich' is a two-verse homophonic song with an old German text. The next two songs (both strongly influenced by the war) have strophic texts by Bruch's daughter Margarethe; 'Der Gärtner als Ulan' (The gardener as a lancer) and 'Wiegenlied im Chiemgau' (Lullaby in Chiemgau), which carries the subtitle 'Wartime 1914'. Ewald Bruch continued the theme of war when he wrote the text for the fourth song, 'Auf eines deutschen Jägers Grab' (On the grave of a German rifleman) in the Vosges mountains in 1915, and the final song, 'Abendläuten' (Evening calls) was written by M. Vorberg to complete the cycle with the favourite Bruch scenario of bells calling the poet back to his homeland.

From the end of 1916 the Bruch household began to feel more serious effects of wartime shortages. Clara's condition was worsening and her stomach cramps became more frequent. She never complained, but continued to attend to her husband's needs, sometimes helped by parcels from Olga Zanders containing bacon, sausage, eggs, butter, fat or fruit.

On 2 October 1916 Bruch began his next choral piece, *Die Stimme der Mutter Erde* (The voice of Mother Earth) for mixed chorus, organ and orchestra Op. 91. The manuscript shows that he finished the work on the 19th, and that it was ready for printing by 1 May 1917 when he made the score Clara's property. The text was 'taken from the Polish' and took up the prevalent wartime mood of patriotism, now tinged with pathos and a yearning for the homeland. The composition (in the

key of E flat major) is in ternary form, a syncopated motif initially
intoned at length by the basses dominating the outer sections. After a
familiar modulation to the mediant key of G major, the sopranos
continue with a *fugato* which is developed together with other
contrapuntal phrases by the rest of the chorus. The climax modulates
to C major at the middle section, and a change of metre from four to
three beats is introduced. This portion of the work is loud and largely
homophonic in character, becoming more fragmented as the
dynamics decrease until the recapitulation of the opening section (with
a return to E flat major and four beats per bar) is reached. The full
chorus now sings the opening phrase of the work in unison, and after a
climax is reached on a chord of D flat its mood subsides to a short
orchestral postlude. The orchestration is thickly textured, incorporating cor anglais, double bassoon, tuba and organ. *Die Stimme der
Mutter Erde* was first performed by the Philharmonic Chorus together
with his earlier *Messensätze* in the Berlin Philharmonie under Siegfried
Ochs on 28 January 1918 in honour of the composer's eightieth
birthday.

As the new decade of Bruch's life approached, honours were
heaped upon him, but they did not compensate for the now critical
material shortages caused by the war. He had received apples from
Bergisch Gladbach, but he and Clara dreaded the approaching winter with its attendant fuel shortages. At the end of October 1917, a
parcel containing Dutch cheese sent him into an ecstasy of gratitude, particularly as butter was a thing of the past. Although Bruch
felt the military situation to be 'very good everywhere', he criticized the Social Democrats and their plans, and at the same time
also chastized the political centre as hesitant, indecisive and infil-
trated by the Jesuits: 'The reins of government trail along the
ground . . . I would suggest that we borrow Mr Lloyd George for
three months. It is true that he is a lying scoundrel (like all his
English colleagues) and an unscrupulous, demagogic rabble-rouser;
but at least the fellow knows exactly what he wants, whereas no
one in our higher and highest circles knows that!'[40]

In spite of these hardships, he celebrated his eightieth birthday on 6
January 1918. Associated events had begun as far back as April 1917
when *Frithjof* was performed with a chorus of 1,300–1,400 singers and
an orchestra of 200. *Gustav Adolf* was performed in Berlin (for the first
time since its composition some twenty years earlier) by the Singakademie on 2 November 1917 to celebrate the 400th anniversary of
the Reformation. This occasion gave the old man particular satisfaction, not least because it served to make a nationalistic point in the
capital of the Reich at a time when the centrist Government was

vacillating again under its Prime Minister Bethmann-Hollweg. Bruch told Francis Kruse that it would be 'a flaming protest by German Protestants . . . a German declaration that we will not let the wool be pulled over our eyes.' Margarethe Bruch was by now taking complete care of her parents, and she organized events for the birthday. At 11.30 on the morning of Sunday 6 January 1918 a delegation of various officials arrived at the flat in Albestrasse. They were attended by the Schultzen-Asten women's choir who sang Schubert's *23rd Psalm* and Bruch's *Altenberger Hymne*, whereupon Margarethe read a poem she had written especially for the occasion. The proceedings continued with a speech by the Mayor of Friedenau (where Bruch had now resided for 27 years) during which he granted the Freedom of the Borough to the composer. The Minister of Culture then presented him with a medal (Kronenorden second class) from the Kaiser, after which Bruch received an honorary Doctorate from Berlin University's Faculty of Philosophy and one from the Faculty of Theology.

On the following day he was honoured with a midday concert presented by the Königliche Akademie der Künste at the Musikhoch-schule, attended by numerous dignitaries of the artistic and academic world. The old man was led by a group of students in traditional gala dress and, on the arm of the President of the Royal Academy of Arts, he entered the hall to thunderous applause. The Director of the Musikhochschule, Hermann Kretschmar, (about to celebrate his own seventieth birthday) delivered a speech in which he praised Bruch's artistic and historical importance. In particular he singled out the music written for male-voice choirs, which had elevated such choral groups to new heights. He also praised Bruch's *Messensätze* as the most beautiful sacred music since Beethoven, and concluded by applauding Bruch's 20-year period as a teacher at the Musikhoch-schule. The Philharmonic Orchestra then launched into a concert which began with the Prelude to *Die Loreley*, followed by the first and second scenes from *Gustav Adolf*, the First Violin Concerto (50 years to the day since it was first performed in Bremen by Joachim) in which Alfred Wittenberg stepped in for the sick Willy Hess, and concluded with two choruses from *Gustav Adolf*. Bergisch Gladbach also made Bruch an honorary citizen on the occasion of his birthday, but Cologne confined itself to the Abendroth performance of *Die Stimme der Mutter Erde*, and to naming a street after him (it lies on the edge of the Stadtwald in the district of Lindenthal, parallel to Brahmsstrasse with the two composers linked by Haydnstrasse).

Probably the most cherished of the gifts he received (together with 400–500 letters and telegrams) was a Christmas tree from the Igeler Hof ('I wept over it' he told Anna Zanders) and several bottles of

Mouton Rothschild 'the crown of all red wines'.[41] Clara had by this time taken to her bed (she did so barely ten days after Max's birthday) and was to remain there for most of the year. Bruch meanwhile set about writing his memoirs, and, to overcome the wartime shortage of paper, he enlisted the help of Anna and Olga Zanders and their family business (the last surviving child of Maria Zanders, Margaretha, had died in 1917).

In the spring, Bruch told Olga Zanders that he had 'only the chapter "Paris 1865" to write; I hope to have completed the whole work before the end of March.'[42] The memoirs were written, but no publisher could be found, and the manuscript was eventually destroyed during the Second World War.

Meanwhile Ewald Bruch, who had so far remained unscathed in his military service, was posted as a lieutenant in the reserve to Tournai in Belgium. On the way there he visited the Igeler Hof for the first time, at the express wish of his father. Bruch was grateful to the children of Maria Zanders, who established a trust fund in 1906 to pay for Ewald's education for a period of five years. The composer was eager for news of his beloved Igeler Hof. His only surviving letter to Ewald regretted the poor weather his son had experienced and went on:

How different the lovely, idyllic Igeler Hof looks in sunshine. Is it not the most lovely, charming and peaceful little spot on earth – on German earth? I would be the happiest man in the world if I could live and work there once again in my life, but my miserable illness makes everything impossible. My longing for Gladbach and the Igeler Hof is often almost a disease, and I weep bitter tears within me that I cannot go there again . . . Mama was especially attached to the late Mama Zanders, your loving godmother, who unfortunately died much too soon for you.[43]

During the summer of 1918 Bruch suffered severe bouts of painful neuralgia, together with asthma and heart failure. After a week in bed he pulled through to face the rigours of survival once again, largely through the purchase of food on the black market. 'Potatoes and butter are often not available', he wrote. 'If from time to time there is a scrap of miserable meat, there is no fat with which to roast it; after such privations, I would walk for hours to eat an ordinary beefsteak or a decent roast of mutton just once again. All of us have deteriorated both physically and morally through this terrible, continual and unendurable malnutrition. And the prices — these profiteers, this dreadful black market! The bitterness is boundless.'[44] In a poignant postscript to this letter, Bruch stated once again that his illness prevented him from travelling, not only to Bergisch Gladbach, but also to Thuringia. Clara (bedridden for six months) presented further problems, and he concluded that 'the only journey that I can still undertake is the one from which no one has returned.'

The twentieth anniversary of Bismarck's death, on 30 July 1918, produced more of Bruch's invective against 'political amateurs' who were ruining the country. He reflected upon another great political leader of the past, Frederick the Great, whose achievements were wasted by his followers. Bruch's example was the defeat of Prussia by Napoleon at the Battle of Jena in 1806, twenty years after the death of Frederick the Great in 1786. The same letter contained an outburst of anti-semitism ominously typical of German sentiments in the two decades following Bruch's death. The shortage of meat ('one must pay 50 marks for a chicken, if you can even get one'), fruit ('we have seen none all summer') and vegetables ('the never-ending carrots and cabbage') led him to write that 'the rich Jews in Charlottenburg have everything, because they pay the highest prices on the quiet.'

By the beginning of October 1918 a revolutionary crisis was developing in Germany, which was to erupt the following month and force the abdication of the Kaiser. This in turn would enable hostilities to end and bring the First World War to its close. Bruch was appalled by the Kaiser's treatment at the hands of his fellow countrymen. Bismarck had toiled for twenty years to secure and strengthen the monarchy, and now the fruits of his achievements were, in Bruch's opinion, being torn apart by the Social Democrats, who, with other radical parties, sought to ruin Germany. The army was betrayed, loyal troops, disarmed and disbanded, were coming home to find no work, food and fuel shortages, and rising inflation. 'I surely believe', Bruch wrote, 'that Germany is now forever totally destroyed — politically, militarily, economically and financially; and this is only through her own fault.'[45] He was shocked to hear that Bergisch Gladbach was occupied by the victorious Allies, for he had under-stood the Rhine's right bank to be a neutral zone. The Kaiser, having abdicated, was exiled in Holland but Bruch made the incredible yet serious suggestion to Anna Zanders that he should somehow be smuggled back to Germany and hidden at the Igeler Hof ('if one can depend upon the absolute secrecy of loyal people') before the Dutch were forced to hand him over to the Allies. The occupation of Bergisch Gladbach by English troops put paid to any further discussion.

A cycle of six songs was now published by Leuckart. These were the *Christkindlieder* Op.92 for soprano and alto solo, four-part female chorus and piano accompaniment to texts by Margarethe Bruch. The first song, 'O holder Herr, O Jesulein', begins *unisono* like its immediate predecessors Opp. 89 and 91, and is followed by passages of *a cappella* writing mixed with accompanied bars, before concluding in chorale fashion. The second song, 'Christi Geburt', is a lilting lullaby in three strophic verses and 6/8 rhythm. The third song (accompanied either by piano or harmonium) is entitled 'Zwei Seelen begegnen sich zur Christnacht im Walde' (Two souls meet in the woods on Christmas Eve) and is for the two female soloists. The dark and sombre (F minor) questions of the alto soloist are dispelled (F major) by the soprano in her response that the light of Christ burns within the heart, and is always visible. This is followed by the lively choral song 'Auf einem goldbraunen Reh' (On a golden brown deer) depicting the laughing and singing Christchild riding through cold snow-covered woods, but kept warm by love. Father Christmas (Rupprecht), follows behind riding a stubborn donkey with a rod, but he is tired and cold as he growls and grumbles his way through the woods. In the third verse the soul, having been offered the choice, selects the way of the Christchild and love. The fifth song, 'Gebet', is an expressive prayer in two verses for choir, again with optional piano or harmonium accompaniment. The final song, 'Christkinds Garten', is the most lengthy and substantial of the six. Written for soloists, choir and with a lively piano accompaniment, it passes through a variety of moods and keys.

Goethe's *Wilhelm Meister* was the source of Bruch's last choral and orchestral work, *Trauerfeier für Mignon* (Funeral rites for Mignon) Op. 93, dedicated to the Berlin Hochschule conductor, Georg Schumann. It is written for double chorus, four soloists (boys in the text but two sopranos and two altos in the score), organ and full orchestra. This composition contains features of much of Bruch's earlier single-movement choral works: the contrasting sections of homophony and counterpoint in both choir and orchestra, a special emphasis on melody and a style which featured both conventional harmony and skilful orchestration to achieve the correct colour and dramatic mood. His device of opening *unisono* is used again, in common with the favoured plagal cadence which concludes it. Prominence is given to one of his favourite instruments, the harp, when it accompanies the unison double chorus at the section 'Seht die mächtigen Flügel doch an' and the four soloists at 'Aber ach, wir vermissen sie hier.' The *Trauerfeier für Mignon* was completed on 24 August 1918 and first performed by the Berlin Singakademie on 5 April 1919. In spite of renewed efforts by Bruch to get the publishing firm of Simrock to take on his new works (it was exactly 50 years since he was first published by them in 1869, but they did not consider the war years to be propitious for the sale or hiring of music), this last choral work was published by the Leipzig firm of Leuckart.

In June 1919, Clara, who had hardly risen from her bed since she took to it eighteen months earlier, soon after her husband's eightieth birthday celebrations, was moved from the flat to a sanatorium, and during the night of 27 August she died in the Berlin Charité Hospital after undergoing an operation. She was sixty-five years old and her already frail health had been broken over a period of six years, first by the death of her son Hans, and then by the war and deprivation which followed. The hospital records show that she had been suffering from cancer of the bowel. With her death Max Bruch lost a faithful and devoted companion of nearly 40 years. By the end of that year he was expressing a lack of interest in life (which held no hope for him or for Germany), and in performances of his own music. On account of the astronomical rise in prices through inflation, he was also forced to give up his favourite cigars and red wine, his last pleasures in life. When he was sent some wine from Bergisch Gladbach for his 82nd birthday, on 6 January 1920, he wrote woefully that it had not arrived and had no doubt been stolen en route.[46] The Social Democrats were at fault here, alleged Bruch, for with them lay the responsibility for the breakdown of discipline among the bureaucracy.

His last published composition was among those written in the first half of 1920. As in the case of Op.77, there is no Op.94, 95 or 96 among Bruch's printed works (though several unpublished works written at this time and later placed in the dubious care of Eichmann could have filled these numbers). The *Five Songs* for voice and piano Op.97 were published by Carl Fischer of New York with an English translation by Alice Mattullath. They consist of typical Bruch sources — a folksong (Spanish), Emanuel Geibel, his daughter Margarethe and Goethe. The gentle Schubertian piano accompaniment of the opening Spanish folksong, 'Mein Liebchen naht, Blumen zu pflücken' (My darling comes to pluck flowers), with its gentle syncopation and arpeggios, is carried in more urgent mood to the second song to Geibel's text, 'Durch die wolkige Maiennacht' (Through the cloudy springtime night). Margarethe Bruch's strophic verse 'Vor dem Fenster mir' (By my window) inspires equally delicate word-painting to portray a rushing brook as the harmony rocks back and forth between G major and its mediant key of B major. 'Morgenlied' is from Goethe's *Claudine von Villabella*. This is a work for which Bruch had composed incidental music when very young, and sought in the immediate aftermath of his son Hans' death in 1913 to continue.

Instead of deriving therapeutic benefit, however, he could not cope with reliving the happiness of his own youth when that of his son had been so abruptly extinguished, and he stopped. That sadness is captured in the rich yet sombre melody of this song. The final song brings the collection to a happier conclusion with a merry *scherzando*, also taken from Goethe (this is another encounter with an admired work which Bruch had set when young), 'Ein Mädchen und ein Gläschen Wein' (A girl and a glass of wine) from *Jeri and Baetely*.

The Berlin correspondent of the *Musical Courier*, Arthur Abell, returned to his native land in 1916, not because of the threat of imminent war between the United States and Germany, but owing to hunger.[47] Abell's friendship was highly valued by Bruch, who wrote a single-movement duet for two violins with piano (and harmonium *ad libitum*) accompaniment, which he dedicated to the journalist and his wife. It was written as an act of gratitude by the composer, who wished to recognize the journalist's championing of his violin music in America (particularly of works other than the First Violin Concerto). 'You have no idea,' Bruch wrote to his ex-publisher, 'what unbelievably affectionate signs are shown me by American violinists just at present. What I experience in Germany is, by comparison, camomile tea!'[48] Abell and his wife were amateur violinists, who used to play duets together 'very nicely'. The E major violin duet was written in the early months of 1920, but was published posthumously in 1922 by Carl Fischer of New York under the spurious title of *Song of Spring* (the title was probably Abell's). The work was based on a passage in *Gustav Adolf* which was a particular favourite of the composer — Scene 10 at letter B for the tenor soloist singing the role of Bernhard, Duke of Weimar. The *Song of Spring* is (like Bernhard's aria) in ternary form, but the middle section of the later work is new material not to be found in *Gustav Adolf*. The piece is inconsequential, with a simplicity of harmony, somewhat crude modulation using the diminished seventh to and from the middle section, and an accompaniment based on the left hand of the piano part of the vocal score of *Gustav Adolf* for the outer sections. An unimaginative middle section is dominated by parallel thirds mirrored in both hands. There are also attempts at orchestral *tremolandi* more suited to the piano score of the original vocal version. Interest in *Song of Spring* is centred entirely on its melodic invention. Bruch himself admitted to a lack of inspiration 'in my old age' in finding new material, when he wrote to Simrock's asking permission to quote from *Gustav Adolf* (which was in their copyright).

At the end of 1919 Bruch wrote two String Quintets (in E flat major and A minor), and at the beginning of 1920 he also wrote a String Octet modelled on Mendelssohn's (though the instrumentation of four violins, two violas and two cellos differed slightly when Bruch substituted a double bass for the second cello). Handwritten copies of the score and parts of the String Quintet in A minor, and the parts only of the String Octet have been discovered in the BBC Music Library, though how they got there remains a mystery. All the material is in the handwriting of Gertrude Bruch, wife of Max Felix. At the end of the score of the Quintet, she wrote (presumably quoting from the original manuscript which went to Eichmann): 'Berlin-Friedenau. 17 November 1918. M.B.' The Octet parts are incorrectly allocated the opus number 97.[49]

Throughout his life, and now at its end, Bruch was close to a violinist, for these works were probably written at the instigation of Bruch's friend Willy Hess. It was in 1897 that Bruch told Fritz Simrock that he preferred 'three whole oratorios with choir and orchestra to three string quartets', yet here he was writing three chamber works in a very short space of time. All three examples of this remarkable return to the genre were entrusted to the care of Rudolf Eichmann. Only one other work was written by Bruch in the year of his death. This was a *Festpräludium* (Festive prelude) for eleven wind instruments and timpani.[50]

During the spring of 1920 Max Bruch's health finally broke down. His daughter Margarethe told Olga Zanders that 'unfortunately I cannot report much good news about my father's health. His old age is now apparent in all manner of serious symptoms. During my absence he often suffered speech impediments, which were considered harmful by the doctors. The slightest excitement gives my father sleepless and painful nights. He tires easily and must be well cared for in every way. He has serious arteriosclerosis, which is weakening his heart. But spiritually my father retains his former freshness. Perhaps his dogged nature will again overcome this spate of recent serious attacks.'[51] Bruch's last letter to Simrock's, although described by them as having been 'written in a trembling hand', nevertheless revealed a lively interest in a performance of *Odysseus* in Berlin which had taken place on 4 May, and performances of *Das Lied von der Glocke* (one in Beuthen, Upper Silesia and the other scheduled in Görlitz with several choral groups amounting to 'about a thousand voices'). Bruch expressed his pleasure that 'the poor, heavily oppressed people of Upper Silesia had found comfort and spiritual uplift in my *Glocke*'. He also eagerly reported that his eldest son Max Felix was planning a performance of *Gustav Adolf* in the New Year of 1921 in Hamburg, where he directed two choral societies. Sadly Bruch was not to live to hear it.[52]

In June Margarethe told Olga Zanders that 'my father has been really ill for the past fortnight. A slight improvement has occurred in the last two days, but one does not know if it will last. His general weakness is very great and remains dangerous. Spiritually he is almost as of old. He suffers all the more for having to lie inactive in bed. I now have a night nurse for him, for we first tried taking it in turns, but could not keep it up' (Margarethe had enlisted the help of an aunt from Vienna to care for her father).[53] One of Max Bruch's last letters was written by dictation to Francis Kruse during the heat of the summer. To the end he dreamed that he would still regain enough strength to make the journey to the Igeler Hof:

It appears to me that somewhat of a lull has occurred in our correspondence. It is solely my fault, but I could do nothing about it. I was already in low spirits at the New Year, but at the end of May a complete breakdown of my strength took place. Since then I have been mainly in bed in this dreadful heat, exhausted and weak. My head is quite good, my thinking clear and precise, but the horrible dizziness will not stop. If only it will go away once and for all! A nurse takes care of me day and night. The whole world is away, I alone had to remain behind in my suffering. You will understand how I could not write under these circumstances.
  . . . If I recover enough this winter, and if a good and thoroughly reliable nurse can be found, I shall go up to the Igeler Hof, which I have not seen for eleven years. I hope you will visit me there, for I cannot travel about much.[54]

A month after her father's death, Margarethe Bruch wrote to Olga Zanders:

He lived for all that was beautiful and blessed from a time now gone for ever. He was so very much a child of Gladbach, in whom to the end such warm, youthful feelings filled his heart, that he constantly felt himself in exile in Berlin. Right up to his last days, he made plans to visit Gladbach in the New Year. Shortly before the end, he described a cornfield, through which he strode towards a beautiful landscape. Many tears flowed in his homesickness for his beloved Igeler Hof. An old friend of his, who visited him a few weeks before his death, wrote to me that he had expressed a wish to her that he might be buried at the Igeler Hof. Now he is peacefully at rest beside my beloved mother, who bore with him in his life so that he could be what he was. She is sometimes thought of too infrequently, but those who knew her know that she was his good guardian angel. Grandmama Zanders also loved her very much. In his last months, my father spoke much of those he had loved in the past. Not only of his wife and son, but also of Maria Zanders, Margaretha,

Richard and Hans. He lived completely in the past, in those lovely days when often Grandmama Zanders would welcome him by decking the columns in the hall with green garlands of fir.[55]

Ewald Bruch wrote of his father's last days:

He was mostly in a kind of coma from which he would rally from time to time. On doctor's orders he was not allowed visitors, and I could only go to him for a few minutes at a time. When he was awake he just said, 'Are you there, my son?' Then he sank back into his dreamy state. In a waking moment he once said to my sister, 'Can I not go to my homeland once again by flying there in a Zeppelin?' We were deeply moved. The love for his native Rhineland did not leave him. In the early hours of 2 October 1920 my father quietly and painlessly fell asleep. At his hour of death, my sister and I were with him. He lay on his deathbed as if asleep, but he had passed away . . . The funeral of my father took place a few days later at the old, evangelical cemetery of St Matthew in West Berlin. A large number of mourners had gathered, including many who had lost touch with him during the last years of his life but wished to honour him. In the cemetery chapel, Willy Hess preceded the clergyman's words with the Adagio from my father's First Violin Concerto. At the end of the service, the funeral procession went to the graveside where the burial then took place. The city later undertook the care of this resting place. Now my unforgettable father rests there with my mother and, since 1963, my sister. She had had the following words carved on the gravestone: MUSIC IS THE LANGUAGE OF GOD.

# Chapter Seventeen

## POSTLUDE

IN ASSESSING Max Bruch as a composer, it is startling that his life of 82 years spanned the lives of so many diverse musical figures, and encompassed so many different significant events in the development of music. It began in 1838 before Wagner stormed the barricades of conventional harmony, and it ended in 1920 after Schoenberg had established serialism. The year of his birth was the year in which Mendelssohn had first thoughts about his Violin Concerto. It was also the year in which Schumann dedicated his *Kreisleriana* to Chopin, who himself was only about half-way through his total musical output. When Bruch died, Stravinsky's *Le Sacre du printemps* had received its first performance seven years earlier, in 1913, Schoenberg's *Pierrot Lunaire* had been given in 1912, Berg was completing his orchestration of *Wozzeck*, and Bartók had just finished his one-act pantomime *The Miraculous Mandarin* (the première taking place in Bruch's native Cologne in 1925). Even more remarkable are the numbers of composers who were born and died within Bruch's lifetime. They include Bruckner, Mahler, Hugo Wolf, Reger, Stainer, Sullivan, Parry, Tchaikovsky, Arensky, Mussorgsky, Rimsky-Korsakov, Scriabin, Dvořák, Boito, Leoncavallo, Bizet, Massenet, Chausson, Chabrier, Debussy and Grieg. Interestingly it was Bruch's colleague and fellow Cambridge doctorand, Saint-Saëns who beat him in the longevity stakes by living from 1835 to 1921.

A study of the life and work of Max Bruch reveals a society now estranged from our own by developments in art and politics. He was unfortunate in living long enough to experience that estrangement. His adherence to the music of his youth brought him into eventual conflict with the music and musicians of his middle and old age. He was born into the world of barely nascent technology, when the first German railway was only three years old, Morse had just invented the telegraph system of communication and photography was also new. When he died, there was already a commercial airline operating regular flights, the radio was about to commence operations and gramophone recordings were on the verge of changing from acoustic to electrical systems.

More significant than lists of names and dates is to consider Bruch's place in the context of the history of music. While the development of music flowed past him, he stood with his roots firmly planted on the banks of mid-nineteenth-century romanticism. Bruch was at his peak of consistent creative inspiration and development between 1865 and 1880. Those fifteen years represent his best work, and were immediately appreciated as such by his public, particularly in view of the excessive praise given to his talents by his teachers Hiller, Breunung and Reinecke, and by the publicity as a *Wunderkind* generated by Ludwig Bischoff. The public responded favourably to his best: to *Frithjof*, *Schön Ellen*, the First Violin Concerto, *Odysseus*, *Das Lied von der Glocke*, the *Scottish Fantasy* and *Kol Nidrei*. His Lieder, choral works, chamber music, symphonies and other concerted works were only partially successful, and, being inferior, they soon found their natural level. His music reflects his training. It is correct in the academic sense of adhering to conventional form and structure, skilfully instrumented or orchestrated (or in the case of his choral music, well written for voice), and it is harmonically safe and melodically strong. It offends no one, but equally it rarely excites through anything other than its emphasis on melodic beauty.

H. C. Colles wrote in Grove (1954): 'Bruch's music gives nothing to discuss and nothing to quarrel about. It is its lack of adventure that limited its fame.' The earlier (1904) edition had not been so harsh because it preceded so many of the drastic changes in music in the twentieth century: 'He is above all a master of melody, and of the effective treatment of masses of sound. These two sides of his artistic achievement . . . have brought him deserved success. Bruch's melody is . . . true, unconstrained, natural and excellent in its structure, broad, impressive and vocal.' Tovey wrote that 'it is not easy to write as beautifully as Max Bruch . . . it is really easy for Bruch to write beautifully, it is in fact instinctive for him. . . . Further, it is impossible to find in Max Bruch any lapses from the standard of beauty which he thus instinctively sets himself.' Gervase Hughes said that Bruch '. . . conscientiously pursued the ideal of absolute beauty — beauty of sound for its own sake'.

George Bernard Shaw was one of Bruch's detractors. Writing in March 1892 after the Crystal Palace performance by Joachim of Bruch's Third Violin Concerto, he said that it was 'like most of his works, masterly in the most artificial vulgarities of the grandiose, the passionate, the obviously sentimental, and the coarsely impulsive . . . Bruch's *Scottish Fantasia* [*sic*] is much better than his concertos; but it is on the strength of the concertos that he is regarded as a sort of contemporary old master, and played by the severe Joachim.' Two years later, however, Shaw wrote differently of *Das Lied von der Glocke*, which had just been performed in St James' Hall in May 1894: 'Bruch's work, passionate and grandiose at best, and lively and interesting at worst, is so very superior to the sort of thing we turn out here, that I cannot, for very shame, insist on its limitations in an English paper. It might well be heard oftener.'

J. A. Fuller Maitland was an admirer of Bruch, and sought to compare him with Brahms to ascertain their relative positions in music. His conclusion (which he described in his *Masters of German Music*) was to place him midway between Brahms and other German contemporary composers. The best of Bruch's works were in Maitland's opinion:

> . . . distinguished by great and easily intelligible beauty, and by the rare quality of distinction . . . Both the music and the man belong to the Lower Rhine country . . . The broadly flowing melodies of his invention suggest the course of such a river as that of his native country, and the absence of any very great heights in his music might be held to support the analogy . . . He is one of those who uphold most worthily the dignity of the art, and if he has not attained to the position of one whose every publication is received by musicians with a reverence due to a new revelation, he has won the hearts of many thousands of hearers by his beautiful creations in certain branches of music — *viz.*, choral works of large design with orchestral accompaniment, and works for violin or violoncello.

German obituaries and entries in musical dictionaries were similarly respectful of Bruch's worthiness as an academically correct and eminent master of his craft, and all lauded his contribution to the choral activities of his native land, particularly the male-voice choir. By avoiding sacred subjects (the *Messensätze* was his only liturgical music, and that was designed as a Missa Brevis for the concert hall), Bruch was restricting his large scale choral works to the sentiments of their own times. The jingoism of the 1870s to the turn of the century was well caught by *Odysseus*, *Arminius*, *Leonidas*, and all the choral works leading up to *Gustav Adolf*. When the sentiment and mood of the age changed, the public demanded other works, but these were not to be found among his compositions.

Bruch was fortunate in having all his works published, even if it took until 1903 before the Genossenschaft der deutschen Tonsetzer (the Association of German Composers) was formed to secure composers their rightful royalties for performances and protection of copyright in their compositions. He, like Brahms, was fortunate in enjoying a good personal relationship with their joint publisher, Fritz Simrock.

As a man Bruch was not everyone's friend. His increasing bitterness at his own isolation from progressive musical developments alienated him from society. He had unquestioned talent as a conductor, and earned the respect of orchestral players, but he thought little of others entrusted with performances of his compositions. Edward Speyer effected an introduction for the English composer Arthur Goring Thomas during Bruch's time in Liverpool:

> Bruch offered to look through his compositions, give him practice in playing from the score, instruct him in form, instrumentation and vocal treatment, take him to rehearsals, and initiate him into the mysteries of the technique of conducting. Goring Thomas fell in with Bruch's proposals, and undertook the fortnightly journeys to Liverpool that winter, which, as he was rather delicate, proved injurious to his health. As to Bruch's splendid programme, not one of the conditions and promises was fulfilled, so Goring Thomas told me afterwards.[1]

Speyer's version of events must be treated with circumspection, for Bruch was, in fact, responsible for the staging in Breslau of Thomas' opera *Nadeshda* in 1890 — at one point he even had to investigate the delayed arrival of the orchestral parts. Thomas wrote to Bruch, saying that he was 'your very true friend and, may I say, pupil'; after the performance of the opera Thomas stated: 'If you find the orchestration good, you must remember that I owe very much to you in that respect, and to your invaluable advice and instruction.'[2] Similar expressions of gratitude can be found in letters from the composers Frederic Cowen and Charles Swinnerton Heap, both of whom had had works performed during Bruch's period in Liverpool.

In a letter to his brother Modest, from Cambridge, Tchaikovsky wrote that 'Bruch is a disgustingly pompous figure'.[3] Although the noble-born Russian composer was probably correct, he also found it difficult to be at ease with the coarse and gruff Brahms. Fuller Maitland, in his fair but sometimes inaccurate article, wrote candidly of Bruch's character:

. . . the best conductor is not always the most popular, however, and it is not to be expected that members of the class from which choral societies are usually recruited should give their due value to the details of artistic excellence, or weigh them against any little jars such as must always arise between a conductor and his choir, unless indeed he is exceptionally diplomatic or exceptionally easygoing. Bruch happens to be neither the one nor the other, but to possess most keen artistic feelings and intolerance of anything short of perfection in performance. . . . If a somewhat blunt manner and an amount of self-centredness that is not common even among musicians prevent his making friends very quickly, or being what is called popular in general society, those who know him best know how whole-hearted is his devotion to his art, how pure are his aims, and how honest and upright he is in every artistic matter, as well as in those which concern everyday life.[4]

Bruch's *bêtes noires*, first the New Germans, Wagner and Liszt, followed by their successors, Strauss, Reger and Pfitzner, apparently thought little enough of his views and opinions to counteract them or argue. Strauss even went so far as to quote from Bruch's First Violin Concerto in early compositions such as the unpublished *Concert Overture* in C, the Violin Concerto Op. 8 and later in the *Alpensinfonie*.[5] Schoenberg, on the other hand, who also wrote a *Kol Nidre* (Op. 39 for speaker, mixed chorus and orchestra dating from 1938) was disparaging of Bruch's work of the same name. 'One of my main tasks was vitriolizing out the cello-sentimentality of the Bruchs etc.'[6]

The last word on Bruch should be given to Bruch himself. Arthur Abell related a conversation he had with the composer in 1907. When asked how Bruch saw his own status as a composer 50 years hence in 1947, compared to Brahms, he replied both wisely and with a great deal of perspicacity.

Brahms has been dead ten years but he still has many detractors, even among the best musicians and critics. I predict, however, that, as time goes on, he will be more appreciated, while most of my works will be more and more neglected. Fifty years hence he will loom up as one of the supremely great composers of all time, while I will be remembered chiefly for having written my G minor violin concerto . . . Brahms was a far greater composer than I am for several reasons. First of all he was much more original. He always went his own way. He cared not at all about the public reaction or what the critics wrote. The great fiasco of his D minor piano concerto would have discouraged most composers. Not Brahms!

Furthermore, the vituperation heaped upon him after Joachim introduced his violin concerto at the Leipzig Gewandhaus would have crushed me. Another factor which militated against me was economic necessity. I had a wife and children to support and educate. I was compelled to earn money with my compositions. Therefore I had to write works that were pleasing and easily understood. I never wrote down to the public; my artistic conscience would never permit me to do that. I always composed good music but it was music that sold readily. There was never anything to quarrel about in my music as there was in that of Brahms. I never outraged the critics by those wonderful conflicting rhythms, which are so characteristic of Brahms. Nor would I have dared to leave out the sequences of steps progressing from one key to another, which often makes Brahms' modulations so bold and startling. Neither did I venture to paint in such dark colours, *à la* Rembrandt, as he did. All this, and much more, militated against Brahms in his own day, but these very attributes will contribute to his stature fifty years from now, because they proclaim him a composer of marked originality. I consider Brahms one of the greatest personalities in the entire annals of music.[7]

In spite of knowledge and love of Bruch's music being limited largely to the one Violin Concerto, there are many other works which are deserving of revival and reappraisal. The conditions and times in which they were written will never recur, nor can they be recaptured, but with a sympathetic awareness of his life and times, and with an appreciation and understanding of his musical philosophy, there is much beauty in the music of Max Bruch which, 150 years after his birth, can please today's audiences as it did those of his own era.

# NOTES

(All letters are to or from Max Bruch unless stated otherwise)

## ORIGINS

1. Bruch, Felix, *Die saarländischen und pfälzischen Ahnen des Komponisten Max Bruch*, 1929
2. *Handbuch der Judenfrage*, ed. 32, 1933

## Chapter One
### CHILDHOOD AND YOUTH

1. The rebuilt tower on this site bears a plaque with the following inscription: *Geburtsstätte des rheinischen Tondichters und Sängers Max Bruch. 6 Januar 1838.* It is unclear why Bruch should have been described as a singer as well as a composer.
2. Bruch, Max, *Childhood and Youth on the Rhine* (unpublished)
3. 29 December 1852
4. 12 March 1852
5. *Niederrheinische Musikzeitung* No. 5, 1857

## Chapter Two
### YEARS OF STUDY

1. *Niederrheinische Musikzeitung* No. 5, 1857
2. *Talks with Great Composers*, New York 1955
3. 20 February 1858
4. *Ibid*
5. *Niederrheinische Musikzeitung* No. 7, 1859

## Chapter Three
### MANNHEIM

1. 3 January 1862

2. Devrient, Eduard, *Meine Errinerungen an Felix Mendelssohn-Bartholdy*
3. Act I, scene 2, No. 5 for soprano soloist and chorus of vine-dressers.
4. Vienna, 3 April 1862
5. The work remains unpublished, the original score being either lost or in the possession of the heirs to the former publishing house of Rudolf Eichmann, to whom it was entrusted for safekeeping during the Second World War by Bruch's surviving children. There is, however, a photocopy in the West German Radio archives in Cologne. An arrangement of the *Canzonetta* for cello and orchestra is in private ownership in Stuttgart, but is not available for inspection.

## Chapter Four
### FOLKSONG AND *FRITHJOF*

1. Published with no opus number by Leuckart in Breslau.
2. to von Beckerath, 19 March 1864
3. to Joachim from Brahms, 30 December 1864
4. Breslau, 9 March 1865
5. to von Beckerath, 24 October 1863
6. from Wilhelmine Bruch, 9 August 1863
7. *Niederrheinische Musikzeitung*, December 1864
8. *Ibid*, 8 April 1865
9. 16 February 1864
10. 16 November 1864

11. 3 January 1865
12. to von Beckerath, 6 January 1865
13. to von Beckerath, 9 March 1865

## Chapter Five
### COBLENZ

1. to Hiller, 10 August 1865
2. *Ibid*, 11 November 1865
3. from Levi, 11 February 1867
4. Clara Schumann to Brahms, 22 December 1866
5. to Simrock, 14 July 1872
6. from Joachim, 17 August 1866
7. *Musical Courier*, 5 July 1911
8. to Joachim, 26 September 1866
9. to Joachim and Moser, 14 March 1912
10. *Ibid*, 17 March 1912
11. to Levi, 21 January 1867
12. from Levi, 11 February 1867
13. to Levi, 4 December 1867
14. *Ibid*, 19 February 1868
15. *Ibid*, 16 April 1868
16. *Ibid*, 26 April 1868
17. *Musical Courier*, 5 July 1911
18. from David, 19 August 1868
19. to Simrock, 26 November 1887
20. to Schrattenholz, 31 January 1913
21. to his family, 24 November 1903
22. to Simrock, 13 June 1885
23. *Ibid*, 27 July 1885
24. Even Bruch's avowed enemy, Richard Strauss, quoted the opening of the second subject of the second movement (rehearsal letter D) in his own *Alpensinfonie* Op.64 (4 bars after fig.80).
25. Tovey, *Essays in Musical Analysis*, Vol.3

## Chapter Six
### SONDERSHAUSEN

1. to Levi, 6 December 1866
2. erster fürstlicher Hofkapellmeister.
3. from Levi, 11 December 1866
4. to Laura von Beckerath, 24 March 1867
5. *Ibid*, 21 May 1867
6. to Clara Schumann, 7 August 1867
7. Kretschmar, *Führer durch den Konzertsaal*, 1890

8. to Brahms, Cologne 22 December 1868
9. *Ibid*, 6 May 1870
10. to Hiller, 26 April 1868
11. *Ibid*, 25 May 1869
12. *Ibid*, 9 December 1869
13. to von Beckerath, 20 November 1868
14. to Simrock, 20 May 1871
15. to Laura von Beckerath, 10 January 1869

## Chapter Seven
### BERGISCH GLADBACH

1. The article is in the Max Bruch Archive, housed in the Musicological Institute of Cologne University, and was published for the first time in the centennial programme book of the Chorgemeinschaft Bergisch Gladbach (formerly Maria Zanders' Cäcilienchor) in 1985.
2. Maria Zanders to Mathilde Bruch, 8 December 1871

## Chapter Eight
### SONDERSHAUSEN: THE COMPOSITIONS

1. from Brahms, 21 February 1870
2. *Musikalisches Wochenblatt* No. 1, 1870
3. to Maria Zanders, 24 April 1865
4. to Brahms, 6 May 1870
5. to Kamphausen, 18 February 1882
6. Tovey, *Essays in Musical Analysis*, Vol.3
7. to von Beckerath, 10 January 1869
8. to Simrock, 13 June 1870
9. to Levi, 29 November 1870
10. to Simrock, 26 February 1886
11. to Spitta, 17 March 1870
12. to Simrock, 5 October 1870
13. *Ibid*, 14 September 1888
14. *Musikalisches Wochenblatt* No.8, 1877
15. Kretschmar, *Führer durch den Konzertsaal*
16. to Laura von Beckerath, Bergisch Gladbach 19 April 1869
17. *Ibid*, 18 June 1869
18. to von Beckerath, 6 August 1869

19. *Ibid*, 14 November 1869
20. *Ibid*, 1 July 1869
21. *Ibid*, 10 January 1870
22. *Ibid*, 9 April 1870
23. *Ibid*, 2 August 1870
24. *Ibid*, 14 November 1869
25. *Ibid*, 2 August 1870
26. from Brahms, 12 June 1870
27. to Brahms, 15 June 1870

14. Lochner, Louis, *Fritz Kreisler*
15. to Simrock, 18 February 1877
16. *Ibid*, 8 March 1877
17. *Ibid*, 2 October 1877
18. Brahms to Simrock, 27 September 1877
19. *Ibid*, 22 November 1877
20. *Ibid*, 18 November 1877
21. *Ibid*, 20 November 1877

## Chapter Nine
### FREELANCE COMPOSER: BERLIN

1. to von Beckerath, 16 October 1870
2. *Ibid*, 20 October 1870
3. Rudorff to Hiller, 29 October 1870
4. to von Beckerath, 9 April 1870
5. *Ibid*, 2 August 1870
6. to Simrock, 4 November 1871
7. *Ibid*, 11 November 1871
8. to von Beckerath, 27 March 1871
9. *Ibid*, 3 November 1871
10. to Mathilde Bruch, 18 September 1871
11. *Ibid*, 21 November 1871
12. to Hermann Deiters, 21 January 1873
13. to Simrock, 27 December 1873
14. *Ibid*, 11 February 1874
15. to Brahms, 22 December 1874
16. to Simrock, 30 November 1874
17. Fuller-Maitland, *Masters of German Music*

## Chapter Ten
### FREELANCE COMPOSER: BONN

1. to Simrock, 30 October 1873
2. *Ibid*, 12 November 1873
3. to von Beckerath, 25 November 1873
4. to Simrock, 27 December 1873
5. to von Beckerath, 6 January 1874
6. from Simrock, 31 December 1873
7. to Simrock, 17 February 1874
8. *Simrock Jahrbuch*, 1921
9. to Simrock, 11 February 1874
10. *Ibid*, 17 February 1874
11. *Ibid*, 1 March 1874
12. to von Beckerath, 25 June 1874
13. *Allgemeine Musikalische Zeitung*, 29 December 1875

## Chapter Eleven
### RETURN TO BERLIN

1. *Musical Times*, 1 October 1879
2. to Stockhausen, 10 August 1878
3. to Simrock, 18 January 1879
4. *Ibid*, 22 February 1879
5. *Ibid*, 27 September 1880
6. *Ibid*, 15 October 1879
7. *Ibid*, 3 June 1880
8. *Ibid*, 30 September 1880
9. *Ibid*, 20 October 1881
10. to Kamphausen, 31 January 1882
11. to Simrock, 9 October 1880
12. *Ibid*, 12 November 1880
13. *Ibid*, 22 August 1880
14. to Hiller, 22 August 1880
15. to Simrock, 27 September 1880
16. *Ibid*, 6 June 1880
17. *Ibid*, 9 October 1880

## Chapter Twelve
### LIVERPOOL

1. Best to Sudlow, 2 February 1881
2. *Ibid*, 2 March 1881
3. *Ibid*, 9 April 1881
4. to Sudlow, 22 July 1880
5. Fanny Bennett to Sudlow, 3 October 1881
6. *Liverpool Mercury*, 6 October 1880
7. to Sudlow, 12 August 1880
8. to Simrock, 9 October 1880
9. to Sudlow, 26 January 1881
10. *Ibid*, 2 February 1881
11. *Ibid*, 22 February 1881
12. Hallé to Sudlow, 4 June 1882
13. to Sudlow, 19 November 1881
14. *Ibid*, 1 September 1881
15. *Ibid*, 27 September 1881

16. *Ibid*, 16 October 1881
17. Liverpool Philharmonic Society Committee Minutes, 17 October 1881
18. to Sudlow, 28 September 1881
19. *Ibid*, 1 December 1881
20. to Alfred Castellaine, 25 January 1882
21. to Sudlow, 24 February 1882
22. *Ibid*, 8 March 1882
23. to Simrock, 30 September 1880
24. to Clara's aunt Adolfine, 16 March 1881
25. from Verdi, 22 October 1877
26. Clara to her aunt Adolfine, 8 October 1881
27. to aunt Adolfine, 22 October 1881
28. *Ibid*, 16 February 1882
29. to Simrock, 19 October 1882
30. Corder to Sudlow, 29 June 1882
31. to Hiller, 7 July 1882
32. *Ibid*, 7 August 1882
33. *Ibid*, 15 November 1882
34. Elgar to A. J. Jaeger, 27 December 1899
35. Wood, Sir Henry, *My Life of Music*
36. to Simrock, 20 March 1886
37. *Ibid*, 16 November 1882
38. Clara Bruch to Margaretha Zanders, 25 November 1882
39. to aunt Adolfine, 27 November 1882
40. to Sudlow, 1 January 1883
41. from Alfred Castellaine, 8 January 1883
42. Isaac Nathan to Lord Byron, 13 June 1814
43. to Simrock, 2 January 1882
44. *Ibid*, 11 November 1882
45. *Ibid*, 9 December 1880
46. to Hiller, 30 November 1881

## Chapter Thirteen
BRESLAU

1. *Boston Evening Transcript*, 17 November 1882
2. *New York Times*, 11 April 1883
3. to Simrock, 26 May 1883
4. *Ibid*, 9 September 1886

5. from Carl Reinthaler, 17 November 1888
6. *Boston Daily Advertiser*, 5 March 1883
7. *New York Times*, 17 December 1882
8. to Hiller, 4 July 1883
9. to Simrock, 12 October 1883
10. from Richard Strauss, 8 December 1889
11. to Richard Strauss, 11 December 1889
12. Hiller to Brahms, 17 April 1884
13. from Hiller, 26 April 1884
14. to Hiller, 29 April 1884
15. Robert Schnitzler to Hiller, 22 May 1884
16. Robert Heuser to Hiller, 30 May 1884
17. from Otto Dethier, 23 May 1885
18. to Simrock, 4 November 1884
19. to von Beckerath, 6 July 1873
20. to Simrock, 19 April 1884
21. *Ibid*, 14 October 1884
22. *Ibid*, 3 May 1890
23. Rosenbaum to Simrock, 11 January 1890
24. to Simrock, 27 September 1890
25. *Ibid*, 14 June 1890
26. *Neue Musikzeitung* No.6, 1885
27. to Simrock, 9 October 1885
28. *Ibid*, 18 December 1885
29. These references occur in letters dated 18 July 1876 and 4 April 1878
30. to Simrock, 26 July 1888
31. *Ibid*, 25 April 1888
32. *Ibid*, 1 February 1889
33. *Ibid*, 16 April 1889
34. to Hans Simrock, 3 November 1904
35. from Andrew Kurtz, 8 January 1888
36. The first melody is No.105 in Johnson's collection. It also occurs in Geminiani's book of violin studies, 'Rules for playing in a true taste' Op.8 (1748), though there it is described as 'an Irish tune'.
37. to Simrock, 10 December 1890
38. *Ibid*, 29 November 1890
39. *Ibid*, 10 December 1890
40. *Ibid*, 15 September 1890

## Chapter Fourteen

BERLIN I

1.   to Simrock, 12 December 1890
2.   to Krause, 7 March 1890
3.   to Simrock, 31 October 1891
4.   to Joachim, 12 March 1891
5.   to Simrock, 11 November 1891
6.   *Ibid*, 1 June 1891
7.   *Ibid*, 31 October 1891
8.   to Joachim, 9 June 1891
9.   to Simrock, 22 March 1892
10.  *Ibid*, 28 March 1892
11.  *Ibid*, 10 May 1892
12.  *Ibid*, 14 July 1892
13.  *Ibid*, 16 July 1892
14.  *Ibid*, 21 March 1893
15.  to Joachim, 9 January 1893
16.  *Ibid*, 27 May 1893
17.  to Simrock, 4 October 1892
18.  *Ibid*, 7 December 1892
19.  Brahms to Simrock, 21 November 1892
20.  *Cambridge Independent*
21.  *Cambridge Review*
22.  *Pall Mall Gazette*
23.  *Punch*
24.  to Simrock, 20 June 1893
25.  Norris, Gerald, *Stanford, the Cambridge Jubilee and Tchaikovsky*
26.  Saint-Saëns, Camille, *Portraits et Souvenirs*
27.  *Pall Mall Gazette*
28.  Stanford, Sir Charles V., *Pages from an Unwritten Diary*
29.  from Joachim, 29 May 1893
30.  Mackenzie, Sir A. C., *A Musician's Narrative*
31.  Speyer, Edward, *My Life and Friends*
32.  Elson, Louis, *Famous Composers and Their Works*
33.  Speyer, Edward, *Op. cit.*
34.  to Simrock, 20 June 1893
35.  *Ibid*, 14 August 1893
36.  *Ibid*, 25 September 1893
37.  *Ibid*, 10 October 1893
38.  *Ibid*, 2 November 1893
39.  Mackenzie, Sir A. C., *A Musician's Narrative*
40.  to Simrock, 17 January 1894
41.  *Ibid*, 24 June 1894
42.  to Philipp Spitta, 17 December 1893
43.  to Simrock, 18 June 1894
44.  *Ibid*, 13 January 1895
45.  *Barmer Zeitung*, 19 January 1895
46.  to Ludwig Spitta, 4 February 1895
47.  to Simrock, 1 February 1898
48.  *Ibid*, 18 June 1894
49.  Brahms to Clara Schumann, June 1895
50.  to Simrock, 13 February 1895
51.  *Ibid*, 12 November 1894
52.  *Ibid*, 13 November 1894
53.  to Krause, 4 March 1895
54.  to Susanne Krause, 16 January 1897
55.  to Simrock, 30 March 1897
56.  to Krause, 5 April 1897
57.  to Schrattenholz, 6 April 1897

## Chapter Fifteen

BERLIN II

1.   to Simrock, 16 January 1898
2.   *Ibid*, 6 December 1897
3.   to Hackenberg, 2 April 1897
4.   *Ibid*, 10 May 1897
5.   'Ein' feste Burg' also appears in *Gruss an die heilige Nacht* Op.62 (as a brass chorale in the work's middle section), and its first phrase occurs at the conclusion of *Herzog Moritz* Op.74
6.   to Simrock, 1 February 1898
7.   to Krause, 14 June 1899
8.   to Vaughan Williams, 31 October 1897
9.   *Ibid*, 5 February 1898
10.  Vaughan Williams to Ralph Wedgwood, 6 February 1898
11.  Vaughan Williams, Ralph, *A Musical Autobiography*
12.  to Carl Hopfe, 23 December 1901
13.  to Simrock, 5 November 1899
14.  *Ibid*, 3 February 1900
15.  *Ibid*, 12 February 1900
16.  *Ibid*, 11 February 1901
17.  *Boston Daily Advertiser*, 13 February 1903
18.  *Ibid*, 14 November 1904
19.  to Simrock, 21 October 1900
20.  *Ibid*, 24 October 1901
21.  to Schnitzler, 13 September 1902
22.  to Maria Zanders, 8 March 1903

23. *Ibid*, 3 April 1903
24. *Ibid*, 12 May 1903
25. *Ibid*, 19 November 1903
26. Clara Bruch to Maria Zanders, 17 November 1904
27. to Olga Zanders, 13 January 1905
28. to Anna Zanders, 9 September 1907
29. to Arthur Abell, 7 February 1911
30. to Francis Kruse, 5 December 1907
31. 8 November 1909
32. to Hess, 15 March 1910
33. to Kroegel, 24 December 1907
34. 23 November 1906
35. to Anna Zanders, 7 May 1908
36. *Ibid*, 23 March 1908
37. to Margaretha Kruse, 21 May 1908
38. *Ibid*, 21 April 1908
39. to Kroegel, 22 October 1908
40. *Ibid*, 9 December 1908

## Chapter Sixteen

### THE FINAL YEARS

1. to Abell, 8 July 1911
2. Maud Powell to Abell, 12 July 1911
3. to Simrock & Co., 22 December 1911
4. to Schrattenholz, 23 November 1913
5. *Allgemeine Musikzeitung* No.40, 1913
6. to Anna Zanders, 31 December 1908
7. to Hans Zanders, 2 July 1910
8. to Anna Zanders, 3 September 1910
9. to Hans Zanders, 28 November 1911
10. 6 November 1912
11. to Kroegel, 26 April 1913
12. to Abell, 30 June 1914
13. Chapter Five, page 75
14. to Kroegel, 13 May 1912
15. to Hans Zanders, 24 July 1913
16. to Kroegel, 19 May 1913
17. to Franke, 23 May 1913
18. *Ibid*, 28 May 1913
19. to Margaretha Kruse, 21 June 1913
20. to Hans Zanders, 4 July 1913
21. to Schrattenholz, 23 November 1913

22. to Olga Zanders, 10 January 1914
23. to Margaretha Kruse, 5 June 1914
24. to Hans Zanders, 2 June 1914
25. *Ibid*, 19 September 1914
26. to Abell, 19 July 1915
27. to his family, 1 April 1904
28. to Schrattenholz, 11 October and 18 December 1912
29. The alternatives listed in the score (not in Bruch's handwriting) are: Spring in the South, Sunny Spring, Symphonic Picture, Symphonic Intermezzo, Merry Intermezzo, Southern Spring, Southern Intermezzo, Spring Day.
30. to Abell, 24 April 1915
31. to Hans Zanders, 6 July 1909
32. to Abell, 26 April 1915
33. *Ibid*, 19 July 1915
34. *Musical Courier*, 26 May 1915
35. *Ibid*
36. *Public Ledger*, Philadelphia, 30 December 1916
37. These versions comprise male-voice choir, mixed-voice choir, organ and brass, and were transposed from E flat minor to F minor
38. 11 September 1916
39. to Francis Kruse, 31 March 1916
40. to Anna Zanders, 25 October 1917
41. *Ibid*, 10 January and 13 February 1918
42. to Olga Zanders, 14 March 1918
43. The Igel Letter, 8 May 1918
44. 16 July 1918
45. 28 November 1918
46. 23 January 1920
47. to Simrock & Co., 14 May 1920
48. *Ibid*
49. The slow movement of the A minor String Quintet is identical to the slow (fourth) movement of the Serenade for String Orchestra (on Swedish melodies, 1916)
50. No score survives, but a reference appears in *Signale* No.78, page 1039, 1920
51. Margarethe Bruch to Olga Zanders, 18 May 1920
52. to Simrock & Co., 14 May 1920

53. to Olga Zanders, 10 June 1920
54. to Francis Kruse, 19 August 1920
55. Margarethe Bruch to Olga Zanders, 5 November 1920

## Chapter Seventeen
POSTLUDE

1. Speyer, Edward, *My Life and Friends*

2. from Arthur Goring Thomas, 9 April and 2 May 1890
3. Modest Tchaikovsky to Peter Tchaikovsky, 10 June 1893
4. Fuller-Maitland J. A., *Masters of German Music*
5. del Mar, Norman, *Richard Strauss*, Barrie & Rockliff 1972
6. Schoenberg to Paul Dessau, 22 November 1941
7. Abell, Arthur, *Talks with Great Composers*

# PUBLISHED WORKS

## OPERAS

*Scherz, List und Rache* Op.1
*Die Loreley* Op.16
*Hermione* Op.40

## ACCOMPANIED CHORAL MUSIC

*Jubilate* Op.3
*Die Birken und die Erlen* Op.8
*Römischer Triumphgesang* for male chorus
    and orchestra Op.19 No.1
Three choruses for male voices and brass
    Op.19 No.2
*Die Flucht der heiligen Familie* Op.20
*Gesang der heiligen drei Könige* Op.21
*Frithjof* Op.23
*Schön Ellen* Op.24
*Salamis* Op.25
*Frithjof auf seines Vaters Grabhügel* Op.27
*Rorate coeli* Op.29
*Die Flucht nach Aegypten/Morgenstunde*
    Op.31
*Normannenzug* Op.32
*Römische Leichenfeier* Op.34
*Messensätze*: Kyrie, Sanctus and Agnus
    Dei Op.35
*Das Lied vom deutschen Kaiser* Op.37
*Dithyrambe* Op.39
*Odysseus* Op.41
*Arminius* Op.43
*Das Lied von der Glocke* Op.45
*Achilleus* Op.50
*Das Feuerkreuz* Op.52
Two male-voice choruses Op.53
*Gruss an die heilige Nacht* Op.62
*Hymne* Op.64
*Leonidas* Op.66
*Moses* Op.67
*Neue Männerchöre* Op.68
*Sei getreu bis in den Tod* Op.69
*Gustav Adolf* Op.73
*Herzog Moritz* Op.74
*Der letzte Abschied* Op.76
*Damajanti* Op.78
*Osterkantate* Op.81

*Das Wessobrunner Gebet* Op.82
*Die Macht des Gesanges* Op.87
*Heldenfeier* Op.89
*Die Stimme der Mutter Erde* Op.91
*Trauerfeier für Mignon* Op.93
Three Hebrew Songs (1888)

## UNACCOMPANIED CHORAL MUSIC

*Five Lieder* for mixed chorus Op.22
*Five Lieder* for mixed chorus Op.38
*Four choruses* for male voices Op.48
*Nine Songs* for mixed chorus Op.60
*In der Nacht* Op.72
*Six Lieder* for mixed chorus Op.86
*Five Lieder* for mixed chorus Op.90
*Christkindlieder* Op.92
Six Folksongs (Welsh and Scottish)

## PIANO MUSIC

*Capriccio* for piano (four hands) Op.2
*Fantasia* for two pianos Op.11
*Six pieces* for piano Op.12
*Two pieces* for piano Op.14

## CHAMBER MUSIC

Septet (1849)
*Three Duets* for female voices and piano
    Op.4
Trio for piano, violin and cello Op.5
*Seven Songs* for two- and three-part
    female voices and piano Op.6
String Quartet in C minor Op.9
String Quartet in E major Op.10
*Swedish Dances* Op.63
Four pieces for cello and piano Op.70
*Lieder und Tänze* on Russian and Swedish
    Folk Melodies Op.79
*Eight Trio Pieces* for clarinet, viola and
    piano Op.83

*Song of Spring* (for two violins, piano and harmonium *ad lib.*)

SONGS

*Six Songs* Op.7
*Hymnus* for female voice and piano Op.13
*Four Lieder* Op.15
*Ten Lieder* Op.17
*Four Songs* Op.18
*Four Lieder* Op.33
*Lieder und Gesänge* Op.49
*Siechentrost Lieder* (with violin) Op.54
*Five Lieder* Op.59
*Five Songs* Op.97
*Twelve Scottish Folksongs* (1863)

WORKS FOR SOLO VOICE WITH
ORCHESTRA

*Die Priesterin der Isis in Rom* Op.30
*Szene der Marfa* Op.80

WORKS FOR SOLO INSTRUMENTS
WITH ORCHESTRA

*Violin Concerto No.1 in G minor* Op.26
*Romanze* for violin and orchestra Op.42

Violin Concerto No.2 in D minor Op.44
*Scottish Fantasy* for violin and orchestra Op.46
*Kol Nidrei* for cello and orchestra Op.47
*Canzone* for cello and orchestra Op.55
*Adagio on Celtic Themes* for cello and orchestra Op.56
*Adagio appassionato* for violin and orchestra Op.57
Violin Concerto No.3 in D minor Op.58
*Ave Maria* for cello and orchestra Op.61
*In Memoriam* for violin and orchestra Op.65
*Serenade* for violin and orchestra Op.75
*Konzertstück* for violin and orchestra Op.84
*Romanze* for viola and orchestra Op.85
Double Concerto for clarinet and viola Op.88
Concerto for two pianos Op.88a

ORCHESTRAL MUSIC

Symphony No.1 in E flat major Op.28
Symphony No.2 in F minor Op.36
Symphony No.3 in E major Op.51
Suite on Russian Folk Melodies Op.79b
Suite No.2 (*Nordland Suite*)
Serenade (on Swedish Melodies) for String Orchestra Op. posth. (1916)

# UNPUBLISHED WORKS

*Ach bleib mit deiner Gnade* (1897)
*Altenberger Hymne* (1913)
*Am Rhein*
*Canzonetta* for orchestra (1862)
*Claudine von Villabella*
Dramatischen Szenen aus Scheffels *Ekkehard*
*Durch Nacht zum Licht* (1919)
*Geistlich gesinnt sein* (1873, orchestrated 1893)

Gesänge bei der Trauung Else Tuczek und Franz von Ankert am 24 März 1897
*Hymne* (1902)
*Hymne an das Vaterland*
*Japsenlied*
*Kaiser Wilhelm-Lied* zum 22 März 1897
*Kleine Präludium* (organ or harmonium) for Hildegard Zanders (1897)

*Lied an die Eltern* (1847)
*Das Lied der Deutschen in Oesterreich*
*Militärmärsche*
*Mindener Fantasie* for piano (four hands)
    (1881)
Piano Quintet in G minor (1886)
String Octet (1920)

String Quintet in A minor (1919)
Suite No. 3 for orchestra with organ
    (1904–1915)
*Venetian Serenade*
*Wächterlied in der Neujahrsnacht* (1888)
*Zum 31.8.1900*

# UNPUBLISHED LOST WORKS

Begrüssungshymne for Maria and
    Richard Zanders
Concert Overture (1854)
*Die Gratulanten*
*Festpräludium* for eleven wind instru-
    ments and timpani (1920)
*Hosanna*
*Jeri und Baetely*
Mass (1858)
Overture to *Jungfrau von Orleans*
Piano Quintet (1858)

Piano Trios (1849, c. 1852, 1855)
*Rinaldo*
*Romanze* for piano
Sonata for cello and piano (1862)
String Quartet (1862)
String Quintet in E flat major (1919)
Suite for orchestra No. 4
Suite for orchestra No. 5
Symphonic Poem *Bilder aus dem Norden*
    (c. 1908)
Symphony in F major (1852)

# BIBLIOGRAPHY

A detailed bibliography of articles from German music books, newspapers, periodicals and dictionaries on Bruch and his music may be found in *Max Bruch Studien*, ed. Kämper (see below).

ABELL, ARTHUR, *Talks with Great Composers*, Philosophical Library, New York 1955

ALTMANN, WILHELM, *Johannes Brahms im Briefwechsel mit Karl Reinthaler, Max Bruch etc, (J. Brahms Briefwechsel: Vol.3)*, Berlin 1908
    *N. Simrock Jahrbuch 1*, ed. Müller, Berlin 1928
    *Cobbett's Cyclopedic Survey of Chamber Music*, Vol. 1 OUP 1929

DEVRIENT, EDUARD, *Meine Erinnerungen an Felix Mendelssohn-Bartholdy*, Leipzig 1872

ELSON, LOUIS, *Max Bruch: Famous Composers and their Works*, ed. Paine, Thomas and Klauser, Millett, Boston 1891

FELLERER, KARL GUSTAV, *Max Bruch: Beiträge zur rheinischen Musikgeschichte Vol.103*, Arno, Cologne 1974

FULLER-MAITLAND, J. A., *Masters of German Music*, Osgood, McIlvaine & Co, London 1894

GYSI, FRITZ, *Max Bruch: 110 Neujahrsblatt der allgemeinen Musikgesellschaft in Zürich*, Orell Füssli, Zürich 1922

HANSLICK, EDUARD, *Fünf Jahre Musik (1891–1895)*, Berlin 1896
    *Aus dem Konzertsaal. Kritiken und Schilderungen aus 20 Jahren des Wiener Musiklebens 1848–1868*, Vienna 1897
    *Concerte, Componisten und Virtuosen der letzten 15 Jahren 1870–1885*, Berlin 1896

HUGHES, GERVASE, *Sidelights on a Century of Music 1825–1924*, Macdonald, London 1969

KÄMPER, DIETRICH (ed), *Max Bruch Studien, zum 50 Todestag des Komponisten: Beiträge zur rheinischen Musikgeschichte Vol.87*, Arno, Cologne 1970

KRETSCHMAR, HERMANN, *Führer durch den Konzertsaal*, Breitkopf & Härtel, Leipzig 1890

LAUTH, WILHELM, *Max Bruchs Instrumentalmusik: Beiträge zur rheinischen Musikgeschichte Vol 68*, Diss, Cologne 1967

LITZMANN, BERTHOLD, *Clara Schumann: Ein Künstlerleben nach Tagebüchern und Briefen Vol.3*, Leipzig, Breitkopf & Härtel 1908

LOCHNER, LOUIS, *Fritz Kreisler*, Rockliff, London 1950

LUYKEN, SONJA, *Max Bruch: Kölner Biografien Vol.17*, Stadt Köln, Der Oberstadtdirektor, Cologne 1984

MACKENZIE, SIR ALEXANDER CAMPBELL, *A Musician's Narrative*, Cassell, London 1927

NORRIS, GERALD, *Stanford, the Cambridge Jubilee and Tchaikovsky*, David and Charles, Newton Abbot 1980

PFITZNER, HANS, *Meine Beziehungen zu Max Bruch*, Langen/Müller, Munich 1938

PIRANI, MAX, *The Music Masters: Vol.3 The Romantic Age*, Cassell 1952

PULVER, JEFFREY, *Brahms* (Masters of Music), London 1926

SAINT-SAËNS, CAMILLE, *Portraits et Souvenirs*, Calmann-Lévy, Paris 1909

SIETZ, REINHOLD, *Aus Ferdinand Hillers Briefwechsel: Beiträge zur rheinischen Musikgeschichte Vols. 28, 48, 56, 60, 65, 70, 92*, Cologne 1958–1971

SPEYER, EDWARD, *My Life and Friends*, Cobden–Sanderson, London 1937

STANFORD, SIR CHARLES V., *Pages from an Unwritten Diary*, Arnold, London 1914

SWALIN, BENJAMIN F., *The Violin Concerto: A Study in German Romanticism*, Chapel Hill, University of North Carolina Press 1941

TAYLOR, STAINTON DE B., *Two Centuries of Music in Liverpool*, Rockliff Bros, Liverpool 1976

TOVEY, DONALD F., *Essays in Musical Analysis Vol.3*, OUP, London 1935

VICK, BINGHAM LAFAYETTE, *The Five Oratorios of Max Bruch*, Ph.D thesis for Northwestern University 1977

WILLIAMS, R. V., *National Music and Other Essays*, OUP, London 1963

WOOD, SIR HENRY J., *My Life of Music*, Gollancz, London 1938

# INDEX

## WORKS BY MAX BRUCH

## INDEX OF NAMES

# AFTERWORD TO THE NEW EDITION

THIS NEW EDITION of my biography of Max Bruch, re-published seventeen years after it first appeared in 1988, corrects some facts and adds new information. It also provides an opportunity for a reappraisal of Bruch's music in the current (2005) repertory. It came as a complete surprise to me when I discovered in 1985 that no biography of Bruch existed, not even in German. When the book was published it clearly alerted orchestras, choirs and recording companies to the fact that there was a wealth of music to be explored, programmed and recorded. However Bruch's three best known works have remained unassailable in the popularity stakes with the public. Since 1996 the London-based radio station Classic FM has held an annual poll entitled 'Hall of Fame', an opportunity for the listening public to vote for its favourite works, three hundred of them played in reverse order over Easter weekend. Taking the poll's second year (1997) as an example, *Kol nidrei* came in at No.280 (in 1996 it had only just made it on to the list at No.300), the *Scottish Fantasy* was up eleven places from No.94 to No.83, but unchanged at No.1 was the ubiquitous first violin concerto, in both years beating Rachmaninov's second piano concerto and Beethoven's *Pastoral* symphony into second and third place respectively. For the five years 1996–2000 the concerto remained top of the poll, in 2001 and 2002 it slipped to second place, while in 2003 and 2004 it dropped to third. Yet despite such popularity, it is rare to hear anyone humming the tune of its *Adagio*, this movement presumably being the reason for its hold on the listening public. It also labels Bruch as a one-work composer, which, as he himself was always at pains to point out, is unfair because there have been just over one hundred published compositions in various catalogues.

The reputation of Max Bruch has been further enhanced by the efforts of his devotees throughout the world. In March 1998 the late Fritz Spiegl organised the erection of a plaque on Bruch's Liverpool home at 18 Brompton Avenue, Sefton Park. In the same year in Germany a Max Bruch Society (Deutsche Max-Bruch-Gesellschaft, www.themen.miz.org) was formed on 3 June in the town of Sondershausen (where the composer worked for the three years between 1867 and 1870, see the article at the end of this Afterword) and the orchestra there (das Loh Orchester) now carries the alternative name of Max-Bruch-Philharmonie. The society's honorary members include conductor Kurt Masur, pianist Justus Frantz, violinist Wolfgang Marschner, and the author. In America, violinist and musicologist Thomas Wood has created a website for the composer (http://pages.wooster.edu/twood/Max_bruch.html). It reports events, performances, research, new publications, recordings and editions as well as providing a forum for discussion among the composer's admirers. Nowadays performances of unfamiliar music tend to depend upon the efforts of conductors or project planners (fairly commonly employed by orchestras or music agencies), but they in turn have to resist accountants who maintain watchful eyes on box-office receipts. In Britain the conductor Richard Hickox programmed a two-concert mini-festival of some of Bruch's orchestral music with the London Symphony Orchestra at London's Barbican Hall in October 1998, before recording most of it. In February 2003 at Liverpool, Gerard Schwarz, the Royal Liverpool Philharmonic Orchestra's American music director at the time, put on two performances of the secular oratorio *Das Lied von der Glocke*.

Between 1996 and 2002 I received monthly bulletins from Tim Gill, at the time in charge of the London orchestral hire library of the music publisher Richard Schauer, part of the German publisher Simrock but now taken over by Boosey and Hawkes. These bulletins listed dates and venues of world-wide performances of Bruch's music by orchestras and choirs, but I was also provided with a retrospective summary of similar hirings between 1980 and 1991. It must be noted that Gill only reported the works of Bruch in the Schauer catalogue, in other words the Double Concerto for clarinet and viola, the Double Piano Concerto, *Scottish Fantasy*, *Kol nidrei*, the three violin concertos (but only Thomas Wood's 1994 edition of the first concerto), Septet, Octet, Swedish Dances, Symphony No.2, *Gruss an die heilige Nacht*, *Serenade on Swedish Melodies*, and a handful of the single-movement concerted works for violin and cello. Therefore, whilst what follows cannot be considered a scientific survey of performances of Bruch's output since my biography first appeared, the fact remains that there has indeed been a marked increase in interest by orchestras, choirs and record companies (see the discography for further details). The Schauer lists containing all the works are far too long to be printed here, but performances of some of the large choral works alone make encouraging reading.

*Moses:* Freiburg, December 1985
     Berlin, February 1988
     London, September 1988
     Basel, November 1990
     Coburg, October 1991
     Hamburg, October 1992
     Arnersfoort, Holland, November 1993
     Olten/Solothurn, Switzerland, March 1996
     Prague, March 1996
     Bamberg, August 1997

Stuttgart, October 1999
Düsseldorf, November 1999
Oxford, March 2000
Nuremberg, December 2001
Miskolc, Hungary, April 2002
*Odysseus*: Hilversum, Holland, October 1981
       London, July 1988
       Hannover, October 1997
       Budapest, October 2000
*Das Lied von der Glocke*: Hilversum, Holland, January 1988
            North German Radio, November 1988
            Saarland Radio, December 1988
            Vienna, February 1990
            Nottingham/London, April 1990
            Karlsruhe, February 1997
            Cologne, October 1997
            Heilbronn, July 1998
            Hannover, January 1999
            Stuttgart, July 1999
            Stade (Germany), November 1999
            Braunschweig, May 2001
            Liverpool, February 2003
*Die Macht der Gesanges*: Stuttgart, May 1998
The orchestral Suite No.1 (*Nordland*) Op.79b was played at Cologne in October 1997, while in London, the author has, since the first publication of this book, conducted the three symphonies, the three violin concertos, *Scottish Fantasy*, *Kol nidrei*, Serenade Op.75, both Double Concertos, Suite No.3, *Jubilate, Amen* Op.3, Swedish Dances, Serenade on Swedish Melodies, Overture to *Die Loreley*, unaccompanied choral songs and *Odysseus*.

Inevitably there are revisions and changes which need to be made to the original text and worklists. An error occurs at the bottom of page 172. Bruch's bride Clara Tuczek was born in 1854, and therefore she was not seventeen, but twenty-seven years old when they married in 1881. It then follows that the description of her voice at the top of the following page is not so 'remarkable' when it came to singing Verdi's Requiem. A similar error occurs on page 329. In 1907 Bruch's projection fifty years hence of the comparative status as a composer between himself and Brahms should therefore read 1957, not 1947. Some works originally listed as unpublished have since appeared in print, much to the delight of players of chamber music. As a consequence of my visit to Sondershausen, two more pieces (Feierlicher Marsch and Intermezzo) can now be added to the list of unpublished works. In the list of Bruch's pupils on page 270 the name of the Finnish composer Ernst Mielck should be included.

He studied with him between October 1895 and May 1896 as a private pupil. According to a reference by Bruch dated 22 June 1896, Mielck was put through his paces in score reading, orchestration exercises, and analysis of the works of the recognised Masters, and under his teacher's supervision wrote a string quartet and an overture for full orchestra. Furthermore, according to Bruch, Mielck developed his natural talent through hard work, became a special pupil who gave him much pleasure to teach, and was assured a promising future.

Since the first edition was published, there have been developments regarding the last three chamber music pieces referred to on pp. 321 and 322. Whilst the A minor string quintet and the string octet have now appeared in print (see New Editions), the manuscript score of the latter has also been found and is now lodged in the Austrian State Library in Vienna. There have been somewhat chequered developments regarding the status of the missing E flat major string quintet. In October 1991 I received a letter from Poole in Dorset. At this point the writer merely asked some seemingly innocuous questions about the quintet including 'You make no further mention of the E flat quintet, does this imply that it is now lost?' and 'I should like to know if you have any idea of where the parts of the quintet may be found.' I replied that to the best of my knowledge the work had vanished, probably into the hands of publisher Rudolf Eichmann, who had been entrusted during the Second World War with several Bruch manuscripts by the composer's surviving children. Over a year later, in February 1993, I received another letter from my correspondent in Dorset, this time informing me that, all along, he owned what turned out to be the parts of this missing work. He sent me a few pages to identify, and sure enough they were in the handwriting of Gertrude Bruch, with the date 6 October 1937 pencilled on the cover page followed by timings for each movement (at 17 minutes the work is shorter by seven minutes than the A minor quintet). These details, which can be verified by the *Radio Times* for the relevant week, were of a BBC broadcast on that date given by the Schwiller Quartet (with an unnamed second violist). Whether by accident or design, the parts were probably left behind on the music stands by the players, and then collected up and deposited in the BBC Music Library together with those of the A minor quintet and Octet, as briefly described on page 322. Somehow the parts for the E flat major string quintet then got separated from the two other works, and were purchased by my correspondent amongst a pile of string music at an auction some forty years later (he could not remember where or when he had 'purchased that bundle'). Happily the work will be edited by the author and published in 2006 under the Simrock imprint.

In 1997, the American Bruch scholar Bingham Vick Jr produced a new English translation of the oratorio *Moses* for his Greenville Chorale in South Carolina, and this text is available for hire. Contrary to my statement on page

298, the manuscript full score of the Double Concerto for clarinet and viola Op.88 turned up at Christie's auction house in London in June 1991 and was bought by the German antiquarian music dealer Ulrich Drüner. In 1999 it was resold by Christie's (having been authenticated by the author at their request), and is now safely lodged in the music department of Cologne University. Some years earlier another work had turned up at a London auction house, this time at Sotheby's on 10 May 1984. It was the 19-page autograph manuscript of a vocal duet dated March 1907 and inscribed as follows: 'Composed for Carmela and Grazia Carbone, *Crux fidelis* (Hymn of Passion). Duet for Soprano and Alto with Piano Accompaniment by Max Bruch'. Its present whereabouts are unknown to the author.

The following amendments update and therefore reorganise Bruch's works as listed on pp. 338–340.

On page 339 the following should be added to the list of Published Works (see also New Editions):

> Piano Quintet in G minor (1886)
> String Quintet in A minor (1919)
> String Octet (1920)
> Suite No.3 for Orchestra with Organ (1904–1915) [a private publication described as Op.88b although it is the prototype from which the later Concerto for two pianos Op.88a was derived]

On pp. 339 and 340 the following should be added to the list of Unpublished Works:

> Feierlicher Marsch (c.1867–1870)
> Intermezzo (c.1867)
> *Crux fidelis* (duet for soprano and alto with piano accompaniment) (1907)
> String Quintet in E flat major (1919)

On page 340 the following should be deleted from the list of Unpublished Works:

> Piano Quintet in G minor (1886)
> String Octet (1920)
> String Quintet in A minor (1919)
> Suite No.3 for Orchestra with Organ (1904–1915) [Op.88b]

On page 340 the following work should be deleted from the list of Unpublished Lost works:

> String Quintet in E flat major (1919)

# MAX BRUCH IN SONDERSHAUSEN (1867–1870)

*This piece presents new research carried out by the author at Sondershausen in June 2001. It appears here using and adapting material from an article written by the author for* The Strad *magazine (Bruch's Violin Concerto, Behind the Notes, pp. 962–7, September 2002), and from a chapter contributed to the book* Max Bruch in Sondershausen *(see the supplementary bibliography). Inevitably there is some repetition of background material on Bruch taken from my biography. It is reproduced here by kind permission of both publishers.*

In Sondershausen's Castle Museum (Schlossmuseum) there are notebooks which list all the concerts Max Bruch conducted during the time he was resident in the town as Court Music Director, while newspapers of the day provide an overview of the Theatre's repertoire for the three years 1868, 1869 and 1870. Remarkably, two unpublished works by Bruch exist in the library of the Loh-Orchester Sondershausen, though both are written in the hand of a copyist. One is a ceremonial march (Feierlicher Marsch) in G major, scored for strings, brass (three horns, two trumpets, and bass trombone) and timpani. It consists of only fifty bars, to be repeated *pianissimo* (the strings muted the second time), at a gentle *Andante* pace, and is probably a work written for a sombre occasion at the time. There is no score, and the parts carry the stamp 'Fürstliche Hofkapelle in Sondershausen', these words encircling the royal crest. The second work is of more interest, an Intermezzo in B major, again with no score and the parts bearing the same proprietorial stamp. But first it would be appropriate to describe Bruch's career during the years just before he came to Sondershausen.

In the 1860s Bruch was beginning to attract attention as a composer, particularly when his cantata *Frithjof* Op.23 for male-voice choir was performed in Aachen in 1864. At the age of twenty-six he had acquired an extraordinary power and facility in the manipulation of large vocal masses; his choral writing was now the work of a completely accomplished musician, solid and effective as well as spontaneous and tuneful. With *Frithjof* he reached to the heart of amateur music-making in Germany by writing for chorus, and by choosing a saga of love, vengeance, heroic deeds and pride of country as subject matter. With such success behind him he began considering the opportunities of a post wherever one might fall vacant. This aspect of his career would preoccupy him for the rest of his life. He suffered the restlessness of the composer/conductor forever travelling, forever worried about money, forever weighing up the advantages and disadvantages of either being a freelance artist or having a permanent position. These concerns were exacerbated when, from January 1881, he had a wife and in due course, four children to support. In the period leading to his first successful application (Coblenz) he was to suffer the disappointments of rejection from the towns of Mainz, Elberfeld and Aachen. It was the highly influential Ferdinand Hiller who played a role in recommending Bruch to Coblenz, where he began work on 2 September 1865 as Director of the Royal Institute for Music and of the Coblenz Subscription Concerts, ten each season between October and March. He stayed for just two seasons, during which time he produced the original version and first revision of his first violin concerto in G minor Op.26. By October 1867 he was in a new post at Sondershausen, as the manuscript of the concerto states twice in the following inscription:

Komponiert 1866 in Koblenz, umgearbeitet 1867. I Auff[ührung] (in der alten Form) Febr. 1867 in Koblenz. Beendigt Herbst (im October) 1867 (in Sondershausen). Von Joachim auf dem Niederrh.[einischen] Musikfest in Köln gespielt (Mai 1868).
Sondershausen 22 Oct. 1867 M.B.

[Composed 1866 in Coblenz, reworked 1867. First performance (in the old form) Febr. 1867 in Coblenz. Finished Autumn (in October) 1867 (in Sondershausen). Played by Joachim in Cologne at the Lower Rhine Music Festival (May 1868).
Sondershausen 22 Oct. 1867 M.B.]

In its archives, Sondershausen's Castle Museum also has a solo violin part for this concerto written in a copyist's hand. It was made for the Concertmeister (orchestral leader) Ulrich, but it may well be the one which Joachim and Bruch used in that autumn of 1867 to make the final changes to the final published version. It is heavily annotated in red ink in the composer's hand, beginning with the opus number which is changed from Op.24 to Op.26 (a similar change can be seen on the manuscript full score now in New York's Pierpont Morgan Museum as part of the Mary Flagler Collection). There are many cuts but the original versions, more extended or more elaborate, are visible. One can also discern bowing changes and a more extensive first movement cadenza, while the original tempo indication for the first movement is changed from *Introduction (quasi Fantasia)* to its current title *Vorspiel* with its speed increased from *Allegro molto moderato* to *Allegro moderato*. This solo part (entitled *Violino principale* and with orchestral cues included) was possibly used by Ulrich on 22 March 1868 at a concert in Sondershausen's Theatre under the composer's direction to celebrate Princess Elizabeth's birthday. This may well have been the second performance of the final version for it was only two months since Joachim played it for the first time in Bremen on 7 January. The manuscript is dedicated to 'Herrn Concertmeister Ulrich zur Erinnerung' on 19 October 1867, just three days before one of the dates listed in the detailed inscription on the full score of the final version. Therefore this manuscript of the solo part marks a step on the road which this piece took before it achieved its final form, and we see Bruch responding to advice sought from the eminent violinists of his day, Otto von Königslow, Ferdinand David, Joseph Joachim, and perhaps Concertmeister Ulrich. Karl Wilhelm Ulrich was born in Leipzig on 10 April 1815, the son of an instrument maker. He studied violin with Heinrich August Matthäi and in 1847, after living and working in Magdeburg, was appointed to the post of leader of the Court Orchestra in Sondershausen (Concertmeister der Fürstlichen Hofkapelle in Sondershausen). On 26 November 1874 he died, still in post after 27 years, in the town of Stendal during a concert tour, but is buried in Sondershausen.

In succession to Friedrich Marpurg (1825–1884), Max Bruch was First Court Conductor in Sondershausen (erster fürstlicher Hofkapellmeister) for three years from the autumn of 1867 to the autumn of 1870 in the service of Princess Elisabeth of Schwarzburg-Sondershausen. He was joined there by his sister Mathilde, who took upon herself the role of housekeeper as well as helping him with artistic matters. Exactly as he had done in Coblenz, Bruch did not cease his activities as a composer when he took up the baton in Sondershausen. The G minor violin concerto and the Symphony No.1 in E flat major Op.28 were both begun in Coblenz and completed in his new residence. The conductor Hermann Levi had persuaded Bruch to write in both concerto and symphonic forms in order to develop his expertise and broaden his experience away from the choral field in which the young man was largely making his mark. Hermann Kretschmar referred to the symphony as 'one of the best known of the period' (Führer durch den Konzertsaal, 1890), which in turn begs an interesting question: who was composing symphonies during the 1850s and 1860s? As far as the standard concert repertoire (overshadowed by Beethoven and Schubert) is concerned, there appears to be a 'black hole' during the quarter century between Schumann's fourth (and last) symphony written in 1851 and Brahms' first in 1876, assuming that one ignores the works of those of lesser renown such as Spohr, Raff, Rubinstein, Sullivan, Gade, and Bruch himself. Today their symphonies may have been recorded, but they rarely find their way into concert programmes. While it is true that during the 1860s Tchaikovsky and Bruckner had each written their first symphonies and Dvorak his first two, their careers were not yet established, and these works made little impact, either at the time or since especially when compared to the last three symphonies each composer subsequently produced. Little wonder then that Brahms delayed for so long before revealing his first symphony to the world.

Meanwhile the first performance of Bruch's first symphony, from manuscript score and parts, took place in Sondershausen on 26 July 1868, and the work was dedicated to Brahms. At this point the discovery of the Intermezzo in the orchestral library of the Lohorchester in Sondershausen takes on an interesting significance. I was first alerted to the possible existence of this work by a letter written by Bruch to his friend Rudolf von Beckerath dated 2 August 1870 from his hillside garden house, a building sadly no longer extant. By this time Bruch had completed his second symphony and was not short of offers from publishers to produce and distribute his music, much of which tended to be choral works with subject matter inspired by the Franco-Prussian war which was raging at the time. In the autumn of 1870 Cranz brought out the patriotic choruses entitled *Das Lied vom deutschen Kaiser* for chorus and orchestra, and in his letter Bruch summarised to von Beckerath what other works were nearing fruition.

Many sketches for the third symphony (**in E major including the Intermezzo in B major from the first symphony**) are already lying around; I am looking forward to and cling to the thought that, having completed the hard work on [the opera] *Hermione*, I shall holiday in the New Year of 1871, either here in my charmingly appointed hillside garden house, or on the Rhine, or anywhere else where I might be able to recover from the [second] symphony. Symphony No.2 will be Op.36, the choruses Op.37, Symphony No.3 Op.38, some songs Op.39, and *Hermione* Op.40.

In fact the songs, subsequently described as five Lieder for mixed chorus, moved up to become Op.38, the choral ballad *Dithyrambe* became Op.39, while the third symphony was not completed until the conductor of the Symphony Society of New York, Leopold Damrosch, commissioned it from Bruch ten years later. When it appeared it carried the opus number 51, and its first performance took place in New York on 17 December 1883. Bruch's reference to the Intermezzo in B major as coming from his <u>first</u> symphony can be confirmed from the advertisements for its first performance in Sondershausen on 26 July 1868, for example in the newspaper *Der Deutsche* No.87 published on 21 July 1868, in which the full programme is listed including the details of the new symphony's movements

Symphony (E flat major) by Max Bruch. (New, Manuscript, for the first time)
I Allegro maestoso. II Intermezzo (Andante con moto). III Scherzo. IV Grave und Allegro guerriero (Finale).

A similar advertisement in No.97 of the same paper carries the same details for the performance which took place three weeks later on 16 August. It follows that this Intermezzo (191 bars in length) was evidently the original second movement of the first symphony with its very curious, almost Schubertian key relationship where the tonic key of Eb becomes (by changing enharmonically to D#) the third degree in B major. In its original form therefore, it also follows that the *Grave* was the introduction to the Finale. Before the work was published Bruch changed his mind and labelled this *Grave* the third movement, though with a timpani roll it still leads into the Finale without a break. In the event the Intermezzo found no place in the third symphony either, and has lain in Sondershausen ever since. The material, in a copyist's hand, consists of a 'Directionstimme' (to be used by the leader of the orchestra) and a total of 27 parts for strings (3.3.2.2.2.), double winds, four horns, two trumpets, and timpani. When the symphony was performed again, on 6 June 1869 at the fourth concert of the Loh Orchestra's summer season, it was advertised as Sinfonie (Op.28). The use of an opus number may indicate that it was now published. It also means that, with the Intermezzo having been discarded, the audience at this third performance was hearing the final version of the symphony with its *Grave* introduction to the finale posing as a somewhat unsatisfactorily short slow movement in the work. More evidence lies further ahead on 15 August, for at this fourteenth concert the discarded movement appears on its own as the fourth item in the programme – Intermezzo (B major) for orchestra by Max Bruch.

By the middle of 1870 Bruch was beginning to feel restless in his Court post at Sondershausen, for although he never changed his regard for the Princess or her family, he did become impatient with Court officialdom. One of the circumstances he took into consideration before making the decision to leave the security of the fixed post was the success he was having with the publication and distribution of his music, in particular by the firm of Simrock with whom he would have an exclusive association for almost the rest of his life. By the beginning of October 1870 Bruch had made up his mind to leave Sondershausen. In spite of an instinctive preference for material and financial security, he was now going to Berlin, and a new phase of his life was about to begin. On Reinecke's recommendation his successor at Sondershausen was Max Erdmannsdörfer (1848–1905), who held the post from February 1871 until 1880.

The archives of Sondershausen's Castle Museum also house a collection of concert programmes of the Fürstliche Hofkapelle, not entirely complete, but by using issues of the newspaper *Der Deutsche. Sondershäuser Zeitung nebst Regierungs- und Intelligenzblatt für das Fürstenthum Schwarzburg-Sondershausen* as a further source, it is possible to reconstruct the programmes of the concerts conducted by Max Bruch during his tenure as Court Conductor in the town from 1867–1870. Although there is some occasional discrepancy between the programme books and the newspaper, the assumption has been made that advertisements in the latter (dated a few days before each concert) reflect last minute changes in programme. Two concerts consisting of different programmes were given each Sunday, the first in the afternoon at 3.30pm and the second in the evening at 8pm. There is a fairly formulaic pattern to the style and content of these programmes. The afternoon event was of a more serious style and content reflected in its choice of works, whereas the evening concerts invariably concluded with three light dances, a waltz, polka, march, gallop or quadrille. On a few occasions the evening programme was repeated a week later at the same time. When Carl Schroeder took up the Hofkapellmeister's post in 1890, bringing with him new players such as Willi Burmester from Rotterdam as well as new pupils for the town's Conservatoire, the conducting of the concerts was shared, with the orchestral leader (in this instance Concertmeister Carl Corbach) taking the lighter evening programmes.

Bruch was fairly catholic in his programming. He conducted all the Schumann and Beethoven symphonies (though the latter's 9th was played, as was customary at the time, without the choral finale), as well as works by Berlioz, Mendelssohn, Schubert, Mozart, Gade, Spohr, Raff, Reinecke and some of his own. New music was performed, often still unpublished and therefore from manuscript parts. The two orchestral Serenades by Brahms were planned, but in the event only the first was played. Soloists often came from within the ranks of Sondershausen's Court musicians, and it was fairly common for special arrangements of works to be made for them to play, such as one for tuba from *Elijah* or a work by Bach for double bass rechristened *Méditation*. Vocalists in the Loh Concerts were not credited, but because their contributions were mostly operatic arias it is fair to assume that these soloists were singers from Sondershausen's Theatre. This institution also supplied its chorus to sing popular choruses by Auber, Gounod or Meyerbeer. Complete finales from operas were given such as the one from *Don Giovanni*, while Bruch even performed works by Wagner and Liszt. Given his growing hostile attitude towards the music of these two composers, it could well have been such encounters with their music which finally caused him to repudiate this school of the New Germans once and for all. His first Concert im Loh, the second of the season, was on Sunday 23 June 1867. The complete list of programmes, with Bruch's own compositions in bold type, is as follows.

## 2. Concert im Loh: Sunday 23 June 1867 afternoon

| | |
|---|---|
| Overture – *Fair Melusine* | Mendelssohn |
| Passacaglia for organ by Bach | orch. H Esser, although according to *Der Deutsche* of 18.6.1867, the Fantasy on Russian folksongs *Kamarinskaya* by Glinka was played |
| Symphony No.4 in D minor | Schumann |
| **Introduction from the opera *Die Loreley*** Bruch | **(first time at the concerts)** |
| Two Entr'actes from *Rosamunde* | Schubert    (first time at the concerts) |
| Overture – *Consecration of the House* | Beethoven |

## 2. Sunday 23 June 1867 evening

| | |
|---|---|
| Overture – *Merry Wives of Windsor* | Nicolai |
| Duet from *Les Huguenots* | Meyerbeer |
| Market chorus from *La Muette de Portici* | Auber |
| *Invitation to the Dance* | Weber |
| Overture – *Fra Diavolo* | Auber |
| *Faust* – Quadrille | Strauss |
| March: *Gruss an Breslau* | Faust |
| *Kieselack* Polka | Conradi |

## 3. Concert im Loh: Sunday 30 June 1867 afternoon

| | | |
|---|---|---|
| Overture to the opera *Jessonda* | Spohr | |
| Cello Concerto (1st movement) | Romberg | (Soloist: Hofmusicus Graf) |
| Masonic Funeral Music | Mozart | (first time at the concerts) |
| Overture – *Aladdin* | Reinecke | |
| Symphony No. 9 in D minor | Beethoven | (first three movements only) |
| Overture – *Leonore* (No.3) | Beethoven | |

## 3. Concert im Loh: Sunday 30 June 1867 evening

| | |
|---|---|
| Overture to the opera *Der Vampyr* | Marschner |
| Romance from *Dinorah* | Meyerbeer |
| Duet from *Faust* | Gounod although according to *Der Deutsche* of 25.6.1867 ballet music from *Stradella* by Flotow was played |
| Finale Act 1: *Don Giovanni* | Mozart |
| Overture – *La part du diable* | Auber |
| Waltz: *Abschied von München* | Gungl |
| Polka-Mazurka: *Sand in die Augen* | Conradi |
| Polka: *Auf Ferienreisen* | Strauss |

Due to the death on 29 June 1867 of the reigning Prince Friedrich Günther of Schwarzburg-Rudolstadt, the concert planned for 30 June was postponed for one week to 7 July. The programme was changed to:

## 3. Concert im Loh: Sunday 7 July 1867 afternoon

| | | |
|---|---|---|
| Overture to the opera *Faust* | Spohr | |
| Fantasia for cello | Servais | (Soloist: Hofmusicus Graf) |
| Masonic Funeral Music | Mozart | (first time at the concerts) |
| Overture – *Aladdin* | Reinecke | |
| Symphony No. 9 in D minor | Beethoven | (first three movements only) |
| Overture – *Leonore* (No.3) | Beethoven | |

## 3. Concert im Loh: Sunday 7 July 1867 evening

unchanged from that advertised in *Der Deutsche* of 25.6.1867 for Sunday 30 June 1867 afternoon

## 4. Concert im Loh: Sunday 14 July 1867 afternoon

| | |
|---|---|
| Overture – *Medea* | Bargiel |
| Aria from *Elijah* | Mendelssohn |
| Symphony No.4 in Bb | Gade |

| | |
|---|---|
| Overture – *Anacreon* | Cherubini |
| March and Chorus from *Ruins of Athens* | Beethoven |
| Overture – *Genoveva* | Schumann |

## 4. Concert im Loh: Sunday 14 July 1867 evening

| | |
|---|---|
| Overture – *La Dame blanche* | Boieldieu |
| Duet from *Les Huguenots* | Meyerbeer |
| Soldiers' Chorus from *Faust* | Gounod |
| Finale: *Lucia di Lammermoor* | Donizetti |
| Overture – *La Muette de Portici* | Auber |
| Quadrille: *Unruhige Zeiten* | Conradi |
| Turkish March | Mozart |
| Polka: *Officiers-Kränzchen* | Gungl |

## 5. Concert im Loh: Sunday 21 July 1867 afternoon

| | |
|---|---|
| Overture – *Egmont* | Beethoven |
| Chorus from *St Paul* | Mendelssohn |
| Symphony No.40 in G minor | Mozart |
| Overture – *Olympia* | Spontini |
| Entr'act & Morning Song from *Joseph* | Méhul |
| Overture – *Der Freischütz* | Weber |

although according to *Der Deutsche* of 16.7.1867 this programme became

| | |
|---|---|
| Overture – *Die Zauberflöte* | Mozart |
| Symphony No.3 in A minor (*Scottish*) | Mendelssohn |
| Prelude to *Lohengrin* | Wagner |
| Clarinet concerto No.4 | Spohr     (Soloist: Hofmusicus Schomburg) |
| Overture – *Olympia* | Spontini |

## 5. Concert im Loh: Sunday 21 July 1867 evening

| | |
|---|---|
| Overture – *Das Nachtlager von Granada* | Kreutzer |
| Aria from *Hans Heiling* | Marschner |
| *Schiller* March | Meyerbeer   [*Torch Dance*, according to *Der Deutsche*, 16.7.1867] |

| | |
|---|---|
| Finale Act 2: *Don Giovanni* | Mozart |
| Overture – *Zampa* | Hérold |
| Waltz: *Isar-Lieder* | Gungl |
| Galopp: *Wandrers Lust* | Frehlde |
| *Irenen*-Polka | Faust |

## 6. Concert im Loh: Sunday 28 July 1867 afternoon

| | |
|---|---|
| Overture – *Calm Sea and Prosperous Voyage* | Mendelssohn |
| Toccata in F for organ | Bach orch. H Esser   (first time at the concerts) |
| Duo Op.140 | Schubert orch. Joachim   (first time at the concerts) |
| Overture – *Die Zauberflöte* | Mozart |
| Clarinet concerto in F minor | Spohr (Adagio & 1st movt)     Soloist: Hofmusicus Schomburg |
| Concert overture in A | Rietz |

although, according to *Der Deutsche* of 23.7.1867, this programme became:

| | |
|---|---|
| Overture – *Calm Sea and Prosperous Voyage* | Mendelssohn |
| Toccata in F for organ | Bach orch. H. Esser    (first time at the concerts) |
| Duo Op.140 | Schubert orch. Joachim (first time at the concerts) |
| Violin concerto | Beethoven    Soloist: Concertmeister Ulrich |
| Overture – *Die Zauberflöte* | Mozart |

### 6. Concert im Loh: Sunday 28 July 1867 evening

| | |
|---|---|
| Overture and Nocturne from *Martha* | Flotow |
| Trio from *Robert le Diable* | Meyerbeer |
| Waltz and Chorus from *Faust* | Gounod |
| Symphony No.8 in F | Beethoven |
| Overture | Kalliwoda |
| Waltz: *Freudengrüsse* | Strauss |
| Polka-Mazurka: *Herzblättchen* | Gungl |
| Polka: *Die Jägerin* | Ziehrer |

According to *Der Deutsche* of 27.7.1867 and its reports entitled *Verschiedenes* (Miscellaneous), Max Bruch was in Zurich where, at a Festival, he conducted a highly successful ('ganz besonders glänzend') performance (with over 700 participants) of his *Scenen aus der Frithjofssage* Op.23.

### 7. Concert im Loh: Sunday 4 August 1867 afternoon

| | |
|---|---|
| Overture – *Julius Caesar* | Schumann |
| Melancolie for solo horn | Klauer    Soloist: Kammermusicus Pohle |
| Symphony No.3 *Eroica* | Beethoven |
| Toccata in F for organ | Bach orch. H. Esser    (repeated by public demand) |
| Violin concerto in Hungarian style | Joachim (1st movement only)   Soloist: Hofmusicus Richard Himmelstoss |
| Overture – *In the Highlands* | Gade |

### 7. Concert im Loh: Sunday 4 August 1867 evening

| | |
|---|---|
| Overture – *Der Vampyr* | Lindpaintner |
| Romance from *Dinorah* | Meyerbeer |
| Ballet from *William Tell* | Rossini |
| Finale from *Stradella* | Flotow |
| Overture – *The Caliph of Baghdad* | Boieldieu |
| Polka: *Die Antilope* | Gungl |
| Waltz: *Empfehlungsbriefe* | Pohle |
| *Saison* Polka-Mazurka | Mendel |

### 8. Concert im Loh: Sunday 11 August 1867 afternoon

| | |
|---|---|
| Overture – *Coriolanus* | Beethoven |
| Larghetto for cello | Mozart    Soloist: Kammermusicus Himmelstoss |
| Symphony No.2 *Ocean* | Rubinstein |
| Overture – *1001 Nights* | Taubert |

| | | |
|---|---|---|
| Symphony No.8 | Schubert | (first time at the concerts) |
| Overture – *King Lear* | Berlioz | |

## 8. Concert im Loh: Sunday 11 August 1867 evening
Programme as Sunday 4 August 1867 evening

## 9. Concert im Loh: Sunday 18 August 1867 afternoon

| | | |
|---|---|---|
| Overture – *Jessonda* | Spohr | |
| Fantasia for flute | König | Soloist: Kammermusicus Heindl |
| Symphony No.3 in A minor [*Scottish*] | Mendelssohn | |
| Suite [No.3] in D | Bach | |
| Overture – *Fidelio* | Beethoven | |

## 9. Concert im Loh: Sunday 18 August 1867 evening

| | |
|---|---|
| Overture – *Robespierre* | Litolff |
| Serenade for horn and flute | Titt'l |
| Trio (Act 2) from *Der Freischütz* | Weber |
| Introduction from *William Tell* | Rossini |
| Overture – *Die Grossfürstin* | Flotow |
| March: *Fürst Bariatinsky* | Strauss |
| *Faust* Quadrille | Strauss |
| Polka: *Aurora Ball* | Gungl |

## 10. Concert im Loh: Sunday 25 August 1867 afternoon

| | | |
|---|---|---|
| Overture – *Prometheus* | Beethoven | |
| Prelude: *Lohengrin* | Wagner | |
| Symphony No.2 in C | Schumann | |
| Overture – *Medea* | Cherubini | |
| Oboe concerto | Diethe | (Adagio and Rondo) |
| | | Soloist: Hofmusicus Hoffmann |
| Overture – *William Tell* | Rossini | |

## 10. Concert im Loh: Sunday 25 August 1867 evening

| | |
|---|---|
| Overture – *Die Lichtensteiner* | Lindpaintner |
| Duet from *Faust* | Gounod |
| Trio with chorus from *Der Freischütz* | Weber |
| *Schwerdterweihe* from *Les Huguenots* | Meyerbeer |
| Overture – *Omar und Leila* | Fesca |
| *Catharina* Quadrille | Bilse |
| Polka-Mazurka: *Die Lachtaube* | Strauss |
| Galopp: *Zechbrüder* | Stasny |

## 11. Concert im Loh: Sunday 1 September 1867 afternoon

| | | |
|---|---|---|
| Overture – *Maria Stuart* | Vierling | |
| Romance for violin and orchestra | Beethoven | Soloist: Concertmeister Ulrich |
| Symphony [No. 41] in C with the fugal finale | Mozart | |
| Overture – *Nachklänge von Ossian* | Gade | |
| Violin concerto | Beethoven | Soloist: Concertmeister Ulrich |
| Overture – *Oberon* | Weber | |

### 11. Concert im Loh: Sunday 1 September 1867 evening

| | | |
|---|---|---|
| Overture – *Die Filibustier* | Lobe | |
| Introduction from *Zampa* | Hérold | |
| Cavatina for trumpet from *Torquato Tasso* | Donizetti | Soloist: Hofmusicus Beck |
| Finale: Act 1 *Lohengrin* | Wagner | |
| Overture – *Alessandro Stradella* | Flotow | |
| Waltz: *Abschied von St Petersburg* | Strauss | |
| Polka: *Etwas kleines* | Strauss | |
| Galopp: *Das Glöcklin des Eremiten* | Bilse | |

### 12. Concert im Loh: Sunday 8 September 1867 afternoon

| | |
|---|---|
| Overture – *Leonora No.1* | Beethoven |
| Overture – *Leonora No.2* | Beethoven |
| *Schiller* Festmarsch | Meyerbeer |
| Overture – *The Hebrides* | Mendelssohn |
| Symphony [No.9] in C | Schubert |

### 12. Concert im Loh: Sunday 8 September 1867 evening

| | |
|---|---|
| Overture – *Die Hermannsschlacht* | Chélard |
| *Coronation* March from *Le Prophète* | Meyerbeer |
| Duet from *William Tell* | Rossini |
| Introduction from *Euryanthe* | Weber |
| Overture – *Die beiden Nächte* | Boieldieu |
| *Conferenz* Quadrille | Keler-Bela |
| Waltz: *Die Prager* | Gungl |
| *Elfen* Polka | Strauss |

### 13. Concert im Loh: Sunday 15 September 1867 afternoon

| | | |
|---|---|---|
| Overture – *Iphigenie in Aulis* | Gluck | |
| Concertino for tuba | König | Soloist: Hofmusicus Ziese |
| Overture, Scherzo and Finale | Schumann | |
| Overture – *Dame Kobold* | Reinecke | |
| Symphony No.8 in F | Beethoven | |

### 13. Concert im Loh: Sunday 15 September 1867 evening

| | | |
|---|---|---|
| Overture – *Les Huguenots* | Meyerbeer | |
| Military concerto for clarinet | Bärmann | Soloist: Militair-Hautboist Strebe |
| Quartet from *Zampa* | Hérold | |
| Finale Act 1 *Tannhäuser* | Wagner | |
| Overture – *Ferdinand Cortez* | Spontini | |
| *Erinnerung an Birda*: Quadrille | Stein | |
| *Motoren* Waltzes | Strauss | |
| *Lucifer* Polka | Strahle | |

### 14. Concert im Loh: Sunday 22 September 1867 afternoon

| | | |
|---|---|---|
| Overture – *Manfred* | Schumann | |
| Symphony No. 9 in D minor | Beethoven | (first three movements only) |
| Symphony No.8 | Schubert | |
| Violin concerto No.6 | Spohr | Soloist: Hofmusicus Richard Himmelstoss |
| Overture – *Midsummer Night's Dream* | Mendelssohn | |

### 14. Concert im Loh: Sunday 22 September 1867 evening

| | |
|---|---|
| Overture – *Der Berggeist* | Spohr |
| Concerto for two oboes | Kiel        Soloists: Hofmusicus Hofmann |
| | and Militair-Hautboist Köhler |
| | |
| Ballet from *Le Prophète* | Meyerbeer |
| Introduction and Bridal Chorus | Wagner |
| from *Lohengrin* | |
| Overture – *Das Thal von Andorra* | Halévy |
| *Nocturnen* Quadrille | Strauss |
| *Die Unzertrennlichen* (Waltz) | Strauss |
| *Helenen* Polka | Bilse |

### 15. Concert im Loh: Sunday 29 September 1867 afternoon

| | |
|---|---|
| *Jubel*-Overture | Weber |
| **Prelude to the opera *Die Loreley*** | **Bruch** |
| Fantasy for double bass | Ernst arr. Stein    Soloist: Kammermusikus |
| | Simon |
| | |
| Symphony No.1 in C minor | Gade |
| Overture – *King Stephen* | Beethoven |
| Ballade and Polonaise for violin | Vieuxtemps    Soloist: Concertmeister Ulrich |
| Overture – *Tannhäuser* | Wagner |

### 15. Concert im Loh: Sunday 29 September 1867 evening (with festive illumination of the Loh)

| | |
|---|---|
| *Festive* Overture | Ries |
| Aria from *Hans Heiling* | Marschner |
| Ballet from *Le Prophète* | Meyerbeer |
| March from *Tannhäuser* | Wagner |
| Overture – *Nurmahal* | Spontini |
| *Wiedersehen* Polka | Herzog |
| *Marien* Waltzes | Gungl |
| *Russischer Zapfenstreich* | |

### Concert in Sondershausen Theatre: Sunday 22 March 1868 evening 7 o'clock to celebrate Princess Elizabeth's birthday. Proceeds donated to the orchestra's widows pension fund

| | |
|---|---|
| Overture – *Calm sea and prosperous voyage* | Mendelssohn |
| Scene and aria 'Ah perfido!' from *Fidelio* | Beethoven    Soloist: Frau Pelli-Sicora |
| Overture – *Manfred* | Schumann |
| **Violin concerto No.1 in G minor** | **Bruch** (new, for the first time) |
| **Op.26** | Soloist: Concertmeister Ulrich |
| *Frithjof* **[Op.23]** | **Bruch**    Soloists: Frau Pelli-Sicora, |
| | Herr Sameck, Sondershausen |
| | Male Voice Choral Society |

### 1. Concert im Loh: Sunday 31 May 1868 afternoon

| | |
|---|---|
| Overture – *Hamlet* | Gade |
| Bridal March from *Midsummer Night's* | Mendelssohn |
| *Dream* | |
| Symphony No.4 in Bb | Beethoven |
| Overture to a Tragedy | Bargiel |

| Concerto No.8 for flute | Fürstenau (new) | Soloist: Kammermusikus Heindl |
|---|---|---|
| Concert-Ouverture | Rietz | |

### 1. Concert im Loh: Sunday 31 May 1868 evening

| Overture – *Fra Diavolo* | Auber |
|---|---|
| Introduction to the same opera | Auber |
| Aria from *Ernani* | Verdi |
| Waltz from *Faust* | Gounod |
| Overture – *Martha* | Flotow |
| Waltz: *Abschied von München* | Gungl |
| March | Bilse |
| Polka | Strauss |

### 2. Concert im Loh: Sunday 7 June 1868 afternoon

| Overture – *Die Abenceragen* | Cherubini |
|---|---|
| Two Entr'actes from *Rosamunde* | Schubert |
| Symphony No.4 in A [*Italian*] | Mendelssohn |
| Overture – *Fidelio* | Beethoven |
| Toccata for organ | Bach orch. H Esser |
| Overture – *Genoveva* | Schumann |

### 2. Concert im Loh: Sunday 7 June 1868 evening

| Overture – *La Muette de Portici* | Auber |
|---|---|
| Market Chorus from the same opera | Auber |
| *Schiller* March | Meyerbeer |
| Finale Act 1 from *Tannhäuser* | Wagner |
| Overture – *Zampa* | Hérold |
| Waltz | Gungl |
| March | Faust |
| Polka | Strauss |

### 3. Concert im Loh: Sunday 14 June 1868 afternoon

| Overture – *Medea* | Bargiel | |
|---|---|---|
| Prelude to *Lohengrin* | Wagner | |
| Symphony No.6 *Pastoral* | Beethoven | |
| Overture – *Nachklänge von Ossian* | Gade | |
| Concerto for violin No.2 | David | Soloist: Hofmusicus Reinboth |
| Overture – *Euryanthe* | Weber | |

### 3. Concert im Loh: Sunday 14 June 1868 evening

| Overture – *Die Felsenmühle* | Reissiger |
|---|---|
| *Geburtstags*-March [Birthday March] | Taubert |
| Ballet from *Le Prophète* | Meyerbeer |
| Duet from *Faust* | Gounod |
| Overture – *Stradella* | Flotow |
| *Die Prager* Waltz | Gungl |
| *Catharinen*-Quadrille | Bilse |
| Polka | Keler-Bela |

### 4. Concert im Loh: Sunday 21 June 1868 afternoon

| | |
|---|---|
| Overture – *Faust* | Spohr |
| Funeral March Op.103 | Mendelssohn   (first time at the concerts) |
| Symphony No.1 in Bb [*Spring*] | Schumann |
| Overture and Entr'act *König Manfred* | Reinecke   (new, first time at the concerts) |
| Concerto for Violoncello | Grützmacher     Soloist: Hofmusikus Graf |
| Overture – *King Stephen* | Beethoven |

### 4. Concert im Loh: Sunday 21 June 1868 evening

| | |
|---|---|
| Overture – *Merry Wives of Windsor* | Nicolai |
| Duet from *Les Huguenots* | Meyerbeer |
| Ballet from *William Tell* | Rossini |
| Soldiers' Chorus from *Faust* | Gounod |
| Overture – *Ruy Blas* | Mendelssohn |
| Polka: *Gruss an Warschau* | Bilse |
| *Faust*-Quadrille | Strauss |
| *Motoren*-Waltz | Gungl |

### 5. Concert im Loh: Sunday 28 June 1868 afternoon

| | |
|---|---|
| Overture – *Bride of Messina* | Schumann |
| Serenade Op. 16 | Brahms   (first time at the concerts) |
| Concert-Overture No.2 in A | Hiller   (new, first time at the concerts) |
| Aria from *Elijah* for tuba | Mendelssohn   (arranged and played by Hofmusikus Ziese) |
| Symphony No. 5 in C minor | Beethoven |

### 5. Concert im Loh: Sunday 28 June 1868 evening

| | |
|---|---|
| Overture – *Der Berggeist* | Spohr |
| Introduction from *Zampa* | Hérold |
| Elsa's Wedding March from *Lohengrin* | Wagner |
| Finale (Act 1) from *Don Giovanni* | Mozart |
| Overture – *Sémiramis* | Catel |
| Waltz: *Ideal und Leben* | Gungl |
| *Schönbrunner* Quadrille | Strauss |
| *Myrthen*-Polka | Conradi |

### Revised programme for the 5. Loh afternoon concert

| | |
|---|---|
| Overture – *Olympia* | Spontini |
| Entr'act from the opera *König Manfred* | Reinecke |
| Suite No.3 in D | Bach |
| Concert-Overture No.2 in A | Hiller   (new, first time at the concerts) |
| Aria from *Elijah* for tuba | Mendelssohn   (arranged and played by Hofmusikus Ziese) |
| Symphony No. 5 in C minor | Beethoven |

### 6. Concert im Loh: Sunday 5 July 1868 afternoon

| | |
|---|---|
| Concert-Overture – *The Naiades* | Sterndale Bennet |
| Prelude: *Die Meistersinger von Nürnberg* | Wagner |
| Duo Op. 140 | Schubert orch. Joachim |
| Overture – *Iphigenie in Aulis* | Gluck |

Concerto for violin                           Rubinstein   Soloist: Hofmusikus
                                                              Himmelstoß
Overture – *Consecration of the House*        Beethoven

## 6. Concert im Loh: Sunday 5 July 1868 evening
Overture – *Lichtenstein*                     Lindpaintner
Trio from *Robert le Diable*                  Meyerbeer
Ballet from *William Tell*                    Rossini
Finale from *Fra Diavolo*                     Auber
Overture – *Die Grossfürstin*                 Flotow
*Victoria*-Waltz                              Bilse
*Astha*-Quadrille                             Dregert
*Alma*-Polka                                  Hertel

## 7. Concert im Loh: Sunday 12 July 1868 afternoon
Overture – *Athalie*                          Mendelssohn
Concertino for two oboes                      Kummer   Soloists: Hofmusikus Hoffmann
                                                              and Capellist Köhler
Symphony No.3 in Eb [*Rhenish*]               Schumann
Overture – *Coriolanus*                       Beethoven
*Kamarinskaya*, Fantasy on Russian folksongs Glinka
Overture – *Roman Carnival*                   Berlioz

## 7. Concert im Loh: Sunday 12 July 1868 evening
Overture – *Rienzi*                           Wagner
Duet from *Les Huguenots*                     Meyerbeer
Aria from *Stradella*                         Flotow
Finale from *Zampa*                           Hérold
Overture – *Le Domino noir*                   Auber
*Norddeutsche Weisen* Waltz                   Gungl
*Troubadour*-Quadrille                        Leutner
*Parade*-March                                Bartholomäus

## 8. Concert im Loh: Sunday 19 July 1868 afternoon
Overture – *Im Frühling*                      Vierling
Passacaglia for organ                         Bach arr. von Esser
Symphony [No.39] in Eb                        Mozart
Overture – *The Ruins of Athens*              Beethoven
Concertino for trumpet                        Wittmann   Soloist: Hofmusikus Beck
Suite in D minor No. 1                        Lachner

## 8. Concert im Loh: Sunday 19 July 1868 evening
Overture – *Yelva*                            Reissiger
March from *Tannhäuser*                       Wagner
Trio from *Der Freischütz*                    Weber
Introduction from *William Tell*              Rossini
Overture – *Das Nachtlager in Granada*        Kreutzer
*Träume auf dem Ozean*                        Gungl
*Jubelfest* March                             Leutner
Polka                                         Ressel

### 9. Concert im Loh: Sunday 26 July 1868 afternoon

| | | |
|---|---|---|
| Overture – *Vom blonden Eckbert* | Rudorff | |
| Concerto for clarinet (Adagio and first movement) | Spohr | Soloist: Hofmusikus Schomburg |
| **Symphony [No.1] in Eb [Op.28]** | **Bruch** | (new, manuscript parts, for the first time) |
| Overture – *Bride of Messina* | Schumann | (for the first time) |
| Entr'acte (No. 3) from the music to *Egmont* | Beethoven | |
| Overture – *St Paul* | Mendelssohn | |

### 9. Concert im Loh: Sunday 26 July 1868 evening

| | |
|---|---|
| Overture – *Der Vampyr* | Marschner |
| March from *Le Prophète* | Meyerbeer |
| Introduction from *Euryanthe* | Weber |
| Finale from *Lohengrin* | Wagner |
| Overture – *Le Bal masqué* | Auber |
| Polka | Bilse |
| Quadrille | Strauss |
| March | Saro |

### 10. Concert im Loh: Sunday 2 August 1868 afternoon

| | | |
|---|---|---|
| Overture – *Rosamunde* | Schubert | |
| Pastorale from the *Christmas Oratorio* | Bach | |
| Symphony No. 2 in D | Beethoven | |
| *Lustspiel*-Overture | Rietz | |
| *Melancolie Morceau élégant* for cello | Schuberth | Soloist: Kammermusikus Himmelstoss |
| Overture – *Ruler of the Spirits* | Weber | |

### 10. Concert im Loh: Sunday 2 August 1868 evening

| | |
|---|---|
| Overture – *Der Freischütz* | Weber |
| Introduction and Fishermen's chorus from *La Muette de Portici* | Auber |
| Duet from *William Tell* | Rossini |
| Finale from *Lohengrin* | Wagner |
| Overture – *Ferdinand Cortez* | Spontini |
| Polka | Strauss |
| Waltz | Gungl |
| March | Faust |

### 11. Concert im Loh: Sunday 9 August 1868 afternoon

| | | |
|---|---|---|
| Kirchliche Fest-Ouverture on the chorale *Ein' feste Burg* | Nicolai | |
| Pastorale from the *Christmas Oratorio* | Bach | |
| Symphonic tone poem *Wallenstein* Op.10 | Rheinberger | (new, for the first time) |
| A *Faust* Overture | Wagner | |
| Introduction & Polonaise for horn on motives from *Der Freischütz* | Stein | Soloist: Kammermusikus Pohle |
| Overture – *1001 Nights* | Taubert | |

## 11. Concert im Loh: Sunday 9 August 1868 evening

| | |
|---|---|
| Overture – *Omar und Leila* | Fesca |
| Introduction and Romanze from *Templer und Jüdin* | Marschner |
| Entr'acte and Brautlied from *Lohengrin* | Wagner |
| Finale from Act 1 *Euryanthe* | Weber |
| Overture – *Filibustier* | Lobe |
| *Souvenir*-Quadrille | Leutner |
| *Festive* March | Bilse |
| *Rosamunden*-Polka | Herzog |

## 12. Concert im Loh: Sunday 16 August 1868 afternoon

| | | |
|---|---|---|
| Overture – *Vom blonden Eckbert* | Rudorff | |
| Symphony No.8 | Schubert | |
| **Violin concerto (op. 26) [No.1 in G minor]** | **Bruch** | Soloist: Concertmeister Uhlrich |
| **Symphony [No.1] in Eb [Op.28]** | **Bruch** | |

## 12. Concert im Loh: Sunday 16 August 1868 evening

| | |
|---|---|
| Overture | Kirchhoff |
| Introduction from *Der Postillion von Lonjumeau* | Adam |
| *Waffentanz* and Chorus from *Jessonda* | Spohr |
| Finale Act 2 from *Don Giovanni* | Mozart |
| Overture – *Le dieu et la bayadère* | Auber |
| *Astha*-Quadrille | Dregert |
| March | Stein |
| *Winterfreuden*-Gallop | Bilse |

## 13. Concert im Loh: Sunday 23 August 1868 afternoon

| | | |
|---|---|---|
| Overture – *In the Highlands* | Gade | |
| Concerto for two violins, cello and strings | Handel (for the first time) | |
| Symphony in D minor | Volkmann | |
| Overture – *Jota aragonesa* | Glinka | |
| *Marche funèbre* | Chopin | |
| *Méditation* for double bass | Bach | Soloist: Cammervirtuosen Simon |
| Overture – *William Tell* | Rossini | |

## 13. Concert im Loh: Sunday 23 August 1868 evening

| | |
|---|---|
| Overture – *Hans Heiling* | Marschner |
| Aria from *Faust* | Spohr |
| *Waffenweihe* from *Les Huguenots* | Meyerbeer |
| Finale from *Oberon* | Weber |
| Overture – *La Dame blanche* | Boieldieu |
| *Nachtfalter* – Waltz | Strauss |
| *Gruss von Breslau* – March | Faust |
| *Kieselack* – Polka | Conradi |

## 14. Concert im Loh Sunday 30 August 1868 afternoon

| | | |
|---|---|---|
| Overture, Scherzo and Finale | Schumann | |
| Concertino for flute | Hacke | Soloist: Kammermusikus Heindl |

Overture – *Calm sea and prosperous voyage* Mendelssohn
Symphony No. 7 in A    Beethoven

## 14. Concert im Loh Sunday 30 August 1868 evening
Overture – *Robespierre*    Litolff
Indian March    Meyerbeer
Trio from *Der Freischütz*    Weber
Finale from *Lucia di Lammermoor*    Donizetti
Overture – *Ruy Blas*    Mendelssohn
Waltz    Gungl
Quadrille    Conradi
Polka    Ziehrer

## 15. Concert im Loh: Sunday 6 September 1868 afternoon
Overture – *Medea*    Cherubini
Concertino for clarinet    Molique    Soloist: Hofmusikus Schomburg
Concerto for two violins, cello and    Handel
   strings
Overture – *Michelangelo*    Gade
Symphony No. 2 in C    Schumann

## 15. Concert im Loh: Sunday 6 September 1868 evening
Overture    Gade
Introduction to *Les Huguenots*    Meyerbeer
Trio from *Faust*    Gounod
Finale Act 3 *Lohengrin*    Wagner
Overture to *Faust*    Lindpaintner
*Königs*-Polonaise    Bilse
*Isar-Lieder* – Waltz    Gungl
*Irenen*-Polka    Strauss

## 16. Concert im Loh: Sunday 13 September 1868 afternoon
Canonic suite for strings    Grimm  (for the first time)
Sinfonia concertante for violin and viola  Mozart    Soloists: Concertmeister Uhlrich
   [K.364]    and Hofmusikus Himmelstoss
Concert-Overture in D minor    Volkland  (new, from manuscript parts, for
   the first time)
Symphony No. 9 in D minor    Beethoven  (first three movements only)
Overture – *Leonore* No.2    Beethoven

## 16. Concert im Loh: Sunday 13 September 1868 evening
Overture und Introduction to *Don*    Mozart
   *Giovanni*
Entr'acte and Hunting Song from *Dinorah* Meyerbeer
Variations for trumpet    Hartmann    Soloist: Hofmusikus Beck
March from *Athalia*    Mendelssohn
Overture – *Die Braut von Kynast*    Litolff
*Die Sprudler* – Waltz    Keler-Bela
*Jubilee* – March    Bilse
*Die Antilope* – Polka    Gungl

### 17. Concert im Loh: Sunday 20 September 1868 afternoon

| | |
|---|---|
| Overture – *Manfred* | Schumann |
| **Prelude to the opera *Die Loreley*** | **Bruch** |
| Symphony No. 3 in A minor [*Scottish*] | Mendelssohn |
| Overture – *Otto der Schütz* | Rudorff (new, for the first time) |
| Concertstück for four horns | Schumann    Soloists: Messrs Pohle, Bauer, Franke and Barthel |
| Overture – *Die Zauberflöte* | Mozart |

### 17. Concert im Loh: Sunday 20 September 1868 evening

| | |
|---|---|
| Overture – *Merry Wives of Windsor* | Nicolai |
| Aria from *Oberon* | Weber |
| Geburtstagsmarsch | Taubert |
| Symphonic poem: *Orpheus* | Liszt |
| Overture – *Martha* | Flotow |
| Waltz | Strauss |
| March | Leutner |
| Polka | Gungl |

### 18. Concert im Loh: Sunday 27 September 1868 afternoon

| | |
|---|---|
| *Jubel*-Overture | Weber |
| *Der Carneval von Venedig* for double bass | Ernst arr. Stein    Soloist: Kammermusikus Simon |
| Symphony No. 3 in A minor [*Scottish*] | Mendelssohn |
| Overture – *Julius Caesar* | Schumann |
| Introduction und Variations on a Russian theme | David    Soloist: Concertmeister Uhlrich |
| Overture – *Tannhäuser* | Wagner |

### 18. Concert im Loh: Sunday 27 September 1868 evening (with festive illumination of the Loh)

| | |
|---|---|
| Overture – *Rienzi* | Wagner |
| Aria from *Oberon* | Weber |
| Concerto for tuba | Sachse    Soloist: Hofmusikus Ziese |
| March from *Conradin* | Hiller |
| Festive Overture | Ries |
| Waltz | Strauss |
| Polka | Gungl |
| Russischer Zapfenstreich | |

### 1. Concert im Loh: Sunday 16 May 1869 afternoon

| | |
|---|---|
| Overture – *Die Abenceragen* | Cherubini |
| Passacaglia | Bach |
| Clarinet concerto | Spohr    Soloist: Hofmusicus Schomburg |
| Overture – *St Paul* | Mendelssohn |
| Symphony No.3 *Eroica* | Beethoven |

### 1. Concert im Loh: Sunday 16 May 1869 evening

| | |
|---|---|
| Overture – *Fra Diavolo* | Auber |
| Introduction from *Fra Diavolo* | Auber |
| Geburtstagmarsch | Taubert |

| | |
|---|---|
| Finale Act 1: *Tannhäuser* | Wagner |
| Overture – *Zampa* | Hérold |
| Waltz | Gungl |
| Marsch | Bilse |
| Polka | Strauss |

## 2. Concert im Loh: Sunday 23 May 1869 afternoon

| | | |
|---|---|---|
| Overture – Suite Op.101 | Raff | |
| Concertstück for flute | Terschak | Soloist: Kammermusicus Heindl |
| Overture – *Hamlet* | Gade | |
| Symphony No.3 [*Rhenish*] in Eb | Schumann | |

## 2. Concert im Loh: Sunday 23 May 1869 evening

| | |
|---|---|
| Overture – *Der Freischütz* | Weber |
| Trio – *Der Freischütz* | Weber |
| *Schiller* March | Meyerbeer |
| Finale Act 1: *Don Giovanni* | Mozart |
| Overture – *Das Nachtlager von Granada* | Kreutzer |
| Waltz | Strauss |
| Quadrille | Leutner |
| Polka | Hertel |

## 3. Concert im Loh: Sunday 30 May 1869 afternoon

| | | |
|---|---|---|
| Overture – *Anacreon* | Cherubini | |
| Concertstück for four horns | Schumann | Soloists: Kammermusicus Pohle, Hofmusicus Bauer, Franke and Barthel |
| Symphony No.8 | Schubert | |
| Symphony No.6 | Gade | |

## 3. Concert im Loh: Sunday 30 May 1869 evening
Programme as Sunday 23 May 1869 evening

## 4. Concert im Loh: Sunday 6 June 1869 afternoon

| | |
|---|---|
| Symphony [No.103] in Eb *Drumroll* | Haydn |
| Overture and Entr'acte from *King Manfred* | Reinecke |
| Three German Dances | Bargiel |
| **Symphony [No.1] Op.28** | **Bruch** |

## 4. Concert im Loh: Sunday 6 June 1869 evening

| | |
|---|---|
| Overture – *Der Günstling* | Frankenberger |
| Duet from *Les Huguenots* | Meyerbeer |
| Bridal March from *Midsummer Night's Dream* | Mendelssohn |
| Finale from *Zampa* | Hérold |
| Overture – *Die Felsenmühle* | Reissiger |
| Waltz | Gungl |
| Galop | Strauss |
| Polka (new) | Kämmerer |

**5. Concert im Loh: Sunday 13 June 1869 afternoon**

| | | |
|---|---|---|
| Concert overture in A | Rietz | |
| Prelude – *Die Meistersinger* | Wagner | |
| Suite No.2 Op.115 in E minor | Lachner | |
| Violin concerto | Beethoven | Soloist: Kammermusikus Himmelstoss |
| Overture – *Consecration of the House* | Beethoven | |

**5. Concert im Loh: Sunday 13 June 1869 evening**

| | |
|---|---|
| Overture – *Hans Heiling* | Marschner |
| Arias from the same opera | Marschner |
| Introduction from *Euryanthe* | Weber |
| Finale: [Act 1] *Lohengrin* | Wagner |
| Overture – *Merry Wives of Windsor* | Nicolai |
| Polka | Bilse |
| Quadrille | Strauss |
| March | Saro |

**6. Concert im Loh: Sunday 20 June 1869 afternoon**

| | |
|---|---|
| Overture – *Prometheus* | Bargiel |
| Two Entr'actes from *Rosamunde* | Schubert |
| *Kamarinskaya* – orchestral fantasy | Glinka |
| Overture – *Oberon* | Weber |
| *Der Gang nach Emmahus* | Jensen  (new – first time at the concerts) |
| Symphony No.8 in F | Beethoven |

**6. Concert im Loh: Sunday 20 June 1869 evening**

| | |
|---|---|
| Overture – *Rienzi* | Wagner |
| Duet from *Faust* | Gounod |
| Waltz and Chorus from the same opera | Gounod |
| Finale from *Stradella* | Flotow |
| Overture – *Ruy Blas* | Mendelssohn |
| Waltz | Strauss |
| March | Leutner |
| Polka | Gungl |

**7. Concert im Loh: Sunday 27 June 1869 afternoon**

| | | |
|---|---|---|
| Overture – *Bride of Messina* | Schumann | |
| Entr'acte from *Egmont* | Beethoven | |
| Scene and aria for horn | Eisner | Soloist: Kammermusicus Pohle |
| Overture in D minor | Volkland | |
| *Harold in Italy* | Berlioz | Solo viola: Hofmusikus Himmelstoss |

**7. Concert im Loh: Sunday 27 June 1869 evening**
Programme as Sunday 20 June 1869 evening

**8. Concert im Loh: Sunday 4 July 1869 afternoon**

| | | |
|---|---|---|
| Overture – *Calm Sea and Prosperous Voyage* | Mendelssohn | |
| Masonic Funeral Music | Mozart | |
| Oboe concerto | Stein | Soloist: Hofmusikus Hoffmann |

| | |
|---|---|
| Ballade for orchestra | Rudorff (new, from manuscript: for the first time) |
| Symphony [No.9] in C | Schubert |

## 8. Concert im Loh: Sunday 4 July 1869 evening

| | |
|---|---|
| Overture – *Ruy Blas* | Mendelssohn |
| March: *Tannhäuser* | Wagner |
| Finale Act 2: *Don Giovanni* | Mozart |
| Introduction from *William Tell* | Rossini |
| Overture – *Yelva* | Reissiger |
| Waltz | Strauss |
| March | Leutner |
| Polka | Gungl |

## 9. Concert im Loh: Sunday 11 July 1869 afternoon

| | |
|---|---|
| Overture – *Struensee* | Meyerbeer |
| Concerto for two violins and strings | Handel |
| Symphony [No.41] in C | Mozart |
| *Romeo and Juliet* (parts 2 and 3) | Berlioz (first time at the concerts) |
| Overture – *William Tell* | Rossini |

## 9. Concert im Loh: Sunday 11 July 1869 evening

| | |
|---|---|
| Overture – *La Muette de Portici* | Auber |
| Market chorus from *La Muette de Portici* | Auber |
| Ballet from *William Tell* | Rossini (on the highest command) |
| Overture – *Martha* | Flotow |
| Polka | Strauss |
| Quadrille | Conradi |
| March | Faust |

## 10. Concert im Loh: Sunday 18 July 1869 afternoon

| | |
|---|---|
| Overture – *Olympia* | Spontini |
| Suite in canonical form for strings | Grimm |
| Solos for double bass: | [transcribed and performed by Kammervirtuose Simon] |
|    Funeral march | Chopin |
|    Meditation on a prelude by Bach | Gounod |
| Overture – *Waldmeisters Brautfahrt* | Gernsheim |
| Symphony No. 9 in D minor | Beethoven (first three movements only) |
| Overture – *Genoveva* | Schumann |

## 10. Concert im Loh: Sunday 18 July 1869 evening

| | |
|---|---|
| Overture – *Les Huguenots* | Meyerbeer |
| *Schwur und Schwerterweihe* from the same opera | Meyerbeer |
| *Ave Maria* | Schubert orch. F Lux (for the first time) |
| Trio [Act 2] from *Der Freischütz* | Weber |
| Overture – *Le bal masqué* | Auber |
| Waltz | Bilse |
| Galop | Frankenberger |
| Polka | Gungl |

### 11. Concert im Loh: Sunday 25 July 1869 afternoon

| | |
|---|---|
| Overture – *Otto der Schütz* | Rudorff |
| Pastorale from the *Christmas Oratorio* | Bach |
| Symphony No.2 in C | Schumann |
| Overture – *Dame Kobold* | Reinecke |
| Violin concerto | Mendelssohn    Soloist: Concertmeister Uhlrich |
| Overture – *King Stephen* | Beethoven |

### 11. Concert im Loh: Sunday 25 July 1869 evening

| | |
|---|---|
| Overture – *Turandot* | Lachner |
| *Schwerterweihe* from *Les Huguenots* | Meyerbeer |
| Trio from *William Tell* | Rossini |
| Rheinlied from *Die Nibelungen* | Dorn |
| Overture – *Ferdinand Cortez* | Spontini |
| March | Saro |
| Waltz | Gungl |
| Polka | Labitzky |

### 12. Concert im Loh: Sunday 1 August 1869 afternoon

| | |
|---|---|
| Overture to a Tragedy | Bargiel |
| **Introduction from the opera** | **Bruch** |
|    ***Die Loreley*** | |
| Solos for double bass: | transcribed and performed by Kammervirtuose Simon |
|   Funeral march | Chopin |
|   Meditation on a prelude by Bach | Gounod |
| Symphony No.3 [*Rhenish*] in Eb | Schumann |
| Overture – *Aladdin* | Reinecke |
| *Harold in Italy* | Berlioz (first movement and Andante – Pilgrims' March) |
| Overture – [*Namensfeier*] Op.115 | Beethoven |

### 12. Concert im Loh: Sunday 1 August 1869 evening

| | |
|---|---|
| Overture and introduction from *Don Giovanni* | Mozart |
| Prisoners' chorus from *Fidelio* | Beethoven |
| Introduction and Bridal Chorus from *Lohengrin* | Wagner |
| Finale: Act 2 *William Tell* | Rossini |
| Overture – *Die Grossfürstin* | Flotow |
| Waltz | Faust |
| Gallop | Strauss |
| Polka-Mazurka | Dregert |

### 13. Concert im Loh: Sunday 8 August 1869 afternoon

| | |
|---|---|
| Overture – *Euryanthe* | Weber |
| Cello concerto | Molique    Soloist: Hofmusikus Graf |
| Symphony No.1 in C minor | Gade |
| Overture and Entr'actes 5, 6, 7 from *Egmont* | Beethoven |
| Overture – *Die Zauberflöte* | Mozart |

### 13. Concert im Loh: Sunday 8 August 1869 evening
Programme as Sunday 1 August 1869 evening

### 14. Concert im Loh: Sunday 15 August 1869 afternoon
| | |
|---|---|
| Overture – *The Water Carrier* | Cherubini |
| Dances from *Orpheus* | Gluck |
| *Sternhelle Nacht*, fantasy for clarinet | Bärmann    Soloist: Hofmusikus Schomburg |
| **Intermezzo (B major) for orchestra** | **Bruch** |
| Overture – *Manfred* | Schumann |
| Symphony No.6 *Pastoral* | Beethoven |

### 14. Concert im Loh: Sunday 15 August 1869 evening
| | |
|---|---|
| Overture and introduction from *Don Giovanni* | Mozart |
| Prisoners' chorus from *Fidelio* | Beethoven |
| Introduction and Bridal Chorus from *Lohengrin* | Wagner |
| Finale: Act 2 *William Tell* | Rossini |
| Overture – *Die Grossfürstin* | Flotow |
| Waltz | Faust |
| Gallop | Strauss |
| Polka-Mazurka | Dregert |

### 15. Concert im Loh: Sunday 22 August 1869 afternoon
| | |
|---|---|
| Overture – *Nachklänge von Ossian* | Gade |
| Symphony in D minor | Dietrich (new, from manuscript parts) |
| Dances from *Orpheus* | Gluck |
| Scherzo from *Wallenstein* Symphony | Rheinberger |
| Overture – *Athalie* | Mendelssohn |

### 15. Concert im Loh: Sunday 22 August 1869 evening
| | |
|---|---|
| Overture – *Der Vampyr* | Marschner |
| Overture – *Euryanthe* | Weber |
| *Schiller* March | Meyerbeer |
| Finale: *Lohengrin* | Wagner |
| Overture – *Fra Diavolo* | Auber |
| Waltz | Strauss |
| Gallop | Gungl |
| Polka-Mazurka | Kämmerer |

### 16. Concert im Loh: Sunday 29 August 1869 afternoon
| | |
|---|---|
| Overture – [*Namensfeier*] Op.115 | Beethoven |
| Love scene and Scherzo from *Romeo and Juliet* | Berlioz |
| **Violin concerto (Op. 26) [No.1 in G minor]** | **Bruch** |
| Symphony No.5 *Reformation* | Mendelssohn |

### 16. Concert im Loh: Sunday 29 August 1869 evening
| | |
|---|---|
| Overture – *Ruy Blas* | Mendelssohn |
| Overture – *Euryanthe* | Weber |

| | |
|---|---|
| *Schiller* March | Meyerbeer |
| Finale: *Lohengrin* | Wagner |
| Overture – *Fra Diavolo* | Auber |
| Waltz | Strauss |
| Gallop | Gungl |
| Polka-Mazurka | Kämmerer |

## 17. Concert im Loh: Sunday 5 September 1869 afternoon

| | |
|---|---|
| Overture – *Michel Angelo* | Gade |
| *Queen Mab* scherzo from *Romeo and Juliet* | Berlioz |
| Overture – *Die Abenceragen* | Cherubini |
| Ballade | Rudorff (manuscript) |
| Duo Op.140 | Schubert orch. Joachim |

## 17. Concert im Loh: Sunday 5 September 1869 evening

| | | |
|---|---|---|
| Overture – *Rienzi* | Wagner | |
| Aria for trumpet from *Nabucco* | Verdi | Soloist: Hofmusikus Beck |
| Trio from *William Tell* | Rossini | |
| Introduction from *William Tell* | Rossini | |
| Overture – *Zampa* | Hérold | |
| Waltz | Gungl | |
| Marsch | Saro | |
| Gallop | Conradi | |

## 18. Concert im Loh: Sunday 12 September 1869 afternoon

| | |
|---|---|
| Overture – *In the Highlands* | Gade |
| Nocturne and Bridal March from<br>  *A Midsummer Night's Dream* | Mendelssohn |
| Fantasy on *Jota Aragonesa* | Glinka |
| Overture – *Julius Caesar* | Schumann |
| Symphony No.4 in Bb | Beethoven |

## 18. Concert im Loh: Sunday 12 September 1869 evening

| | | |
|---|---|---|
| Overture – *Merry Wives of Windsor* | Nicolai | |
| Solo for trumpet | Suppé | Soloist: Hofmusikus Beck |
| Elsa's Bridal March from *Lohengrin* | Wagner | |
| Trio from *Der Günstling* | Frankenberger | |
| Overture – *Das Nachtlager von Granada* | Kreutzer | |
| Quadrille | Dregert | |
| March | Faust | |
| Polka | Strauss | |

## 19. Concert im Loh: Sunday 19 September 1869 afternoon

| | |
|---|---|
| Symphony Op.12 | Reinecke (for the first time at the concerts) |
| Nocturne and Bridal March from<br>  *A Midsummer Night's Dream* | Mendelssohn |
| Concert overture in Eb | Tausch (new, from manuscript parts) |
| Symphony No.4 in Bb | Beethoven |

## 19. Concert im Loh: Sunday 19 September 1869 evening

Programme as Sunday 12 September 1869 evening

## 20. Concert im Loh: Sunday 26 September 1869 afternoon

| | |
|---|---|
| Overture – *Jubel* | Weber |
| Scherzo from *Wallenstein* Symphony | Rheinberger |
| Concerto for double bass | Stein    Soloist: Kammervirtuosen Simon |
| Overture in D minor | Volkland |
| Introduction and variations on a Russian folksong | David    Soloist: Concertmeister Ulrich |
| Symphony No.5 in C minor | Beethoven |

## 20. Concert im Loh: Sunday 26 September 1869 evening (with festive illumination of the Loh)
Programme as Sunday 12 September 1869 evening

## 1. Concert im Loh: Sunday 5 June 1870 afternoon

| | |
|---|---|
| Overture – *St Paul* | Mendelssohn |
| Pastorale from the *Christmas Oratorio* | Bach |
| Fantasie for flute | Doppler orch. König |
| | Soloist: Kammermusikus Heidl |
| Symphony No.2 in D | Beethoven |
| Overture – *Bride of Messina* | Schumann |
| Dances from *Orpheus* | Gluck |
| Overture – *Consecration of the House* | Beethoven |

## 1. Concert im Loh: Sunday 5 June 1870 evening

| | |
|---|---|
| Overture – *Egmont* | Beethoven |
| *Schwerterweihe* from *Les Huguenots* | Meyerbeer |
| March from Suite No. 2 | Lachner |
| Romanze and Finale Act 1 *Tannhäuser* | Wagner |
| Overture – *Zampa* | Hérold |
| Waltz | Strauss |
| March | Saro |
| Polka-Mazurka | Kämmerer |

## 2. Concert im Loh: Sunday 12 June 1870 afternoon
## The [first] wedding anniversary of his Highness [Karl Günther] the Prince Regent

| | |
|---|---|
| Concert-Overture in A | Rietz |
| Three movements from *Romeo and Juliet* | Berlioz |
| Fantasiestück for clarinet | Kalliwoda    Soloist: Hofmusikus Schomburg |
| Symphony No. 4 in D minor | Schumann |

## 2. Concert im Loh: Sunday 12 June 1870 evening

| | |
|---|---|
| *Jubel*-Overture | Weber |
| Finale from the unfinished opera *Lorelei* | Mendelssohn |
| *Schiller* March | Meyerbeer |
| Waltz and Chorus from *Faust* | Gounod |
| **(Fireworks in the interval)** | |
| Overture – *Rienzi* | Wagner |
| Waltz | Gungl |
| Polonaise | Bilse |
| March | Strauss |

### 3. Concert im Loh: Sunday 19 June 1870 afternoon

| | |
|---|---|
| Symphony No. 1 in C | Beethoven |
| Entr'acte from the music to *Egmont* | Beethoven |
| Overture – *Leonore* No. 1 | Beethoven |
| Symphony No.9 in D minor<br>(first three movements) | Beethoven |
| Overture – *Leonore* No.3 | Beethoven |

### 3. Concert im Loh: Sunday 19 June 1870 evening

| | |
|---|---|
| Overture – *Der Templer und die Jüdin* | Marschner |
| Duet from *William Tell* | Rossini |
| *Ave Maria* | Schubert orch. F Lux |
| Entr'acte and Hunting Song from *Dinorah* | Meyerbeer |
| Overture – *Merry Wives of Windsor* | Nicolai |
| Polka | Strauss |
| Quadrille | Leutner |
| March | Gungl |

### 4. Concert im Loh: Sunday 26 June 1870 afternoon

| | |
|---|---|
| Overture – *Julius Caesar* | Schumann |
| Serenade in D [Op.11] | Brahms (for the first time) |
| *Queen Mab* Scherzo | Berlioz |
| Symphony in D minor | Dietrich |

### 4. Concert im Loh: Sunday 26 June 1870 evening

| | |
|---|---|
| Overture – *Robespierre* | Litolff |
| Nocturne from *A Midsummer Night's Dream* | Mendelssohn |
| Wedding March | Taubert |
| *Ständchen* | Schubert orch. E Stein |
| Overture – *La Muette de Portici* | Auber |
| Polka-Mazurka | Neumann |
| *An der schönen blauen Donau* | Strauss |
| Polka | Kämmerer |

There is some uncertainty over the concerts on 3 July 1870. While there is no printed programme for this date in the collection, *Der Deutsche* for 21.6.1870 announces the programme for the 4 Loh Concert as above but then announces it again a week later on 28.6.1870 for 3 July. While the programme content for both afternoon and evening concerts remains the same, items 2 and 3 in the afternoon (Brahms and Berlioz) are now swapped around.

### 5. Concert im Loh: Sunday 10 July 1870 afternoon

| | | |
|---|---|---|
| Overture – *Ruy Blas* | Mendelssohn | |
| Two Entr'actes from the music to *Egmont* | Beethoven | |
| Concerto for two metal flutes | Fürstenau | Soloists: Kammermusikus Heindl and his pupil Rudolf Keil |
| *Ivan IV (The Terrible)* | Rubinstein (new, for the first time) | |
| Symphony No. 3 *Eroica* | Beethoven | |

### 5. Concert im Loh: Sunday 10 July 1870 evening

| | |
|---|---|
| Overture – *Der Freischütz* | Weber |
| *Waffentanz* and Chorus from *Jessonda* | Spohr |
| *La Campanella* | König |
| Chorus from *Die Walpurgisnacht* | Mendelssohn |
| Overture – *Fra Diavolo* | Auber |
| Polka | Strauss |
| Quadrille | Gungl |
| March | Bilse |

### 6. Concert im Loh: Sunday 17 July 1870 afternoon

| | | |
|---|---|---|
| Overture – *The Fair Melusine* | Mendelssohn | |
| Symphony [No.4] *Die Weihe der Töne* | Spohr | |
| Concerto for violin | Beethoven | Soloist: Concertmeister Uhlrich |
| Symphony No.8 in B minor | Schubert | |
| Overture – *Euryanthe* | Weber | |

### 6. Concert im Loh: Sunday 17 July 1870 evening

| | |
|---|---|
| Festival Overture | Ries |
| Elsa's Wedding Procession from *Lohengrin* | Wagner |
| March: *Vom Fels zum Meer* | Liszt |
| Duet from *Der fliegende Holländer* | Wagner |
| Overture – *Der Zweikampf* | Hérold |
| Polka-Mazurka | Kämmerer (new) |
| Waltz | Strauss |
| Polka | Wick (new) |

### 7. Concert im Loh: Sunday 24 July 1870 afternoon

| | | |
|---|---|---|
| Overture – *The Water Carrier* | Cherubini | |
| Introduction [*Adagio*] and Fugue for strings | Mozart (for the first time) | |
| Concertstück for four horns | Schumann | Soloists: Kammermusikus Pohle, Hofmusikus Bauer, Franke and Bartel |
| *Ivan IV* (*The Terrible*) | Rubinstein | |
| Symphony No.3 in A minor [*Scottish*] | Mendelssohn | |

### 7. Concert im Loh: Sunday 24 July 1870 evening

| | |
|---|---|
| Overture – *Tannhäuser* | Wagner |
| *On the Wings of Song* | Mendelssohn orch. Marpurg |
| Prelude to *Faust* | Gounod |
| Finale Act 1 *Don Giovanni* | Mozart |
| Overture – *Omar und Leila* | Fesca |
| Mazurka | Gungl |
| Polonaise | Bilse |
| Polka | Strauss |

Concerts conducted by Bruch in 1869 and 1870 which either preceded or followed the Loh-Concert series were as follows.

**Benefit Concert on 30 January 1869** to raise funds for a memorial to Johann Sebastian Bach in Eisenach. [Concert zum Vortheil des Denkmals Johann Sebastian

Bachs in Eisenach 30. Januar 1869], and this programme was repeated in its entirety exactly a year later to the day for the same purpose.

| | |
|---|---|
| Suite [No.3 in D] | Bach |
| Pastorale from the *Christmas Oratorio* | Bach |
| Violin concerto in A minor | Bach      Soloist: Hofmusikus Himmelstoss |
| Passacaglia | Bach orch. H Esser |
| **Final chorus from *Frithjof*** | **Bruch** |
| Scenes from *Idomeneo* | Mozart |
| Symphony No. 4 in D minor | Schumann |

Vocal soloists: Frau Pelli-Sicora, Fräulein Constabelli and Herr Bertoni from the Opera, Fräulein Lammert from the Fürstliche Hofkapelle, and the Liederhalle Male Voice-Choir

In this next concert Bruch very unusually includes one of his own choral works, surrounds it with the music of the composers he most admires, only to conclude with a work by the one he came to hate most, Wagner, 'a brilliant man, who strives with great energy and exceptional talent for undoubtedly the wrong goals', as he wrote just one month earlier to Rudolf von Beckerath (9 April 1870).

### Concert of the St Cecilia Society, Hall of the Hotel Münch: 15 May 1870

[Concert des Cäcilienvereins im Saal von Hotel Münch 15. Mai 1870]

| | |
|---|---|
| *Frühlingsbotschaft* | Gade |
| Duet from *Der Berggeist* | Spohr |
| *Walpurgisnacht* | Mendelssohn |
| ***Die Flucht der Heiligen Familie* [Op.20]** | **Bruch** |
| Quintet | Hiller |
| Finale Act 1 *Lohengrin* | Wagner |

On 4 September 1870 a concert was given to raise funds for soldiers from the area who were wounded fighting in the Franco-Prussian War, which had begun that year. Curiously for such an occasion, the programme concluded with the first performance of Bruch's second symphony.

[Concert der Fürstlichen Hof-Capelle im hiesigen Theater zum Besten der Verwundeten der im Feld stehenden vereinigten deutschen Heere, unter Leitung des Hof-Capellmeisters Max Bruch, sowie unter gefälliger Mitwirkung der Damen Fräulein Ad. Braun, Fräulein M. Lammert und des Herrn Musik-Direktors L. Rakemann.]

### [Concert im Theater:] Sunday 4 September 1870 evening at 7 o'clock

| | | |
|---|---|---|
| Overture – *Egmont* | Beethoven | |
| Aria: 'Ocean, thou mighty monster' from *Oberon* | Weber | |
| Piano concerto in A minor | Schumann | Soloist: Music Director Rakemann |
| Concert aria | Mendelssohn | Soloist: Mlle. Lammert |
| Elfenreigen and Hochzeitsmarsch from *A Midsummer Night's Dream* | Mendelssohn arr. for piano solo by Liszt Soloist: Music Director Rakemann | |

Two Lieder:                                        Soloist: Mlle. Braun
a: *Abendreihen*                    Grädner
b: *Frühlingsnacht*                 Schumann
**Symphony No. 2 in F minor Op. 36**   **Bruch** (new, for the first time)


## Concert given by the Court Orchestra and the local Liederhalle (Choral Society) in the Court Theatre on Saturday 24 September 1870 evening at 7 o'clock

[Concert der Fürstlichen Hof-Capelle unter Mitwirkung der hiesigen „Liederhalle" im Fürstlichen Theater, Samstag, den 24. September 1870, abends 7 Uhr]

| | | |
|---|---|---|
| *Jubel* Overture | Weber | |
| 'Dir will ich diese Lieder weihen' | Kreutzer | performed by the Liederhalle |
| *Das deutsche Lied* | Kalliwoda | performed by the Liederhalle |
| Piano concerto in Eb [*Emperor*] | Beethoven | Soloist: Musikdirector Rakemann |
| | | |
| *Kriegslied* (poem by Geibel) | König | performed by the Liederhalle |
| 'Die Wacht am Rhein' | Wilhelm | performed by the Liederhalle |
| Overture – *Beethoven* | Lassen (new, for the first time) | |
| Symphony No. 5 in C minor | Beethoven | |


## Concert im Loh: Sunday 25 September 1870 [evening] (with festive illumination of the Loh)

| | | |
|---|---|---|
| *Kriegerische Jubeloverture* | Lindpaintner | |
| Cavatine for flugelhorn | Donizetti | Soloist: Hofmusikus Beck |
| *Coronation* March | Meyerbeer | |
| Finale Act 2 from *Wilhelm Tell* | Rossini | |
| Festival Overture | Ulrich | |
| March to the song 'Was ist des Deutschen Vaterland' | Golde | |
| March to the song 'Die Wacht am Rhein' | Pieske | |
| Pariser Einzugsmarsch | | |


## Concert by the Saint Cecilia Society in the Schützenhaus Hall, 25 December 1870

[Aufführung des Cäcilienvereins im Saal des Schützenhauses 25. Dezember 1870]
*Elijah*                        Mendelssohn


## Music and Theatre repertoire in Sondershausen from 1868 to 1870

(Bruch's period as Theatre Conductor begins with the season starting January 1868, and his operatic repertoire is summarised at the end of this list).

**1868**

| | | | |
|---|---|---|---|
| 1 January | Die Hochzeit des Figaro | Opera | Mozart |
| 3 January | Aschenbrödel | Comedy | Roderich Benedix |
| 5 January | Die alte Schachtel | Farce with songs | Pohl/ Musik: Bial |
| 8 January | Der Königslieutenant | Comedy | Gutzkow |
| 10 January | Die Jüdin | Opera | Halévy |
| 12 January | Bajazzo u. seine Familie | Romantic play | Marr |

| | | | |
|---|---|---|---|
| 13 January | Joseph in Egypten | Opera | Duval/ Mehul |
| 17 January | Der 30. November | Comedy | Feldmann |
| | Die beiden Helden | Comedy | Marsano |
| | Hermann und Dorothea | Farce | M: Lange |
| 19 January | Graupenmüller | Farce with songs and dance | Salingre/M: Bossenberger |
| 20 January | Der Barbier von Sevilla | Comic Opera | Rossini |
| 22 January | Treue Liebe | Play | E. Devrient |
| 24 January | Fidelio | Opera | Beethoven |
| 26 January | Hinko | Play | Birch-Pfeiffer |
| 27 January | Czar und Zimmermann | Comic Opera | Lortzing |
| 29 January | Erziehung macht den Menschen | Comedy | Görner |
| 31 January | Tannhäuser | Opera | R. Wagner |
| 2 February | Otto Bellmann | Farce with songs | Kalisch/M: Conradi |
| 3 February | Die Entführung aus dem Serail | Opera | Mozart |
| 5 February | Die Jäger | Play | Iffland |
| 7 February | Fidelio | Opera | Beethoven |
| 9 February | Ludwig der Eiserne | Play | A. Rost |
| 10 February | Lucia von Lammermoor | Opera | Donizetti |
| 12 February | Das Glas Wasser | Comedy | E. Scribe |
| 14 February | Der Wasserträger | Opera | Cherubini |
| 16 February | Ein ganzer Kerl | Farce with songs | Salingre/M: Bial |
| 17 February | Die weisse Dame | Comic Opera | Boieldieu |
| 19 February | Unsere braven Landsleute | Play | Bouzy |
| 21 February | Die Verschwörung der Frauen | Comedy | Artur Müller |
| 23 February | Der Tower von London | Play | A. Bahn |
| 24 February | Robert der Teufel | Heroic Opera | Meyerbeer |
| 26 February | Ein Vormittag in Sanssouci | Comedy | Mühlbach |
| | Duett aus „Romeo u. Julia" | | |
| | Das Lied von der Glocke | | M: Lindpaintner |
| 28 February | Die Jüdin | Opera | Halévy |
| 1 March | Der Freischütz | Romantic Opera | Weber |
| 2 March | Fra Diavolo | Comic Opera | Auber |
| 4 March | Günther von Schwarzburg | Play | Theodor Apel |
| 6 March | Die Nachtwandlerin | Opera | Bellini |
| 8 March | Ein Kind des Glücks | Play | Birch-Pfeiffer |
| 9 March | Die lustigen Weiber von Windsor | Comic Opera | Nicolai |
| 11 March | Das Urbild des Tartuffe | Comedy | Gutzkow |
| 13 March | Alessandro Stradella | Opera | Flotow |
| | Traumbilder | | Nyhlsen/M: Lumbye |
| 15 March | Berliner Droschkenkutscher | Farce with songs | Weirauch/M: Hauptner |
| 16 March | Herzog Richelieu und Fräulein Gabriele von Belle Isle | Play | Holbein nach Dumas |
| 17 March | Die lustigen Weiber von Windsor | Comic Opera | Nicolai |
| 20 March | Faust und Margarethe | Opera | Gounod |
| 23 March | Aschenbrödel | Play | Bendix |

| 24 March | Die Anne Liese | Play | Hermann Hersch |
|---|---|---|---|
| | Der Liebestrank | Operetta | Gumbert |
| 25 March | Die Stumme von Portici | Opera | Auber |
| 27 March | Don Juan | Opera | Mozart |
| 30 March | Die zärtlichen Verwandten | Comedy | Bendix |
| 31 March | Die beiden Schützen | Comic Opera | Lorzting |
| 25 December | Der Troubadour | Opera | Verdi |
| 27 December | Das Nachtlager in Granada | Romantic Opera | Kreutzer |
| 30 December | Gute Nacht Hänschen | Comedy | A. Müller |

## 1869

| 1 January | Robert der Teufel | Romantic Opera | Meyerbeer |
|---|---|---|---|
| 3 January | Der Glöckner von Notre Dame | Play | Birch-Pfeiffer |
| 4 January | Die Regimentstochter | Opera | Donizetti |
| 6 January | Ein Lustspiel | Comedy | Benedix |
| 8 January | Die Jüdin | Opera | Halévy |
| 13 January | Der Waffenschmied von Worms | Comic Opera | Lortzing |
| 14 January | Das Geheimnis der alten Mamsell | Play | Moßberg |
| 15 January | Die Jüdin | Opera | Halévy |
| 17 January | Philippine Weiser | Play | v. Redwitz |
| 18 January | Die Selige an den Verstorbenen | Comedy | K. Friedrich |
| 20 January | Fidelio | Opera | Beethoven |
| 22 January | Der Sonnwendhof | Play | Mosenthal |
| 24 January | Der Maschinenbauer | Farce with songs | Weirauch/M: Lang |
| 25 January | Czar und Zimmermann | Comic Opera | Lortzing |
| 27 January | Die relegirten Studenten | Comedy | Benedix |
| 29 January | Czar und Zimmermann | Comic Opera | Lortzing |
| 31 January | Steffen Langer aus Glogau | Comedy | Birch-Pfeiffer |
| 1 February | Martha | Opera | Flotow |
| 5 February | Der Freischütz | Romantic Opera | Weber |
| | (Debut: Minna Lammert als „Agathe") | | |
| 7 February | Der artesische Brunnen | Farce | G. Raeder |
| 8 February | Die Mönche | Comedy | Tenelli |
| 10 February | Die Loreley | Play with Songs | Hersch/M: Neswadla |
| 12 February | Der Prophet | Opera | Meyerbeer |
| 14 February | Die Maurer von Berlin | Humoresque | Emil Pohl |
| 15 February | Flotter Bursche | Operette | Suppé |
| | Vormittag in Sanssouci | Comedy | Mühlbach |
| 17 February | Die Hochzeit des Figaro | Comic Opera | Mozart |
| 19 February | Der Prophet | Opera | Meyerbeer |
| 21 February | Aus bewegter Zeit | Character picture | Pohl/M: Lang |
| 22 February | Bürgerlich und romantisch | Comedy | Bauernfeld |
| 4 March | Der Störenfried | Comedy | Benedix |
| 5 March | Goldbauer | Play | Birch-Pfeiffer |
| 7 March | Unruhige Zeiten | Farce with songs | Pohl/M: Conradi |
| 8 March | Die Selige an den Verstorbenen | Comedy | Clairville |
| 9 March | Düweke, das Täubchen von Amsterdam | Play | Mosenthal |
| 11 March | Der Günstling | Opera | Frankenberger |
| | (Minna Lammert as Dunia) | | |

| 12 March | Zehn Mädchen und kein Mann | Operetta | Suppé |
| | preceded by Arias and Recitatives from *Ernani* by Verdi | | |
| 14 March | Pech-Schulze | Farce with songs | Salingré/M: Lang |
| 15 March | Die Compromittirten | Comedy | Julius Rosen |
| 16 March | Zehn Mädchen und kein Mann | Operetta | Suppé |
| 17 March | Der Freischütz | Romantic Opera | Weber |
| | (Minna Lammert as Agathe) | | |
| 19 March | Ein moderner Barbar | Comedy | G.v. Moser |
| | Aria from *Barber of Seville* | | Rossini |
| | Scenes and Duets from *Les Huguenots* | | Meyerbeer |
| 21 March | Der Günstling | Opera | Frankenberger |

## 1870

| 1 January | Böse Zungen | Play | H. Laube |
| | Prolog | | Herzenskron |
| 2 January | Die Stimme von Portici | Opera | Auber |
| 3 January | Kanonenfutter | Comedy | J. Rosen |
| 7 January | Lucrezia Borgia | Opera | Donizetti |
| 9 January | Das Turnier zu Kronstein | Comedy | Hohlbein |
| 13 January | Die bezähmte Widerspenstige | Comedy | Shakespeare |
| 14 January | Der Freischütz | Romantic Opera | Weber |
| 16. January | Unter der Erde | Character picture with music | Elmar/M: Suppé |
| 17 January | Margarethe | Opera | Gounod |
| 18 January | Doctor Treuwald | Comedy | Benedix |
| 20 January | Die Anne Lise | Play | Hersch |
| 21 January | Czar und Zimmermann | Comic Opera | Lortzing |
| 23 January | Preciosa | Play with songs | Wolff/M: Weber |
| 24 January | Der Freischütz | Opera | Weber |
| 26 January | Revanche | Comedy | Birch-Pfeiffer |
| | Garibaldi | Farce | I. Rosen |
| 28 January | Die Zauberflöte | Opera | Mozart |
| 30 January | Pfeffer-Rösel | Play | Birch-Pfeiffer |
| 31 January | Der Platzregen als | Comedy | Raupach |
| | Eheprocurator | | |
| 2 February | Gegenüber | Comedy | Benedix |
| 4 February | Marie | Comic Opera | Donizetti |
| 6 February | Lenore | Play with Songs | Holtei/M: Eberwein |
| 7 February | Die Hochzeit des Figaro | Comic Opera | Mozart |
| 9 February | Das Kätchen von Heilbronn | Play | Kleist |
| 11 February | Martha | Opera | Flotow |
| 13 February | Der böse Geist Lumpaci Vagabundus | | |
| 14 February | Der verwunschene Prinz | Comedy | Plötz |
| | Rübezahl | Operetta | M: Conradi |
| 15 February | Robert der Teufel | Opera with Ballet | Meyerbeer |
| 16 February | Deutsche Modedamen | Comedy | Görlitz |
| 18 February | Robert der Teufel | Opera with Ballet | Meyerbeer |
| 20 February | Ein Mädchen vom Ballet | Character pictures | Germamer |
| 21 February | Don Juan | Opera | Mozart |
| 23 February | Die Grille | Character picture | Birch-Pfeiffer |
| 25 February | Die Hugenotten | Opera | Meyerbeer |

| 27 February | Reichsgräfin Gisela | Play | Wegener |
|---|---|---|---|
| 28 February | Stradella | Comic Opera | Flotow |
| 2 March | Die Amnestie | Play | A. May |
| 4 March | Margarethe | Opera | Gounod |
| 6 March | Marie | Comic Opera | Donizetti |
| 7 March | Sie hat ihr Herz entdeckt | Comedy | Königswinter |
|  | Das Schwert des Damokles | Comedy | Putlitz |
|  | Rübezahl | Operetta | Conradi |
| 8 March | Die Hugenotten | Opera | Meyerbeer |
| 9 March | Muttersegen | Play | Friedrich |
| 11 March | Marie | Comic Opera | Donizetti |
| 13 March | Pariser Leben | Operetta | J. Offenbach |
| 14 March | Robert der Teufel | Opera with Ballet | Meyerbeer |
| 16 March | Die Amnestie | Play | May |
| 18 March | Die lustigen Weiber von Windsor | Opera | Nicolai |
| 20 March | Klein Geld | Farce with songs | Conradi |
| 21 March | Das Haus Haase | Comedy | F. Wehl |
| 23 March | Doctor Faust's Hauskäppchen [performance for children] | Farce with songs | M. Hebenstreit |
| 25 March | Der Templer und die Jüdin | Opera | H. Marschner |
| 27 March | Wallenstein's Tod | Tragedy | Schiller |
| 28 March | Der Templer und die Jüdin | Opera | H. Marschner |
| 30 March | Er ist eifersüchtig | Comedy | A. Eltz |
|  | Der alte Student | Play | v. Maltitz |

**Summary of Bruch's operatic repertoire (32 operas in alphabetical order by composer) conducted in Sondershausen between January 1868 and March 1870**

| Fra Diavolo | Auber |
|---|---|
| La Muette di Portici | Auber |
| Fidelio | Beethoven |
| La Sonnambula | Bellini |
| La Dame blanche | Boieldieu |
| Les deux journées | Cherubini |
| Lucia di Lammermoor | Donizetti |
| La figlia del regimento (Marie) | Donizetti |
| Lucrezia Borgia | Donizetti |
| Alessandro Stradella | Flotow |
| Martha | Flotow |
| Der Günstling | Frankenberger |
| Faust | Gounod |
| La juive | Halévy |
| Das Nachtlager in Granada | Kreutzer |
| Czar und Zimmermann | Lortzing |
| Die beiden Schützen | Lortzing |
| Der Waffenschmied von Worms | Lortzing |
| Der Templer und die Jüdin | Marschner |
| Robert le diable | Meyerbeer |
| Le Prophète | Meyerbeer |
| Les Huguenots | Meyerbeer |

| | |
|---|---|
| *Die Zauberflöte* | Mozart |
| *Le Nozze di Figaro* | Mozart |
| *Die Entführung aus dem Serail* | Mozart |
| *Don Giovanni* | Mozart |
| *Die lustigen Weiber von Windsor* | Nicolai |
| *Il barbiere di Siviglia* | Rossini |
| *Il Trovatore* | Verdi |
| *Tannhäuser* | Wagner |
| *Der Freischütz* | Weber |

# ADDITIONAL BIBLIOGRAPHY

BAUR, UWE, *Max Bruch und Koblenz (1865–1867)*. Eine Dokumentation (Beiträge zur mittelrheinischen Musikgeschichte Nr 34) (Schott, Mainz 1996)

FIFIELD, CHRISTOPHER, *Bruch, Max (Christian Friedrich)*. Article in *The New Grove Dictionary of Music and Musicians*, ed. Sadie, Stanley, Vol.4, London, New York etc 2001 pp. 454–6

———, *Bruch's Violin Concerto, Behind the Notes*. Article in *The Strad* pp. 962–7, September 2002

KÄMPER, DIETRICH, *Bruch, Max*. Article in *Die Musik in Geschichte und Gegenwart. Allgemeine Enzyklopädie der Musik* ed. Finschner, Ludwig, Personenteil 3, Kassel, Basel etc. 2000, col. 1028–34

LARSEN, PETER (ed), *Max Bruch in Sondershausen (1867–1870)*. Musikwissenschaftliches Symposium (Hainholz Musikwissenschaft Band 8, Göttingen 2004). Contributors and articles:

    *Manche entschiedene Vortheile* – Peter Larsen

    *Max Bruch und Philipp Spitta* – Dietrich Kämper

    *Max Bruchs Wechsel von Koblenz nach Sondershausen* - Uwe Baur

    *Max Bruch und Johannes Brahms* – Claudia Valder-Knechtges

    *Max Bruch and Sondershausen* – Christopher Fifield

    *Marginalien zu Bruch aus Berliner Archiven* - Robert Schmitt Scheubel

    *Max Bruch und die musikalische Schottland-Romantik* – Andrea Marxen

RIEDERER-SITTE, PETRA, *Max Bruch. Briefe an Laura und Rudolf von Beckerath* (Die Blaue Eule, Essen 1997)

SCHWARZER, MATTHIAS, *Die Oratorien von Max Bruch*. Eine Quellenstudie (Beiträge zur rheinischen Musikgeschichte Heft 141) (Merseburger, Kassel 1988)

# NEW EDITIONS

Violin concerto No.1 in G minor Op.26 (violin and piano ed. Thomas Wood)
Elite Edition 4021 N Simrock London/Hamburg, 1994 (orchestral material available for hire)
Violin concerto No.1 in G minor Op.26 (violin and piano ed. Michael Kube)
No.708 G Henle Verlag, Munich, 2003
Romance in F for viola and orchestra Op.85 (viola and piano ed. Norbert Gertsch)
No.785 G Henle Verlag, Munich, 2004
Romance in F for viola and orchestra Op.85 (version for violin and piano ed. Norbert Gertsch)
No.791 G Henle Verlag, Munich, 2004
Piano quintet in G minor (1886; without opus number) (ed. Rudolf Lück)
EG 152 Edition Gravis, Bad Schwalbach nr Wiesbaden, 1988
String quintet in A minor Op. posth (1918) for 2 violins, 2 violas and cello (ed. John Beckett)
GM 1352 Edition Kunzelmann, Adliswil/Zürich, 1991
String octet Op. posth (1920) for 4 violins, 2 violas, cello and double bass (ed. Thomas Wood)
Elite Edition 4034 N Simrock London/Hamburg, 1996

# SELECT DISCOGRAPHY

The focus of this discography is on the composer's lesser known symphonic, instrumental, choral and chamber music. Recordings of Bruch's violin concerto No.1 in G minor Op.26, the *Scottish Fantasy* Op.46 and *Kol nidrei* Op.47 far outnumber his other music, therefore not all are listed. Where only the name of another composer is stated in brackets, that composer's violin concerto may be found coupled with music by Bruch e.g. Violin Concerto No.1 Op.26/(Brahms). The following abbreviations are used:

CO   Chamber Orchestra
O    Orchestra
PC   Philharmonic Choir
PO   Philharmonic Orchestra
RC   Radio Choir
RSO  Radio Symphony Orchestra.
SO   Symphony Orchestra.

## CHORAL

*Odysseus* Op.41 Kneebone/Maultsby/Nylund/Lange NDR RC/Budapest RC/NDR PO, Hannover/Botstein      Koch 3-6557-2

*Das Lied von der Glocke* Op.45 Selbig/Graf/Bleidorn/Eckert Singakademie Dresden/ Choristers of the Saxon State Opera, Dresden/Dresden PO/Rademann Thorofon DCTH 2291/2

*Moses* Op.67 Volle/Gambill/Whitehouse Bamberg Chorus and SO/Flor  Orfeo C438 982H

*Moses* Op.67 Shaw/Gulley/Broussard Greenville Chorale and SO/Vick (live performance sung in English)      IP0015

*Schön Ellen* Op.24/Serenade for strings Op. posth./Swedish dances Op.63 Braun/Laske/ Kantorei Barmen-Gemarke/Wuppertal SO/Hanson    MDG Gold MDG 335 1096-2

*Kyrie, Sanctus and Agnus Dei* Op.35/*Damajanti* Op.78/*Jubilate* Op.3 Baranska/ Towarnicka/ Matusek Cracow PC/PO/Bader      Koch 3-1253-2

Lieder für gemischten Chor Vol.1 Opp.38/60/71/72 Konzertchor Darmstadt/Seeliger Christophorus CHR 77195

Lieder für gemischten Chor Vol.2 Op.86/Seven Scottish and twelve Welsh folksongs Konzertchor Darmstadt/Seeliger      Christophorus CHR 77211

*Gruss an die heilige Nacht* Op.62/*Die Flucht der heiligen Familie* Op.20/(Hugo Wolf *Christnacht*) Inoue-Heller/Schreckenbach/Wilke/Thiem/Berlin PC/Berlin Radio SO/Gronostay      Koch 313 013 H1

## VOCAL

Two excerpts from *Hermione* Op.40: Setzt Ihnen nach!/Allein, allein mit meinem Gram Franz Hawlata/WDR Orchestra, Köln/Froschauer      Capriccio Records 10781

Excerpts from oratorios: The Art of Emmi Leisner (rec. 1924) Ich wob dies Gewand (*Odysseus* Op.41) /Aus der Tiefe des Grames (*Achilleus* Op.50) Preiser Records 89210

## ORCHESTRAL

Symphonies Nos.1–3 Opp.28, 36, 51/Swedish dances 1–7 Op.63 Leipzig Gewandhaus O/Masur   Philips 420 932–2

Symphonies Nos.1–3 Opp.28, 36, 51/Romance Op.42/Adagio appassionato Op.57/In memoriam Op.65/Konzertstück Op.84   Accardo/Leipzig Gewandhaus O/Masur Philips 462 164–2

Symphonies Nos.1–3 Opp.28, 36, 51 Gürzenich PO Cologne /Conlon   EMI 5 55046 2

Symphonies Nos.1–3 Opp.28, 36, 51/(Schreker Prelude to a Grand Opera) Gürzenich PO Cologne /Conlon   EMI 575157

Symphony No.1 Op.28/Overture *Die Loreley*/Suite for large orchestra on Russian folk melodies Op.79b/Romance for viola Op.85   Moog/Rheinische Philharmonie/ Balzer ebs 6071

Symphony No.1 Op.28/Violin concerto No.3 Op.58 Mordkovitch/LSO/Hickox CHAN 9784

Symphony No.2 Op.36/Violin concerto No.3 Op.58 Krecher/Wuppertal SO/ Schmalfuss   MDG 335 0868–2

Symphony No.3 Op.51/Violin concerto No.2 Op.44 Mordkovitch/LSO/Hickox CHAN 9738

Symphony No.3 Op.51/Suite for large orchestra on Russian folk melodies Op.79b Hungarian State SO/Honeck   Naxos 8.555985

Suite [No.3] for orchestra with organ [Op.88b]/(with works by Wagner, Handel and Grieg) Wisskirchen/Bayer PO/Koch   Bayer CD 1996–02

## CONCERTOS

Violin concertos 1–3 Opp.26, 44, 58/*Scottish Fantasy* Op.46/ Serenade Op.75 Accardo/ Leipzig Gewandhaus/Masur   Philips 462 167–2

Violin concertos 1/3 Opp.26, 58/(Sarasate *Navarra*) Hanslip/Ovrutsky/LSO/Brabbins Warner 0927–45664–2

Violin concerto No.2 Op.44/Romance Op.42/Adagio appassionato Op.57/Double concerto for clarinet and viola Op.88 Israelievitch/Katkus/Chadash/St Christopher CO of Lithuania/Lipsky   Fleur de son 57925

Violin concerto No.1 Op.26/(Brahms) Little/Royal Liverpool PO/Handley EMI 5 74941 2

Violin concerto No.1 Op.26/(Brahms) Zuckerman/LPO/Los Angeles PO/Mehta RCA 8287 6552682

Violin concerto No.1 Op.26/*Scottish Fantasy* Op.46/Romance Op.42 Rosand/North German Radio PO, Hannover/Wyneken   Vox Classics VXP 7906

Violin concerto No.1 Op.26/(Elgar) Menuhin/LSO/Ronald/Elgar (rec. 1931/32) Claremont CD GSE 78–50–79 LI

Violin concerto No.1 Op.26 Menuhin/LSO/Ronald rec. 1931   Biddulph LAB 031

Violin concerto No.1 Op.26 Menuhin/Philharmonia O/Susskind EMI Legend 5577660

Violin concerto No.1 Op.26/(Mendelssohn) Menuhin/LSO/Boult EMI CDZ7 62519–2

Violin concerto No.1 Op.26/Prelude to *Die Loreley*/(Spohr No.9 *Gesangsszene*) Marschner/Loh Orchestra, Sondershausen/Richter   Marioton MMV 2134

Violin concerto No.1 Op.26/(Mendelssohn/Vieuxtemps No.5) Cho-Liang Lin/Chicago SO/Philharmonia O/Minnesota O/Slatkin/Tilson Thomas/Marriner Sony SMK 64250

Violin concerto No.1 Op.26/(Mendelssohn) Mutter/Berlin PO/Karajan   DG 4000312

Violin concerto No.1 Op.26/(Mendelssohn) Bell/Academy of St Martins-in-the-Fields/
Marriner    Decca 421 145–2
Violin concerto No.1 Op.26/*Scottish Fantasy* Op.46/ (Mendelssohn) Kyung Wha
Chung/RPO/Kempe    Decca Legends 4609762
Violin concerto No.1 Op.26/(Tchaikovsky) Kyung Wha Chung/RPO/Kempe
Decca 417 707–2
Violin concerto No.1 Op.26/*Scottish Fantasy* Op.46 Kyung Wha Chung/RPO/Kempe
Decca 4485972
Violin concerto No.1 Op.26/*Scottish Fantasy* Op.46/(Vieuxtemps No.5)
Heifetz/National SO/Sargent    RCA 09026617452
Violin concerto No.1 Op.26/*Scottish Fantasy* Op.46 Hoelscher/Bamberg SO/Weil
EMI CDZ 25 3061 2
Violin concerto No.1 Op.26/(Lalo *Symphonie espagnol*) Stern/Philadelphia O/Ormandy
CBS CD 45555
Violin concerto No.1 Op.26/(Beethoven) Oistrakh/LSO/Matacic    EMI mono
CDM7 69261
Violin concerto No.1 Op.26 Schneiderhahn/Bamberg SO/Leitner    DG 4775263
Violin concerto No.2 Op.44/(Busoni/Strauss) Turban/Bamberg SO/Shambadal
Claves CD 50–9318
Violin concerto No.2 Op.44/(Paganini No.1) Rosand/Bavarian RSO/Richter
de Rangenier/Saarland RSO/Steinberg    Vox Classics VXP 7905
Violin concerto No.2 Op.44/Suite for organ and orchestra Op.88b
Brusch/Mikkelsen/Tübinger Ärzteorchester/Kirchmann    ebs 6049
Violin concerto No.2 Op.44/*Scottish Fantasy* Op.46 Perlman/Israel PO/Mehta
EMI Classics    CDC 49071
*Scottish Fantasy* Op.46/(Brahms Double/Glazunov) Heifetz/Feuermann/London
PO/RCA Victor O/Philadelphia O/Barbirolli/Steinberg/Ormandy (rec. 1934/39/47)
Naxos 8.110940
*Scottish Fantasy* Op.46/Serenade Op.75 Fedotov/Russian PO/Yablonsky
Naxos 8.557395
*Scottish Fantasy* Op.46/(Lalo *Symphonie espagnol*) Little/Royal Scottish National
O/Handley    EMI 5 66119 2
*Scottish Fantasy* Op.46/(Mozart Sinfonia concertante and Duo/Hindemith) David
Oistrakh/Igor Oistrakh/Horenstein/Hindemith/LSO/Kondrashin/Moscow PO
Decca Legends 4702582
*Kol nidrei* Op.47/Canzone Op.55/Adagio on Celtic motifs Op.56/*Ave Maria* Op.61
Berger/Polish National RSO/Wit    ebs 6060
*Kol nidrei* Op.47/Canzone Op.55/Adagio on Celtic motifs Op.56/*Ave Maria*
Op.61/Double concerto for clarinet and viola Op.88 Ostertag/Schlechta/Schloifer/
South-West RSO/Boder    Aurophon AU 031455
*Kol nidrei* Op.47/(Dvorak/Elgar) Casals/Czech PO/BBCSO/LSO/Szell/Boult/Ronald (rec
1936/1937/1945)    EMI Great artists of the century 5629522
*Kol nidrei* Op.47/Adagio on Celtic motifs Op.56/Canzone Op.55/*In memoriam*
Op.65/Adagio appassionato Op.57/Romanze Op.42 Soh/Coray/RPO/Griffiths
Gallo CD-692
Double concerto for clarinet and viola Op.88/Eight pieces for clarinet, viola and piano
Op.83/Romance for viola Op.85 Caussé/Meyer/Duchable/Lyon Opera O/Nagano
Erato 2292–45483–2
Double concerto for clarinet and viola Op.88/works by Mendelssohn/Crusell/Spohr
etc. King/Imai/LSO/Francis    Hyperion 22017

Double concerto Op.88 (version for violin and viola)/Romance for viola Op.85/*Kol nidrei* Op.47 (version for viola)/(Walton Viola concerto) Bashmet/Tretiakov/LSO/ Järvi/Previn     RCA 09026 63292 2
Concerto for two pianos Op.88a/Fantasy Op.11/Swedish dances Op.63 Berkofsky/Hagan/Berlin SO/Herbig     Vox Allegretto     ACD 8169
Concerto for two pianos Op.88a/(Mendelssohn Concerto for two pianos) Katia and Marielle Labèque/Philharmonia O/Bychkov     Philips 432 095-2
Concerto for two pianos Op.88a/(Mendelssohn/Mozart Concerto for two pianos) Guher and Suher Pekinel/Philharmonia O/Marriner Chandos     CHAN 9711

## CHAMBER MUSIC

Eight pieces for clarinet, viola and piano Op.83/Piano trio Op.5  Ensemble Instrumental Contrasts     Discover International DICD 920194
Eight pieces for clarinet, viola and piano Op.83/(Mozart *Kegelstatt* Trio K.498) The American Chamber Players     Koch 3-7029-2 H1
Eight pieces for clarinet, viola and piano Op.83/(Mozart *Kegelstatt* Trio K.498/ Schumann *Märchenerzählungen* Op.132) Hilton/Imai/Vignoles     CHAN 8776
Eight pieces for clarinet, viola and piano Op.83/(Reinecke Trio Op.264) Kegelstatt Trio Amsterdam     Erasmus WVH 061
Eight pieces for clarinet, viola and piano Op.83/(Reinecke Trio Op.274) Tudorache/Gridchouk/Riolo     Pavane ADW 7386
Eight pieces for clarinet, viola and piano Op.83/Swedish dances Op.63 (version for clarinet and piano) Klöcker/Sebestyen/Genuit     BR 100060
Eight pieces for clarinet, viola and piano Op.83/*Kol nidrei* Op.47/Romance for viola Op.85 Plane/Dukes/Rahman     ASV 1133
Eight pieces Op.83 (version for clarinet, cello and piano)/(Robert Delanoff Trio (1965)) Budapest Piano Trio     Thorofon CTH 2248
String quintet in A minor/String octet/Septet Bronx Arts Ensemble Premier PRCD 1048
String octet/Piano quintet/String quintet in A minor Ensemble Ulf Hoelscher cpo 999 451-2
String quartets Opp.9/10 Mannheim String Quartet     cpo 999 460-2
String quartets Opp.9/10 Academica Quartet     Dynamic CDS 29
String quintet in A minor/(Brahms String quintet Op.3) Allegri Quartet/Ireland naim naimcd 010
Piano quintet/(Nordgren and Borodin Piano quintets) Pihtipudas Quintet Edition Abseits     EDA 001-2

## OTHER WORKS WHICH, AS FAR AS IS KNOWN, ARE NOT TRANSFERRED FROM LP TO CD AND MAY INTEREST THE READER

*Scherz, List und Rache* Op.1 (One-act comic opera with piano accompaniment)/Lieder und Gesänge Op.49 Reisk/Protschka/Fäth     Glauss/Beaumont/Freyer (pianists) Capriccio C30 034 1-2
*Waldpsalm* Op.38 No.1/(Deutsche Volkslieder by Brahms and others) Schreier/ Dresdner Kreuzchor     Telefunken 6. 48085 DT
*Gruss an die heilige Nacht* Op.62/(instrumental Christmas music by Bach, Handel and Haydn) Günther/Rheinische Singgemeinschaft and SO/ Günther Garnet G 40 118
*Kleine Maria* Op.86 No.2/(Lieder by Brahms, Rheinberger, Richter, Becker, Grieg) Alsfelder Vokalensemble/Helbich     Thorofon Capella MTH 195

*Weihnachtslied* Op.60 No.8/(*Die Dreikönige*/Lieder by Reger/Burkhard/Kodaly/
　　Raphael) Bildhauer/Kölner Kantorei/Hempfling　　Cantate 620.001
*Herr, schicke was du willt*/(Motets from the Renaissance and Romantic eras) Kölner
　　Kantorei/Hempfling　　Aulos FSM 43 517 AUL
*Lasst uns das Kindlein wiegen* (Choral movement) Matkowitz/Heinrich Schütz Kreis,
　　Berlin　　PV NC 4
Serenade for string orchestra on Swedish melodies (Op. posth)/(Suites and Serenades
　　by Schubert/Volkmann/Weber and Reger) RIAS Sinfonietta/Starek
　　Schwann Musica Mundi VMS 2054
Piano trio Op.5/(Widor/Schumann/Marschner) Göbel Trio Berlin
　　Thorofon Capella ATH 213
Septet (1849)/(Mendelssohn Octet Op.20) Berlin Philharmonic Octet
　　DGG 2532 077
Eight pieces for clarinet, viola and piano Op.83 Brahn/Craford/Brügger
　　Da Camera Magna SM 92912